Robert Carver

was brought up in Cyprus, Turkey and India. Educated at the
Scuola Medici, Florence, and Durham University, where he
read Oriental Studies and Politics, he taught English in a
maximum security gaol in Australia, and worked as a BBC
World Service reporter in Eastern Europe and the Levant.
Four of his plays have been broadcast by the BBC. He has
written for the *Sunday Times*, the *Observer*, the *Daily Telegraph*
and other papers.

ROBERT CARVER

The Accursed Mountains

Journeys in Albania

Flamingo
An Imprint of HarperCollins*Publishers*

Flamingo
An Imprint of HarperCollins*Publishers*
77–85 Fulham Palace Road,
Hammersmith, London W6 8JB

www.**fire**and**water**.com

Published by Flamingo 1999
9 8 7 6 5 4 3

First published in Great Britain by
John Murray (Publishers) Ltd 1998

Copyright © Robert Carver 1998

The Author asserts the moral right to
be identified as the author of this work

ISBN 0 00 655174 2

Set in Adobe Palatino

Printed and bound in Great Britain by
Clays Ltd, St Ives plc

For my late parents, Richard and Dorothy,
who made it all possible,
and who would have been very proud

'The tongue is soft yet chews everything.'
The Kanun of Lek Dukagjin

Contents

Contents

Illustrations

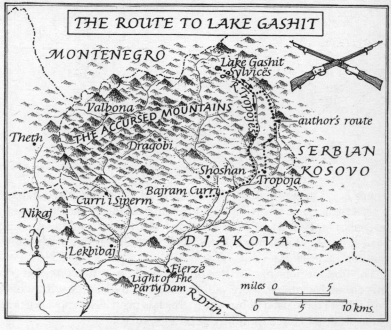

THE ROUTE TO LAKE GASHIT

MONTENEGRO

Lake Gashit
Sylvicës

R. Tropojë

Valbona

THE ACCURSED MOUNTAINS

author's route

Theth

Dragobi

SERBIAN
KOSOVO

Shoshan

Bajram Curri

Tropoja

Curri i Siperm

Nikaj

DJAKOVA

Lekbibaj

Fierzë
Light of The
Party Dam

R. Drin

miles 0 ——— 5

0 —— 5 —— 10 kms.

ALBANIA
in context

AUSTRIA HUNGARY

SLOVENIA

CROATIA

ROUMANIA

SERBIA

BOSNIA
HERZEGOVINA

ITALY

MONTENEGRO

SLAVO-
Skopje
MACEDONIA

BULGARIA

Rome

Durrës
Brindisi

Tirana

Istanbul

Salonika

Jannina
GREECE

TURKEY

Athens

miles 0   100   200

0   200   400 kms.

Author's Note

There is no agreement on the spelling of Albanian place names. Gjirokastra is also known as Argyrocastro and Gjirokastër; Peskopi as Peşkopia; Tírána as Tiranë – and so forth. I have used the spelling easiest for Anglophones to cope with, usually in line with James Pettifer's *Blue Guide*.

The umlaut presents further problems; there is no consensus on this either. Inevitably, there will be those who disagree with where and when I have used it, but again this has been as in 'most normal' examples that I have found from other sources.

The Italian and Greek reported speech is as it was heard, regardless of grammar. The Albanians learnt their Italian under Fascism, when the 'voi' rather than 'lei' form was used for 'you'. To have 'corrected' this would be to have falsified actuality.

Acknowledgements

There are a surprising number of books in English on Albania. Unfortunately, many of them are out of print and difficult to find. For me the best were *Journals of a Landscape Painter in Albania* by Edward Lear, *High Albania* by Edith Durham, *Sons of the Eagle* by Julian Amery and *Biographi* by Lloyd Jones. In addition, *Captured by Brigands* by Gjerasim Qiriazi (Albanian Evangelical Trust, PO Box 288, Wrexham, Clwydd) gives a sharp insight into the world of the traditional Albanian brigand. A clear and unbiased short history is Miranda Vickers' *The Albanians: A Modern History* (I.B. Tauris, 1995). A useful guidebook is James Pettifer's *Albania: The Blue Guide*. The *Kanun of Lek Dukagjini* is invaluable but difficult to find. Many of the facts and figures I have quoted from the pre-1997 collapse come from Derek Hall's *Albania and the Albanians*. *BESA*, the magazine edited by Miss Primrose Peacock for the Friends of Albania Society, has also provided – and still does provide – much very useful specialised information of all matters Albanian.

In order to safeguard those who helped me in my journeys I have changed many names, elided places, and even altered people's physical descriptions. This is no mere affectation: many Albanians who helped British liaison officers in the Second World War were hunted down afterwards by the Communists, tortured and then murdered.

Obviously, then, many of those to whom I owe most cannot be mentioned by name here. To all those people in Albania who helped me so unstintingly, and whose information made this book possible, I offer my heartfelt thanks – *falerminderit, shumë, shumë, shumë.*

To those who can be mentioned I would like to thank the following for their advice, help and information: Miss Primrose Peacock; Mrs Kit Evered; Mrs Sandra Lula-Meredith; Miss Dervla Murphy; Mr Patrick Leigh Fermor; Dr Tom Winnifrith; Mr Joe Medhurst; Mr Peter Hopkirk; Mr William Dalrymple; Mr Peter Levi; Mr Norman Lewis; and Mr Michael Moran.

Acknowledgements

The blame for any errors of fact, or indeed any contentious or politically incorrect opinions expressed in this book, are, of course, to be laid at the feet of the author, not to any of the above.

To my editor, John R. Murray, an especially warm encomium is due – for having had faith in an untried travel writer in the first place, and for having shown exemplary patience, good humour and sound sense in steering the project through the turbulent currents, even white-water rapids which such a book perhaps inevitably involved: not so much a publisher, more a secular saint.

Not least, cordial thanks are due to my brother Ian in Hong Kong for having kindly allowed me to live in his *residence secondaire* while I wrote this book.

Robert Carver
London, January 1998

Prelude

IN EARLY 1991 in London I interviewed for BBC Radio 3 the distinguished travel writer Patrick Leigh Fermor, who surely knows more than anyone now living about Greece and the Balkans. In 1933, at the age of eighteen, he had set out from the Hook of Holland to walk to Constantinople. His adventures, recounted in measured, elegant prose, have enthralled readers for generations.

As the BBC microphones were being put away away, the interview over, Mr Leigh Fermor and I sat back and caught our breath, winding down after the stress of recording. We were in the rooms of his publisher, John Murray, in Albemarle Street. The famous picture of Lord Byron clad in traditional Albanian costume gazed at us impassively: beside it hung a portrait of the turbaned Bokhara Burnes, the nineteenth-century Central Asian explorer.

I had recently inherited my father's house in Cyprus, and Mr Leigh Fermor had lived for decades in the Peloponnese. We talked of water and the lack of it, and of our olive trees, and what sort of apricot trees did well in rocky soil. He had hard, thick, stubby fingers and powerful hands, I noticed, just like any Mediterranean peasant who works the land. This was the man who had captured a German General in Crete in the Second World War, I kept reminding myself; who had lived disguised as a Cretan shepherd for years in the White Mountains, organising the resistance against the Germans.

Finally, I asked him my question, the question that I had been wanting to ask him for years: 'If you were eighteen now, today in 1991, and you wanted to go somewhere – somewhere right off the map, with no tourists or modern development – where would you go?'

He frowned and thought hard for several moments. We had

already spoken of how Greece had been largely despoiled by tourism and concrete. 'Epirus – the north, the mountains. Albania if you could get in there. That's where I would go. You might have a chance of finding places up there.'

It was 1991 and Communism still ruled in Russia. Albania was all but hermetically sealed off from the world. Nevertheless, the germ of an idea began to sprout in my mind. I started to read about Epirus and the nineteenth-century despot Ali Pasha of Jannina, about King Zog, forced to flee into exile when the Italians invaded in 1939, and about the dictatorial regime of the Communist leader, Enver Hoxha, who had died in 1985. And what I read made me thirst the more to try to get into this extraordinary country.

PART 1

The Flight of a Swallow

Into Toskeria

Sultan Murat sat astride his steed
And observed the prisoner bound hand and foot:
His advanced age, his wounds, his chains . . .
'Albanian', he inquired, 'Why do you fight
When you could live differently?'
'Because, Padishah', replied the prisoner,
'Every man has a piece of sky in his breast
And in it flies a swallow.'

Sultan Murat and the Albanian
Fatos Arapi (*b.* 1930)

1

Albanian Approaches

Into a State of Fear

As WE DROVE closer to the frontier it seemed that I was approaching a war zone. The road blocks which outside Florina and Kastoria had been discreet, camouflaged behind trees, manned by two or three police only, were now frank and unashamed, striped poles or upturned oil barrels barring our way. The Greek military were in control here: young conscripts with automatic rifles and machine-guns, middle-aged Special Forces officers with paunches, clad in all black uniforms. We had to slow down and pull to a halt beside each of the posts. My driver spoke to the soldiers in his rapid, Macedonian-accented Greek, explaining who we were. But this wasn't enough. At each post a Special Forces man would make me get my passport out for him, and then examine it, frowning, as if he expected it to be false.

'You say you are British. Tell something to me in English', they demanded in English, unsmiling.

'I live in London and I am going into Albania to work. I'm a writer', I replied.

We were waved on then, each time, and moved forward through a landscape emptied of life. There were low stone houses with red tiled roofs, old and dilapidated; but the people had long departed. On either side of us the mountains of Macedonia rose up, green and with trees on the lower slopes, but becoming wild and untenanted. We were driving down a twisting cone which steadily narrowed, a defile of rock and grey-white scree, a thin ribbon of sky above us.

Between the checks my driver, a bald man in his late fifties with a mouthful of broken teeth and watery blue-grey eyes which he blinked all the while, gave me discouraging advice. 'Keep your bags with you all the time. Never let them out of your sight. Don't let an Albanian touch them. Put your money down here', he indicated his crotch, 'be very, very careful all the time. They are great thieves and a foreigner is a good prize. I will find you a driver at the frontier to take you to Korça. It will cost 4,000 drachma, possibly 3,000. Never go off the roads on your own, never. It is extremely unsafe. They all have knives and many have guns. Be very, very careful.'

I felt my stomach tighten. I lit yet another of the driver's cigarettes. This advice was nothing new. I had spent the last two weeks in the border country and everywhere, everywhere, when I had mentioned to Greeks that I was going into Albania the reaction had been the same. In Psarades one old lady had actually burst into tears and thrown her apron over her head, crying 'Aeii! They will murder you and eat you up!'

Petros, her son, more rational though no less pessimistic, had said: 'Don't trust them at all. They smile and they smile and they try to gain your confidence – then they rob you and kill you. When our police arrest them and throw them in gaol before sending them back over the border, they have to take away all their knives and all their money. Otherwise they kill each other in prison.'

'Do they give the money back?'

'Of course', said Petros. 'Just before they put them over the border they give them the money and make them run off, one at a time, to give each a chance to get clear of the others.

No one knows how many illegal Albanian migrants have poured into Greece since the Communist regime fell in 1991 and the borders became permeable for the first time in fifty years. The Albanian government admitted to 200,000. The Greeks claimed there were nearer a million. In Albania there were estimated to be between 3.5 and 4 million people in all: so perhaps a quarter of the population had fled to Greece, all young, all male.

I had seen them for weeks now, ever since I arrived in Athens. They were unmistakable, clad in ill-fitting old clothes, many with unfashionably long hair and sideburns. They were lean and unsmiling and grimy, carrying sacks or battered hand luggage, their faces burnt dark by the sun. They slept rough, worked as day labourers where they could and begged or stole where they could not. They were tall, fair people, lighter in hair and skin than the Greeks, and many of them had long noses and reddish freckles on their faces:

they looked like Irish Celts, but with bleak, unsmiling faces and eyes of flint.

They had a fearsome reputation among the Greeks: they were murderers, thieves, rapists. Every Greek had a horror story: apartments burgled, cars stolen, hold-ups, stabbings and killings late at night. Yet I had seen a young Albanian boy, scarcely more than a child, shyly buying bread in Kastoria, offering the stern baker's wife the crumpled drachma notes with a provincial adolescent's lack of confidence. I couldn't believe all the horror stories. Other people, in England, old Albania hands, had told me of great hospitality, of the kindness and sweetness of the ordinary people; how as a perfect stranger one would be invited into a house, offered coffee and *loukoumia*, a spoonful of jam in a glass of water; asked to stay, plied with food, raki, home-cured tobacco. It used to be like this in the Greece of my childhood, forty years ago, before tourism and industry and the European Union made the Greeks as bad-tempered and rich as the rest of Western Europe.

I wanted to believe in this more pastoral, more optimistic vision of Albania, a country which had been sealed off from the world for fifty years by Enver Hoxha. There were villages in the north, I had read, where the way of life had continued virtually unchanged since the fifth century AD: where families still dressed in traditional costume, lived in fortified stone houses, slept on sheepskin rugs and lived on their own corn, yoghurt and fruit. Villages without cars or tractors, where oxen, mules and donkeys were all they possessed. This seemed so unlikely in 1996 that perhaps it might even be true.

Very few people I spoke to had been to Albania, and most of those had been only to the south of the country, below the Shkumbin river, to Toskeria, where traditionally the people had always been more open to foreign influence. It was impossible to separate the rumours from the reality. When pressed, most of the Greeks who told these tales of rape and murder had never actually been into Albania at all: it was always someone else who had been robbed by an illegal immigrant, never they themselves. My watery-eyed driver was the exception. He had not been robbed but he had been into this state of fear.

'I have been to Korça.'

'What is it like then?'

He paused, caught between melodrama and truth, a traditionally Greek dilemma.

'Very nice', he admitted finally. 'Old and run down and shabby of course. Hasn't seen any paint since before the last World War – but nice.'

'Restaurants?' I suggested. Some Greeks had said I should even take food with me as there was nothing to eat.

'Very good restaurants. Very cheap. You eat for two or three dollars – a whole meal. Beer, wine, everything. Friendly people. There are cafés, under the trees, they walk about in the evening . . . the whole town . . . in the streets . . . there are almost no cars . . .'

'Like Greece used to be, then, after the Civil War?'

He became animated, suddenly: 'That's it! Just like Greece used to be after the Civil War. No cars, much poverty, broken houses, donkeys and mules, no work – but . . . but . . .'

'. . . a sweetness?' I suggested.

'Yes. A sweetness.'

*

I had spent the last two weeks moving about in Greek Macedonia. I had told myself that this was because I wanted to feel out these border lands, long disputed between Serbia, Slavo-Macedonia (the former Yugoslav Republic of Macedonia), Bulgaria, Albania and Greece. This was only part of the truth. I was scared of going into Albania on my own, knowing no one, not speaking the language. I wanted time to pluck up courage. The state of fear I was going into was my own.

I had caught the night sleeper from Athens to Salonika. In my compartment was a man from Salonika going home and a Pontian Greek, small and wizened-looking, from the Black Sea coast of Russia. Although he had been in Greece four years, the man from Salonika had problems understanding his archaic Greek. The third traveller was an Albanian – my first. He was a thickset, stocky fellow in his late thirties, with a bull neck and tree trunks for legs. He was festooned with bags and cases, smartly dressed in new casual clothes. His friends had entered the carriage in Athens and explained to us that he was Albanian, that he spoke no Greek, and that we were to look after him on the journey. Though I did not realise it at the time, I was watching for the first time the Albanian custom of passing on *besa* for a guest.

Besa is usually translated as 'truce', or 'word of honour'. When a guest is accepted into an Albanian house he is granted *besa*. This means his safety and honour become the responsibility of the whole *fis*, the extended family or clan. To allow any harm or insult to come to a guest is the deepest disgrace than can befall an Albanian. To insult a guest is to insult the whole *fis*. A foreigner protected by *besa* has an invisible army all around him. No one will risk harming him: to do so could provoke a revenge feud, or *hakmarre*.

I had read of all this, but couldn't yet comprehend that it was a living reality, rather than some arcane piece of folklore. More than this I came to understand that it was in fact *besa* which, in the absence of any real law or authority, made everyday existence in Albania possible.

I had mugged up a few words in Albanian, and tried these out on my fellow traveller. The result was gratifying, if unexpected. He fell on me like a long-lost friend, and poured out a great litany of woes in Albanian, only a fraction of which I understood. He had been travelling in Greece and Turkey for the last month. He was not, he repeated, not an illegal immigrant. He had a passport and proper visas – not false ones. He got out his passport and showed it to all of us. The Pontian and the Salonikan entered into this drama with authentic Greek curiosity.

'Eh . . . eh . . . tell me, what is he saying?' they kept demanding of me as we rolled slowly out of the hot Athenian night into the cool of the countryside. The carriage windows were all down and the lights from distant villages flashed like fireflies. It was early May but already Athens was burning with summer heat.

His name was Agron Tafilitsa, our Albanian, and he was a cyclist – a professional cyclist. He had won the Tour d'Albanie in 1987 – champion, he told me proudly (the word was the same in Albanian as English). He lived in Tirana and immediately invited me to visit him and stay with his family there. He wrote down his name and address in my little book in a beefy, childish hand. He had been away from Albania for a month and no one – no one – had spoken Albanian in Greece and Turkey. He had been so, so lonely. I was the first person he had spoken to in Albanian.

I relayed this in my poor Greek to the little wizened Pontian and the man from Salonika, a broad-shouldered, laughing type in his early forties with gold teeth and wavy brown hair. He was a truck driver, he told me later, and a great lover of *rembetika* music.

'Eh – what religion is he, then?' the man from Pontia asked me.

'Orthodox? Musselman? Katolika?' I enquired of Agron. He thought about this for a moment. 'Communist?' I suggested. 'Enver Hoxha?'

A look of supreme distaste came over his face. He grimaced and made as if to split. 'Enver Hoxha – Jo, jo, jo – diktatura, shum kek'. Dictatorship – very bad.

He was from a Moslem background, he added, but he was a secular man, like most Albanians. He never went to the mosque, and drank beer when not in training.

'How many religions do they have in Albania then?' asked the little Pontian.

'Three, and a few Protestants. And Bektashi dervishes too', I replied.

'Aeii, Aeii!' exclaimed the Salonikan, and shook his head. Albania for both of these two Greeks was somewhere unimaginable, further than the moon. Yet the border was less than a morning's drive from Salonika. I got out my large-scale map and showed them how close it was: they wondered silently, pointing at the strange names of towns written in the unfamiliar Latin alphabet: Korça, Leskoviku, Gjirokastra, Tepelena, Fier, Tirana, Peshkopi, Radomirë, Kukes, Bajram Curri, Shkodra.

'It's all mixed up', said the man from Salonika. 'There are Greek towns and Turkish towns all jumbled in there', he said when I recited these names off to him. 'Are there Greeks up there then?' he asked.

'There are certainly Greeks up there – whole villages of them.'

'There are Greeks everywhere', added the Pontian. 'I was in Kazakhstan for years and there are regions there entirely populated by Greeks, villages, towns full of them.' I hadn't known this. I asked him how they had got there.

'After the Civil War, the Communists retreated, taking lots of people with them into Yugoslavia and Albania. Hundreds of thousands. They were spread out when they arrived – some in Hungary, some in Albania, many in Russia. A whole lot went to Kazakhstan.'

We sat in our hot little carriage rocking northwards through the night, a Pontian, an Albanian, a Greek from Salonika and a Briton, each wondering at the diversity, the complexity of a world that had thrown us together like this for an instant, unmatched dice in a casting box soon to be flung apart again, never to reassemble.

There was a locked cabin at the end of the carriage where the steward kept the towels and bedding. In here was a sort of silver metal samovar for hot water you could get to make tea or coffee.

I had debated long and hard with friends in England what to take with me as small presents to give to people in Albania. After weighing up the merits of postcards of Princess Diana, packets of needles and miniature chocolates, I had settled on Earl Grey teabags: these were British, light to carry plenty of and convivial without any possibility of giving offence.

As the steward had put in an appearance and his cabin was unlocked, I now distributed three of these to my travelling companions. Agron immediately insisted on giving me a *frappé* cup in return. *Frappé* is iced instant coffee, which the Greeks drink all through summer. The cup was a plastic traveller's version of this pavement café drink: one opened the package, added cold water, shook the cup then removed the cap. Voilà. Cold, frothy coffee. I was secretly pleased that I had managed to give an Albanian, my first Albanian, a small present before he had been able to give one to me.

Agron and I thanked one another profusely, our right hands on our hearts, in the traditional Albanian manner. 'Faleminderit, shumë', we said. Curiously, only the Pontian refused my teabag offering, though I insisted hard he take it, for a friend, for his children, for luck. But he wouldn't. There was something sly and odd about this gnome-like man. With his sparse hair and gross, ancient features he looked like a Silenus. He said he was going to Salonika but he had no luggage; when we awoke in the morning an hour before we arrived at our destination he had vanished from our lives, like a wraith.

*

We ground on and up in the Peugeot 304 on the twisting mountain road towards Albania. It had been difficult to find a driver willing to take me to the border crossing, though it was only a little over half an hour's drive from the village of Psarades, where I was staying. This was the last place in Greece, isolated on a sliver of the shore of Lake Prespa, a pocket of Hellas in mountainous land surrounded on three sides by water, Albania and Slavo-Macedonia. Ironically, I was less than a kilometre from Albania at Psarades: all I had to do was walk down a cart track by the shore of the lake, and cross a low hill – that was the border. But it was out of the question: the whole area seethed with Albanian illegals hiding up in the thick woods, moving only at night. Patrols of both the Greek and Albanian armies were constantly on the move and both sets of border guards had a reputation for shooting first and asking questions afterwards. There had been several fatalities along this frontier in the last few years: each side blamed the other. In Psarades an elderly shepherd had told me grimly: 'I found one of them, early this spring, just after the snows had melted, a cursed Albanian. He was asleep in a clearing, exhausted. I cut his throat and hung his head from a tree, as a warning for the others. I've lost ten sheep in a single year to those thieving vagabonds.' I thought he was joking at first, but he pulled out a large knife and flourished it: 'With this – see!'

'We don't go further than half an hour's walk down that track', Germanos Papadopolous told me later in his taverna, which was set back a few metres from the waterfront in Psarades.

'There are figures moving across the hillside constantly. Walk off to the right for ten minutes and you are in Albania. The French built the track in 1916, when they occupied this region. They were going to drive a road right through to Korça, but they didn't stay long enough to complete it.'

In the strange jigsaw of modern Balkan politics perhaps nothing is more bizarre than the short-lived French Republic of Korça, which lasted from 1916 to 1920. In the collapse of the Ottoman empire in this part of Turkey-in-Europe a number of contending forces had struggled for ascendancy: the Serbs, the Greeks, the Bulgarians, the Slavo-Macedonians and the Albanians had all sought to impose their rule over these debatable lands, populated by an ethnic rainbow of Balkan peoples. And the Powers, too, had their fingers in the pie: the Austro-Hungarians wanted to extend their empire as far as Salonika; the French and the Italians both had visions of colonies and spheres of influence. Korça had a long tradition of French culture. There was a lycée, whose best-known graduate was probably Enver Hoxha, who had returned later from an uncompleted university education in Montpellier to teach at his alma mater in the 1930s.

Psarades had become Greek and Korça – or Koritsa, as some Greeks still called it – part of Albania. You could gaze across the lake to the snow-capped mountains of Albania a few tantalising kilometres away; little fishing boats belonging to Albania, Greece and Slavo-Macedonia pottered about in their own territorial waters. I had surprised an Albanian bark with a small, noisy outboard motor as it was nosing towards a rocky bay well inside Greek waters. The two men spotted me and roared, or rather spluttered away back into Albanian waters; then stopped, anchored and watched me, bobbing about in their own wash. I wondered what they were up to.

I mentioned the boat to Germanos that evening in the small village store which doubled as a bar for the few men of the village. The owner, a choleric type with a barrel chest and a mop of grey hair, was mending blue plastic fishing nets with a large needle, his two bottle-nosed sidekicks holding great swathes of the stuff between their outstretched arms like women with knitting wool.

Germanos had told me earlier that in Psarades they had nothing to do with the Albanians or the Macedonians. Yet when I entered the bar all the men, including Germanos, had been conversing in Macedonian. When they saw me they switched to Greek immediately.

'There's been an accident over on that side', Germanos explained. 'A boat with a party of schoolchildren capsized in a storm over the weekend and all of them were drowned. That boat you saw would have been Albanian police, out looking for the bodies. They've had permission.'

It was a fluent, plausible reply; but I didn't quite believe it. The two men in the bark had not been police and their behaviour had reeked of subterfuge. That morning a Greek army helicopter had chattered in low across the lake and hovered for a long time over Psarades, checking. There was a uniformed man inside with binoculars; I could see him clearly, so low was the helicopter. He was sweeping to and fro, to and fro, looking for something, or someone. Eventually the helicopter had vanished over the mountains in the direction of Florina, the nearest Greek town.

Psarades was a bit of a mystery. Behind the counter of the one small store were shelves stacked with a compendium of Scotch whiskies, including several single malts, and duty-free style litre bottles of The Famous Grouse. There was also a large quantity of French brandy and a wide selection of American cigarettes: strange provender for a tiny fishing village, surely. I had the feeling I had stumbled on a Balkan *Whisky Galore*: the Albanian boat I had disturbed would have been bringing in smuggled liquor and tobacco to a prearranged cache, from where the Greek boats would collect it that night. The lake shore was riddled with ancient caves and grottoes, many of which had been refuges to Orthodox monks and hermits in the remote past.

The men in the store-cum-bar were all locals and not particularly welcoming. They were drinking raki, the colourless spirit distilled from grapes or plums, a Balkan cousin of grappa. The owner had a tumbler with four fingers of neat Scotch, which he replenished at regular intervals. All the men sported grog-blossomed cheeks and faintly luminous noses. Not hard to imagine what went on here during the long winter evenings.

I ordered a Metaxa brandy and offered round cigarettes. Conversation flickered in Greek and English. Germanos spoke excellent Canadian-accented English. His trajectory was typical of this odd, orphan-like village. As a small boy he had been swept up in the Communist retreat after the Civil War. He had spent his youth in Budapest ('a wonderful city, wonderful') and his early adulthood in the Ukraine. Then, in the '60s, he had managed to emigrate to Canada, where he had made enough money to marry a local girl from Psarades who was also in Toronto. The couple had returned home and opened a fish restaurant for the summer tourists. He also had a boat with a powerful engine – for fishing, he told me – or for taking tourists out to see the ancient churches hewn into the lakeside caves.

Few foreigners visit Lake Prespa because it is so remote, but in summer coach parties of Greeks come up for the day. There was even a hotel, recently completed, across the bay. I had wanted to stay with a Greek family in the village – there were rooms to rent, I knew. But Germanos has steered me into the hotel, arranging for me to pay no more than I would have done with a family. He was friendly and helpful, but he didn't want me in the village. I don't think he quite believed I was a writer. He may have suspected I was some sort of European Commission snooper.

The weather was intermittently rainy; clouds boiled over the lake from the mountains of Macedonia; but after Athens this damp and coolness were a relief. I went for solitary walks along the lake shore, gazing across the still waters into the mountains of Albania. Massive, gaunt and severe, their peaks snow-stained and barren, lit by shafts of fitful sunlight and shadowed by black rain-heavy clouds, they called for the brushes of Edward Lear.

No wonder Lord Byron had loved Albania so much! If ever a landscape deserved to be called Byronic, this was it. There was such a sombre, brooding melancholy amid the grandeur. I saw my first Albanian eagles here, a pair of them soaring high up in the thermals over the peaks.

The vegetation around the lakeside was a strange blend of Mediterranean and northern European: there were daisies and buttercups by the track, but Aleppo pine and cedar too, and great stands of beech higher up. Cicadas hummed from the grassy banks and water streamed down from the hills in thin rivulets.

*

Although we were still in Greece, we had left Greece: the army no longer patrolled the road and there was no attempt to control the groups of Albanians we could see making their way across the rocky countryside. My taxi driver pointed to a flock of sheep and goats grazing beside the road. These were tended by a tall shepherd and his two sons, who all waved to us.

'Albanian tourists . . .', was the driver's laconic comment.

'Vlachs?' I asked. He nodded.

The Vlachs had moved throughout the Balkans with their herds for centuries. They spoke a variant of Roumanian, and were thought to be the remnants of the Roman legions which had once garrisoned the eastern parts of the empire. Under Communism they had been 'settled': now they were on the move again.

'When the Communists fell, the first thing they did was empty the prisons – not of political prisoners, but of murderers and rapists. They took them to the border and said "There is Greece. Don't come back." So the first wave of refugees were the worst elements, and we have had many murders: Albanians killing Albanians, Albanians killing Greeks. Many have guns and knives. Our police round them up, give them a beating, then deport them. They wait for a week or so, then creep back. Often they are exploited by Greeks. Last week a trailer pulled by another trailer turned over and fell off the road and over a cliff. It was full of Albanians, who were all killed. The driver, who was a Greek, fled. The police are still looking for him.'

'Why did the Albanians strive so hard to get into Greece?' I asked. 'What did they earn?'

'In Albania there is nothing, no work. In Greece a Greek labourer earns 100,000 drachma [£300] a month. An illegal Albanian with no papers will work for 30,000 drachma a month. In the summer they come over for the fruit-picking round Edessa. They depress the labour market and make our unemployment much worse. But they don't stay. They save, then go back. In Albania you can build a house for 3 million drachma [£9,000] which would cost 30 million in Greece.'

I kept the driver talking. It helped keep my nervousness in check. I was smoking too many of his cigarettes.

Suddenly we were at the border. There were just two small concrete shacks separated by a hundred yards of broken road. All around us, on both sides of the frontier, milled Albanians with ragged clothing and unkempt hair. They were trying to sell cartons of cigarettes, soft drinks, bottles of Bulgarian mineral water. They importuned, begged, crowding up close to us and gazing mournfully into our eyes. This was a scene from the remotest regions of Anatolia, from Central Asia even.

There were no cars, no tourists, nothing. We had a coffee at a stall outside the tiny Greek customs-house, and smoked a last cigarette. An olive and a glass of water, I thought, the traditional last offering to the condemned man in Ottoman Turkey. Then I went inside the hut and handed the Greeks my passport.

'Where are you going, and why?' a moustachioed official asked me peremptorily, aggressively rude.

'Albania', I replied, 'Korça, Tirana – to work.' He said something I didn't catch to a colleague, and they both laughed bitterly. He slapped my passport back at me dismissively.

My Greek taxi driver had found an Albanian driver with a Mercedes to take me to Korça for 3,000 drachma. He was already parked on the Greek side. I paid the Greek driver and shook his hand. I suddenly felt very alone and vulnerable. My bag was locked in the boot of the Mercedes and I got inside. We bucketed over the broken concrete into Albania.

There was no barrier, no attempt at control or surveillance. We could have driven straight on. But the driver stopped, and indicated for me to go into the Albanian customs post.

Inside, in the gloom, I made out three policemen in smart blue uniforms with red-banded peaked caps and Sam Browne belts with automatics in leather holsters. They ushered me past the deserted guichets and into their inner sanctum, where a wooden chair was provided. My British passport was passed around and inspected with great interest. I had to fill out a short immigration form which was smudgily printed in Italian and Albanian.

There was a single metal-framed bed of ancient, school dormitory, design in the office, on which the night shift was sleeping soundly, still fully dressed in his uniform, his cap and shoes resting on a wooden chair by his head.

'I soldi . . . i soldi . . .', said one of the other policemen to me, rubbing his fingers together. I gave him the five dollars required for my visa, and he wrote out a receipt.

The police all smiled at me as if I had just passed a difficult exam. My passport was stamped, and I was officially inside Albania. They all shook hands with me before I left.

Tourism was clearly in its infancy here.

We drove down a terrible road, pocked and cratered as if it had been recently shelled by mortar fire. On either side were rows of mushroom-like concrete swellings with gun slits, the notorious bunkers of which Enver Hoxha had created hundreds of thousands to defend Albania from an imperialist attack which never came. And everywhere, people. Old men in grey, baggy suits and flat caps: small children in shorts and plastic sandals; women with head-scarves and long dark dresses; policemen dapper and smart in blue uniforms, with Kalashnikovs and moustaches; young long-haired dandies of yesteryear in leather jackets and winkle-picker shoes. There were no cars and few bicycles; instead there were mules, donkeys and horses. I felt as if I had just stepped back fifty years, to the immediate post-war world, and had entered a remote Central Asian republic, Kazakhstan, say, or Tajikistan.

All the houses looked as if they had been bombed in the last few months: we passed several large buildings, evidently once collectives of some sort but each now roofless and gutted, burnt out during the 1991 anti-Communist revolt.

'Democrat? Communist?' my clean-shaven, middle-aged driver demanded of me. Noticing the dollar bill pinned to the nodding dog on his windscreen and the miniature portrait of President Sali Berisha, it was not hard to guess his own sympathies.

'Democrat', I replied diplomatically. He cheered loudly and hooted his horn as we swayed past a battered, overloaded bus. He and the bus driver exchanged the two-fingered Democrat V for Victory sign, and hooted madly. From the back of my taxi came another cheering voice. I turned in surprise. On the back seat lay a uniformed policeman, lolling on his elbow, a rose in his mouth, a Kalashnikov cradled in his arms. It seemed we were taking the morning shift home.

'Welcome to the Albania', he said to me carefully, while smiling broadly. 'I am learning the English. I want to go to America.'

2

Optimistic Massages

Prelude to a Balkan Election

'The Party of optimistic and hopeful massages'

Zeri i Popullit, official Socialist Party organ, English page.

'THIS WAS NOT a very intelligent predicted candidate', was Gabriel's mild post-mortem comment as we trudged limply from the Socialist Party headquarters in the direction of the Army Officers' Club in Korça.

'Prospective candidate', I corrected. It was part of our arrangement that while Gabriel would translate for me I would try to buff up his already excellent English.

'Yes, I'm sorry. But of course, he is not a real candidate, in a sense, but what we call a Turk's head.'

The candidate I had interviewed was a cross-eyed fellow with a straggling beard and a rambling manner. It turned out he didn't know the Socialist platform, and wasn't even a member of the Party. We had sat for several hours waiting for a superior candidate to put in an appearance, but in vain. The Socialist Party headquarters was housed in an Italian colonial villa of peeling stucco: the window frames were cracked and long unpainted, the shutters falling off their hinges. Morose villagers in muddy boots hung about in the foyer waiting for someone to hear their grievances; from behind closed doors muffled voices could be heard as a hidden cabal discussed strategy. There was an ancient, broken Gestetner duplicating machine someone was trying to get working, and a single telephone, around which sat several middle-aged men who bore a collective air of patient expectancy, as if Enver Hoxha might suddenly ring up and tell them what to do.

The Socialist Party had once been the Party of Labour and before that the Albanian Communist Party. In the last five years it had been trying desperately to regain the power it had lost when the dictatorship fell in 1991: this election, people were saying, was their last chance. Widespread disillusionment with Dr Sali Berisha's Democrat Party government was reported, especially from the villages, which still contained 65% of the country's population. The rebirth of capitalism and the influx of foreign goods and money from the West had largely benefited the towns. People were saying this election was going to see either a return to a modified form of Communism, or else the permanent eclipse of the old ways.

The armed uniformed guard who normally stood outside the Officers' Club had vanished. Gabriel and I slipped discreetly inside the porticoed entrance. The club's espresso coffee, made with a genuine Italian machine, was not only the best in Korça but also the cheapest.

We sat at a table in a cavernous high-ceilinged, open-plan café with plate-glass windows supported between square, severe concrete pillars. The floor was marble and cool underfoot, an inset kilim design in multicoloured chips of stone marking the entrance. Groups of elderly men in old-fashioned grey suits and flat caps sat talking slowly in low voices, most of them smoking acrid local cigarettes: old Communists, though none of them looked particularly military.

'Are we allowed in here?' I had asked Gabriel nervously when we first ventured into what had become by now a regular haunt of ours. He had shrugged, and beckoned a waiter who wore a long white apron of the sort I had only seen before in posters by Toulouse-Lautrec of *fin de siècle* Parisian cafés.

'Who knows? There are no rules any more, really. No one is sure what is allowed and what isn't. Anyway, you are a Western writer on an official mission . . .'

A Westerner of any sort, I had soon came to realise, was a rare and wonderful bird, allowed almost any licence. The Communist past, fifty years of isolation and self-imposed blockade, had been swept away: Albania was itself now to become Western. So far this had manifested itself only in small ways: Greek and American cigarettes proudly proffered; Italian chocolates and wine for sale in the tiny stalls that had sprung up along the dusty roadsides; Mercedes Benz taxis and American-style jeans and T-shirts; a lively free market in dollars and drachma by the old bazaar.

But of Westerners themselves there were none in evidence: the terrible shortages of 1991–3 which had brought in trucks with foreign aid had now passed. Today the market was full of imported food of all kinds for those who had the money to buy. Most of the aid workers had moved on to zones of fresher crisis. I had assumed Korça would be hosting gaggles of curious antipodean backpackers and little groups of yelping foreign journalists in for the general election; but I seemed to be the only outsider in town.

Gabriel was a tall, fair-haired man in his early forties. He was strongly built and nattily dressed in light-coloured casual clothes of distinctly foreign cut. He wore gold-framed glasses, and looked more British than I did. He was proud of the Western impression he made, though also quietly proud of being Albanian. Constantly, discreetly, he tried to put a positive spin on things for my benefit. He was a strong Democrat Party supporter; but he was also a *dirigiste* with an authoritarian streak.

'The government should have stopped . . .' was a favourite refrain of his. To be a Democrat in Albania, I realised, was not necessarily to be a democrat, just as to be Socialist implied no belief in any socialist doctrine: the levers of power, the positions of preferment were what people wanted from politics. Ideology seemed to count for very little.

'What is a Turk's head?' I asked, as we sipped our thimblefuls of coffee, each served deferentially by the waiter with a tumbler of cold water. I unwrapped a sticky cake topped with synthetic cream which I had bought in a nearby pastry shop, and ate as Gabriel talked.

'In the days when Albania was fighting the Ottomans, the Sultan used to send hordes of Turkish soldiers here to fight – hordes is right, no? – and of course in those days both sides cut off the heads of those they killed as trophies. There were so many Turks' heads displayed in Albania that the phrase came to mean "worth nothing, valueless". We use the term now in politics to mean "a man of straw", as you say in English. That candidate, for example – if he is elected, if he – he will never sit in Parliament. He will be given another token post somewhere, and a real Communist who would never be elected because of his record under the dictatorship, he will be substituted. This is allowed under the current temporary constitution.'

Gabriel was not only a translator: he was my guide through the complex labyrinth of Albanian culture I had stepped into. He spoke fluent Greek, Italian and Macedonian as well as English. He had travelled to Greece and Italy and even to England, was well read and an accomplished musician. Yet until the fall of Communism he and his whole family lived under a constant shadow of fear: they had bad *biographi*.

Every Albanian who graduated from high school had a dossier with the Sigurimi, the Communist secret police. Details of an individual's family and ancestry were all entered into this *biographi*, which was constantly updated. To have a father or uncle who had been a Zogist, or a supporter of the right-wing Republican Balli Kombetar party, was enough to damn one. Education, a good job, preferment, an apartment to live in, all these depended upon good *biographi*.

Gabriel had been forbidden higher education. He had trained as a musician and managed to join a local orchestra as a cellist. But in secret, at home, he had studied and learnt languages.

'I listened to the BBC World Service in English. It was extremely dangerous: ten years in gaol if you were caught. So that way I learnt English from the radio, and from an old dictionary I managed to find. I also got hold of American, English and European novels. Jack London, Dickens, Dumas, Zola. I taught myself. Being in the orchestra was safe – it was completely unpolitical.'

Had he managed to talk to other people like myself, internal *émigrés* who were also studying secretly, listening to foreign radio stations, I asked.

'No. It was too dangerous. There were Sigurimi spies everywhere. You couldn't trust anyone. I didn't even tell my sister what I was doing. My father knew, because he used to listen to foreign radio stations too, alone at night when everyone else was asleep. You could tell who was listening to the BBC though, at school. We were all mad about sport and it was safe to talk about that. One or two people gave themselves away by knowing the results of international matches a few days before the results were announced on Albanian state radio. You knew then they'd been listening to 'Sports

Round-Up' on the BBC in English. But you didn't say anything. It could have been a trick.'

With the fall of Communism the new Democrat government had been desperately short of trained, experienced people who were not compromised by service with the old regime. Gabriel, in spite of not having a university degree or a teaching qualification, had taken a crash course as an English teacher and now held a job in a high school in Korça, a coveted post which paid $75 a month. The former teachers from the Communist regime had all been exiled to remote villages: as in Soviet Russia, to live in a 'cultured' town such as Leningrad or Moscow was a sought-after privilege. Next to the capital Tirana, Korça was generally held to be Albania's most 'cultured' town. Again, as in Russia, 'culture' did not mean Mozart and poetry readings: rather, a sense of civility and order, of amenity and courteous manners. To be learned and speak foreign languages, to know about the West, to be able to use abstract, rhetorical language, not to work with one's hands, to be a member of what in Tsarist Russia had been called the intelligentsia – to be an engineer, a doctor, a schoolteacher, a journalist – this was to be 'cultured'.

Gabriel was nothing if not cultured. Everyone knew him in Korça and everyone deferred to his undoubted superior status. The schoolteacher in provincial Albania was still the pillar of the community he had once been in, say, nineteenth-century Scotland or Russia. In a town where there were no bookshops, no libraries, nothing to read except a few ill-printed newspapers from Tirana, Gabriel had many books and was well read, in Albanian, Greek, Macedonian, Italian and English. It quickly became apparent to me that he was vastly more intelligent, worldly and knowledgeable than any of the hopelessly ignorant parliamentary candidates of all parties I was seeing.

'I was asked to stand for the Democrats', Gabriel admitted, when I asked him about this, 'but I refused . . .'

'Why?'

'I have no university degree from Tirana. It is impossible to get anywhere without this, to be taken seriously. Also . . . at present things are going well for the Democrats, but if the Communists ever got back again . . . I would be ruined, my whole career gone. I would have to go back to playing the guitar at weddings, as I did under the dictatorship.'

This was no exaggeration. If the Communists got back, then all Democrat Party supporters would suffer the consequences: gaol, execution or exile to the remote villages. Gabriel had survived the terror and the purges of the Hoxha years by keeping his head down. He was married with two children. His father, Georgio, was in his sixties and had diabetes. Gabriel had responsibilities to his *fis*, of which he would soon be the head.

'If you were twenty?' I asked.

'If I were twenty, I would have left for England or America in 1992', he said with finality. The 'England' was put in out of courtesy to me. He meant America, of course: every other intelligent Albanian over forty I met said exactly the same thing.

'Green card is the god of Albania', Gabriel told me quietly, as we strolled about the leafy boulevards of the town, part of the late afternoon *volta* where the town took its ease, where friends were greeted, ice creams slowly eaten, new clothes paraded.

Green card, or *grincardi* as it had been Albanianised, was the landed immigrant's visa for the United States. Everywhere we went Gabriel would say to me: 'She – that girl over there – she has just won the *grincardi* lottery. Her whole family leaves next week for Milwaukee.' Fifty thousand green card visas had been allocated to Albania on a lottery basis that year, I was told. Every winner could take their whole family.

'The winners suddenly find they have far more cousins in their family than they ever knew', Gabriel said, deadpan. You could buy your way into one of these departing families easily; it was common knowledge, merely a question of money.

There was a long tradition of Albanian emigration to the United States, dating from the 1880s. 'Better to be a dog in America than a man in Albania' was a traditional nineteenth-century saying. To my surprise I could quote this, even to fervent Albanian patriots, and get only complete, unqualified agreement. America was a paradise, uncritically accepted by all, Communist and Democrat alike. Everyone dreamt of *greencardi*.

Korça was the centre, by all accounts, of one of the most developed, prosperous regions of the country: but it was desperately poor, with an economy and an agriculture dating from the pre-war era. Everything the Communists had built was shoddy. If it had not already fallen down or been destroyed it would collapse within a few years. No one was bothering to repair anything. They just started again from scratch, using Greek bricks, Greek cement, even Greek sand to build their houses – paid for with drachma earned in Greece.

In 1991–2 the destruction of the Communist economy had been all but complete. Virtually all the factories and collective farms had been looted and burnt out. Even the thousands of hectares of orchards had been cut down. 'We thought America would make us a white cheque', I was told, naively, by Albanian after Albanian. Even the term 'white cheque' (for 'blank cheque') was a curiosity. There were no cheques in Albania, no credit cards, just cash, soggy, crumpled notes from the Communist era with pathetic pictures of old-fashioned steam trains and Chinese-style lorries on them, the technological *dernier mot* in Enver Hoxha's epoch. Or else, these days, dollars, drachma and Italian lire.

Albania had been hermetically sealed off from the world since 1945. Gabriel aside, everyone I met showed a staggering ignorance not just of the rest of the world, but of what had happened there. Conversations suddenly ground to a halt when someone would ask 'What is a hippy?' or 'Who is Freud?' What could you say?

'Albanians are like people standing in a pit, their eyes just above the ground', Gabriel told me once very earnestly. 'Their horizons are very near. They can see almost nothing. Westerners are like men standing on a hill. They can see far horizons, know about great rivers and seas of which we know nothing.'

It was to his great credit that Gabriel not only recognised this, but could admit it to himself and to me, a Westerner. In over two months travelling, meeting Albanians every day, he was almost the only one who had this degree of insight or humility. Most were, in varying degrees, puffed up with that combination of egoism, pride and national chauvinism known to scholars as 'Albanianism', an ideology adopted by Enver Hoxha's regime from the nationalists, and strenuously propagated. Indeed, even Gabriel still had faith in officials and officialdom, in solutions promulgated in Tirana and carried out by cadres, educated men like himself.

He had asked me frankly what I had thought of his school. I said frankly that it was falling apart. There were waist-high weeds in the playground, the windows were broken and the lavatories were filthy and stank. There were no books, let alone computers or sports equipment.

He agreed, mildly: 'It is a scandal. The government should do something, spend more money . . .'

'You and your fellow teachers should do something, Gabriel', I proposed. 'Get the pupils in after lunch and set them to weeding the playground. Organise a raffle or a cake sale among the parents to raise money to buy glass for the windows, paint for the walls and pay for a cleaner to wash out the lavatories.'

Gabriel looked away from me, embarrassed.

'This is the government's job. It is a scandal . . .'

Gabriel was an *effendi*, when the chips were down. He would not get his hands dirty, would never be seen doing or even supervising degrading manual work, and nor would his fellow teachers or pupils. At home he was waited on by his wife or his mother. At work he hectored and lectured, a dogmatic authoritarian who would brook no interrruption. In his leisure he sat around the cafés drinking beer and smoking cigarettes, preferably in the company of status-giving foreigners such as myself. Gabriel went on about how 'Western' he himself was , and how 'Western' Albania really was, yet he was himself a figure who could be found more readily in Syria, Egypt or Turkey than in England or America – Westernised but not Western.

I had realised within a few days of arriving in Albania that nothing would ever be done to clean up and rebuild the country, because that was always and would always be 'someone else's' job. No one took any responsibility for anything. Everyone liked to talk politics, but no one would ever actually do anything to change things: to speak of reform, repair, replacement was to have achieved it. The Albanian intelligentsia lived in a cloud of glorious rhetoric in which problems were the fault of others. I disconcerted them most by being concrete.

'They are ashamed', Gabriel had told me about the politicos I had interviewed, 'because you ask them' "How much will this cost?" and "Where will you get the money?" No one has ever asked them this before and they do not know the answers. This is the Western way and they are not used to it.'

He had a bicycle, a small folding Raleigh model given to him, like his two computers, his colour TV set, and his library, by English friends. His bike was his substitute car, the car he desperately wanted but could not afford. Every day he wheeled or rode it to his school, some ten minutes from his family's flat. He always carried his class books on it, in a parcel. He could have walked, but he never did. He never carried the books, ever: they were always strapped to the bike.

Indeed, I had never seen him carry anything at all. It was a mark of the cultured urban man not to carry things. The fact that I had a bag with me always, holding books, notepads, pens, cameras, odds and ends, was regarded, I knew, as incongruous and puzzling. I was obviously a Western man of culture: why then did I have a bag?

I had a flash of intuition as we sat drinking beer one afternoon at a pavement café.

'Gabriel, tell me, do you have the word *hamal* in Albanian?'

'Yes, of course.'

'What does it mean?'

'It means a low person, a poor, ignorant person. A person of no culture.'

Now, *hamal* in Turkish means a porter. The men who had loaded and unloaded cargo on their backs from the *caiques* in the Istanbul of my youth had been called *hamal*. But it also meant more. It was a term of mild abuse in Turkish. It meant exactly what Gabriel had told me. I had begun to realise that though Albanians claimed they had no Ottoman roots, that these had been pulled up and destroyed completely, the truth was otherwise.

For all its superficial French and Italian veneer, the pre-war stucco villas with red tiled roofs, the new pizza parlours and Mercedes taxis, Korça was still at bottom a provincial Ottoman town, stuck in a historical time warp. As in Russia and Eastern Europe, Communism had acted like a deep-freeze, preserving largely unchanged patterns of behaviour, architecture and prejudices from the period before the First World War. Even in my childhood in the 1950s and 1960s in Cyprus and Turkey the old-fashioned world still to be found in Korça had been all but swept away.

Gabriel never asked me how, as an Englishman, I knew the word *hamal*, or why I had asked about it. Like all Albanians, he was intensely self-centred and oblivious to any oblique agenda I as a foreigner might have. As in other orientalised countries, on an individual basis Westerners were always assumed to be without guile, to be naive and easily cheated: yet *en masse* Western civilisation was rather seen as threatening, potentially all-powerful, to be railed at when one was strong enough, placated and kow-towed to when weak, and aped at all times by the cultured. Gabriel in himself reflected this paradox: he was very protective of me – I sometimes almost felt as if I were in his custody – yet he would launch into one of his nationalist monologues, if allowed to, at the drop of a hat. The gist of this was always the same: the West must help Albania, since the West was rich and strong, Albania poor and weak. And in particular the West must help him, Gabriel. How could he get a new, a better computer? How could he set up a private school? As the representative of the West there present, it was obviously my duty to help him . . .

*

Although Gabriel lived only ten minutes from the Illyria Hotel, and I had a map of how to get to his family's apartment block, it had not been easy.

I had checked into the Illyria on arriving, a grim concrete Soviet-style mausoleum in the central square which had been recently 'privatised'. This, I learnt, meant that it had been given to a northern, Gheg family, supporters of Dr Sali Berisha – himself a Gheg. I had paid $15 a night; the rate for Albanians was $2 a night. Everything in Albania had two unofficial prices: as expensive as possible for the foreigner, as cheap as possible for the Albanian. The logic of this was unassailable: the foreigner was rich and could pay, the Albanian was poor and could not.

There was no running water in the Illyria, no electricity, and the lavatories were piled high with encrusted excrement. There were bloodstains and worse on the walls of my furnitureless cell, and the bed sagged like a hammock. Apart from that, it was fine. It was by far the best hotel in Korça.

The unsmiling girl at the reception desk spoke a few words of Greek, Italian and English. In all of these she was equally unhelpful. The map I produced, which showed both the Illyria and Gabriel's apartment, was puzzled over by her and all her relatives. They handed it back to me with smiles and noddings of the head, signifying they understood nothing. To shake the head in Albania is to agree, to nod to disagree or indicate a negative.

'Boulevarde Fan Noli?' I asked, pointing to the main street leading off from the Illyria, one side or the other, left or right. They nodded again. Either they didn't know or they weren't going to tell. Maps only became legal in 1995, I was later told. There weren't any for sale anywhere. I never met anyone in all Albania who could read the ones I had brought from London with me.

There was not much to do in a waterless, electricityless decaying Soviet hotel cell, so I went out and walked the streets of late afternoon Korça. The town was afoot, *piano piano*, taking the air; the *volta*, a custom widespread in southern Italy and Greece was in full swing. I had the impression I had just stepped into the post-war world of an Italian neo-realist movie: *Rome, Open City*, say, or *The Bicycle Thieves*.

There were no cars, few bicycles, rather more mules and donkeys; and above all, men in shabby, baggy suits and women in long dresses. Only the young had adopted the universal uniform of jeans and T-shirts.

I attracted considerable attention as I walked about, looking for street signs. I was evidently pretty well the only foreigner in town. There were no street signs. The old Communist ones had been removed and the new Democrat ones not yet put up; no one had any idea where Boulevard Fan Noli was. It transpired later, Gabriel told me, that I had been in it all the time I had been asking people. I later learnt this was a highly Albanian situation.

I had already tried to phone Gabriel from both Greece and the Illyria: of course the phones did not work. I was beginning to realise that in Albania more or less nothing worked, nothing was available, and no one knew anything. There were virtually no shops in Korça, that I could discover, merely a couple of booths and stalls selling potato chips, biscuits, cigarettes (all imported from Italy or Greece) and a large open bazaar. The stalls were like African *dukas*.

*

I had discovered Gabriel's block of flats, eventually, on my own, after several hours. I had stopped people who spoke fragments of Greek, Italian and even Turkish, but no one had understood either the map or me. They had simply gaped at me, or grinned and shuffled with embarrassment.

'They are not used to dealing with foreigners', Gabriel explained later. 'They are simple people. Or even if they are not, they pretend to be. It is always safer not to know anything at all in Albania. To be stupid is never to be punished, only to be a threat . . .'

As I progressed gradually out of town, the pocked tarmac road ceased and a pot-holed dirt track snaked between ten-storey blocks of concrete Stalinist flats, instant slums surrounded by a littoral of grassless, treeless waste-ground scarred with disused bunkers, gipsy encampments, burnt-out trucks and heaped refuse. It was like the outskirts of any Third World town, though without the usual vibrant undercurrent of trade, of small shops, wheeled stalls, buyers of snacks and sellers of gewgaws.

Sagging, stained, obviously already collapsing, these blocks looked as if they had been put up by amateurs: the bricks were small, deformed and ill-laid, the solidified mortar oozed out like toothpaste, any old how. The only building work as poor as this I had ever seen was the Ghetto wall in Warsaw which the Germans had forced the Jews to put up in 1941, slave labour of another sort.

It turned out that some of these Korça blocks had indeed been put up by amateurs, workers from factories who had 'volunteered' to build their own apartments in the afternoon. It was a curiosity of Albania that even those few who claimed to be working in offices did so only until 12 noon, as they always had, it seemed, even at the height of Communism. Everything shut down at midday, for the rest of the day. I met with looks of blank incredulity, even horror, when I said that in the West people regularly worked from 9 or 9.30 in the morning to 6 or even 7 or 8 in the evening, later even in some cases. No one made the correlation between the short working day and merely token effort put into official tasks and the poverty, disorder and decay all around them.

Capitalism in Albania meant Western patterns of consumption, not of production. Rich countries were rich, and that was that, immutably: it was thus their duty to help by giving money, cars, food, trucks and clothes to poor countries like Albania, so they too could become rich. In spite of the popularity of capitalism and the post-1992 reforms, there was still a stigma attached to being rich, having money, doing well: it was regarded as more than faintly immoral.

'Soviet formalism is a disease we still suffer from', Gabriel had told me in relation to the old-fashioned teaching methods schools still used. The Soviet-style textbooks had been removed, but the new ones used the old pedagogic methods. 'We need people from the West to come and teach us', he added. You can 'overthrow' Communism, as Albania had: harder is to change the ingrained cultural mores of centuries. Much of what the West habitually criticised as 'Communism' in Eastern Europe had little to do with a Marxist regime and rather more to do with long-established traditions and habits. Albania was the heir to Levantine and Balkan ways, not just those of Communist Eastern Europe. Already, within a few days of being in the country I had heard echoes of so many places I had been before, and of Turkey most of all.

*

Gabriel had been out when I finally found his apartment. His father, Georgio, and mother, Emira, were in, and were expecting me.

Gabriel was at the Albanian centre of a network of English people who for the last ten years or so, even before the fall of Communism, had been helping Albanians with training, gifts, money, books and equipment. There was a regular means of communication through the factory at which Gabriel's wife Eleni worked: there they had a fax machine and telephone maintained by Germans; these always worked, it was claimed. The *fis*, the clan, knew who I was and what I was doing.

I was welcomed as if an old friend. I offered to take off my shoes at the door, as I knew this was the custom of the country, but was told not to bother. Gabriel never took his shoes off in his own apartment, I later noticed, though both his parents and his wife did.

I was offered a cup of herb tea, and Mr Georgio, a slim, slight figure in his sixties with a merry smile and a bald pate, conversed with me easily in Italian, which he had learnt during the Occupation and still spoke fluently in spite of nearly fifty years' lack of use. Italian, rather than Greek or French, was still the lingua franca; and it was to Italy that Albania looked, rather than Turkey or Greece. Italian television was usually the favoured channel, Italian songs the most popular, and Italian wine and food the most eagerly consumed, when they could be afforded. The male side of Gabriel's family were Greek Orthodox and they all spoke good Greek. Emira was a secular Moslem, but Italy was where their tastes and aspirations lay.

Their two-bedroom apartment was very small indeed, and crammed with bulky Greek furniture. Six of them lived there, the children sleeping in the living room on the couch. There was a large colour TV, two computers and shelves lined with books: all the fruits of contact with the English since the fall of the dictatorship. 'In 1991 we had nothing – sticks only – everything we have is thanks to Democracy', Gabriel told me. Democracy meant aid, patronage, goods from the West, just as Communism had meant the same from the East. Albania was a professional client state. It had been bankrupt since its inception in 1913 and had just gone on borrowing money and scrounging goods and aid ever since. None of this was ever paid back; instead, new patrons of a different political hue were sought. Albanians would wave any flag you liked as long as they were paid for it, until the inevitable row and split.

Gabriel's family were all staunchly, fiercely for the Democrat party of Sali Berisha. To return to Communism at the forthcoming election would be for them, I realised, a great catastrophe. Albanian politics are neck or nothing. If you win, you gain all. If you lose you end up exiled, in a labour camp or shot dead. To them every Westerner was a very real friend, an ally and a pledge for the future. I was welcome, doubly welcome for all this.

'We are very, very, very grateful to Mrs Thatcher and Mr Bush. They are like saints to us, for never surrendering to the Communists, always fighting them and giving us hope. Only because they were so, so strong for so many years were we able to struggle from our prison and become free.'

Mr Georgio's sincerity was transparent. Now retired, he had been a vet, working in the villages.

'The stupidity, the ignorance, the sheer malevolence of the Communists is impossible to describe to you. They have ruined the country completely. Look around you. I remember the Zog period and the Italians, when we had a gold currency, prosperity, everything – richer by far than Greece before the last war. The Fascists were saints and holy men compared to Hoxha and his band of criminals.'

'What about Enver Hoxha himself?'

Emira, Mr Georgio's wife, emerged from the tiny kitchen annexe at the sound of the monster's name.

'Enver Hoxha – skata, skata!' she shouted, waving a wooden spoon in the air.

'Hoxha – merde!' translated Mr Georgio, in case I hadn't got the message. It was the same with all Democrat supporters I spoke to. Objectivity in Albanian politics was a contradiction in terms: you loved or you hated, and almost everyone I spoke to in the towns loathed Enver Hoxha. In the villages, though, it was a different story.

3

Broken Land

The Enemy behind Your Head

VOSKOPOJA LAY IN the mountains at over a thousand metres, some twenty-four kilometres from Korça up the worst dirt track I had ever suffered. On the plains near Korça, in green fields behind the tree-lined road, peasants stooped, hoeing and weeding by hand; in the bald, treeless mountains they had given up the struggle. Up here the trees had been cut down in 1991 when the fuel ran out. No one had replanted, because planting was the responsibility of the government in Tirana, and they no longer cared.

In this region many of the people were from the Greek minority. Since the fall of Communism they had abandoned their villages and gone south into Greece itself; whole villages now lay empty and abandoned.

On the outskirts of old Voskopoja I saw a lean man with a thin face dressed in a battered grey suit and flat cap, trying to plough a field with a crude museum piece of a wooden implement, ineffectually dragged along by a tiny donkey. I wanted to stop and photograph this impotent symbol of contemporary Albania, but I could feel Gabriel's disapproval overpowering me. This was all so shamefully primitive, so uncultured. Better by far to stop in the cafés of Korça drinking beer and talking up Democracy and the West.

I had been expecting a grand ruin, a sort of dilapidated Antioch or Salonika. After Constantinople, Voskopoja had been the second city of Turkey-in-Europe. By the middle of the eighteenth century it had a population of 30,000, with another 20,000 in its environs. Then called Moschopolis, it had developed into an important entrepôt positioned half-way along the overland route between Constantinople and Venice. The first printing press in the Balkans had been established there in 1720: Greek books had been printed, and many Orthodox churches built. But the wealth of the city had aroused the jealousies of local Moslem beys, who had massacred the Christians and burnt the town several times. Now Voskopoja was a tiny village. There were a few scattered, crumbling Ottoman stone houses hatted with wooded shingles, which sat astride great cobbled boulevards built for ampler days. There were no cars up here; no bus service, no shop – nothing.

The few people in the broken streets, some as blond as Austrians, gazed at us with bovine lack of interest. If Korça was Italy *circa* 1948, then the mountain villages were at African bush level. These were Orthodox Vlachs, settled shepherds. There were 800 people and two functioning churches. Since 1991, 200 of the young men and five complete families had left for Greece.

The shy young village priest was roused from his siesta to open up the grandest of the seventeenth-century churches, St Nicholas. The church was in a pleasing state of benign neglect: there were wild flowers growing between the paving flags in the courtyard and moss on the stone gate pillars. Nevertheless, it had to be kept locked against theft. In the Hoxha years this confident, massy stone building had been used as an army barracks, and then as a food store. There were delicate Byzantine-influenced seventeenth-century frescoes in bad condition on the walls inside and out: the Communist soldiery had picked out the eyes, just as I had seen the eyes picked out of the faces on the election candidates posters in Korça. Belief in the Evil Eye was still strong: but it wasn't something Gabriel ever wanted to talk about.

I greeted Father Thomas in Greek, and he smiled and looked embarrassed. I had assumed he was a Greek, but he was a new priest and only spoke Albanian. Hoxha had all the Albanian Orthodox clergy imprisoned or shot, and so in 1992, when religion was allowed again, many had come up from Greece. They preached in Greek and an Albanian translated for the congregation. Some had been accused of using the pulpit for Greek irridentist propaganda. The Albanian Orthodox Church became autocephalous in the 1930s after a long struggle, but how could they not be dependent on their brethren in Greece?

A gaggle of curious small children waited for us outside, but they were too timid and too inexperienced to beg. They followed us at a distance, like lost sheep. Gabriel spoke kindly to them, as a good schoolteacher knows how to. They chirped back at him innocently and reached up to hold his hands. They were so easy to lead, you realised, so trusting in tall, strong patriarchal figures. This was how Enver Hoxha used to be photographed, the Father of his People, trusting little children in national costume with their hands in his.

The taxi driver, a middle-aged Korça man with dyed hair who wore smart slacks and a natty blue short-sleeved shirt, was already in the sole village café. Gabriel came with me to translate for the priest, but then he too made for the café. He could see no charm here, only squalor and ignorance.

I wandered about the ruins of this curious place by myself for half an hour before joining them. A few children said 'Yassu' to me halfheartedly; their elders simply stared. Donkeys grazed on garbage in the streets: I discovered one broken, rusting Communist-era tractor abandoned in a field. There were fruit trees in the walled gardens and TV satellite dishes on some of the houses. No one was working in the abandoned fields.

A fierce political argument was in full swing in the café when I arrived: Gabriel and the taxi driver for the Democrats, three rustic villagers and the café owner for the Socialists. We drank Greek beer and soft drinks and smoked Greek cigarettes, Assos brand, all of which I paid for. No one had any money.

There was almost nothing in the café: a few chairs, two tables, bottles of drink and cigarettes. No food, no coffee machine even.

'The Berisha government has done nothing for us! Our young men go away to Greece! The cities have stolen all the good things!' This was the villagers' line. They were thickset, loud, Balkan peasants: they bellowed and thumped the table. Communism, you could see, had not been so bad for them. Tirana provided everything, of a very poor quality but without question: seeds, tractors, fuel oil, cloth, salt, a hedge-teacher, a visiting doctor. Now all that had stopped. And their economy was in ruins. Cheap food had poured in from Greece, produced under subsidy by the EU agricultural policy. They could never compete with their locally grown crops. So they had given up. They herded a few sheep, and subsisted. If this was a typical village, I realised, the Berisha government was in for trouble at the election.

'If you take everything out of your houses which has come since Democracy – your TVs, washing machines, furniture, clothes – then your houses will be ready for whitewashing [i.e. completely empty].' This was Gabriel's bellowed response. Political argument seemed to rest entirely on a material plane, who had got what from whom.

The villagers resented the privatisation of land, too, and blamed the Democrats. The first privatisation had offered land for sale. Some villagers had bought. Then, those who had hung back had been given their land. That was unjust.

Gabriel hadn't wanted me to come up here, hadn't really wanted to come himself. He had given me his rosy, townee view of the new Albania; this belligerence and crudity were not part of it. No wonder the intelligensia hated the villages: this was where you were exiled to if you lost out. Up here in places like this all the former town-dwelling Communist Party teachers and doctors now worked, exiled by the Democrat government. There was still no independent employment for functionaries: you went where the party bosses sent you, or emigrated. This, or worse, was where Gabriel would be sent if the Socialists got back in at the election. No wonder he was full of nervous tension.

There were two local lads back from Greece on a visit. They sat listening to the political debate but not contributing. Only the heads of families expressed opinions, never the sons or womenfolk. They were dressed smartly in jeans and fashionable shirts. They spoke good Greek and looked me straight in the eye when they addressed me. By contrast, their fathers would look at the ground, sniggering like yokels, avoiding one's gaze.

'Have you left for good or will you come back?' I asked one of the smart lads.

'We have to pretend we will come back one day, for the sake of their pride. But we can never do so. Our place is in Greece', one of them replied, *sotto voce*. They were Orthodox, with Greek names: Vasili and Yiorgo. Like millions of other Illyrian and Epirote Albanians over the centuries, they would be absorbed into Hellas without trace.

As we bucketed back down the terrible track we passed an ancient Chinese-made lorry swaying up to the high pastures, crammed with villagers. They stared at us in our Mercedes taxi with a bovine peasant stare that was Asiatic in its intensity and indifference.

'Even if the whole country votes Communist and I am the only Democrat left, I will never change, never, never', swore the taxi driver vehemently. 'They can shoot me. I will not change.' Gabriel translated this to me with ill-disguised approval. But the villagers made up 65% of the Albanian population. How many, I wondered, still clung to the past?

We picked up a villager, clad in now ragged early 1990s Western charity-aid clothing. He carried a gunny sack over his shoulder. He was walking to another village, miles below his own. He had set off from his mountain home at 6 a.m. It was now 3 p.m. He sat in the front seat, by the driver, and smoked a pungent home-cured roll-up. His Albanian was thick and harsh. He quite ignored Gabriel and myself in the back, but talked to the driver, only in a monologue, the lonely hours on the track pouring out of him.

He paid the driver 100 lek (about one dollar) when he got out, even though I was paying for the whole expedition. This was normal in Albania. He strode away with his sack over his shoulder.

'They live in shit and fuck their sisters', Gabriel had said to me before, with a *moue* of distaste, this of Albanian villagers in general.

*

I had moved out of the Illyria Hotel into Popi's apartment. Popi was Gabriel's sister, a plump, jovial lady in her early forties, divorced, with a loutish-looking nineteen-year-old son, who spent his time lounging and drinking beer with his friends in the bars on money his mother gave him. He was unemployed and obviously unemployable. She worked as a shoemaker in her own eighth-floor Stalinist flat, peddling away on a foot-driven treadle machine installed on her covered balcony. This ancient model had been given to her by English well-wishers. An electric machine would have been useless, as the power was often cut in the winter for weeks at a time. The power was off when I arrived, as it happened.

'Two schoolteachers from Pogradeç crashed into a high-tension electricity pylon in a friend's car. They could not drive properly. They were killed, and now there is no electricity', Gabriel had told me simply, as if this were an everyday occurrence: which in fact it was. There was no driving test in Albania. You just paid the police $10 for a permit. Spectacular crashes were common.

There was no water either, except between 2 and 4 p.m. on the days that there was any pressure. Sometimes the water was off for a month at a time. Then they had to go down with their buckets to a friend's house, which had a well. They cooked on little Greek camping gaz burners when the power was off. In the winter, with no electricity or water, deep snow outside, they often went to bed at 6 p.m. just to keep warm. No wonder there were so many children everywhere.

All the bathrooms had crude galvanised iron holding tanks installed, slung from the ceilings. These filled, very slowly, when the water pressure was up, and you had to make the contents last. Popi's bathroom boasted a Western lavatory, from Greece. In Gabriel's family apartment, as elsewhere in the country, the reeking *alla turca* with its treacherous corrugated footprints ruled supreme.

Under the Communists Popi had worked for twenty-six years in a shoe factory, which had employed three eight-hour shifts, working twenty-four hours a day. For this she had earned $6.50 a month.

'We did exercises in the mornings, Chinese style, in the Mao Tse Tung period. After we broke with them that stopped. Twice a day the siren blew and we had to go down into the bunkers for air-raid practice.'

There had been very little food for the last ten years of Communism. 'One litre each of oil, milk, sugar and meat per family per month, no matter how many people in the family. One kilo of bread per family every two days. Often there was not this much food in the shops for your *talone* [coupons]. Wine, raki and vegetables were not rationed, and people made or grew them themselves. One bakery was called the 'Death Breadshop' because so many had collapsed and died of starvation while waiting in the queues. All this time Enver Hoxha and his clan were living in luxury in Tirana and in their palaces, taking holidays in Italy and France.'

Popi had gone without a meal a day for a year in 1970 to buy a black and white TV. 'By twisting the aerial in the summer months you could sometimes get Italian TV. This was because Hoxha installed a temporary booster transmitter so he could receive his favourite RAI programmes from Italy at his villa by the shores of Lake Ochrid, a few kilometres away.' Popi had believed CP propaganda until the late '70s, when friends who had been contract workers abroad told her about life in the West.

Popi had built her own apartment with her workmates from the factory in the afternoons. It had taken her five years to get the required points. She had bought it in the 1991 privatisation for $100, on borrowed money. Then, she had been earning $2.50 a week. Now, the flat might be worth $3–4,000. It had heavy Greek furniture, a glass-cased wall cabinet with cheap glassware on display, all new since 1991. The rugs and bedcovers were garish, factory-produced goods from Turkey.

Popi spoke fluent colloquial English, though nothing like Gabriel. Her British friends had given her a two-week holiday in England. What had she thought of it?

'Very clean, very rich. But there is no family life and everyone works so much, all the time. And the women are hard, like men, and men soft, like women. In England the women are beating the men, I think.'

She had seen me brewing my morning tea in her tiny kitchen, and had thought: 'Ah, just like a woman', as she later told me. No Albanian man lifted a hand in the house. Popi's husband had been ejected from the *fis* by Gabriel 'for beating her too severely', as Gabriel had told me himself, explaining the absence. Gabriel's wife Eleni always looked at her husband with fear, I thought. And once, when she and I were alone in an office, she helping me send a fax, I caught a look in her eye of pure terror: she thought I might be going to rape her. Women never allowed themselves to be alone in a room with men who were not kin. 'Cigarettes on the table, a woman in bed' was an Albanian saying I had already heard, meaning help yourself, no permission required.

Popi warmed to me. She was lonely without a man. She sat like a Dickensian heroine, struggling on making crude leather shoes all day for the village market. She would have liked to go out and sit in cafés and drink beer, but even in cultured Korça this was something only the men did.

'I am not interested in other women', she told me shortly, when I suggested she organise an outing with her female chums. She was the first Albanian I met who didn't want to go to the West. She had seen England and didn't like it. Given the terrible state of Albania, this was a harsh indictment of Britain.

All around her apartment block was the usual waste-land of ruined trucks and scattered garbage. Hoxha had settled the gypsies in these blocks: as many as 20% of Korça's people were Romanies. Now they were moving out again, trading in horses and mules, selling gold and silver, tinkering. They made their campments between the tower blocks, sleeping in tents and cooking over open fires. In Korça, as in Voskopoja, Albania was returning to only recently abandoned pastoral ways.

Popi liked the gypsies. They were her neighbours in the block, and their children kept dropping in for treats – a slice of white bread with oil and sugar, this the standard Albanian kids' breakfast. White bread, made from Greek flour, was still a novelty and a luxury. Popi had a washing machine, a new cooker and a big colour TV, like her brother – all gifts from English well-wishers – but no books or computers.

'Enver Hoxha was a chief devil of all the little devils. He ate up the whole country', she told me, with real hatred in her voice. I was paying her $10 a night for my lodgings, without food. She earned $2.50 for an eight-hour day from her shoemaking, 'when there is the work'. Sometimes there was no demand for a week at a time. She had a brand of soap called Fax from Turkey, Greek biscuits and Bulgarian soap powder. Nothing was made in Albania any more: only some poor quality fruit and vegetables were grown.

All the Democrat Party propaganda about 'building capitalism' was guff: Albania had slipped into a bankrupt, post-colonial fate, its ruined economy unable to compete on any level. Everything was imported, even the soap. The money to pay for all this came from foreign loans, emigrants' remittances or slave labour like Popi's.

Food was as dear or dearer in Albania than in the EU or America, where mostly now it all came from. Gifted food aid was sold in the market openly, for high prices. Yet the wages were below sub-Saharan and 90% of the people were without work. The dole was $12 a month: enough to buy one loaf of bread a day.

Yet after Hoxha's Communism this was a paradise. 'Like day after night', Georgio told me fervently. He had a fixed pension, $15 a month. He had diabetes and ate only vegetables, drank his own home-brewed raki, and for him this was freedom and plenty. The Sigurimi could no longer arrest you and send you to the gulag for fifteen years for complaining about the quality of the tomatoes in the shops, as they had before 1991.

There was a black joke people used to tell in secret about the camps. Two political prisoners were talking on their arrival at the notorious Burrel gaol. 'I got ten years. What did you get?' asked the first. 'I got fifteen', said the second. 'What for?' asked the first. 'Nothing', replied the second. 'Listen', riposted the first sharply, 'If we are going to be friends you're going to have to be honest with me. For fifteen years you must have done something – ten years is the sentence for nothing.'

Gabriel was a fund of these jokes, including many about Enver Hoxha. You got ten years if you were caught telling one in Communist times. Then they used to refer to Hoxha as *dulla* – queer, or faggot – in these jokes to avoid punishment. Hoxha, like Kemal Ataturk, was widely believed to have been bisexual: he was reported to have had a male lover with him throughout the partisan years during the Second World War. This man had been sent to the camps, as a reward, instead of being shot during the purges. He had even survived, it was claimed, and was still living. There were many jokes about Hoxha's prodigious sexual appetites, as there must have been surely about the nineteenth-century despot Ali Pasha, Lion of Jannina, who was both bisexual and a paedophile, his harem containing hundreds of pretty children of both sexes, stolen from his subjects: he had even attempted to seduce Lord Byron, to no avail.

The Albanian state-run Democrat Party-controlled TV news was full of the forthcoming election. In the north the police had uncovered a Communist plot: a Socialist-Communist mayor had been handing out drugged cigarettes to known Democrat voters. These cigarettes were to put the smokers out for the count so they would miss the election altogether. A Democrat Party-appointed general in Tirana solemnly swore this was true. Another alleged scandal emerged: the Communists had a list of all the Democrat voters, who after their victory were going to be shot. Then there was the 'parallel process': the Socialists were alleged to have prepared a second set of blue electoral slips, which were to be substituted by hidden members of the old Sigurimi, to 'prove' a Socialist victory. Now the colour of the slips had been changed at the last moment to foil this dastardly plot.

'Do you believe any of this?' I asked Popi as we watched together, she translating for me.

'It is possible. After what we have been through we can believe anything. In Albania we do everything in the bad way.'

*

Getting Gabriel up to Lin, a village by Lake Ochrid was not easy. There was a nice fish restaurant near by, which was to the good: but it was another village.

I had insisted, gently.

'I know two pretty girls – not prostitutes – respectable girls – we could take with us', had been his response. Gabriel was a married man with three children.

'Won't your wife object?' He looked at me as if I was crazy. 'No girls, Gabriel.' He shrugged. It had been worth a try.

'Albanian hospitality', Edward Lear had written in the mid-nineteenth century, 'largely comprises of you buying a chicken and your hosts helping you eat it.' Nothing had changed. If anything was to be done, the Westerner had to pay for it: taxis, food, drinks, cigarettes. Everyone was broke. I was paying Gabriel as my translator, and buying all his food in restaurants along with my own. He loved it, being paid for what he most enjoyed: stuffing himself on imported luxury foods, while spouting away in a foreign language. He loved touting me round town, too, during the *volta*, introducing me to all his aquaintances, speaking loudly in English or Italian, showing off. Like all the Korça people, he had a distinctive gait, half penguin roll, half drunken sailor, all at 20% of the normal European metropolitan speed. When you talked to an Albanian as you were walking they would stop and face you to reply. There was no hurry for anything, ever.

On the Lin trip we had taken along Mr Slovki, Gabriel's brother-in-law. The ostensible reason for this was that Mr Slovki had the use of a factory car, which would save me the taxi fare: the real reason was that Gabriel was bored with talking to just me. Also he wanted to get me to buy both of them a big lakeside fish dinner. He lost out on the girls, but won on the brother-in-law.

The factory was a 1930s-style horror, built in the post-war years of steel, glass and rough concrete: rows of silent girls in white protective cloth caps were bent over antique sewing machines. German supervisors stalked the corridors. Cowed managerial Albanians sat in chaotic, paper-strewn offices looking depressed. I could not help thinking of Steven Spielberg's recent film *Schindler's List*. It was just as he had portrayed the Jewish factory in wartime Kraków.

This was an illusion, however. The girls here were being paid $100 a month – to Gabriel's $75 as a teacher – and this was the last such enterprise still functioning in Korça. They made clothes for the export market, for Germany, brand name Jolly Roger. All the cloth was sent in bolts from Germany by rail, the finished clothes sent back.

This explained why all Gabriel's family were so well dressed in Western clothes. Like everyone concerned with the enterprise, they stole cloth from the factory by the bolt, and made up their own clothes at home – and had done so all through the Communist years when it was a state enterprise. Gabriel was quite open about this theft.

'Otherwise we would have been naked for forty years', he had assured me. There was no shame or guilt in stealing from the state. Everyone did it. Nor from foreigners: they were so rich. Now the factory was privatised, owned by three Albanian-Americans and Mr Slovki. Everyone still stole, just the same. That was the Albanian way: everyone stole from everyone else.

Gabriel was often used at the factory as an interpreter or translator. Waiting for Mr Slovki to join our expedition, he settled into the office familiarly, and started talking loudly. A short-haired, skinny German woman in her thirties was speaking on the phone in German. She paused and said to Gabriel in English: 'Would you do me a big favour? Just stop talking while I'm trying to make a business call.'

Gabriel bridled. He had evidently never been spoken to like this by a woman before.

'Yes, indeed, I could do you this one big favour, of course, with no difficulty at all', he huffed in English, his voice heavy with sarcasm. The German woman ignored him and continued her call.

I avoided Gabriel's eye: he had been shamed in front of me, his prestige-conferring foreign friend, by a foreign woman. No

Albanian woman would ever have dared speak to a man like that. 'Long hair, short wits – a woman' was an Albanian aphorism.

*

At Lin, an hour's drive away, neither Gabriel nor the brother-in-law had wanted to get out of the car, a smart new Japanese model.

'There it is', Gabriel indicated, from the roadside. 'Now we can go to the fish restaurant . . .'

The village, a noted beauty spot by the shores of Lake Ochrid, nestled on a hillside, a collection of old stone single-storey cottages with red tiled roofs. The lake was blue and sparkled in bright sunlight: beyond, across the other side of the lake, the snow-capped mountains of Macedonia rose craggily.

'Drive down and park, please', I insisted. Reluctantly, they complied. I got out and started to wander down the little lanes between the houses.

Gabriel and Mr Slovki hung about the car miserably. They hated it absolutely. The town and the village were at war, I now realised. This was enemy territory. If you left a car unattended, people stole the hub caps and the wing mirrors, within minutes. Every car had to be garaged under armed guard. Outside their family, everyone was at war with everyone else.

A few villagers approached me shyly. I spoke to them in Greek. They replied in French, which I found odd, surely a relic of the old 1920s Korça Republic.

After ten minutes of agony, Gabriel forced himself to join me. He couldn't bear not to be there, mediating. Immediately he began to bully the villagers in a jocular, patronising manner. This was a Democrat, I had to keep reminding myself, not a Communist commissar.

The villagers remained stolid: they had seen his type before many times before.

'They are idiots. They know nothing', Gabriel said to me, in English, smiling with complicity. He began to lecture them on politics.

Gabriel: Are you going to vote Democrat, then, after all the good things they have given you?

Villager: Sali Berisha should have lightened our ploughing [i.e, no we
    are not, he should have sent us tractors].
Gabriel: Take out everything you have got from your houses since
    Democracy and they will be ready for whitewashing!

The villagers looked at him silently and stonily.

'You see. To this they have no reply', Gabriel chortled to me
proudly. This was the level of political debate in provincial Albania
in May 1996.

On an unrepresentative straw poll of just two villages, it seemed
pretty clear to me that the Democrats were going to lose the election
unless they managed to rig it.

An old woman doing her washing at the village pump smiled at
me and asked where I was from. 'England', I replied. 'And him?'
pointing to Gabriel. 'Korça'. She shook her head in disbelief. 'No,
he's not from there.' Gabriel was absolutely delighted at this. 'At the
Greek border in 1992 the guards, too, thought I was foreign –
because of my clothes and my culture', he told me proudly.

I realised that I had to escape from Gabriel soon. I was in his protective custody, and would always be fighting to try to see what he
didn't want me to see. I also realised with faint distaste that his
family had probably collaborated with both the Italians and the
Germans during the war. Mr Georgio loved singing old Italian
songs when he was tipsy: I had prompted him with 'Giovinezza',
the Fascist anthem, and he had sung it off without a blink, remem-
bering all the words after fifty years. Westerners, people like me,
were the new occupiers, the people with the power and money in
Albania. Already there were American troops, and NATO divisions
on exercises. Even the borders were being patrolled by the EU.

We drove back through the lakeside town of Pogradeç, a smaller,
scruffier version of Korça, though the pavement cafés were absent.
The streets were full of morose young men with no work and
nothing to do. The lake was beautiful: still and blue, a few primitive
fishing boats at anchor by the pebble shore, which was littered with
plastic detritus.

We drove through the enclave by the lake set aside for Hoxha and
his clan, discreet pastel-painted Italianate villas set in a park, now
lushly overgrown. There was a police guard with a machine gun, to
keep out Albanians. Gabriel explained that I was a foreigner, and so

we were let in. It had an eerie feel, like a campment of the tents of Genghis Khan frozen in aspic, after the death of the Great Leader. The Democrats didn't use it, just as Hoxha hadn't used Zog's palaces. Albanians still feared the Eye.

*

The man who owned the fish restaurant was short and muscular, with a shock of thick grey hair and a bold, brutal, suntanned face sporting a beaky nose: a tough commander of a Roman legion, an energetic provincial who with a bit of luck might rise high, even become Emperor.

He had been the biology and athletics teacher of the Pogradeç High School in Communist days. The red-speckled trout of Lake Ochrid were famous; in Byzantine and Ottoman times they had been taken to Constantinople by fast runner, on mountain ice, for Emperor and Sultan. In Hoxha's imperium they had been reserved exclusively for the high officials of the CP. Any local caught fishing or eating fish was sent to the camps for fifteen years. This hadn't stopped the athletics teacher. He was a strong swimmer.

'I used to go out into the lake on dark nights, naked and oiled against the cold, to fish with a net. There were patrol boats but they never saw me. It was how I fed my family – we would have starved otherwise.' He was the fittest, the best-built Albanian I ever met.

The restaurant was a visible product of the Democrat reforms. The ex-teacher had been able to build a pleasant little house next to a vineyard right by the lakeside. There were plastic tables and chairs outside under shady trees; we could have been by Lake Garda. Nothing like this had ever been allowed by Hoxha; then, everything good had been reserved for the high officials of the Party. A great part of the pleasure Albanians got from things was the knowledge other Albanians didn't have them. A suggestion to share by a foreigner was always evaded: only family and clients deserved whatever was on offer. One of the reasons foreigners were listened to with such avidity was that they gave information free.

Gabriel and Mr Slovki made straight for the indoors restaurant, this right by the road. It was a beautiful warm spring day, the sun shining brightly from a blue sky, the lake inviting.

'Let's sit outside', I suggested.

They didn't want to. They found another little enclosed wooden booth, hidden away in the garden, but hot and stuffy, with plastic windows.

'I think we should sit here', I said, and moved three chairs to a table under a tree in the open air. There was nothing they could do. I was paying for this treat. Why didn't they want to sit outside, be visible? We were the only guests. There was no one else around for miles. It was a puzzle. In Korça Gabriel liked nothing better than to sit at the pavement cafés under the shade of the old linden trees planted by the French, greeting his pals as they rolled past. Perhaps it was because this was the country, or because they felt they might be seen and reported. I couldn't work it out.

'What would you like to drink?' Gabriel asked me. We sampled the house red wine. It was home-made but adequate. It cost $2 a litre, wildly expensive by Albanian standards. I agreed to a litre.

Unwisely, I did not check the price of the trout, which Gabriel ordered for the three of us in Albanian, without reference to me. Little plates of garlic yoghurt, tomato salad and home-made bread appeared, a *meze*. The host stood us a glass of home-made raki apiece. 'Gëzuar!' we said, raising our glasses, 'Health!'

The host sat with us while his wife prepared the fish. He knew Gabriel and Mr Slovki well. I asked him through Gabriel if it would have been possible to escape from Albania in the Hoxha years by swimming the lake to Yugoslavia on the other side: it was only about a mile away, even less. Even I could have made it, on a dark moonless night, I thought.

'All Pogradeç people were under a 6 p.m. to 6 a.m. curfew to prevent escapes', he replied, 'but yes, it would have been very easy. There were patrol boats, but in winter or in storms they rarely went out. The trouble was if you got over to the other side the Titoists made you appear on TV and denounce the Hoxha regime, in exchange for political asylum. Then your family in Albania would all be sent to the camps. No one could do that to their family. So almost no one ever tried.'

The secret of Hoxha's grip on the country was explained. Albania was imprisoned by its tight bonds of kinship. I had met Russians and Poles who, under threat during purges, had simply vanished, gone to the mountains or to Siberia; this was always possible and easy. No one followed you to Tashkent or Alma-Ata, to the high

Tatras. In Poland I had met noblemen from Warsaw who had spent years alone as foresters in the southern mountains: the Communists couldn't have cared less. In Albania no one would do this: the sense of family was too strong. Gabriel had already told me that the families of those sent to the gulag were allowed to accompany them, as in Russia in the Tsar's time.

'Hoxha loved this area. He had a studio built at the state fish farm, where he would go and work all day', the ex-athletics teacher told us. 'He used to stroll through the villages, dropping in on people unannounced. One old lady prepared him coffee, gave him raki and *loukoumia*, welcoming him as a guest as she would anyone. After his food taster had made sure these were safe, Hoxha sat down and ate and drank. He was so pleased with this village and he ordered a feast for the people, providing meat and wine. Everyone ate and drank, made music and had a wonderful time. Hoxha sat and watched, and was pleased. As Hoxha was leaving, a man from the village threw himself in front of the official Mercedes and cried out: "Oh Great Leader, I have been blind from birth! The doctors here can do nothing for me. Send me, please, to Europe, where the doctors can cure me!" Hoxha's bodyguards and Sigurimi pulled this man away roughly, and Hoxha drove on. The man was given fifteen years in the camps under Article 55 (Agitation, Betrayal and Propaganda) and his family were all sent to the gulag. Thus ended badly a day which had begun well with much joy, and all because a simple man had asked his ruler for a boon.'

Gabriel translated this for me in spurts, slowly, as the man recounted it. The way it was told made this vignette sound like a biblical parable, or else a story from the *Arabian Nights*. The standard greeting to Enver Hoxha had been 'Take years from our lives, Great Leader, and add them to yours!' In Ottoman days in Turkey and its empire part of the oath of allegiance to the Padishah had been 'Let Allah cut years from my life and add them to his.'

The fish arrived, well presented in a metal dish and garnished with parsley. It was delicious, firm-fleshed and moist, more like salmon than trout. A curiosity of this fish was that the only other place it could be found was Siberia, in Lake Baikal. I complimented mine host on the sauce, a mixture of tomato, garlic, herbs and wine. Was it traditional in his family, or had he invented it himself, I asked.

'Many people have tried to get the secret of his sauce but I will not tell them', he replied. He had interpreted my question as a request for his trade secret.

I had begun to recognise that Albanians never offered information to one another, never helped each other, except for favours or money. Everyone strove to get the better of the other by cheating or stealing. Duplicity and trickery were the currency of everyday life: the cunning man, the successful cheat or swindler, was greatly admired. Honesty, frankness, fair trading were all despised as naïve. Cynicism was intelligence, fairness stupidity.

The athletics teacher now presented me with a large, brightly coloured schoolchildren's folder illustrated with Mickey Mouse and Pluto, and with 'Hollywood World' printed on the top. Inside were architectural drawings for an ambitious hotel-restaurant complex. There was to be a swimming-pool, fifty bedrooms, a vast restaurant seating 500 people. The ex-teacher wanted to put this up on his lakeside site, which at present had four plastic tables in the garden and four indoors.

It would cost $150,000 to build, he explained. He wanted 100% capital input and 20% on top of this 'for myself, for my ideas'. Would I like to invest?

This, then, was the real reason we had come here. Gabriel and Mr Slovki looked at me expectantly, as if I might pull out a wad of greenbacks and agree on the spot. All foreigners were rich. All foreigners were gullible, too, and easily cheated. They came with 'aid' and 'development money', with trucks and clothes and machines and gave these to just anybody, for nothing. This was the Albanians' experience of the West in the last five years, after all. Why should they think any differently?

'Have you a business plan?' I asked. A long conversation between the ex-teacher and Mr Slovki now ensued in Albanian as it was explained what this was. No, he hadn't.

'Have you approached any banks?'

He had no cousins who worked in the state bank, so he could not get a loan. After five years of a pro-capitalist Democrat Party government there were no foreign banks in Albania; they were still illegal.

Mine host's son, a goofy blond youth of about nineteen, dressed in a track suit, was sitting in on this discussion, saying nothing.

'Why don't you get a group of local businessmen to club together to send a representative to Salonika, with all your business plans, to approach commercial banks there for development loans?' I suggested. There was a bus service every day from Korça to Salonika. It took five hours and cost $20. Some Greeks had already invested in southern Albania. There were French, Italian and American banks in Salonika. It wasn't such a radical idea.

'You could send your son there', I suggested.

'If I was sent to Salonika I would never come back', replied the son promptly, with absolute conviction. His father did not look at all surprised or put out by this admission.

'One in every three was a spy in the Hoxha years', Mr Georgio had told me earlier. 'You could not even trust your wife not to denounce you.' One in every three was feared to have been a spy, as in the Ottoman Empire. Now, with Communism ostensibly abolished, you couldn't even send your own son to Salonika – he wouldn't come back. But the foreigner was expected to invest $150,000 in a fantasy. Apart from us there were no clients at the restaurant, and there was no tourism in Albania: the border with Macedonia was closed, and all cars had to be guarded with guns against thieves and bandits. The amazing thing was, over the years, foreigners had invested in Albania – and lost everything, time and again.

'No', I said firmly, closing this pointless discussion. 'I don't want to invest in anything.' The folder was put aside. It had been worth a try. Perhaps one day a suitable mug would arrive, *inshallah*.

'Shall we have another plate of fish?' suggested Gabriel.

I had had more than enough. 'Not for me', I replied.

'I think we will have one more dish', Mr Slovki said to no one in particular. He spoke quite good English, but never talked, normally, when Gabriel was there. Why keep a dog and bark yourself? Mr Slovki spoke to the restaurateur in Albanian, and another dish of fish, seven or eight large pieces, was immediately brought to the table. It had clearly been ordered and cooked with the previous one, and was all ready. The foreigner would pay, so why not?

Gabriel and Mr Slovki tucked in with energy, swiftly scoffing the lot. I watched them impassively, now knowing I would be cheated on the bill, too. It was an unspoken contractual agreement that in exchange for buying their meals, the Albanian 'friend' you were with made sure you were not overcharged in the restaurants, which always happened otherwise. If there was one consistent trait all Albanians shared, it was to charge the foreigner the absolute maximum the market would bear. But here the unwritten rule was to be broken, for the ex-teacher was Gabriel's pal, and I had been set up.

I had been expecting the bill to be about $15, which it would have been in a Korça restaurant. It came to well over $30: almost two weeks' salary for Gabriel. I was handed the bill expectantly. They all watched me to see how I would take it.

It was clear I was upset. The atmosphere changed immediately and became frosty. They all knew they had gone too far. I had told Gabriel repeatedly that I was not in Albania on a grant, that no government or charity or organisation was paying for me. That I had a strict budget of $10 a day of my own money, to pay for my food and transport: and it was true.

'You knew how much the fish was going to cost, didn't you?' I told him. He avoided my eyes, wriggling like a child caught lying.

'It is very expensive', he said, hopelessly. In London it would have been nothing, but we were not in London. If he had said before we arrived 'Look – this is going to cost you $30 – is that okay?' I would not have been upset. But he hadn't, because he knew I would not have agreed. I had been told fairy-stories about *besa* and Albanian honesty and trust, about looking after the foreign guest. It was a con, I realised: these people were crooks who lied and fawned on you for advantage, and then cheated you when they had lulled you into believing their lies.

I paid the bill without comment and walked back to the car. The restaurateur came after me, cringing now and offering cigarettes and coffee. He realised he had overdone it. They all knew I was writing about Albania. What kind of things did they expect me to say about them? I remember a Turkish waiter telling me, in 1994, when a tourist had just been shot dead in the bazaar in Izmir: 'Write something nice about us for a change!' What could you say? 'Come to Turkey! Only One Tourist Shot Dead Today!'

But you were supposed to say only nice things, write only honeyed phrases: to do otherwise was to be 'hostile', to be 'unfriendly'.

Gabriel sat with me in the back of the car on the return to Korça instead of in the front with Mr Slovki. He fawned on me and tried to make amends with soothing words. He had great expectations but saw he had jeopardised them. He was stuck without foreigners to help him and his *fis*. He wanted to set up a private school to teach English and computing. He had asked my advice on this, tried to draw me into a patron-client relationship so I would feel committed to 'helping' him with money, books and equipment, as other English people had. He wanted me to intervene for him with his chief patron in England, to get this man to give him an IBM-compatible computer so he could use Windows 95. It was eating him up that his computers were not 'modern' enough.

Gabriel had two computers already, both of which he very rarely used: they were symbols of Western power and culture. He wouldn't take them down to the school to teach the children with: that would be to dilute his power. He used them as Enver Hoxha had used his 'French culture', picked up at the Korça Lycée and Montpellier University, to awe and impress other Albanians.

Gabriel had a good *biographi* in England: he had been anti-Communist; he helped aid workers, journalists and other travellers. He was pro-Democracy, pro-Western. Now he realised I could put in a bad report, and he would get some bad *biographi* with his patrons. This was the way Gabriel thought. He had already told me he knew that in the West 'everyone had a *biographi* just like in Albania, but with the bank, the employer, the police, everybody'. Like his sister Popi, he had been to England for two weeks, paid for by his English patrons. He was half-Westernised, but only half. He had the veneer, the clothes, the gold-framed specs, the command of foreign languages. But he thought like a feudal Albanian.

I had refused to intervene to try to get him the IBM computer he craved. When I got back to England I rang his English patron and explained the situation. But he knew the score: 'Oh, don't worry. Gabriel is the next Enver Hoxha – I've told him that many times. Those two computers he's got already aren't his, you know. They were sent out from a charity, and he just stole them *en route*. They were meant for a children's home.'

In Albania foreigners were a source of both plunder and of status: their 'culture', so admired, was also like an object to possess. To be 'cultured' was like having a Mercedes or a pack of genuine Marlboro cigarettes. It was to have got something Albanians themselves couldn't produce, but could only fake. The country was awash with imitation products – fake Marlboro cigarettes, Levi jeans, Lacoste shirts – and with imitation Western people, too, in dark glasses, Italian clothes, driving stolen Mercedes. For forty years Albania had been an imitation Soviet, a huge collectivised Potemkin village, in reality operating on clan and tribal lines. That had collapsed. Now it was an imitation of capitalism, a fun-fair democracy.

Whatever the ostensible 'system' the real basis for all Albanian endeavour was deceit, fraud and theft: a few pashas living on the backs of their slaving peons.

*

We drove back, largely in silence, through the green countryside, down a dead straight avenue built by the French and planted by the Italians with poplar trees on either side. Many had been cut down for fuel, but none had been replanted.

I was starting to see Albania as country where only foreigners had planned and built things, a former colony which was acted upon, itself only reacting.

Albanians waited until others came – Italians, Russians, Chinese, now the West – and then sought to gain personal and clan advantage from them. All the talk of Fascism, Communism and Democracy was a blind: these were costumes Albanians put on and took off to flatter and deceive foreigners, to convince them they had allies. Where was the evidence for all the billions of dollars of aid the Russians, the Yugoslavs and the Chinese had invested in the country since 1945? Hoxha and his clan had devoured it. Where had the billions of Western dollars that had poured into the country since 1991 gone? To people who stole computers and never used them: on big fish dinners, foreign furniture, imported beer, cigarettes, biscuits, bananas and other treats. No one worked unless they were forced to. No one did anything except for themselves and their clan.

Gabriel put on a tape of local Korça music, by a singer called Emira Babaliou. They were old songs, from the period of the Italian occupation. They were lovely, melancholy ballads of love, loss and regret, aching and beautiful. Gabriel, the musician, had orchestrated these for Babaliou, who had already left for America on *grin-*

cardi: there would be no follow-up album. He had laid a bossa nova rhythm behind the melody, which gave the tunes a strange, Brazilian feel. The guitar work, by contrast, was intricate and Spanish-sounding. How much of it was original, how much pastiche? Had some Italians from Mussolini's legions picked up this guitar style during the Spanish Civil War? It spoke of Andalusia, not Naples.

The music changed the landscape for me: the broken, destroyed orchards, their fruit trees cut down in 1991, the burnt-out houses and collectives we passed, the ragged peasants on donkeys and mules now illustrated not Balkan ruin. Rather, I was transported as if back to 1948, to the Italian *mezzogiorno* of the early films of the neorealists, De Sica and Rossellini. It became a pastoral, the figures gliding slowly as in a ballet.

This was the last gasp of the last of such traditional European peasant economies. Teams of oxen were ploughing, the men in rough homespun cloth and bare feet goading them with sticks; women in bright headscarves jogged along on mules, balanced earthenware clay water pots dangling from ropes on each side; small boys in ragged shorts herded ducks along the sides of the road; a tubercular-looking old man in a brown suit sat on a wooden harrowing chair, tugged over a field by two mules. All this had passed in Italy and Greece, Portugal and Spain. Nor, surely, could it last here under the hot breath of a subsidised international agrobusiness.

Gabriel and Mr Slovki refused to notice any of this archaic backdrop: it was simply not happening. They willed all this unculture away.

*

When we got back, Gabriel insisted that he buy me a beer, though neither of us wanted one. I had to agree, and had to let him pay. I insisted on the local Korça beer, not imported Amstel. This was half the price and twice as good. But even that had been originally brought in by the Italians in the '30s. The label was still in Italian, with the old design of an alpine lakeside castle unchanged through all the Communist years: 'Birre Pilzen – Grand Prix Hors Concours – Selenik 1935-9', it read. The recipe was old, too, and unchanged, hoppy and full, like the beer in Cyprus, still brewed to a colonial standard, something brought in by outsiders. I always tried to insist we drank Korça beer. 'If you do not support your own industries you will end up as an African colony', I warned Gabriel and his pals. But to them imported was best, anything Albanian *skata*.

Safely back in Korça, Gabriel was in a pensive, self-critical mood. He put his opened hand twelve inches in front of his face, in his own direct eye-line. 'My enemy is not here', he said, 'but here – ', and he clapped his other hand to the back of his neck.

4

Surviving the Whirlwind

Nests of Gentlefolk

NOSTRADAMUS HAD A donkey. One day he thought: 'I'll see if I can get this donkey of mine to do the same amount of work with one day's food less.' So he made the donkey toil as usual, without its food for that day. It succeeded – the animal kept working exactly the same.

'Surely, then', reasoned Nostradamus, 'he can be trained to do without two days' food.' This, too, was a success. The donkey went on working as before.

'Well then, certainly I can train my donkey to do without food altogether', Nostradamus concluded. So he stopped feeding his donkey – and the donkey went on working as before.

'So, I have succeeded!' exclaimed Nostradamus in triumph, 'I have trained my donkey to work without food!'

On the seventh day – a Sunday – the donkey dropped dead all of sudden. Nostradamus then flew into a great rage and cursed the dead donkey, beating its lifeless corpse with his stick.

'Cretin! Idiot donkey! Just when you become useful to me, just when I have succeeded in training you to work without food, you go and die on me!'

'Nostradamus was understood to be Enver Hoxha, the donkey Albania', Gabriel explained to me, in case I hadn't understood.

'I met Hoxha once, in the last years of his life', he continued. 'I was in the Korça orchestra and was on holiday by the sea at Vlora, with some friends. Suddenly we were recalled urgently. It was baking hot and the car we had been sent broke down. The chauffeur stopped another car from an enterprise *en route* and took spare parts from it – "important Party business!" He drove all day and night. When we arrived in Korça he was so tired he almost killed someone by knocking him over. We had to dress up in folk costume and play for Hoxha. He was very old by then, and wrinkled. His face was covered with fine pink powder to hide his decay. The whole thing was being filmed.'

Like all ageing dicatators, Hoxha feared his own end. Once he visited an old woman in Gjirokastra with his court. She was a distant relative and quite unafraid of the tyrant. 'You will live long!' he said to her, indulging her.

'No, no – you and I are both very old. We shall be dead very, very soon!' exclaimed the old woman vehemently.

Hoxha turned pale and started trembling. No one ever dared speak to him like this: it must be a prophecy. Everyone in Hoxha's entourage trembled. This was a man who liked attendants to follow after him on his tours, planting roses in his footsteps, where he had trodden, setting apple trees where his eye had chanced to fall on a bare patch of hillside.

Ramiz Alia, court sycophant and eventual successor to Hoxha, stepped in swiftly: 'No, no, Great Comrade Hoxha', he said lightly but seriously, 'You will live to be a hundred because that is in your family blood line, but you will get another twenty years from Socialism, too!' All the entourage clapped this piety with enthusiasm.

Hoxha relaxed, and smiled. The situation was saved and another savage purge perhaps averted.

Gabriel and I were still friends in spite of the fish-dinner coolness; but the days of wining and dining at my expense were over. I now ate alone, modestly, on food I bought in the bazaar. 'I have to save the $30 I have already spent', I told him, and it was true. Gabriel handed his whole pay packet to his father, who managed the family's expenses. Everyone was still paid in cash in Albania, a wodge of folding notes in an envelope every two weeks. Eleni, Gabriel's wife, did all the shopping for the *fis*. I had asked Gabriel to come with me to buy fruit in the bazaar once, but it was clear he had never shopped before. He didn't know how to choose fruit, or weigh it, or what the price should be. Budgeting, shopping and making-do were women's work. So how could one expect such coddled men to be responsible for themselves? If they got money or credit, they simply blew it on beer, cigarettes and big blow-outs, a nation of working-class irresponsibles. And this, during the summer of 1996, was what the whole of Albania was doing with the foreign aid that should have been restarting the economy: it was candy-floss capitalism. They had seen all this gaily coloured consumerism on Italian TV: now they too could have it. Work was what Communism had tried to make them do.

*

Gabriel hadn't wanted me to visit Rahman. He knew where he lived, but wouldn't show me or take me there. I found my own way to his shop, in spite of the lack of street signs, and received a rapturous welcome.

Rahman was a small, energetic, bald fellow in his late forties. Under capitalism he and his wife had set up as hairdressers, with equipment provided by English well-wishers. They had a salon in a run-down central block, barred and locked against thieves, with equipment from Italy and England. They were working hard, doing a thriving trade, a complete contrast to Gabriel, who was full of hot air but no action.

Rahman's eldest daughter, who was in her mid-teens, spoke good English. They insisted I come to their home for supper the next day. Gabriel – normally breathing over my shoulder when I composed a newspaper article on his computer, trying to mis-correct my English and prevent me saying critical things about the Democrat Party – was vague and distant about Rahman and his family. And they were cousins of his, too.

I took Italian wine and biscuits as gifts, which were received without thanks or comment, in the Albanian style. Rahman's home was a flat in a Stalinist block on the other side of town. Rahman took me there himself after work, guiding me through a ruined park where wizened old men sat cross-legged in little circles on the thin grass, each of them clad in a grey suit and a flat cap, living relics of Communism. They were pensioners, Rahman told me, just killing time.

Inside his apartment, Rahman had transformed the place. New Italian furniture, Italian tiles on the floors, a huge colour TV and VHS, a modern cooker, a large fridge. His children were smartly dressed and everything was neat and clean: the contrast with Gabriel's family's shabby, scruffy flat was marked.

But here there was no conversation. Rahman spoke a little English, but no one apart from him expressed any opinions. His eldest daughter translated my questions and her father's cryptic answers deadpan. She had a fiancé, called Toni, who looked Greek and had in fact been in Greece and spoke some English. He had worked illegally in the town of Drama for several months, seven days a week, paid 30,000 drachma a month where a Greek doing the same job would have been paid 60,000 or 80,000, he claimed. He had resented being treated 'like a third-class citizen'. 'Most southern Albanians are better educated than the Greeks. All they have is money.' Greek and Albanian Epirus had only been separated in 1913; before that, Greeks and Albanians had wandered up and down the land since antiquity and before. The curse of the modern nation-state had severed these provinces and caused all the problems: the two places were as alike as Northumbria and the Scottish Borders.

Toni was an evangelical Christian, recently converted, as were Rahman and his whole family, though by origin they were secularised Moslems, and Toni Orthodox.

We sat in embarrassed silence. I was guest of honour. Although it was hot and dry, I had to ask for a glass of water as we sat waiting interminably for dinner, being cooked by the women in the kitchen. A silent younger daughter was dispatched to get it, and serve it to me. No coffee was offered, no raki, no bon-bons: this was very un-Albanian.

If Rahman was reticent, Toni was open. He, not being yet part of the family, and speaking English, was allowed to talk to me directly.

Without a passport, he had walked across the border into Greece at night, guided by local villagers on either side for money. Most of the Albanians in Greece, he said, 'were from the north', though this meant Vlora and Durrës rather than Ghegeria, it later transpired. They had knives and guns, and often fought. Taking a sack of food with them, they would walk by night, sleeping during the day, for a week. Making for Florina or Kastoria, they would then get a taxi on to Salonika or Athens. Buses were avoided, as they were known to be stopped by the police. The Greeks pressurised the Albanians they caught to claim Greek ancestry and name. If they agreed to do so, they were often given papers. Sometimes the police asked them: 'What was your grandfather's name? Quickly! Quickly!' Confused, the Albanians often replied 'Mustafa' or 'Ahmet' – and were promptly chucked back over the border again.

Since 1991 many Albanians of Moslem origin had given their male children Greek names so they could eventually escape into Greece. Others had new Albanian identity papers issued, giving Greek names: this only cost $10 in bribes at the local *bashkir*, or town hall. In Edith Durham's day, in 1908, in the northern highlands, it had been the fashion for Catholic Albanian tribesmen to give themselves Moslem first names to add to their baptismal Christian names, 'because they liked the sound of them', but also probably because it stood them in good stead with the Ottoman authorities. Religion and ethnic identity in the Balkans were as much a matter of convenience as anything else.

The Franciscan priests in the north had always had to grow moustaches or they were not recognised by their parishioners; the Pope had given them a special dispensation to do so, and also to carry personal side-arms. One such friar, on leave in Italy, was arrested by a carabiniere as an imposter for sporting a Browning automatic and a full set of whiskers.

Many were the stories of sudden changes of faith in Albania, often due to outraged pride. One whole village threatened to turn Turk unless the Sunday Mass was delayed to allow them to get down for the start from their high pastures. The priest refused. So they all trooped down into Shkodra and converted *en masse*. Later they repented, and wanted to go back to Catholicism, but it was too late.

Toni confirmed what the Russian teacher at Gabriel's school had already told me: that to get into Greece legally, with a work visa, cost $1,000 to the Greek consular officials. A US visa cost $6,000 in bribes, only available in Tirana, where intermediaries fixed it. German and British visas were impossible to buy. No one wanted to go to France: they hated Moslems and were pro-Serb.

I pieced together Rahman's story slowly. He didn't mind my asking questions, and evidently regarded me with affection: I was a friend of his good friends in England. But he didn't volunteer anything. When I asked him if he knew any Enver Hoxha jokes, he said he didn't. So I told him one, but halfway through he said he knew it.

'Why didn't he tell it to me?' I asked the daughter. 'Because I was afraid', she translated for him. Then she added: 'He is joking.' But was he? Was that comment her interpretation, or his own words?

'As a hairdresser you hear lots of things', Rahman said. 'You have to respect the clients' confidence.' He had been a barber under the Communists. His father had had a barber's shop in the Zog and the Italian time: he had hung on the wall a portrait of Mussolini, with King George of the Greeks on the back. As the Italians and Greeks invaded, retreated and re-invaded, he had turned the portrait round and about.

'Every Albanian has two flags', Rahman told me, 'the one he is waving and the one he is holding behind his back.' I told him about Hoxha's food taster, which he hadn't known of, but which didn't surprise him. 'I expect Berisha has a food taster too', he commented.

With Gabriel I had visited the school in Korça where the Albanian language had first been taught in the late nineteenth century. Three of the founding teachers had been murdered, one by the Turks with poison in his coffee, one by poisoned *loukoumia* given to him by a Greek Orthodox priest, the third pushed out of a window in a hotel in Constantinople by persons unknown, but presumed to be the Ottoman secret police. One of the few things Greeks and Turks were agreed upon pre-1913 was the undesirability of fostering Albanian nationalism.

The food finally came. Chips, fried meatballs, fried spam, and a dollop of bottled mayonnaise: a grease-up special. Lemonade was added to the Italian wine. The whole family cut their food first with knives, then ate it with forks only, like peasants. No one spoke as we ate.

The TV spewed out multicoloured rubbish from Italy. There was an Italian game-show on, which by chance had an Albanian girl, very beautiful, as one of the mannequins: she got a big round of applause from Rahman's family when her nationality was announced. They all watched avidly as a collection of modern jewellery was displayed, commenting on the value. But when two rival craftsmen from Bologna and Florence were set against the clock to put complex ruby and diamond brooches together, the whole family lost interest and turned away. Work, craftsmanship, how the West was won, none of this mattered to them.

After we had finished eating, Rahman showed me a clip of a video someone had sent him from America on hairdressing. Gripping stuff.

Rahman had started doing fancy, bourgeois ladies' hairdressing illegally in Communist times. Some copies of an Italian magazine called *Estetica* had been sent to a library by mistake; a friend had stolen them and then sold them on to Rahman. That had given him ideas, some styles, and got him started. Then his new English friends, tourists met on holiday at Lake Ochrid, had been importuned for supplies. The next year they had returned with basic kit for him – scissors, razors, shampoo, conditioner, hairdryers – all quite unobtainable in Albania, of course.

When had they started to doubt Communist propaganda, I asked? 'We believed everything until 1991. Then we saw on foreign TV that things were better in the West', the daughter said.

She wasn't translating now but speaking for herself. 'A foreign language is a weapon in the struggle of life', Enver Hoxha had claimed, plagiarising Mao Tse Tung. The old, patriarchal Albanian order was being undermined by the girls' skill at these new, important languages.

'In 1982, during your miners' strike', she added, 'we saw the news and we felt so sorry for the British, starving and beaten by the Fascist police. "Why don't you make a revolution like us?" we thought.'

The next day, when we were sitting at a café drinking beer again, Gabriel said to me: 'Of course, Rahman was Party secretary of the Communist Barbers' Union during the Hoxha years.'

*

Gabriel had produced a pal of his called Azem, who spoke French: he was a thin, dark-haired, intense type, who even managed to resemble a Gallic intellectual. Like Enver Hoxha, who had studied at the French Lycée in Korça, he was a local French teacher. Hoxha had been a student at Montpellier University. His enemies said he had failed his exams there. His supporters claimed King Zog had ended his bursary when a critical article in *L'Humanité* on the monarchy was traced back to Hoxha, even though he'd used the pen-name Lulo Malesore. 'Malesore' meant 'noble man of the mountains' in the Gheg north, where Zog's *fis* came from. Hoxha was a Tosk from the south: treason and impertinence combined.

French culture still meant something in Albania, above all in

Korça. Camus' *The Outsider* had been a best-seller when it had been translated after the fall of Communism: the fate of Sisyphus, eternally rolling that rock up the hill, had a peculiar resonance for Albanians.

I had mentioned to Gabriel that I'd lived and worked in France for three years: he wanted to check out how good my French was, hence Azem. Gabriel wasn't sure what I was worth.

'We have the worst Western foreign experts sent to us', he told me in disgust on another occasion. 'Two Irish were sent from the EU in Brussels. They spoke a very bad English, "Brrr-iaou . . . brr-antriu . . . brr-anpiin . . ." mumbling like this, eating their lips' (and here he demonstrated, flubbing his lips with his fingers). 'No one could understand them. They were also stupid and patronising. They told us how to make raki. We have been making raki for hundreds of years.'

I spoke to Azem in French: my stock immediately rose with Gabriel, who could not contribute. He sat there gasping like a landed fish. When he tried to speak French only Italian came out, which Azem neither spoke nor understood.

'When I first went to Greece in 1991, I asked my parents what Salonika was like', Azem told me. '"Like Korça", they said. When I got near, at night, in the bus, I saw the lights shining on the horizon and I became afraid. "Oh, God", I thought, 'This is going to be like New York."'

'I walked round the streets of this great, modern, shiny city in a daze. I kept asking people: "Is this enterprise private, too?" It seemed impossible that such large stores did not belong to the state. Even the poor dressed like the rich. How could Salonika have become like this in such a short time, when before the war it was like Korça? I felt very ashamed of Albania. I worked illegally for several months and then travelled to Italy, France and Switzerland. I liked Switzerland very much. It impressed me deeply – so clean, so well ordered. I would like to live there very much.'

Would he consider leaving Albania for ever? 'If I were twenty-one, yes, certainly, but I am forty-one. I have a family and children and am building a house. It cannot be.'

We drank our beer and smoked. It was difficult to find any Albanian cigarettes now. What had happened to the famous Tarabosh tobacco from Shkodra, I asked Gabriel. 'Marlboro have beaten them. L & M have conquered them. Assos have destroyed them completely', he intoned without irony.

I found one brand called Drino, packed in crude cardboard with no cellophane. These cost 13 leks for twenty, or 13 US cents, and were very short with no filter. They were poorly rolled, and had the faintest reminiscent whiff of the Israeli brand Avion, which we had been given as a free issue in the kibbutz in 1969: these were so terrible that even the poorest Palestinian beggar would refuse one if you offered it to him. If you rolled a Drino in your fingers, held vertically, the tobacco trickled out, like the Victory cigarettes in George Orwell's *1984*.

Gabriel had heard of neither George Orwell nor *1984*. I had begun making a list of the things Gabriel – by far the most well informed and educated Albanian I met – had never heard of: surrealism, sado-masochism, inferiority complex, Freud, post-modernism, F. R. Leavis and George Steiner were some of them. The only modern English or American author he had read was Graham Greene, and before that Jack London.

We would sit and talk at our regular pavement café, a two-table affair served by an effusively subservient old man with a bald head and an exaggerated smile. We were his only customers; drinking beer in cafés was too expensive for most Albanians.

'That man was the head of the Sigurimi in Korça.' Gabriel indicated a tall, slim, blond man in his early thirties, conventionally handsome, who was holding the hand of his young daughter as he bought her an ice cream.

Across the road from us, in the overgrown garden of a once fine, now ruined Italian villa, a gypsy was being berated by a policeman in uniform: the gypsy had tethered his horse there to graze. He was made to take the animal away, holding the rope halter in his hand.

Elsewhere in Korça during the *volta*, I had seen a uniformed policeman greet a civilian friend in the street, kissing him four times on the cheeks, *à la française*. The two men had gripped each others' coat sleeves as if they were drowning.

*

'Take me to someone who remembers the Italians and Zog', I asked Gabriel; and he did.

Albanians knew almost nothing of their own past. Gabriel had been astonished to learn of the 10,000-strong Albanian SS troop, the Skanderbeg Division, raised in Kosovo by the Nazis in the war. He knew about the Hoxha years, but nothing before except Albanian nationalist propaganda he had learnt at school.

Andreas was Gabriel's great-uncle. He had been born in 1915, in a village near Korça. His father had been a Vlach shepherd who took his flocks into Greece in winter, up into the mountains round Korça in summer. His whole family had settled in a village in 1927, when Andreas was twelve, then later had moved into Korça.

Andreas seemed to be a very old man indeed: stooped, bent and feeble. His wife was equally ancient, though more energetic. They sat in their Ottoman-era stone house and blinked at me as I asked my questions through Gabriel.

Their house was spacious. They had a large fridge and a TV. On the living room floor was a fine large dowry kilim, woven by Andreas' wife, Yola. Gabriel was very polite and deferential, translating directly without intervention. 'I am like a machine', he told me, 'I translate what people say – if they make a mistake I translate that too.'

In the 1920s in Korça, Andreas told me, there had been very few cars, perhaps half a dozen. To go to Tirana you had to wait until a lorry taking food went, and then ride up on the sacks: you might have to wait three or four days. His father had told him that the Ottoman time, before 1908, was very bad. There were Turkish soldiers and they could attack you in the hills, steal everything and murder you. No one punished them.

In the Zog time the Prefect of Korça was a Gheg, as was the head of the police. There had been a secret police chief too, also a Gheg: he kept files on people, had paid informers, and was much feared. 'You can say the Zog regime was half a dictatorship', Andreas concluded. Zog had never come to Korça. He stayed in his palace in Tirana.

You could buy Italian, French and Greek newspapers easily in Korça in the 1930s. It was easy to go to Greece and Italy, too. There was no paper money, people had gold napoleons. There was no bank in Korça before the Italian businessmen came in the mid-1930s. People buried their money in tin boxes sealed up, either in their gardens or in the walls of their houses. The Communists shot many people who refused to tell them where their gold was hidden.

A school friend of Andreas was shot for not handing over the family gold. He died with the secret: no one now knew where it was hidden. This happened to many families. The Communists confiscated any gold they found.

The Italian time was a good time. The Italians were polite, cultured and brought in goods from Italy, 'though not of the first quality because of the war'. Had the Germans and the Italians got on well? 'Of course, they were both Fascists and Nazis – they were the same *fis*.'

The Germans had been billeted in every house, three to a room, but only for a few days. They were distant and formal. They didn't eat with the families or talk. If you left them alone, they left you alone. If you attacked them they took terrible revenge. They were only passing through.

Andreas had started listening to the foreign broadcasts of the Voice of America and the BBC in the 1950s, but not very often. If you were denounced you got fifteen years.

I had already learnt from Gabriel that the East German radio sets made in Albania under licence had a shortwave band. At first this was so Albanians could listen to Radio Moscow, then to Radio Peking after the break with Russia. When they broke with China, no one thought to stop production of this model, so Albanians with radios could always get Western stations, if they dared. Andreas believed all Western broadcasts. He knew the Communists were lying about everything in the country and outside.

His father had spoken perfect Greek. He himself spoke it badly. His wife spoke it rather better, and – rare for an Albanian woman – she kept interrupting her husband in his narrative and correcting him. But then they were Vlachs, really, by origin, not Albanians.

They didn't talk to anyone about anything during the Communist period: it was too dangerous. When Hoxha had been friendly with the Yugoslavs, many of them had come across and bought up goods with worthless dinars, which Hoxha made equal to leks. Products vanished for ever from the shops. Another very bad time was after they broke with Russia, when there were serious shortages, especially wheat flour. Maize bread from the north was introduced: it was hard and poor in quality. In Zog's time merchants grew very rich from bringing in grain from Serbia, Slavo-Macedonia and Greece, where it was cheap.

I asked Andreas if he thought Hoxha was a good man who took the wrong road, or an evil man who wanted to oppress and hurt Albanians. Andreas and his wife both now thought he was an evil man.

They had been married in the Albanian Orthodox Church, by a visiting bishop from Connecticut, USA, having coronets (the same word in Albanian as English) put on their heads. Andreas showed me the black and white wedding photographs. After 1967 priests disappeared and all icons were collected from people's homes when Albania became the first officially atheist state in Europe.

Was Andreas frightened of foreigners now? Did he think they were spies? No, he was not frightened of them. What would they spy on? All was open and free. Democracy was a good thing.

As we sat and talked, to and fro, Yola moved in and out of the kitchen serving us raki, *bons-bons* in wrappers, *loukoumia* and coffee, in that order. She spoke some halting Greek to me directly. Their raki was noticeably better than Mr Georgio's.

Andreas had been a pharmacist. Once, in Hoxha's time, a relative of Albanian descent had visited from America. He asked Andreas to record a message for other relatives in the States on a tape recorder. Andreas had done so, but afterwards 'had felt terrible and could not sleep for fear'. The next day he asked for an interview with the police chief and told him what he had done. He didn't think it was added to his *biographi*, but he wanted to make a clean breast to the Sigurimi so he could not be accused to having hidden such an incident. No action was ever taken against him.

*

The election grew near. The Socialists had found me an ex-Minister from the former transitional government to interview. He was thin and wiry, in late middle age, with gold teeth and sparse, dyed hair. He chain smoked, though calmly and deliberately.

Gabriel wanted to translate for him, but the ex-Minister preferred to trust to his own slow English, which proved adequate to the task. He clearly didn't trust Gabriel. Once again, Gabriel sat there like a mute fish, unable to take part in the conversation, but unwilling to disengage.

The ex-Minister was experienced and intelligent: he knew

France, Italy and Germany. He had a young Socialist newspaper-man with him, bearded and in his late twenties, who spoke French and who had worked in Lyon.

'About half the Socialist Party are old-style Stalinists, the other half European-style Social Democrats', the ex-Minister told me. 'I am one of the latter group. In the long run we must prevail: there's no future in Stalinism.'

'What about this election?' I asked.

'Already there have been many, many irregularities. We fear it will not be fair. We fear Berisha's appointees will not allow the election to be honest. Almost all the mayors are Democrat supporters and they control the polling stations.'

What would the Socialists do if they felt the election was unfair? The ex-Minister thought for a moment, lit another cigarette and said: 'We will not embark on any adventures.'

*

The night before the election was Gabriel's birthday. I was invited to a family celebration at the family's flat. Popi was there, too, and all the children. I sat next to Mr Georgio, as guest of honour. The children ate in a separate room. The women served us food. Mr Georgio poured us his home-made raki. Popi drank this, too, and Eleni.

We had a Greek-style *meze*, then soup and meat with chips and salad. I had brought a bottle of Italian wine and biscuits, as my contribution. I heard Popi ask Gabriel in Albanian how much my wine had cost, assuming I couldn't understand. '300 lek', he told her, in Albanian. This was $3: more than a day's wages for her.

Mr Georgio gave the only toast of the evening: 'To the victory of the Democrat Party'. Everyone raised their glasses, even the elderly grandmother, dressed entirely in black, who otherwise said nothing.

'I am very worried', Gabriel confided to me later, as we walked the silent, pitch-black streets. 'If they lose tomorrow, we lose every-thing. We are not ready for a change. I hope the Democrat Party do rig the election – it will be better.' It was out in the open at last. Gabriel was a Democrat, but not a democrat.

With him earlier, I'd gone round the new Orthodox Cathedral

which was being built with Greek money in the centre of town. I had pointed out a huge inlaid marble Star of Vergina set into the floor. 'Do you know what that is?' I asked him. Gabriel, Orthodox by origin, admitted he didn't.

'That is the sign that was on Philip of Macedon's shield, found at the excavation of his tomb. It is the symbol of Greek Macedonia. It's on all their banks, shops, tourist maps, local government signs. It's like Skanderbeg's double eagle for them – not a religious but a national symbol. What do you think the Greek tour guides are going to say to the Greek schoolchildren they bring here in twenty years time?'

'"See! There is the sign of Macedonia on the ground in our Orthodox church, proving this is really and has always been our own Greek Macedonian territory"', I intoned.

This subterfuge shook Gabriel. He was Orthodox, but an Albanian patriot. The architect of the new cathedral was a Macedonian Greek, from Salonika. The old cathedral had been knocked down by the Communists; the *bashkir*, or prefecture, was now on the original site. The new one would be right opposite.

We had gone round the town again, and I had pointed out the Star of Vergina symbol worked into the iron railings of balconies, walls and gates of Greek houses from the 1900s and 1920s.

'What does it mean?' Gabriel asked me, genuinely puzzled.

'Perhaps so the Greek soldiers knew which houses were owned by Vlachs and Greeks – houses not to loot or burn', I suggested.

When the Greeks had finally been made to quit Korça after the First World War occupation, they had buried some 'Greek antiquities' from elsewhere underground, so they would be able to dig them up again one day to 'prove' Korça was really settled by ancient Greeks, when they eventually marched back in again one day. The Albanians had learnt about this trick, and dug them all up again in front of the foreign press, who then exposed the plot.

Albania was so fragile, with so many enemies. Even the supporters of Democracy didn't really believe in its ability to rule them without fraud.

People afterwards asked me whether the 1996 election was fair or not. What could I say? In Korça I saw nothing irregular, except that the police were actually inside the voting centres, which apparently they should not have been. Everything was quiet and orderly. 'Our French culture', said one policeman to me proudly.

On the day of the poll I met the Socialists at noon, after touring the electoral centres. They were angry and emotional. 'There has been widespread fraud and rigging', they claimed, 'especially in the villages.'

Gabriel was very happy. 'We shall win now, and democracy will continue.' He meant by this that the Democrat Party would continue in power. That, I realised, was what Albanians meant by 'democracy'.

Albanian state TV reported that the whole election had been correct and fair. Reuters reported 'allegations of widespread fraud' on satellite TV. The Socialists pulled out of the election at 6 p.m., and their observers withdrew.

Gabriel had been a translator for a Bulgarian observer at the 1991 transitional elections: there had been widespread intimidation and rigging in the villages by the Communists, then in power. The Bulgarian had made an official protest.

In the Hoxha years voting in elections was compulsory. Party workers came round and rousted out people at 6 a.m., even the sick. Everyone was given a printed slip of paper with the Communist candidate's name on, and was watched closely as they put it in the urn. The radio kept up a constant, excited barrage: 'It is 6.15 and already 48% of Albania has voted!' Hoxha's candidates always secured 97% of the vote.

In the 1996 elections the voters were given a slip of paper with all the candidates' names on: they crossed out those they didn't like. There were international observers at most polling stations. I met some young Flemish Belgians, who were from a European Socialist Guild. They claimed there had been 'serious fraud'.

The celebrations now began. With the Socialist candidates all withdrawn, the Democrat party claimed a landslide: there would only be nine opposition seats in the new parliament. I was asked anxiously by Gabriel and his friends what the West would do. I said I didn't know, but things didn't look hopeful.

Up and down the streets of Korça cars and trucks roared to and fro, all evening and into the night. 'Sa-li Ber-i-sha!' the all-male mob chanted in five syllables, madly waving EU and Albanian flags. These were the *rrugaças*, or street roughs, who a year later were to pull Berisha's regime into the dust after the pyramid schemes failed.

Now, though, all over the country, as we saw on TV, the same boulevard theatre was being acted out. Albania was the only place I had ever seen the European Union flag, the golden circlet of stars on its blue field, genuinely sported by enthusiastic people. Many cars flew it for sympathetic magic: they so wanted to 'get into Europe'.

As the night progressed, the *rrugaças* got more drunk and more aggressive. Hard liquor was being passed around, swigged from the bottle. The police looked on benignly: their jobs were safe. If the Socialists had won, they would all have been sent back to the villages again, unemployed. Every single public service job was a political appointment.

In the streets of Korça there were no functioning street lights and the pavements were all broken, the roads deeply pot-holed. Yet when I was introduced to the Mayor, I noticed his office had elegant new Italian furniture, fax machines and expensive carpets. The Mayor and his young aides were well-dressed in smart Italian clothes. In his twenties, he looked like a TV executive from Naples or the south.

All but 5% of his budget came from Tirana, from the Democrat central government. People in Albania didn't like paying taxes, he told me. Or paying for electricity: they preferred to connect themselves up illegally to a power line. They were supposed to pay local taxes, but most didn't. The tax collectors accepted bribes to exempt them. Korça had negotiated a $25 million loan from a German bank: this would help matters a lot, when it came through.

'He has been all over Europe, and to America five times', Gabriel told me with awe, before I was presented. 'He has been to places in America even Americans cannot afford to go into.'

This was a curious but very Albanian notion: in the Hoxha time there was part of Tirana permanently forbidden to ordinary Albanians known as 'the Block'. Here the senior Party and their families lived, in Western bourgeois style and comfort.

The Mayor was the first person who asked me questions about places outside Albania. What did I think of Refah, the fundamentalists in Turkey? And Egypt? Roumania? Roumania had very strong potential with oil and industry, he thought. His administration was going to receive training in local government from Britain, he said proudly – a case of the blind leading the blind if ever I heard of one. I taught Gabriel the meaning of 'a jobsworth', telling him he'd soon be needing it.

'Albanians always go to extremes', the Mayor told me, 'to the extreme end of communism, and now I think to the extreme end of capitalism.' In this prediction he was certainly proved correct.

'We will be the first Eastern country to be in NATO', he also opined, and in this he wasn't wholly wrong either, Albania later being the first ex-Communist country to be occupied by NATO soldiers.

*

The day after the election the Socialist headquarters was like a morgue. There was no one to be seen, only pop music coming from a loudspeaker. 'When they were in power you got ten years for listening to that music. Now they play it to show how they've changed', said Gabriel bitterly.

There had been a cabaret show from Tirana the night before on state TV. A middle-aged male singer warbled away emotively into the mike. 'He served twenty years for singing the Beatles' "Let it be" in the Hoxha years', I was told. That night he sang 'Summertime' in English, as a symbol that now songs could be sung in English, all thanks to Democracy.

'Maybe he was gaoled for being such a bad singer', I suggested. No one laughed at this. The pain, the horror of the recent Communist past was still too fresh in their minds.

As we walked past the Socialist HQ, keeping in the shade of the roadside trees, a man suddenly rushed out of the building. He ran close, pulled up his camera, and took my photograph, head and shoulders; and then rushed back into the building again.

'What was that about?' I asked.

'For your *biographi*', Gabriel said in a matter-of-fact voice.

The day before, complaining to me bitterly of voting irregularities, the Socialists said that they hadn't been able to take photos of intimidation 'because they hadn't got the cameras'. Poor organisation for a party that had been in power since 1945.

*

The day before I left Korça I was walking with Gabriel in a rundown part of town. His confidence had returned after the Democrat

73

election victory. He was giving me a variation of his long mono-
logue-lecture on how Western Albania was, and how the West must
help them. We were walking by an old crumbling mosque with a
broken minaret, the call for prayer sounding from above. A man in
baggy breeches and a white fez was beating his donkey to try to
make it move. A group of gypsies in bright costumes were squatting round a fire, while barefooted children played happily in an
open sewer that ran, stinking, through the street. Broken lorries and
rubbish surrounded us.

'Stop talking for a minute, Gabriel, and just look at where we are.'

He stopped, stared round, then looked at me. 'I can see nothing',
he said.

'That is exactly the trouble.'

We climbed up to the Martyrs' Memorial, where a huge concrete
Socialist Realist statue of a partisan, gun in hand, stood guarding
the graves of the dead fighters. A man in a battered suit came out of
a cave and hailed us: I thought he was a tramp, but he was the
guardian, paid by the state, still, to safeguard the monument
'against vandalism and sacrilege'.

We looked at the gravestones, each marked with a name and the
Communist star. 'Most of them didn't die fighting', Gabriel said.
'They brought them in from village graveyards after the war and
reburied them. The only people the partisans ever fought were
Zogists and Balli Kombetar. They planted vines all over this place,
but they died of phylloxera.'

Below us in town a solitary tall brick chimney stack belched out
black smoke, covering Korça with smog. 'The Chinese built it with
very old technology, but the filter broke years ago. It would cost
$500,000 to replace, so they just left it', Gabriel told me. When it
worked, this plant generated all Korça's electricity.

I looked down on the town, the inner ring of red-tiled colonial
Italian villas and Ottoman houses giving way to the tower blocks of
the Hoxha years. With the chaplet of mountains all around and the
tiara of pollution, it looked more than ever like a Soviet invention in
Central Asia.

That evening we drank beer again and smoked cigarettes
together in the café. The next day I was to leave for Gjirokastra. I
had given Gabriel two novels in English for his birthday: E.M.
Forster's *Howards End* and a spy thriller about Kim Philby.

It was Philby who had betrayed to Soviet Russia details of the Anglo-American post-war invasions of Albanian Royalists. Hoxha's men had been waiting for the parachutists, and shot them upon arrival. Very few survived.

'Was that true?' Gabriel asked me. 'I thought it was just Communist propaganda.'

Gabriel was the first and the last Albanian I ever saw reading a book of any kind in any language: CNN had beaten them; RAI had conquered them: BBC had destroyed them completely.

5

Albania–Africa

Through the Grammos Mountains

'IT IS A GOOD road from Korça to Gjirokastra, built by the Italians before the war', Mr Georgio had told me earnestly, trying to allay my fears. 'Very few buses fall over the cliffs, except in the winter rains.'

It was a terrible road. It could not really even be called a road, rather, a rough track hacked like a knife wound through the mountains. It was too narrow for all but a slim jeep. Yet we drove up and up, winding round the corners, in a very old, stout, faded blue Greek bus, which still had Larissa shown on the front as its destination.

At every corner we would slow to walking pace: but still the loose shale and earth under the offside wheels would crumble and spin off, falling thousands of feet below with a dry rattle that seemed to echo in my throat. If this was a good Albanian road, what was a bad one like?

We never made more than 35 kilometres an hour – mostly under 15. I felt like getting out and walking much of the time, for my own safety. The bus constantly swayed from side to side and bucketed up and down. The driver had passed out thin plastic shopping bags before we started: most of the peasants started vomiting when we began to rise up through the first few low mountain passes.

We climbed and we climbed: still the high Grammos Mountains loomed ahead of us in massy bulk, a grey and white, craggy doom. It was like entering a country of mythological giants. You really expected to see a Cyclops up ahead on the track, surrounded by black, shaggy goats the size of yaks.

This was an impossible, magnificent country, fit only for bear, wolf and bandit. It was up here that the partisans had lived and trained in the Second War, descending to fight; through these moun- tains that Smiley and Maclean, the first British emissaries to the guerrillas had infiltrated from Greece. With enough food and ammunition you could live up here for ever.

We had crept up from the warm, fertile plain of Korça, misty still in the early morning, the road lined on either side with tall poplars, reminiscent of Lombardy or the Po valley.

The peasants on board were mainly from the Greek minority vil- lages; they looked at me shyly and whispered to each other in soft Greek. The bus was only half full when we started at 6 a.m. Mr Georgio had walked down with me, my bag slung over the handle- bars of Gabriel's Raleigh bike. The streets of Korça were being swept with water by gypsy women in long, bright, multicoloured dresses. They used witches' brooms of long switches bound together round a wooden haft. A tramp with a long white beard sat outside a bank- rupt, boarded-up Communist-era enterprise, piling cardboard on a small fire to warm himself in the morning chill. Rubbish was being laboriously shovelled into a metal cart. Korça, which had seemed to me when I first arrived as a broken, destroyed place, something out of Central Asia, now appeared as a town with a civic tradition, street cleaners, rubbish collection. Before the war Korça was known as 'le petit Paris', I was told in Gjirokastra.

The night before I left I had gone into the living room to pay Popi. Three gypsy women were sitting on the floor cross-legged, watch- ing a large black man in glasses reading the financial news from Washington on CNN. The gypsies looked like an illustration by Augustus John, hair tied up in red and yellow bandanas, silver coins on chains dangling from their brows, bare feet and hennaed hair. One of them had turned to look at me, and smiled: 'The dollar is up again', she said happily. As well as horseflesh, the Albanian gypsies traded in currencies. I had been invited in to the living room on another occasion to take coffee with Popi and her next door neighbour, an old gypsy woman who looked like the agèd Geronimo. She gazed deep into my eyes very intently, and then smiled: 'He has a good face' she said in Albanian to Popi, who told me in English. I found this verdict both unaccountably touching and reassuring. Enver Hoxha had a soft spot for the gypsies and never persecuted them – except by forcing them indoors. His own mother was dry and he'd had a gypsy wet-nurse when he was a baby: 'That is why my complexion is somewhat dark', he used to joke in later years. I often wondered how both the Albanian Jews and gypsies escaped extermination by the Germans in the war. Perhaps it was simply too difficult, that the Germans were always in too tenuous a position themselves. Apparently there were no Jews now left in the country. The small community had all left for Israel in a body after the fall of Communism.

*

Fields of maize gave way to ruined orchards, many of them lifeless, mere rows of stumps, destroyed in the 1991 rising against Communism – a rising of slaves against masters – or burnt for fuel in the shortages afterwards. Albanian Socialism had created an agricultural helot society, a latifundia where forcibly collectivised peasants worked for the state on starvation rations, their produce confiscated and sold to support a tyranical ruling élite. When that system collapsed, the peasants destroyed the collective farms and orchards so they could never be made to work in them again, whatever happened.

Now the peasants had returned to herding sheep and goats up on the mountain slopes, as they had before 1945. Enver Hoxha's family had been wealthy Moslem proprietors from Gjirokastra, owning much land in the Greek-minority border villages. Here the Christian peasants toiled for them under conditions of semi-slavery. Hoxha nationalised this peasant-serf economy, like everything else: the whole of Albania was to be his fief. Khruschev had criticised the Albanian Communist Party for being dominated by 'the sons of Beys and Aghas'. The reference to Hoxha himself was clear and infuriated him, in no small way influencing the break with the Soviet Union. Photographs of the early Communist partisans in the mountains tell the whole story: groups of young, weedy-looking townee intellectuals in plus fours and raincoats *alla franga*, overgrown café-society students, surrounded by shy, stocky, blank-faced peasants with Martini-Henry rifles and bandoliers. Hoxha had hated his own father, all his family in fact, except his uncle.

Now the land was returning to its past. Where wheat had once grown, gaunt men with sickles now cut the long grass for winter hay. Field after field had been abandoned, gone wild, poppies glowing like rubies amidst the swaying emerald grass and pale, feral wheat.

There were two gypsy boys on the bus, sitting at the front. They were very dark, with wild black hair. They sang and beat their hands in time on the metal of the seat front. The driver played Greek *rembetika* on the tape machine. The gypsies' rhythm and beat were their own, not in time or counterpoint to the recorded music. The heads of the old peasant women were swathed in black scarves; the men wore open-necked shirts and rough old suits with mismatching flat caps. These country people carried wicker baskets full of food they had bought in Korça, covered with old, patched napkins of white linen. The bus would stop in the middle of nowhere and let them off: they bade no one farewell, but stumbled silently away down rocky tracks into hidden valleys. There were no houses visible in these lower pastoral highlands above Korça.

I had the eerie sense of passing through a remote part of Greece I did not know, somewhere around the year 1948.

Soon we were finished with agriculture altogether. Dense green-black forests of pine rose amid the wildest desolations of rockface and sheer mountain cliff. Lord Byron and Edward Lear both said the mountains of Albania knocked those of Greece into a cocked hat, and as far as the Grammos were concerned no one could possibly dispute their judgement. We were shadowing the Greek border all the way: it lay a few kilometres to our left, over the impossible ranges.

I thought Dhori Qiriazi was a businessman or functionary at first. He wore smart glasses and boasted a row of pens in his shirt pocket. He had a tie on, and wore trousers with creases. I sat opposite him deliberately right from the start, and soon we started up a conversation. He was in his forties and spoke some Greek and was travelling alone. He came to sit next to me, delighted to have company. Although no distance in kilometres, this journey to Gjirokastra would take seven or eight hours because of the mountains and the bad road.

'The Communists never repaired the roads', Dhori told me. 'They didn't want people to travel around. They themselves had planes and helicopters to move about in, or strong Benzes which could cope with the roads. This one is as the Italians left it. When there is a landslide, the villagers just fill it in with loose earth, and it soon goes again. In winter it's ofen closed for weeks, or impassable with snow. A truck slipped off last week in heavy rain – everyone on board killed – one whole family riding on the top of the sacks. It rolled over and over . . .'

We passed wreck after wreck below us, trucks, buses, cars that had slid off the road and tumbled down thousands of feet. I had never been on such a ghastly road before. I could not bring myself to look over the edge of the cliffs which we crept round so cautiously. I gripped the metal bar in front of me in futile terror much of the time and compulsively sucked boiled sweets from Syria, Al Sabah brand, which were strongly acidic, like the sweets of my childhood. I'd bought them in the bazaar before leaving Korça.

All the books warn one about this road, but the reality was far, far worse than I had imagined. I really did not give us much more than a 50% chance of arriving in Gjirokastra. Every ten minutes or so we would oh-so-nearly slide off the edge, the wheels grasping desperately with such thin purchase on the crumbling soil. I lit cigarette after cigarette and tried to keep looking up, up at the spectacular crags above us: see the Grammos and die.

Dhori Qiriazi was originally from Berat. He was a qualified mechanical engineer, but when his enterprise had closed in 1991 he went to Greece. Now he had a flat in Athens and regular papers: he sold lottery tickets in the streets. He was proud of this job, and said he earned 'very good money'. His wife and family still lived in Berat in their apartment. He had just come from visiting them there, then on to see friends in Korça. Now he would go to Saranda on the coast to visit some of his own family, then go back to Athens again. He was loud in his contempt for the wilderness through which we were passing: 'Po . . . po . . . po! Skata . . . skata!' he would say, grimacing at the mountains.

Yet even in the wilderness, in the very highest passes, perched on crags and hidden in narrow valleys, there were bunkers built by Hoxha. These and the occasional enormous Socialist Realist concrete statues of heroic partisans waving their rifles from rocky eminences gave the landscape a surreal quality, as though some eccentric billionaire had commissioned Christo and Salvador Dalí to combine to create a satirical Communist-Paranoid theme park in this remote Balkan wilderness.

Right up high in amidst these passes we came to Leskoviku. It looked like a small town on my map, but was nothing but a crumbling village with broken concrete apartments and old cottages half in ruin. There were cows and sheep in the streets and a bitter wind blew down off the high Grammos.

The bus halted and we ran into the only café. Here men in grey suits sat round drinking raki and smoking. There was no heating, no fire, and the electricity was off. The owner had installed a large brass-plated colonial-style fan overhead, which hung lifeless and futile. There was an Italian espresso machine, which of course didn't work as the power was off – as it had been for the last three days. We drank raki and smoked cigarettes, stamping our feet to keep warm. There was nothing to eat. Dhori had brought some fatty Greek salami and offered me chunks. He paid for my raki before I could get my money out. Raki cost 10 lek (12 cents) a shot. A hundred years ago, with charcoal from the mountain trees and wood fires instead of the dead electrical heaters and machines, we and the villagers would have been warm and comforted with hot coffee: Communism, in aping the 'modernity' of the West, had simply destroyed what little had existed before.

Outside, spindly, ill-looking young men stood about morosely in the streets. A thin, youthful Orthodox priest in robes and high hat mooched about hopelessly. His pasty, bearded face was covered with boils and his nose seemed to be being eaten away. 'Sifiliticos!' Dhori whispered to me, and I confess I had thought the same thing.

'Skata!' said Dhori with disgust. 'No money, only skata – Albania – Africa!' His open hand waved round, encompassing all Leskoviku, then he beat the air with it in short, chopping movements, and grimaced, miming giving the place a beating. In lieu of hot coffee we drank cold *frappé* in plastic cups, brought across from Greece, only an hour and a half away by a mountain footpath.

No wonder the young men walked for a week at night, sleeping during the day to get to Salonika or Athens! The full devastation of ruined Albania now hit me. How could anybody stay here who had two legs to walk out on? Dhori was shivering. He was *en route* for Athens, which was already melting in summer heat, and he wore only a short-sleeved cotton shirt. We were at almost 4,000 feet, or so a faded sign claimed. The Communists had attempted to get some enterprises going in Leskoviku, but these had all failed and were now burnt out and abandoned. There were supposed to be some fine nineteenth-century beys' houses but, walking round to keep warm, I couldn't see anything but ruins. The 1913 boundary commission deprived the Albanian Moslem landowners of many of their estates in Greece, and the village of Leskoviku had clearly never recovered.

When we left the bus was crammed full, and no wonder. I was surprised everyone in town hadn't quit. Being a beggar in Athens suddenly seemed incredibly attractive after Leskoviku. Apparently, there had been no bus from Korça for three days: they had all broken down in the mountains. This was the sort of place the losers in Albanian politics got sent to: this was where the Democrats had been determined not to risk being sent back to. What were a few stuffed ballot boxes compared to the appalling risk of living out one's life in Leskoviku? It was up in places like this that the Communists had been exiled since 1991. Gabriel had confessed to me that the best teachers and doctors were now all in the villages. It was a problem for him: his own children were receiving an inferior education from Democrat Party teachers, newly down from the villages. What could he do? For fifty years to get anywhere in Albania you had had to be a member of the Party; inevitably the careerists, the men of talent and ambition had joined. Now those that had not thrown in their lot with Berisha were up in places like this, no doubt burning with resentment and aching for revenge.

*

Although grossly overloaded, the bus had at least stopped swaying and bucketing. There were even patches of unbroken asphalt. But we kept rising. As if in some symbolic move signifying a grand climacteric, the bus driver stopped playing *rembetika* as we crawled through the highest passes, and put on Whitney Houston instead. The gypsies at the front had long ago fallen silent, racked with motion sickness. Curious that Albanians, the poorest and most oppressed of peoples, naturally gravitated to black soul music, and to Greek *rembetika* from Asia Minor, both the rhythms of injustice, loss and despair. 'To be without rhythm' had been a criticism both Albanian political parties had used against each other in the election campaign.

My head hurt and my sinuses had become dry. I wanted to be sick but couldn't. My whole body ached and my bones felt as if they had all been disconnected from each other. I wanted to lie down and go to sleep peacefully for several years.

As we came down the other side of the range, a ragged gang of youths waved us to a halt, blocking the road. Of course, bandits: what else could complete such a scene?

We slowed to a halt. The door was opened a fraction for negotiations. There was a long altercation. The bus driver did not want to let the mob on board. We'd had a police escort with a Kalashnikov for the first hour, to get us through the established highway robbery zone near Korça. He had got down and left us hours ago; in the mountains you were on your own.

The youths forced their way on board, prising the door open with their fingers, though in truth there was almost no room for them. They were very young, the oldest in his late teens. Most of them were between fourteen and eighteen. The youngest, a blond mite with grey eyes, could not have been more than six or seven. They smelt of woodsmoke and their boots were caked with mud. Not bandits, refugees.

There were no doubting where they had come from: Greece, over the passes. They were hungry and tired and very thin. These were the people I had been seeing all over Greece, people who had fled from a failed country, a province of the former Ottoman empire that had ruined itself. These boys were the soldiers recruited by the Sultan for so many centuries to fight his wars. 'Albanian, will you go to hell?' asked the Turk in the old Ottoman proverb. 'What is the salary?' had come the Albanian's answer. Now the Turks had gone and the Sultan had no more use for these soldier-boys. They were tough and bold and dulled with poverty and tiredness, these refugees: yet they made jokes and laughed, though almost asleep on their feet.

There was a sort of leader, a young man of perhaps nineteen. He had been to Greece before several times. The others were all beginners. He had shown them what to do and how to survive, for a fee. Often these leaders were themselves killed by the band once they got across the border, to avoid payment. Now, usually, the money was given to the leader's *fis* in advance before they started, so he was carrying nothing to steal. This band of lads was from Vlora. All this Dhori told me, in Greek, as he chatted away to them like a kind old uncle. The friendliness of ordinary Albanians towards one another in public was in marked contrast to either the voluble aggression of the Greeks or the slow reserve of the Turks. Once again, and not for the last time, the Albanians reminded me of the southern Irish.

I passed a boiled sweet to the little boy with blond hair, when I next ate one myself, and I gave one to Dhori at the same time, so it did not appear as a patronising gesture. The boy thanked me gravely in Albanian, hand on heart and asked Dhori if I was a Greek.

'He is from England', Dhori replied.

'Is England part of Greece?' the boy asked. And then: 'How do you say "thank you" in Greek?' Six or seven years of Vlora, then two months of Greece; that was his entire world.

'Efharisto', said Dhori, slowly. The boy tried it, but couldn't manage. They had been in Greece for over two months, this band, yet no one had given this child the opportunity to learn say 'thank you' in Greek.

He took at least five minutes to get the wrapping paper off the boiled sweet. One of the older boys had a carton of blackcurrant juice he had brought with him from Greece. He drank some, then offered it to his friend. Though obviously thirsty, his friend refused.

'Bere, bere!' the boy said, thrusting the carton at him, and smiling. 'Drink, drink!' Pride and honour fought thirst and fatigue. In the end he allowed himself to be persuaded: he only meant to take a polite sip, you could see. But it was too much for him, and he drained the carton. His friend smiled on, and patted him on the back.

'Good boys' said Dhori affectionately, as though their schoolmaster.

A long and increasingly acrimonious argument had started between the bus driver and the leader of the band. The driver was insisting they paid or get off. From time to time, to emphasise his point, he would slow down, then stop, and throw open the front door dramatically. None of the band moved. The leader would then go into a long and eloquent sob story, and evidently make some minor concession, at which we would start on our way again.

Finally, the bus driver lost his temper. He stopped, turned off the engine and stood up, haranguing the refugees. Pay or get off, was his unambiguous message. A few crumpled 100 lek notes, each worth about $1, were now reluctantly passed over the heads of the standing passengers from the group leader; one man, separate it seemed from the main group, offered a 10,000 drachma note, worth £25 sterling. The bus driver raged: he had no change for such a large foreign note; the man must pay in lek or get out. But of course the man had no lek. The driver berated him mercilessly. Reluctantly, infinitely slowly, this sacrificial victim got out with his sack. He stood hopelessly by the side of the road, staring at us as if at a passing lifeboat in mid-Atlantic, his useless drachma still held in his hand. The wind whistled down from the mountains pitilessly, preternaturally loud in the absence of engine noise. We drove on, leaving him there.

Now, after five hours of climbing, the high passes slowly gave way, and we descended. Signs of life appeared once again. We drove through a mob of sheep and goats, the ragged herdsman leaning on his stick, staring at us deeply as we passed.

Below, in a deep-cut valley where a great fall of water tumbled out of a gap in the cliff face several hundred feet above us, there on a greensward lay three shepherds taking their ease, lying on their sides, conversing, their rifles stacked in a triangle beside them. Even in the Communist period the shepherds had been allowed rifles against the wolves and bears.

Abandoned fields surrounded us once again; then fig trees appeared, olives and grapevines. We passed men on mules and women leading donkeys. For five hours we had seen no motor traffic of any sort. There were signs now even of some fields still under cultivation.

'You will come to a bridge', Mr Georgio had said, 'A good bridge made of steel, built by the Italians. After this the road forks: to the right are Berat and Tepelena, to the left is Gjirokastra.'

It was as he said, the rusty Bailey bridge spanning the river, a footpath on either side for armed guards to patrol. We trundled across it at a walking pace. The thick struts under us rattled like great clashing wooden spoons. Nothing had changed here since 1939. It was easy to imagine the Italian engineers and soldiers who had built this road, this bridge, before the war. It was an heroic endeavour by any standard: what a wild adventure it must have been for them. Before this, to get from Korça to Gjirokastra you had to go on horse, over the mountain passes.

We turned left, and stopped to let off the refugees and other passengers bound north. Cold streams descended down the mountain side into roadside pools; here people had set up little *dukas*, selling soft drinks and snacks and bananas imported from Greece. Like Poland after the fall of Communism, Albania was mad for bananas: they were a little bit of instant capitalism, forbidden fruit for so many years. In the markets of Korça they were twice as expensive as in London, yet people bought them. When I had commented on their dearness, Gabriel had said: 'Many hands touch bananas.' In Poland the children of the Party élite had been nicknamed 'banana-kins' by other Poles: they were the only ones who ever got to eat this luxury fruit under Socialism.

We had seen no food for over five hours, but now we were on the main road, such as it was – a broken, pot-holed two-lane track – from Greece to Tirana. Trucks roared past, blaring their horns, loaded with provender and treats for the capital. Here you could buy Greek biscuits and chocolate at the roadside.

In the mountains we had passed through villages where the only sign of life had been peasants loading milk into a collective truck, using plastic buckets, this to be made into yoghurt or cheese. Georgio – a vet all his life – warned me against ever drinking milk in Albania. 'Brucellosis is widespread: the milk is neither boiled nor pasteurised.' For this reason he and his family, and all Orthodox Albanians I met, drank no milk but only ate yoghurt, which was reputedly safe. The infant mortality in the villages was still at sub-Saharan levels.

We rolled down the road towards Gjirokastra, half empty again. Dhori was busy writing his name in my book in a thick childlike hand. 'Come to Saranda – tomorrow! I will show you everything. It is so beautiful!'

We passed a smart new Mercedes with TR number plates, signifying Tirana. It had come off the road and lay on its side in a ditch, nose pointing to the capital. The owner sat on the side of the overturned car smoking a cigarette, as though his donkey had just died on him. Albanian driving was still at the Mr Toad stage, heavy on the accelerator and horn.

We passed a stagnant lake, gilded with green scum. Boys were carefully washing tins of soft drink and bottled water from Greece in this stagnant brew. Dhori looked on approvingly: 'Turizm – very good!' Beside the lake an old man was belabouring his donkey, which refused to budge: this was tourism Albanian-style, the picturesque without the tourists.

We came to the outskirts of Gjirokastra and as in Turkey stopped well before the centre, where other connecting buses waited. Everyone except me and one young mother and child got out. The bus, I had been told, would eventually go up the hill into the centre of town. The driver disappeared for a meal. I sat there for half an hour. The young mother gave up and left.

Outside, a large black pig rooted around in the wayside garbage. There was a petrol station near by, the first I'd seen since Korça, selling Dracoil. Petrol came in two state brands, Dracoil and Lekoil. In spite of five years of 'capitalism' there were very few foreign enterprises established in Albania. It was too risky to invest, and it was said the Albanian government always wanted too much in bribes.

Eventually, I got my bag and started walking up the hill. It was a steep climb. Gabriel had drawn me a map, like a six-year-old child's scrawl. It had taken him ages. But it was useless, as the bus had not stopped where he'd said it would, and the streets had no names, the houses no numbers.

After fifteen minutes of walking the bus roared up and stopped beside me. I climbed on board again. There was now a drunk at the front, shouting at the driver. He turned his attention to me: 'Anglisht? Anglisht?' he cried, waving a bottle at me in rage and aggression. He evidently knew who I was from the driver. I ignored him. He continued shouting at me, pushing his face into mine, his breath hot and stinking of raki. 'Why doesn't he talk? He must be a Socialist he's so silent!' the drunk finally cackled at the driver. The driver said nothing.

When the bus stopped finally, I got out and walked away into the labyrinth of winding lanes of old Gjirokastra.

6

Little Castles of Stone

Of Ruins and Assassins

THE FIRST ATTEMPT to murder and rob me was a hopelessly amateur affair.

I was walking alone in the old mountain-top citadel of Ali Pasha. The place was weed-strewn and deserted. It was mid-afternoon, very hot, cicadas loud all around. I had just passed the 1950s American 'spy-plane' allegedly shot down by the Communists – who had no anti-aircraft guns – and which was still proudly on display as a trophy, when I became aware of two men following me.

I glanced round: one of the men ducked behind a pillar. I walked on, and turned a corner, not altering my pace. I was out of their sight now, and I found purchase in a crumbing wall and scrambled up to a buttress some twenty feet above ground level. Ducking down amidst weeds and high grass, I looked back the way I had come. The two men were slowly and intently following my path: they both had knives drawn.

I ducked down again in the weeds and waited. I heard their feet crunching past below me. I let them get twenty metres or so further on, out of earshot, then jumped down and ran back the way I had come. They thought they had me cornered. There was no way out the way they were going. But I had a map, and I knew that, too.

I ran back past the circular stage where in Communist times the annual folk music festival had been held. Here a group had sung the hit tune *Tungjakjeta Enver Hoxha* – 'Long Life to Enver Hoxha'. Now the stage was abandoned and ruined like everything else. I ran past a dark green Chinese-era soft-top truck parked in a cavernous passageway, past the Second World War artillery pieces abandoned by the Italians, still displayed as trophies. Here, at last, there were armed guards with Kalashnikovs. Half an hour before they had shooed me out of the abandoned political prison which sat up on a higher level, into which I had clambered through broken strands of barbed wire. There was a firing squad wall still pocked with bullet holes and stained with encrusted, ancient blood. The last view the executed had was of a magnificent amphitheatre of mountains all round, soaring to snow-covered peaks over which, in late May 1996, the eagles of Albania could still be seen dipping and gliding. The doors of the prison cells were all missing but the bars at the windows were still in place.

It was my black shoulder bag and my beard which gave me away as a Westerner. I went back to Angeliki's house and shaved off the beard straight away, smoked three cigarettes one after the other and had a pot of Twining's Earl Grey tea to calm myself down. Then I forced myself to go out in the streets again, without the bag, passport stuffed down my trousers. It was not dangerous, I told myself; no would try to murder me, as long as I kept within sight of other people.

Gjirokastra was not like Korça at all. The mountains surrounding it were grander, more noble and austere. The men in the streets were sullen and aggressive, and there were no women to be seen out of doors. There was no evening *volta*. By 9.30 everyone was locked and bolted indoors. There were more cars, which drove around the narrow lanes pointlessly, endlessly, too fast and too noisily. There was no work going on; rather, a mood of suppressed anger and imminent violence hung in the air. No one smiled as they had in Korça, and the heavily armed police seemed like an army of occupation. The Greek minority's pro-Hellenic candidate from the thinly disguised OMONIA Party had won the election here, with the Socialists in close second place.

The only place that was busy was the Greek Consulate, which issued visas. Outside stood mobs of ragged Albanian men under an outsize Hellenic flag, waiting to be called inside. There was always a crowd of several hundred here waiting until noon, when the offices closed for the day. They came from all over southern Albania, and here they stayed until they got their precious bit of paper which meant escape. The rest of the upper town, all old stone Ottoman houses built like little forts, roofed with thick, rough granite slabs the French call *lauzes*, was deserted. It was picturesque, with a fine

Ottoman mosque and minaret, wealthy beys' and merchants' houses from the nineteenth century – but it was dead.

Gjirokastra was really an overgrown village; you could walk round it in half an hour. I was the only Westerner in town.

In Gjirokastra there were 'dozens of restaurants,' according to Gabriel, and 'many, many shops': in fact there were three restaurants, two of which were closed. All the shops bar one in the upper town were boarded up. In 1991 at least half the population had been ethnic Greek. Many had already left, many more were planning on leaving. All the business had slid down the hill, to the main Tirana-Greece road. Here there was a supermarket and little kiosks, people walking about, cars and trucks. The atmosphere was more relaxed, too.

Gjirokastra had the ruins of tourism: a Communist-brutalist hotel, monuments, museums, even Hello-Johnnies who said 'Do you speak English? French? Italian? German?' as I passed them in the central square outside the hotel. But when I replied 'Ochi – katalaves Elleniki?' they looked at me blankly.

Gjirokastra had been Hoxha's home town, and in the Communist years it had money and attention lavished on it, and was given the title 'Museum City'. That was all past. No money was flowing in here from Tirana now, only up from Greece, from the emigrants.

*

Angeliki was in her early forties, pudgy and overweight, with dyed black hair, a sad, hangdog expression and liquid, pained eyes. She was a relative of Gabriel's, and it had been arranged through him that I stay with her.

'She has had the misfortune never to be married. You must be very careful not to make scandal', Gabriel had told me seriously. Not to be married, not to have children in Albania was regarded as a catastrophe. Angeliki's brother and his family were away, visiting Gabriel's clan in Korça. Angeliki was alone in the family house.

Gjirokastra and Korça had a tradition of intermarrying. Many, perhaps most, marriages in Albania were still arranged, usually with families belonging to entirely different *fis* in other towns. I had assumed that Angeliki's family would be as pro-Democrat as Gabriel's, being kin. This was far from the case. Angeliki was a strong Communist, as were all her close family. It was not uncommon, I learnt, for a family of one political stripe deliberately to ally itself through marriage with their opponents, as a means of securing advantage and influence if and when their own faction was out of favour. 'A man marries his wife's village', Gabriel had told me. As in other tribal, clan-based societies, elaborate kinship networks were the working basis for economic and political as well as simply reproductive endeavours. As James Pettifer has pointed out in a perceptive article, in 1962 of the 58 members of the Communist Party Central Committee under Hoxha no fewer than 28 were related, and eight were married to each other, thus operating on traditional clan lines.

'Like a big mafia', Gabriel had said; but his own *fis* operated in exactly the same way. The only people whose houses he ever took me into were his relatives.

Angeliki's family house was a large and comfortable Ottoman-era Greek-style building, stone-built, detached and on two storeys, the double front doors opening onto steps which led straight down to the granite-paved street. The rooms were light and large, the high ceilings elaborately panelled in wood with intricate carving. The house had not been subdivided during the Communist era, indicating influence within the Party.

I was given the absent brother's master bedroom. It had pre-war Greek furniture, a double bed, a Chinese-era electric fan and Chinese factory-made rugs on the wooden floors.

Angeliki rarely went out, except to shop. She sat indoors and watched Italian TV, which she did not understand, rather than Greek TV, which she could at least follow. She read *Zeri i Popullit*, the Socialist Party daily, and smoked Marlboro cigarettes surreptitiously, as this was still regarded as 'fast' for a woman of her generation. She spoke some Greek, but not very much. The whole family were Orthodox but secular.

The arrangement was that I would pay $10 a day, without food; but Angeliki was an old-fashioned Albanian lady, and having a man in the house was an excuse for her to cook, and cook and cook . . . All those frustrated family meals she had never been able to prepare she now made for me. Fried eggs, fried cheese, *burek*, chips, fried goat's meat with yoghurt, giblets with macaroni, great mounds of food were all prepared while I sat with coffee, raki and cigarettes, waited on hand and foot. 'You could be pressed to death slowly by *loukoumia* and female attention', I wrote in my journal: 'they would wash your feet and dry them with their hair if you let them.' The strongest contrast with the West was this devotion, this completely uncomplaining and delighted attention the Albanian women paid their men inside the home. Coming from the abrasively post-feminist world of London, these attentions were both touching and embarrassing: they were also for me a reminder of my childhood in 1950s colonial Cyprus. As a little boy I had been fed and fussed over by Greek maids and nannies just like Angeliki.

Unlike the Korça ladies I'd met, advanced in their *petit Paris*, Angeliki had no pretensions at all to being either modern or Western. I was a man, the man of the house, in the absence of any other. Everything thus centred around my comfort and gastronomic demands.

She managed to round up three of her young nieces and a nephew, who were brought in to complete the ersatz family circle. Thus I would be seated at the head of the table, while the oldest niece, perhaps five years old, solemnly served me raki. Angeliki would then dole out chips and fried cheese, and yet more goat's meat. 'Gëzuar!' I would say, raising my glass, 'Health!' 'Gëzuar!' Angeliki would reply raising hers, and the children would pipe up the chorus. In the corner the Italian TV blared away inanely. The nieces and nephew chattered on to Angeliki in Albanian, while I smiled on, a vicarious, mute patriarch.

This was as close as Angeliki would ever get to being married. It was only because all the other adults were away that she was able to stage this charade at all. I felt so sorry for her, that something as paltry as a strolling Western traveller was all she would have as a temporary surrogate. She even became bold enough to smoke her cigarettes openly indoors in my company, when she saw I did not disapprove.

Dr Shkrelli from next door was called in early on in the proceedings to help out on the conversational front. Albanian women do not expect their men to do anything except talk with one another, or go out to the cafés to drink raki and talk politics.

Dr Shkrelli was in his late forties, hair going, waistline gone. He was a physician by profession, a cardiac specialist. He chain-smoked Greek cigarettes and had a slight paunch, the first I'd seen in Albania. He spoke good Greek and reasonable Italian. Like all the intelligentsia I met in Albania, he was slowly dying of provincial ennui and welcomed the chance to pass the time with a Westerner.

Since 1991 he had worked for several years in Greek hospitals, and still went down to Jannina virtually every week to attend to patients.

Gjirokastra is part of Epirus, and Jannina has always been the capital of the province. In Ali Pasha's day the Albanians ruled the roost; now the Hellenes held the south of this ancient, disputed territory. Just as Korça looked to Salonika, so Gjirokastra looked to Jannina, not many miles away. Berat, Vlora, Tirana were all remote, far-off foreign places in the minds of Gjirokastriots.

From Dr Shkrelli I had the full Albanianist plaint: the betrayal of the West; Albanians treated worse than Moroccans or black Africans; Skanderbeg the saviour of Christendom; the Anglo-American betrayal after the Second World War; the crime caused by Albanians in Italy the fault of the Italians for 'not giving Albanians longer visas', etc, etc.

I replied that Albania had abandoned the West, not the other way round: for 45 years we had been denounced as decadent and consigned to the scrap heap of history. King Zog ran away, refused to fight, and never tried to return during or after the war. King George of the Hellenes, by contrast, returned with his Royalist forces from Egypt to fight the Communists. The Zogists and Balli Kombetar refused to attack either the Germans or the Italians. Why should the British fight for people who would not defend their own interests? As for Skanderbeg, he served the Ottomans faithfully for decades, converted to Islam, fought against Christian armies for the Sultan – and only turned his coat when it was convenient. His son sold his Albanian inheritance to the Venetians and went to live in Italy, abandoning Albania for ever. Where were the Albanian *palekari*, the 'proud warriors', at the Turkish siege of Constantinople? In Albania, Albanians only ever fought for themselves, or as mercenaries. As for the Italians, why should they allow any Albanians into Italy at all, or Greece for that matter?

Dr Shkrelli ignored all this completely. Albanians did not argue, I had noticed: they simply made speeches, and then did not listen to any rebuttal or counter-arguments but continued with their monologue regardless after you had finished, as if you'd never spoken.

The Greeks, he went on, now they were a weak and cowardly parcel of people. No use at all, like women: all brag and with no pride and no honour. Albania has produced many, many scientists and intellectuals, far greater than those of Greece.

Even if this were true, I replied, it did not follow that Greece should therefore accept, as it had, upwards of half a million or more penniless Albanian refugees – few if any of them distinguished scientists or intellectuals. And how was it that the Albanians hardly fired a shot against the invading Italians in 1939, whereas the 'cowardly' Greeks fought bravely and strongly against Mussolini in 1940–1, and threw his armies back almost into the sea, suffering terribly for their stand by bringing down the wrath of Hitler and the might of the German army on to themselves?

'The defeated Greeks came through here as beggars in 1941', Dr Shkrelli continued, as if I had not spoken. 'We gave them bread. "Psomi! Psomi!" they cried. And we gave them bread. We were rich then, we had gold. They were so poor. Now they are rich because Europe has helped them. Getting into the EU was the only clever thing the Greeks ever did – and the only stupid thing the Europeans ever did. They are not Europeans but a Balkan people, like us. They will be a Trojan horse inside Europe.'

You might have thought that with these sentiments Dr Shkrelli didn't like visiting Greece. This was far from the case: he adored the place.

'I love the night life, the music, the *bouzoukia* – I am mad for the *bouzoukia*. Ah, the restaurants of Jannina and Athens . . .' he enthused again and again.

I thought then of Mustafa Kemal Ataturk, the Macedonian-born father of modern Turkey, whose parents were both Albanians; of how he loved to go into the Greek tavernas of old pre-First World War Salonika and Constantinople, to drink ouzo and sing and dance with the Greeks. Yet he threw in his lot with the Turks, as had so many Albanians in the past five centuries, and succeeded in expelling the Greeks from Asia Minor, and wrenching Turkey into the twentieth century. Hitler was an Austrian with a complex about his Jewish past, his Schickelgruber relatives: the first thing he did when he took over Austria after the Anschluss was order the destruction of the cemetery where his dubious ancestors lay buried and of all the church records. Kemal Ataturk was a Macedonian Albanian, a man who, according to his biographer, Lord Kinross, once said of the Turks in 1920, when he was trying to make a new army of them to fight the Allied occupation forces: 'They are hopeless. You can do nothing with them. If only one could convert them to Christianity . . .' Outsiders often made the best, and the most dangerous, modernisers and reformers: Hitler ended by cursing the Germans for having failed him.

Dr Shkrelli despised Greeks and loved Greece: Ali Pasha had employed both Orthodox Greek and Moslem Albanian troops in his army, and Roman Catholic highlanders from Mirdita, too: when one faction refused to slaughter their co-religionists, he was always sure the others would fall upon them with enthusiasm. Moslem Albanians had ruled Orthodox Greeks for centuries: that was their pact with the Ottomans. Now the Greeks had got the better of them, had backed the twentieth-century winning side, Europe and America. Albanian resentment was that of former top dogs, now unfairly relegated by history: obviously the West owed it to them to make up the shortfall. Dr Shkrelli resented not being on top of the Greeks, that was all. He liked their culture in the way some English liked the Irish: as an overlord to an amusing, entertaining underdog.

Dr Shkrelli had passed two out of three vital medical exams in Greece. 'Then I was failed for the last exam by Greek professor who hated me and who was a strong Communist,' he told me bitterly. And so he had had to leave the Greek hospital and return home. Albanians, it seemed, were somehow always destined to fail that last, vital third exam.

*

All the museums in Korça had been closed while the Tirana government prepared to cleanse them of their Communist propaganda. In Albania 'propaganda' had no negative connotations: if you were a Democrat you freely admitted to the superiority of your own side's propaganda.

In Gjirokastra the Enver Hoxha Museum had been cleansed, and was now open again, renamed the Ethnographic Museum. Every trace of Hoxha or the Communist era had been expunged. Instead,

there was an anodyne collection of nineteenth-century folk costumes, implements and furniture, much of it bought from Turkey,
apparently, as there was little left from this era still in Albania. It was
housed in the fine, large stone-built fortress-house where Hoxha
himself was born, though this too was something of a forgery, as the
original had been burnt down by the Greek army in 1916 and later
rebuilt.

The woman who looked after the place darted out of her office
when I arrived, demanding five dollars entrance fee. We compromised on one dollar.

'What is your tongue?' she enquired.

'English', I replied.

'Good, then I will speak this, and you will correct my wrongs.'

In her office four large-eyed children were engaged in devouring
a loaf of grey bread from a sheet of newspaper on the desk: I had
disturbed the family elevenses.

'Where are all the Hoxha exhibits?' I asked, as we walked round,
she helpfully pointing at things, saying: 'This is knife cutting,
cutting . . . this is old chair, too, too old . . . this is oven for making
breads . . .'

She became defensive at the mention of the former Great Leader.
'All Communist exhibits taken to Tirana,' she claimed, 'This not
Hoxha museum, before, but Partisan Museum.'

I opened a small wall cupboard idly; inside were stacked all the
Hoxha portraits and exhibits from the old regime. After all, who
knows? The Communists might well be back again one day.

Hoxha's cult of the personality exceeded any in the Communist
world, save perhaps that of Kim Il Sung of North Korea, who had a
gold statue made of himself which people had to bow down to in
the central square of the capital. The one thing Hoxha never did,
though, was have his face put on the banknotes. This was for fear of
defacement by his enemies, or worse, the use of his image for
cursing him or other occult sabotage.

Hoxha was superstitious and, like many Albanians, gave great
credence to the power of dreams. He never travelled if he had had
a bad dream, for fear of an accident. For this purpose, and to deflect
assassins, he employed a *sosi*, or double. Originally a dentist from
the Gheg north, this man had been discovered by the Sigurimi and
brought to Tirana, where he was given plastic surgery and taught to

walk and talk exactly like Hoxha. The surgeons and his trainers were then put in a bus, and pushed over a cliff into the Adriatic, to secure the secret. This double often used to impersonate Hoxha in public, opening stadia, visiting factories, making speeches, being filmed as the Great Leader. He was kept in a villa in the Block in Tirana when not needed: he had no clothes of his own, nor indeed any identity save that as Hoxha's double. He had to read what Hoxha read and develop similar tastes in French literature and Marxist dialectics so he could perform convincingly. Even his food was measured to keep him the same weight as the Great Comrade.

Only the memory of his wife and two little daughters kept this exalted prisoner sane. He was even taught how to perform if ever shot by an assassin, to look optimistic and hopeful for the cameras, just in case he survived: as of course he necessarily would, for Hoxha would not have been the one actually stopping the bullet.

When Hoxha finally died, this *sosi* was given some clothes by his guards and told to disappear. His wife and daughters, of course, had been shot by the Sigurimi in the first week of his training. They now told him this apologetically. Devastated, he escaped from Tirana, but was of course a marked man. Everywhere he went people fled at the sight of him: the spirit of the monster come back to haunt them. He was attacked and beaten, shouted at and insulted, spat on and screamed at. Even small children fled from him in tears.

Finally, in deep anguish and despair, he found refuge in one of the gulag camps of the exiles in the south, where they had never seen films or TV, and so did not know what Hoxha looked like. Here Hoxha's double lived on in obscurity until the fall of Communism in 1991. Then, like everyone else, he tried to escape to the West. He returned to Tirana and climbed over the wall into the West German Embassy. The other refugees screamed and attacked this ghost of the dictator who had followed them even here.

In deep depression the double attacked his own face with a knife, putting out one of his eyes and disfiguring himself appallingly, so he would no longer resemble Hoxha. He gave up all attempts to escape to the West and went back to the gulag camp, where he died shortly afterwards.

*

When I mentioned to Dr Shkrelli that I was planning to go to Saranda and Butrint by bus he looked horrified: 'You cannot! It is too dangerous. You must go by taxi. I will arrange it.'

In his eyes, Westerners, as honorary *pashas*, had to travel by Mercedes taxi: anything less demeaned their status and, by association, the status of all they knew and those with whom they were staying. The bus was for low types, villagers and peasants.

Like Gabriel, Dr Shkrelli ached for his own car, 'so I can go to Saranda at the weekend'. Saranda, a seaside port virtually overlooking Corfu, had long been advertised to me as the earthly paradise. Butrint was a noted classical site, an ancient Greek city, possibly founded by the Trojans, where Andromache was reputed to have lived.

As a destination, Butrint went down with Dr Skhrelli less well than Saranda. At Saranda one could lounge in cafés, listen to *bouzoukia* and talk politics. In Butrint there was nothing but old stones and snakes.

Over three days three different 'cousins' were brought round for lengthy negotiations to see what the market would bear for this trip. The bidding started at $150 and slid down, over time, to an acceptable $15. Dr Shkrelli couldn't decide whether to accompany me or not. On the one hand, it would get him away from his family for the day and there would be a café stop in Saranda for sure. On the other, there was Butrint: all those stones and snakes.

In the end he couldn't resist, but jumped in the taxi at the last moment, in the front, with the driver, much to that man's relief: a whole day just with a Westerner would have been hard to take. Albanians hate being alone, and treats paid for by foreigners should be shared with relatives if possible. Needless to say there was no question of any of the women accompanying us.

The road to Saranda took us over the low coastal range. Once on the other side, immediately we left the Balkans and entered a Mediterranean zone. The temperature rose by 15° and there were suddenly olive and orange trees, the latter all dying or dead through lack of attention. Hoxha had insisted all this area be planted with citrus trees, but no one knew how to look after them. All the oranges and lemons in southern Albania now came from Greece, like everything else except yogurt, raki and goat's meat.

The road was pocked and holed as if by an artillery barrage. We passed through a Greek minority village, where amid the destruction an old church was being restored with care and taste.

Saranda had attractive palm trees and a seaside esplanade, but that was all. The town was an ugly sprawl of Communist-era grey cement boxes. The one hotel was a peeling, leprous concrete tower which looked like a south London council block in bad repair.

We sat at the one seaside café which was open and had espresso coffee as good as any in Italy, orange juice from Greece and Bulgarian mineral water. The taxi driver-cousin was of course part of the treat and so joined us. We sat next to the water, which was delicately perfumed with raw sewage, this evidently debouching straight into the sea untreated. There was only one ship left, a small rusted freighter lying on its side in shallow water, which had evidently run aground while attempting to flee with refugees in 1991.

We were the only people sitting out. The whole town was deserted, yet it was a beautiful summer's day in early June. Where were all the much-vaunted tourists, I enquired.

'It is too early', said Dr Shkrelli tersely.

'When do they come then?'

'Later. July, August. Many come: Germans, French, Greek, Italians . . .'

'How many come? Ten thousand a year?'

'Yes, yes, ten thousand. Many ten thousands.'

'Where are all the restaurants?' I continued relentlessly. Saranda was very small and I couldn't see any sign of them. Where did these tens of thousands of tourists eat? How many restaurants were there, actually?

'Eight', said Dr Shkrelli, after considerable thought, but with great conviction.

So eight restaurants fed ten thousand people, over the two-month season, I computed wonderingly. They must be very big restaurants.

We had passed a police road block on coming into this tourist paradise. According to Dr Shkrelli, this was 'to stop the wrong people getting in'. It was also to extract money from the motorists and bus drivers. Every Albanian policeman had a little roundel at the end of a stick, showing red on one side for 'Stop' or green for 'Go' on the other. These were each deployed when he saw a likely-looking mark.

Dr Shkrelli instructed me as to the form when we, too, were

motioned to stop: 'Take off your sunglasses, say nothing and look stupid', he instructed. I did as he said. Dr Shkrelli then went into a long story to the policeman about how he was taking medicine for the Saranda Chief of Police, whose children were ill: this tale got us through without a bribe. 'If they knew you were foreign we would have had to pay double and in dollars', Dr Shkrelli told me. Had the policeman really believed such an unlikely tale?

'They are very stupid – otherwise they would not be policemen', Dr Shkrelli replied with equanimity.

The delights of Saranda seemed to have paled since the doctor had been here last. He became gloomy: 'All Albanian tourists now go to Greece. It was better when the Russians were here. Then there were bands playing music and dancing and ice cream. After the Chinese came, all that stopped and it became very puritanical.' I reflected that it was a sad seaside resort indeed which harked back to the Stalinist Russian era as its heyday.

There was a mild tussle over the drinks bill at the café, but I was graciously allowed to pay in the end. The subject of lunch was now foremost in the doctor's mind.

'There are many, many wonderful fish restaurants on the way to Butrint,' he said, hope in his voice. On hearing the words 'fish restaurant' alarm bells started to ring.

'We go on to Butrint now, not to any restaurant', I said firmly. Dr Shkrelli sighed, but acquiesced.

The road to Butrint followed the coast. Corfu was so near you felt you could reach out and touch it. I could see people on the beaches there, and windsurfers darting across the sea quite clearly. Over on this side there was nothing except rubbish-strewn beaches with signs reading 'Mines – Beware' and the endless concrete bunkers, some of which had been painted in pleasing patterns, bright blues, yellows and greens, to surreal effect.

There were no restaurants and few houses for that matter, merely half-built concrete skeletons which had been abandoned for lack of money. We did find a petrol station where we were able to fill up. Here the owner had placed a votive figurine painted bright blue on the perimeter wall, to avert the Evil Eye and to prevent misfortune falling on his establishment. On close inspection this turned out to be a Barbie doll with blonde hair and blue eyes. The owner had been in Italy and spoke some Italian.

'Why a Barbie doll?' I enquired. Traditionally, I had read, these statuettes were made of clay.

After a moment's thought the owner replied: 'To be modern.'

*

We picked up two paying passengers *en route*, one of whom spoke good English. He was an elderly gentleman, and a state archaeologist, it transpired. I was in the back, sandwiched between two loudspeakers that blared out *bouzoukia*. 'I love this music!' exclaimed Dr Shkrelli, quite oblivious that at that volume I might not.

When we arrived, there was a short debate as to how many entry tickets to the site I had to buy as a Western *pasha*. The bidding started at fifteen, then fell to ten, and stuck for a long time at five. I refused to buy any more than two, which was finally accepted, these at a dollar each. 'He is so important he counts as twenty-four witnesses at a trial' was how one tribal bigwig was described to Edith Durham in 1908 in Ghegeria.

Obviously, Dr Shkrelli and the taxi driver did not have to purchase any tickets at all, being Albanian. The archaeologist hung around, expecting to be hired as a guide, but as I already had a book printed in England, giving an exhaustive description of the site, he was superfluous. He sloped away disconsolate.

I tried to get Dr Shkrelli and the taxi driver to stay in the taxi. They had no interest in the site. However, the Albanian fear of allowing any individual endeavour to take place unsupervised overcame their horror of wild country places.

They followed after me round the site timidly, crying out every five yards 'Come back! Come back! You are leaving the group!' or 'No, no! Do not step off the path! There are snakes in there!'

Butrint was a fine classical Greek site in a state of pleasing neglect, lushly overgrown with thick bush and densely aromatic shrub, wild olive trees emerging from cracked antique pavement and grotto. I was sorry to see that British archaeologists had been allowed in to do their usual level best to destroy the delicate atmosphere by erecting large, ugly and quite unnecessary signboards at every point, tokens of the vanity of the archaeologists, which merely obscured the stones and statues about which they purported to inform. The over-regulated, over-signposted world of contemporary Britain, with its incessant nannying and chivvying was brought back to me in a rush. Bruce Chatwin believed that all museums should be looted every fifty years. The museum at Butrint was closed, of course, but in line with Chatwinian theory, it was comprehensively looted in March 1997.

'Your Prime Minister John Major has promised much money for this site, but he has not yet paid!' claimed Dr Shkrelli in a voice dark with grievance, as if this were personally my fault.

'That is very unlikely. The British government is notoriously mean about culture', I riposted.

A bizarre sight awaited us at the Roman footbaths, if that is what they were. A middle-aged Albanian – with a beard, strangely, and clad in robes of antique cut – was pacing round and round barefoot in a small circular stone pool filled with a few inches of muddy water. He was muttering angrily to himself. He wore thick white make-up on his face and was obviously in a foul mood. What was he doing?

I positioned myself in a nook to observe. Some event, surely, was planned.

A large, sumptuous coach now swung into view, bearing Tirana number plates. It carried on its side the legend AlbTurizm, and from its sighing doors emerged a party of waddling, elderly American Midwesterners, each wrapped in characteristic brightly coloured flannel baby-clothes, a protective floppy sunhat on each head. They were followed by their minders, young, slim Albanians with charming smiles, who all wore sombre three-piece suits in spite of the stifling heat of the day. Each of these displayed a characteristic bulge under his left armpit, indicating automatics lodged in shoulder holsters.

AlbTurizm was one of the few Hoxha-era foreign currency-earning rackets which had survived into the Democrat *raj* still in the hands of a Communist *fis*.

The portly Midwesterners were gently shooed and led towards the robed sage, who still paced about, angrily muttering.

When he spotted his prey, the ersatz philosopher began to declaim even more angrily and loudly in what I took to be ancient Greek. In this I was immediately corrected by Dr Shkrelli, who claimed it was ancient Illyrian, of which he was doubtless an adept.

The tourists, like some obtuse species of herbivorous animal which could not see what was in its own obvious best interest, kept ignoring their keepers and the performer, instead gasping, oohing and aahing at the old stones and ruined buildings. I now realised that I was a privileged spectator at an ancient and all but extinct ritual: the Communist-era collective tourist experience. Once rites like these had been performed across the Eastern bloc world, from Dresden to Sakhalin. Sadly, by 1996 they were for the most part at one with Nineveh and Tyre.

The actor declaimed on, even more angry at being ignored. I could see his point. He had probably been waiting there for hours in the blazing heat, paddling round and round, and now it was all for nothing. The Midwesterners clearly had no culture.

'Look', I said to Dr Shkrelli, indicating discreetly the actor's bare arm, 'A fine example of an early 5th-century BC gold wristwatch.'

He did not laugh. Neither irony nor sarcasm seemed to take much purchase on the Albanian imagination: humour revolved around pratfalls and *mut*. Norman Wisdom is the acme and idol of all Albanian comedy. Dr Shkrelli and the driver both ardently yearned to join this alluring group. Who knows what proximity could not provide? It was all I could do to prevent an amalgamation.

We were not to escape without another try at a fish dinner. On the way back we stopped at a half-built concrete skeleton which claimed to be a restaurant. The owner asked me if I would like to invest £50,000 in his establishment. He said he had already spent $35,000 on the roofless ruin achieved so far.

'The English', I said, 'can go to the United States without visa or *grincardi*. We can invest our money in America. Why then would any English want to invest in Albania?'

This was received in silence by all as a self-evident truth. Economics having failed us, the subject of fish dinners came up, and menus were proffered.

I lit a cigarette and stated flatly that I was not hungry and did not want to eat. This was true. Angeliki had given me a mountanous fry-up of goat's giblets and offal, washed down with copious draughts of raki for my breakfast, this as a sovereign against the possible dangers of the day's adventures ahead.

Dr Shkrelli and the taxi driver found, too, that they were not hungry, after all, and the menus disappeared.

As we drove back through Saranda we had to slow down for a mob of gawpers which had gathered by a brand new 4-wheel drive Toyota that had just turned over into the ditch. The police were too busy with this contretemps to try to extract any money from us, and we were waved on.

All the way back we passed wrecked Communist-era fish farms and agricultural enterprises, all burnt out and destroyed.

'America and the West must make all this good again', said Dr Shkrelli. 'It is their duty now we are their friends. Why do they not come with money to give us? It is a shame to them, it blackens their faces.'

Livestock wandered the road, justifiably lugubrious expressions on their faces. One large ruminating donkey had established itself in the central portion of the road and would not budge, despite much horn-blowing by our driver. In the end we had to creep round it, almost sliding off the edge of road.

We almost stopped to buy honey from a stall, but Dr Shkrelli decided against it. He couldn't, however, resist the cherries a few kilometres further on. He bought a kilo, but I refused them politely when offered.

'Are they better in England?' Dr Shkrelli asked. He had asked me the same about Butrint, too.

A week later in Tirana I was talking to Carruthers of the British Embassy about my trip in the south. 'Didn't eat or drink anything in Saranda I hope?' he enquired.

'Why?' I asked.

'Well, cholera's just broken out there.'

I expressed my skepticism. All over the Near and Middle East diplomatists in the capital tend to regale you with tales of cholera having just broken out in those provinces you have either just come from, or are just going to.

'Well', said Carruthers, 'One of our secretaries at the Embassy went down there for a weekend and came back with it. She's in a hospital in Brindisi as we speak. The Wop docs think it was the fish dinner she ate.'

7

Saying Goodbye to the Church

Tales of the Black Market

'PIMPING IS QUITE a good career now, or else smuggling drugs. If you are leaving school today in Albania, you have three choices: you can emigrate to Greece or Italy; you can stay here and get a job paying no money; or you can say goodbye to the church . . .'

Away from his parents, in whose company he was always respectful and silent, Egrem could be quietly voluble. He was just eighteen and about to leave school, so such career decisions were important. Whereas Gabriel, the schoolmaster, had always been trying to steer me away from anything which smacked of a lack of culture, Egrem was overflowing with frankly counter-cultural lore, and not inhibited by defensive national pride.

He was a slight, dark-haired, olive-skinned boy, the good looks of his round, gently smiling face temporarily gilded by a mask of adolescent spots. He was the apple of his doting mother's eye. In her presence he always seemed to shed five or six years, becoming puppyish and supple. With me he was always a polite, attentive, discreet little monster.

He spoke good English and had passed his Cambridge First certificate. He had been to England already, the guest of Dr Cider and his family. In Gloucester, Egrem had managed to wangle himself an illegal job earning £2 an hour selling vegetables in a fruiterer's, to the detriment of his studies. Dr Cider was a noted expert on the Vlachs and their language, one of the few Englishmen who had detailed practical knowledge of southern Albania, through which he often walked on foot during the summer months, striding from Vlach village to Vlach village in search of errant or simply changing phonemes like some scholar-gipsy of yore. It was through Dr Cider's kindness that I had been offered such a warm welcome by Egrem's family, which was not, incidentally, Vlach, but rather secular Moslem, recently converted to evangelical Christianity. Though they lived only a few hundred yards from each other in Gjirokastra, Angeliki's *fis* had never heard of Egrem's.

*

I was sitting in Egrem's parents' flat one afternoon, the TV whispering out a pirated satellite rock video from MTV. Egrem's younger brother Bardhyl, aged sixteen, was also there, the two boys smart in neat blue jeans, leather belts and western cowboy-style shirts. The rock video was about a group of long-legged and scantily clad blonde American prostitutes and their black macho pimps: there was much assertive, transgressional smoking of cigarettes, slapping of white female faces, elaborate crane-shots of flash Cadillacs cruising the rain-slicked streets of a big city, close-ups of sexy whores trawling their wares from the kerbside, heroin being injected in public lavatories, scantily clad white female dead bodies being wheeled into morgues. It was well made in a consciously rough-cut street style, all shot in grainy black and white. I wondered how much of the dense racial and sexual subtext these two Albanian boys understood.

'What did you think of that?' I asked Egrem. He smiled faintly, as to an impossibly straight oldster who could hardly be expected to grasp such arcane street culture.

'Oh, we have this in Albania, too. The pimps kidnap young girls, mainly from the north in Ghegeria, and take them to Italy to be prostitutes. They are sold for $1,000 each, and the man who sells expects a percentage of the profit each girl will earn, from the man who buys. This trade is usually done inside the *fis* to stop cheating. They like to get the girls young – fifteen to sixteen – and they take them to special houses in Durrës, where they are raped by many men and taught all the tricks. Then they are smuggled into Italy to work on the streets, and beaten often by their owners to keep them in line.'

Egrem's knowing smile remained unchanged through this litany. His father, Dhritero, was busy in the kitchenette, preparing a lunchtime fry-up. Dhritero was the only Albanian man I ever saw at work in the house.

I was shocked. Not just by Egrem's easy acceptance of this trade, and by his immediate grasp of such a milieu on TV, but by his lack of shame: Gabriel or any of his friends would have strenuously denied this sort of Albanian criminality for being 'shameful', therefore not really happening.

'What about AIDS?' I asked.

'They have this now in Durrës and Vlora and the north. The Ghegs bring it back from Italy. They will not use condoms because of their pride, so they come back and infect all their families. Even in Communist times they could not wipe out syphilis in the north.'

Like most Tosks, Egrem had a low opinion of the Ghegs. I told him I was going north, into Ghegeria. His cockiness evaporated instantly. He looked genuinely alarmed, the smug grin wiped from his face.

'I would not advise it. It is very dangerous. The Ghegs are violent and untrustworthy. You will be attacked and maybe killed.'

He was deadly serious. There had been talk of Egrem accompanying me on my travels as a guide-cum-interpreter. He had suddenly seen a vision of himself being dragged off into the wild tribal highlands. But then Egrem thought Tepelena was 'violent and dangerous' too, and that was only ten miles up the road. For him all of Albania outside Gjirokastra was dangerous.

Like so many other Albanians I met, the only thing he could think of was how he could get out for good. He couldn't give a damn about the elections: 'I don't care who wins', he told me: 'Dictatorship can never come back.' His elders were still all obsessed with the minutiae of Balkan politics, ancient tribal resentments: he couldn't give a toss.

'I have a visa for Greece but I do not want to go unless I can pretend to be English. I despise the Greeks and they treat Albanians very badly. They are like women, the Greeks, with no courage or pride. No Albanian denies being an Albanian in Greece.'

I forbore from pointing out that he himself intended to pass himself off as an Englishman.

Wouldn't it have been better, I suggested, if southern Albania had been incorporated into Greece for the last fifty years? Egrem paused and thought: 'For the money, yes. For the people, no.'

A Greek visa cost $400 in bribes from the consulate, Egrem claimed. A thousand were issued every day. The visa officers were changed every month, so rich were the pickings: these jobs were in the gift of the ruling Greek Socialist Party, PASOK, and as such always went to the Party bosses' relatives, 'just as in Albania'. The customs officers on either side of the crossing from Greece at Kakavia made fortunes in bribes. Egrem himself had been offered a job as a customs official by relatives, but he had been too young at the time to take it. The whole Kakavia customs racket was entirely sewn up by one large Gjirokastra *fis*. The bribes were enormous: every Albanian officer took $20,000 a month, and they were only allowed to stay in the post for a month a year to give others a chance. Every car or motorbike or truck had to pay a bribe to get in. None of this money ever got to Tirana. Tirana controlled the bribes for vehicles coming in from Durrës. This was how the élite lived, from these bribes, as there were no taxes to steal from, and industry had collapsed.

Everyone stole who could, from the humble village policeman upwards: the political resentments were from those who had been deprived of such opportunities. Fatos Nano, leader of the Socialists, had been head of an interim administration. He had been accused of stealing $7 million of Italian food aid in 1991, when the country was starving: he was in gaol in Tepelena, serving a long sentence for this crime. His supporters said this had all been trumped up by Sali Berisha, that Fatos Nano had not had time to steal anything, as he had not been in power long enough. The Democrats said the evidence against Nano had been shown in open court, reported by Western journalists, and was undeniable.

I asked Egrem what he thought. 'They are all thieves,' he said simply. I had asked Gabriel, too, if he had thought Berisha's hands were clean. He had frowned and looked worried: 'Yes, I want to believe so', he had replied. But to my question 'Who do you think will win the election?' he and all the others had always answered with whoever they wanted to win: what you believed and what you wanted were the same.

Egrem, as a potential pimp or black-marketeer, knew the prices of everything illicit in Albania. A Kalashnikov cost $1,000, an automatic pistol $600, a genuine Greek passport $2,000, and a false US passport – 'but good enough to get across all borders between Balkan countries' – was $3,000. It cost $400 to be smuggled into Greece across the passes and 'many thousands' to be taken by illegal boat into Italy. A medical degree allowing one to practise as a doctor – this also included Greece, where such certificates were recognised as valid – cost $5,000, but you had to go to Tirana in person to get one.

On a more mundane level, it was going to cost Egrem $5 to get his school leaving certificate. You could either sit the exam, or pay the teacher $5. He couldn't be bothered to sit the exam: $5 was nothing to him. His master plan was to try to pass himself off as an Englishman on one of the Greek islands for the summer, earn and save $15,000 as a waiter, and then buy a Greek passport and go to England. He knew people in England. With a Greek passport he could live and work there legally.

I had no idea how much of all this information was adolescent fantasy and how much the truth: I could hardly check with his parents. 'Saying Goodbye to the Church' was the Albanian expression used by those young people who had decided to adopt a life of crime. Many of the Albanians who went to Greece had only the intention of stealing, Egrem told me. Passports were the most coveted items, particularly American or Western European. These would be brought back and sold in Albania for $6,000 each. Even small children went to Greece to steal. In Albania stealing was not worth while. Houses were well guarded, and if you were caught the family cut off your nose and ears. In Greece all you got for stealing was a beating from the police, which was laughable. A beating to an Albanian was like a shower of rain.

I asked why I had not seen any of these earless, noseless Albanian thieves in my travels. 'The families hide these people because of the shame. You will never see crippled people, insane people or deformed people in the streets, unless they are professional beggars or have no family. They are hidden, or sometimes killed secretly and buried in the gardens at night', Egrem explained equably.

Like many Albanians, Egrem had overambitious hopes for me at first: a three-day taxi trip to Berat and Tepelena costing $150 had been proposed, with many a fish dinner no doubt envisaged *en route*. A simple bus trip to Tepelena, costing $2, was my riposte. Egrem accepted this with good grace.

Egrem's father, Dhritero, had overwhelmed me with hospitality. He was a great friend of Dr Cider, and my short introductory letter opened all doors.

Dhritero had been a career officer in the Albanian army under the Communists. He was a short, balding energetic man, with a great big smile. He was always bobbing up and down, getting me soft drinks and beers, cigarettes and sweets, grinning and patting me on the back.

Now under Democracy he ran a small kiosk opposite a high school, selling candies and Coca-Colas, exercise books and pencils. He was very happy. He was delighted to have survived a regime which had killed so many of his friends and colleagues. He bubbled over with love of life. He was the happiest Albanian – perhaps the only happy Albanian – I ever met.

He had been a believing Communist until 1990. He had accepted all the Party's propaganda until very late. He cried when Enver Hoxha had died in 1985. Then he realised when the Democracy movement started that Communism was a tyranny and Hoxha had been a dictator. He had started to learn English in the 1960s, because his wife, Mimoza, was an English teacher by profession; but his senior officers had put in reports on him for 'learning a useless language'. 'What are you going to do: become an American spy or defect?' they had asked him. So he stopped learning English. One of his best friends had been sent to Russia to study. This friend had once been overheard to remark that in Russia the food was better than in Albania, you could go to dances and enjoy yourself with women at the weekend, and moreover the Russian army was better armed and better trained than the Albanian. This scandalous statement had resulted in a public show trial, after which the officer had been cashiered and sentenced to fifteen years in the camps under Article 55 (Agitation, Betrayal and Propaganda).

Dhritero had a large picture book of Hoxha's life, which he took out and showed me.

'A few years ago there were mountains of these. Now there are none to be found anywhere', he told me. He pointed out the Politburo surrounding Hoxha, and his senior chiefs-of-staff, announcing about each, one by one: 'Shot – shot – fifteen years – poisoned – shot – twenty years – died in a helicopter crash – shot – shot– shot – pushed off a cliff – shot – shot' and so on, interminably. Dhritero's graphic, spartan English was well up to this grim recital.

There were photos of Hoxha in the early partisan days, up in the mountains, photos I'd seen before in English books: yet these were different. All the British liaison officers, Captain Julian Amery, Smiley and Maclean *et al.*, had been airbrushed out. Hoxha had even bulldozed the British military cemeteries to try to destroy the last vestiges of evidence of British help in his rise to power.

And there, also, was an early partisan photo of Hoxha with Mehmet Shehu airbrushed out, too. Mehmet Shehu, a tough brigade commander in the Spanish Civil War, had played Trotsky to Hoxha's Lenin, largely forming and creating what little military competence the Communist partisans could lay claim to. Shehu had once boasted to Colonel Smiley that he had himself personally cut the throats of more than seventy Italian prisoners. Smiley believed him.

The inevitable murder of Shehu by Hoxha was clouded in mystery. As with the death of Ali Pasha, there were several conflicting versions. The standard account was that during a politburo meeting Hoxha and Shehu had had a falling out and Hoxha had told Shehu to step into an adjoining room so they could sort out their differences in private. Once alone with his old chief-of-staff, Hoxha pulled out his pistol and shot Shehu dead. Other accounts claimed that Shehu had been found alone, peacefully lying on his bed fully dressed, with a pistol in his hand and a mortal head wound which would have been impossible for him to have inflicted himself. The senior politburo were reputed all to have underground passages dug between their villas in the Block in Tirana, so they could visit one another unbeknown to the others. These tunnels were guarded by armed and trusted members of their *fis*. It was said that the day Shehu was murdered, his own guard had mysteriously been called away elsewhere, and so the assassins had been able to gain entry to Shehu's villa without difficulty by the secret passage.

Hoxha had a particularly brilliant film-star smile, which he used to devastating effect: he was said to give an extra high-wattage version of this smile when he shot his victims. He always made sure he shot enemies himself, so he knew they were dead. The quarrel with Shehu was rumoured to be about his son, who had supposedly married a girl from an enemy *fis*, thus casting shame on Hoxha and his *fis*. Evidence was still coming to light, and scholars were studying these grisly internecine Communist Party murders. Every night the Berisha-run state TV would put on some black and white archive film showing Hoxha making secret speeches to the politburo. One concerned the purging of his once powerful rival Koci Xoxe. 'What did he know – *mut!*' exclaimed Hoxha, making the vulgar Albanian upward jerk of the left hand, which signified 'Shit!'. 'What was he? *Mut!*' concluded Hoxha contemptuously. Albanians place great emphasis on public respect and decorous comportment. Such a speech showed Hoxha in a vulgar light.

'He spoke a filthy Albanian, using all the filthy words the Albanian language was capable of', Gabriel had concluded with disgust about this performance. Yet Gabriel himself loved nothing more than to tell *mut* jokes to me in private; it was the public revelation of the use of such terms by a national leader which covered the speaker in shame: no culture at all.

It was interesting to watch the evolution of Hoxha's uniforms over the years in Dhritero's picture book. Just as Tito's costumes became more and more elaborately Soviet over the decades, so Hoxha's came to resemble those of a Ruritanian neo-Fascist generalissimo of Latin American dimensions. And so often he wore knee high jackboots, I pointed out to Dhritero.

'"Always wear jackboots", Stalin advised Litvinov', Dhritero told me in response. Dhritero had, as an Albanian army officer, followed obligatory courses in Marxism-Leninism, where such aphorisms were common currency.

The picture book revealed another side to the dictator: Hoxha the Podger. Always plump, he had visibly swelled over the years into a fleshly sybarite: he was very fond of Italian cooking, and had a personal chef trained in Rome. All the delicate provender for the high Communist élite had been imported from Italy and France. The Berisha regime had inherited the archive of invoices and backlogged order forms. These had been published, showing how well the old Communists had been living while the rest of the country starved. Dhritero was vehement in his contempt for the old regime: he thought the Democrats' rule was a paradise by comparison. He was a very decent man, I thought, and the fact that he had remained a Communist for so long spoke volumes for the effectiveness of their propaganda, and the isolation of the country from outside sources of information.

Mimoza said of her husband, when he was not there: 'His men loved him like a father and believed everything he told them. When Democracy started, he explained the charter of the United Nations to them, and taught them about freedom and human rights. He was posted by the Communists to remote places as a punishment, and in the end he had to resign from the army without a pension or anything, after much trouble and persecution. But it was too late to send him to the camps – the Communists had lost power by then.'

Mimoza was an intense, highly serious woman in her forties, humourless and inclined to lecture. She spoke precise, formal English of great correctness, but without feeling. Egrem her son, by contrast, used his English like a pair of elegant, slightly decadent silk gloves.

*

Ali Pasha's stone-built castle at Tepelena was massive and imposing from the outside, dominating the river valley from a rocky eminence, glowering down gloomily in spite of illumination under a brilliant sky.

Inside the walls, there was nothing. The elaborate Italian formal gardens once tended by captured Italian slaves, the elegant houses and buildings described by Lord Byron and his companion John Cam Hobhouse, all had been swept away. There was nothing now but a warren of shacks, mostly inhabited by gypsies, who stared at Egrem and me as we picked our way through the vegetable gardens and across little streams of sewage.

Everything that had once spoken of the great Vizier Ali Pasha's glory and greatness had vanished, except the very stones of his fortress walls: and these had been pillaged in part for building material. Yet Ali had once been the absolute ruler of southern Albania and all Epirus, his sons ruling in the Morea and other parts of Ottoman-occupied Hellas. In the early 1990s, when James Pettifer came here, Ali Pasha's crest carved in stone had still lodged high in the wall over the entrance gate through which Lord Byron's horse had picked its way in 1809. Now, in the summer of 1996, this crest-stone had been prised out and stolen, no doubt sold in Greece, like the contents of the citadel museum in Gjirokastra, which had been despoiled by the curator's family in 1991, its antiques and finely jewelled weapons sold to dealers in Athens.

In England it was a charge lodged against President Berisha that he had given Mrs Thatcher, Mr John Major and other Tory party luminaries Albanian antiques which had been stolen from public museums. Yet in Albania public property was always plundered by those in power; Enver Hoxha, like Ali Pasha, had robbed the entire country and all those in his thrall. Albania was still feudal: the public purse was that of the ruler.

I had set off with Egrem at 8 a.m. from Gjirokastra. The bus broke down almost immediately and we waited while the driver descended, pulled up the bonnet and tinkered with the engine. Then we rolled on again in the early morning sun. The seller of tickets distributed bright red plastic shopping bags gratis to the vomiting classes, in this case small children and the elderly, who, as if on cue, started puking immediately.

The bus fare to Tepelena was 100 lek each, or $1. I slid the money to Egrem and he paid for both of us. As a foreigner, whenever I tried to pay the price would rocket to fantastical figures, hundreds of dollars sometimes being demanded. In restaurants, when I went in alone, I was always cheated. In the Veneziana in Gjirokastra the waiter had short-changed me by 500 lek or $5 on a 450-lek meal, claiming I had only given him a 500 lek note instead of the 1,000 lek I had in fact given him.

'You should have pulled a policeman in from the street and told him to give the man a beating', Egrem had advised me when I recounted this. 'Policemen have been told by the Democrat government to help foreigners. You are their friends. He would have got a very bad beating, this waiter.'

There had been a Vlach couple at the Veneziana, who had observed the process of my being cheated with a sniggering fascination. The woman spoke a little English, as she was a schoolteacher.

'Are you very angry?' she asked me, still sniggering. I said I was, because being cheated made me feel bad about Albanians, which I didn't want to do.

She smiled broadly at this and translated my remark to her husband, an officer in the Democrat Special Forces. He gave a sinister smile and said nothing. He then informed me, through his wife, that he was in Gjirokastra to get a visa for Greece, as he needed expert medical treatment from a Greek hospital, which he would receive free, being an Albanian. His lip curled contemptuously as he spoke of the Greeks. 'My husband despise the Greeks, he hate them', said his wife happily. They came from Berat, and worked in

Kukova, or Stalin City that was. I made a mental note to bypass both places.

On the subject of beatings, I had asked Egrem if the Albanian police would feel confident enough to beat a doctor or a professor.

'They would regard it as an honour and a privilege to beat a doctor or a professor', he had replied with absolutely no trace of irony. I had asked Toni, the *fiancé* of Rahman's daughter in Korça, if the Albanian police took bribes. 'They are men – of course they do', he had replied. That naïveté of mine now seemed a very long time ago. In Albania everyone who possibly could took bribes.

The road to Tepelena was the main artery from Greece to Tirana. The police were out in force, even this early in the morning, collecting cash. The bus driver had an open locker stuffed full of crumpled lek notes above his head. When we were waved in by the police he would slow down and stop, grab a handful of notes, slip out of the bus, and pay off the cops by the rear nearside wheel at the back. This happened every five minutes or so on this stretch of road, near town. It made the journey very slow. Many people prefered to travel on night buses to avoid these delays; but on the other hand the unlicensed, un-uniformed bandits operated at night, and they often forced the buses off the roads at machine-gun point, and then stole everything, including in some cases the clothes the passengers stood – or rather sat – up in. The bus drivers carried pistols to protect themselves from hijackers on board, but this was no protection from determined men with machine-guns. None of this highway robbery had happened under the Communists, everyone told me, Democrat and Socialist alike, because everyone had been too terrified. And, of course, there had been almost no buses or cars to travel about in either, in those days.

'What happens if the drivers argue or don't pay enough?' I asked Egrem.

'They smash the "ears", that is, the side mirrors on the front; first the driver's, then if you don't pay, the passenger's. Then you get an extra fine for having broken mirrors.'

'Do any of the car drivers shoot the police when this happens?'

'No. This is because there is another policeman to the side with a machine-gun who would kill everyone in the car.'

This wasn't the case in Ghegeria, I later discovered. Up there police were slightly more chary about highway robbery: there had been several instances where the families of police had been identified and their flats firebombed after such extortion, whole piles of them all incinerated together.

The punishment for being caught with an illegal pistol was theoretically five years in gaol, and for a 'white arm', or knife, three years, Gabriel had told me. Yet already by the summer of 1996 this law could not be enforced. The bus drivers weren't supposed to have pistols but they often did, and the police winked at this infringement, knowing the risks. In many cases, especially in the north, the drivers were ex-police or Special Forces, as it was such a risky job. A hijacked Mercedes minibus was worth several men's life earnings, and as such made an enviable prize. New papers could always be bought and the vehicle then sold in another city. Inevitably, drivers were being held up and murdered by their passengers for their vehicles, especially taxi drivers with Mercedes.

None of this was reported in either the local or the foreign press. Foreign journalists now rarely travelled outside Tirana, and then only cautiously, with guards or in convoys. The country was slipping back into a lawlessness it had not known for fifty years. It was evident nothing could stop this collapse, which was why so many Albanians were desperate to leave. My journey had become a race against time. Was I going to be able to see what I had set out to, including the badlands of highland Ghegeria, before the whole shaky edifice of Democrat-run Albania folded around me?

I had pooh-poohed the risks of this trip before I arrived in the country, but in the cold light of day it was obvious that there was an ever-increasing chance I was not going to get out alive. My passport alone was worth $6,000 on the black market.

Egrem had taken me to his uncle, who ran a guest house in Gjirokastra. Staying there was a Dutch boy called Jan, whippet-thin and ginger-haired. He was bicycling through southern Albania. He had a smart, obviously expensive new bike and was clad top to toe in stylish multicoloured lycra. It was Jan who confirmed that the elections had been rigged.

'They were a farce. I saw them stuffing the ballot boxes with Democrat votes after the Socialists pulled out. They now claim to have got 87% of the vote, the Democrats.'

Jan had been to a Socialist rally after the election to protest, where he had been beaten by the police, along with everyone else. He took off his shirt to show his welts. He also had a nice set of colour photos of these, to show his friends back in The Hague, evidence of the progressive equivalent of a holiday sun-tan.

'Isn't it risky, cycling round the country?' I asked. He considered this for a moment, and then said:

'Yes, I suppose so. The police stop me and ask for money all the time, but I don't give. Sometimes I have to wait half an hour. But I don't think they have the courage to shoot a foreigner.'

He had just cycled from Korça to Gjirokastra over the road on which I'd come. It had taken him three days. *En route* he had slept in schoolrooms, on the teacher's table, as there had been no lodging available. I asked if he was going into Ghegeria.

'What is that?' he asked, puzzled. He had been to Albania twice before, but knew nothing of the country's history or geography.

'It is the north, the mountain highlands', I said.

He looked at me as if I was a dangerous escaped lunatic. 'You cannot go up there. The tribal blood feuds have all come back and they are shooting each other and any outsiders.' I told him I was intending to go up there anyway.

'You are completely mad', he pronounced with absolute conviction. He himself was about to head for Saranda and the ferry to Corfu. 'This country is getting ready to explode – and soon', was his parting comment.

Everything except staying at home behind locked doors was dangerous in Albania. The further you got from home, the more risks you took and the more dangerous things became. Albanians, and those foreigners they affected with their nervous fears, were as a result pessimistic and passive. No one wanted to risk much or travel far. Yet Albanians were often forced to travel, whereas foreigners could choose. Everyone tried to avoid doing so alone, and made friends on the bus with other people as soon as they could. This is what the Middle Ages, or even the eighteenth century, must have been like, I realised, this constant sense of risk and fear. It wasn't romantic or glamorous in the least, just demeaning and numbing. I found I wasn't frightened so much as angered by this atmosphere of constant menace and oppression.

Yet Tepelena, so full of terrors to Egrem, seemed no different to me from Gjirokastra. It was a smaller, scruffier version of a southern Albanian town: a shabby Ottoman centre, peeling Communist apartment blocks, an old Soviet-style hotel, one or two pavement cafés with modern plastic chairs from Greece. I offered to buy Egrem a Coca-cola at a café; it would have been pleasant to sit there in the sun and admire Ali Pasha's fortress walls and muse on Lord Byron, Fate and the ruin of men's ambition. But no – Egrem didn't even dare sit down and relax in Tepelena.

'They are bad people here, dangerous and violent. Better to wait until we get back to Gjirokastra' was his response; and he kept on walking. Did he think he would be poisoned, perhaps?

There was a strong police presence on the streets, uniformed and plain-clothes men with Kalashnikovs slung over their shoulders. Tepelena was the only place I saw the Communist-era partisan martyrs' statues still complete with their embedded red stars; elsewhere, like every other symbol of Communism, these had been prised out and destroyed. The museum was shut here, too. Tepelena still had a Communist mayor, apparently, one of the few towns to have held out against the Democrats. As a result, ballot box stuffing here was likely to have gone the other way. I asked who had won Tepelena in the first round of the election, but Egrem didn't know or care. He just wanted to get home again. He followed me round, trailing like an anguished child forced to accompany an adult on some senseless and risky outing.

The next day was a Sunday, and the second round of the elections was due to be held. The Socialists were still trying to mount demonstrations, which they hoped would turn violent, leading to people being shot by the police. This in turn could lead to the old Communist Party seizing power again in a *putsch*, on a wave of public anger at the deaths. This, after all, had been the prelude to the Democrats' electoral victory in 1991, after the Communists had massacred people during earlier pro-Democrat protest marches. The trick of Albanian governance was to stop mobs of people massing against you.

The police in Tepelena were herding the children from the schools as we walked about, and telling them to stay home and not go out. There wasn't an official curfew, but if you didn't keep moving in the streets the police gave you the hard Albanian stare which needed no translation.

'It is National Children's Day today in Albania', Egrem told me. 'Do you have this holiday in England?'

'No', I replied, 'We celebrate instead a national holiday called King Herod's Day.'

Egrem accepted this without comment, which led me to suspect his conversion to evangelical Christianity had not included much Bible reading.

I walked across the main road and into the trees, making my way down a steep slope towards the river valley where the Drinos meets the Vjosa. The trees and undergrowth were thick and green, the water glittering silver below in the sunlight. The mountains rose on either side like steep Scottish crags. Lord Byron had compared Tepelena and its citadel to Walter Scott's Branksome Hall, and indeed the atmosphere was somehow more Scots Highland than Balkan.

A group of woodcutters dressed in homespun, with axes on their shoulders, were trudging down the path to the footbridge which crossed the river. Two men leading donkeys laden with firewood were coming across the bridge slowly towards town, the planks creaking under their weight. This bridge had been put up by Ali Pasha in the early 1800s and had remained largely unchanged since then. It was a simple affair of wood on stone pillars with a thick hawser for a handrail, sufficient only for men and donkeys. Two villagers who had clearly been on a buying expedition to Tepelena were now making their way slowly down the path towards the bridge behind the woodcutters. Like characters from an early film by Polanski, they were carrying between them an immense piece of archaic furniture, a hall hat-stand and built-in mirror, with hooks and curlicues for umbrellas and walking sticks. It was clearly of pre-war Greek provenance, a copy of a *fin de siècle* French design. Where had they got it from? Where were they taking it? The mountains of the interior started the other side of Ali Pasha's bridge: there were no trucks or cars over there, just a muddy footpath. For how long were they going to walk with this monstrosity?

I followed them across the bridge and watched them disappear slowly into the lush green interior. There was no indication of the political strife which animated the towns down here, just two hundred yards away from Tepelena itself.

No one bothered with the countryside: no police patrolled, no one marshalled school children or tried to prevent demonstrations. Afghanistan started the other side of the bridge.

Poor Egrem had reluctantly followed me across the bridge. He looked so miserable, as though he was going to be eaten by bears. 'I think we should go back now . . .', he kept whispering to me.

'No, no. Let's walk for a couple of hours up into those nice-looking mountains', I said cruelly, watching the sheer horror of this notion sink in.

'We cannot,' he said faintly. 'It is too . . . too . . . dangerous.'

*

Ali Pasha had been known as 'the Lion' when successful and 'Black Ali' after his fall from power. Born between 1745 and 1750, he started life as a sheep-stealer and bandit but rose by cunning and violence to rule much of southern Albania and northern Epirus. He played off Christian against Moslem, Greek against Albanian, and used stratagems to eliminate his enemies, such as gifts of robes infected with smallpox. His spies and assassins operated all over the Balkans and his own guests sometimes used to have their heads cut off and presented to other guests on silver platters during drunken orgies.

Ali boasted to Lord Byron that he had personally murdered 30,000 people, and that he would certainly kill as many again if he lived long enough. For a spring clean he would murder his whole harem, usually having them drowned in the lake at Jannina. His own wife was among his victims. He was an enthusiastic lifelong pederast and paedophile, sending his agents out to steal pretty boys and girls for his harem. The great powers of the day, England and France, both sought his support with emissaries, gold and weapons.

Famously, Ali warred against the Christian Suliotes and, after long battles, killed or exiled all the men and drove the women and children to throw themselves off the cliffs to their death, thus giving the Victorians wonderful subject matter for illustrated prints showing half-naked mothers in an emotional state hurling tiny infants to their doom.

So sated was Ali's pet tiger with human victims that he often refused to devour the condemned, and was eventually exiled to a provincial town as punishment. Ali enjoyed watching his victims being tortured slowly to death, especially if they were young and beautiful. Though he could not read or write, he was not without imagination; he had a recalcitrant page-boy soaked in spirits, then had the lad fired out of a cannon so he could watch him being burnt to death while flying through the air. A Greek who had stolen some property belonging to plague victims was thrown into boiling oil to disinfect him, and the gypsies who murdered his son's wife, Zobieda, and her illegitimate child by Ali were all strangled by deaf-mute black dwarves, who could never speak of the deed.

'You think I am cruel', said Ali to a visitor, after hanging a parcel of men from the branch of a nearby tree, 'but you do not know these Albanians and Greeks as I do. This is the only thing they understand.' Enver Hoxha would certainly have agreed.

In the end the Porte became tired of Ali's quasi-disloyal flirtations with the Christian Powers, and sent an army against him, which Ali was too mean to suborn with bribes, thinking – wrongly – he could defeat it.

'A vizier is a man covered with honours, seated upon a barrel of gunpowder which may be blown up by a single spark', said Ali of his own plight. President Sali Berisha would certainly not have disagreed with that, either.

In the end Ali was murdered and his head sent to Constantinople. All his children betrayed him, but they too were executed. Ali's great treasure, supposedly sunk in Lake Jannina, has never been found. Lord Byron reported that Ali was very charming, and had a beautiful singing voice. He was the precursor of Albanian independence and an authentic monster by any standards.

*

We caught a bus back that was bound from Elbasan to Saranda, and which would pass through Gjirokastra on the way. It was full of rough peasant types, short and dark, many of them with gypsy features. They were dressed poorly, in Western charity clothing. Where was their next load of clothing going to come from, I asked myself. Hoxha's factories had all closed down or were export-only affairs, like the Jolly Roger in Korça. Who was ever going to set up textile factories, or anything else for that matter, in Albania again?

8

With the Old Communists

'The West must help us . . .'

'THE COMMUNISTS BUILT a complete factory at Pogradeç for producing false Marlboro cigarettes. This was run by the Sigurimi. The machinery was of the first quality, made in Swizerland. These false Marlboro were identical to the genuine ones, including the packets and cellophane – until you smoked one. They were filled with cheap Albanian tobacco and tasted disgusting. The Sigurimi exported all these cigarettes across Lake Ochrid clandestinely and sold them to the Yugoslav secret police for dollars. The Yugoslavs, who had trading rights with the West, were known as a good source of Western contraband throughout the Eastern bloc, so these false Marlboro were sold in Russia, Ukraine and Central Asia as the real thing, for hard currency. They were even used as currency in these places. This factory is still producing false Marlboro, but it has been "privatised" and a Democrat Party *fis*, formerly Communist but now allied to Berisha, controls it. Today the cigarettes are sold inside Albania, and also exported to Italy by the smugglers.'

Timoshenko was the first Albanian who admitted to still being a genuine Communist, not a pretend Socialist. He was in his early thirties and was a friend of Angeliki's family. Like the Great Leader, he was a bit of a podger himself, with chubby cheeks and a spare tyre round his tummy. He was a construction engineer and spoke good English. He'd had an American Peace Corps volunteer as a paying guest for six months in the immediate post-Communist period, from whom he'd learnt the lingo. He was a mine of information about illegal Albania. He confirmed all the prices and services Egrem had told me about. I asked him about corruption in the Democrat Party ranks.

'They are all corrupt, right up to the very top. Berisha has salted away vast fortunes stolen from foreign aid in bank accounts in Italy, Greece and Switzerland. Nothing gets done in Albania without a bribe – all into the Democrats' pockets.'

Dr Shkrelli was sitting in on this session *chez* Angeliki, and as a pro-Democrat I asked him if he thought this was true. 'Probably', he admitted. 'You only have to look at what happens at Kakavia to see the fortunes that are being made. Why should the politicians stay clean?'

The absence of tractors in the country regions had been explained to me as well. The EU had purchased a consignment of Chinese tractors to replace the old Soviet-era 1950s models, which had all broken down completely. These relatively modern machines had been 'sold' to southern Albanian farmers on easy credit, with no deposit. Every single one of them had been driven straight across the border by the new owners into either Greece or Macedonia and resold. The men returned with flocks of sheep and goats, which they were now herding once again as their grandfathers had before Communism had collectivised agriculture and forced them to grow wheat and other foodstuffs for the cities. They would never repay a penny of these 'loans' for the tractors to EU.

'As many as twenty sheep are now being butchered every day in Gjirokastra', Egrem had told me wonderingly. This in a society where until the fall of Communism few ever saw any meat in the shops. Their wheat now came from the EU and America, as food aid: no one could ever compete with that, so why bother?

Like Dr Shkrelli, Timo was bored with his provincial fate. He invited me into his family home, a fine fortified Gjirokastra house as big as the one owned by Hoxha's *fis*, and only a hundred yards away. It had been built in 1822 and was obviously the family residence of wealthy Moslem beys, Timo's ancestors. The *fis* had enjoyed high favour in the Communist period and had kept the whole house undivided as their own.

Timo was still resolutely pro-Communist, against all the evidence. Soviet and Eastern European technology and industry were still 'very strong'; the French 'had bought Russian jets and aircraft technology'; the Kalashnikov (actually an ancient, primitive Second World War design) was 'the best rifle in the world – used even by Western armies'; many Western armies 'were equipped with Soviet weapons which were better than their own'. Interestingly, all of this entirely fallacious superiority which Timo still attributed to Eastern Europe was military, not economic or social.

I pointed out that I had been to Soviet Russia, Czechoslovakia and Poland and he had not, and that not one of these things he believed was true. 'You may have been there, but I believe what I believe', he replied firmly.

Albanian education, both at school and in the home, relies on learning a set of formulae by rote, and being able to repeat this word perfect. The pupil is not expected to question, analyse or challenge any of this information. To doubt or question what one's school-teacher or father told one was a sign of disrespect, rebellion and dis-obedience, casting shame on all involved. As a result, most Albanians could not, in the Western sense, think critically about or even evaluate for accuracy information which differed from what they had been taught to believe, or what was in their family inter-est to support.

Timo had learnt that the Soviet bloc had strong industry – hydro-electric power, mines, chrome – stronger than the West. He still believed it, and simply would not listen to any counter-evidence. To think otherwise would be to admit that his father and teachers had been wrong, and his clan enemies – Democratic Party supporters – were right for having backed the winning side. Pragmatism would thus be betrayal. In a culture where honour and shame regulate every aspect of life, Albanians were forced into accepting rank absurdities and even dying for them. No one could choose whether or not to inherit a blood feud or a political commitment. The only way out was to emigrate and so cease to be beholden to feudal Albanian obligations. Even so, male members of families had been known to be given passports and tickets to Italy and even America, there to seek out and murder clan enemies with whom their own kin were in blood. Inside Albania apparently random murders by com-plete strangers were due to this implacable rule of inherited honour and obligation, which had survived all Communist attempts to nationalise the blood feud. For forty-five years every Albanian had owed the state blood if they transgressed, but with the privatisation of the economy had come the privatisation of revenge and the blood feud as well. The state no longer got involved, and individuals and families killed each other as they had in the time of Zog and before.

'Greece is no good', Timo continued, 'Albania has better country-side and better beaches. Soon Albania will take all Greece's tourism.'

The seductive chimera of tourism and its wealth has haunted many a philo-Albanian optimist, including Queen Geraldina.

'No it won't', I replied. 'No one will ever come to a country where police with machine-guns stop people in cars and demand money, and where foreigners are cheated by Albanians every time they buy anything.'

Silence.

Timo never riposted to my arguments. It was easy to understand why Albanian politics descended into abuse, fighting, torture and shooting so quickly: none of them listened to anything anyone who might differ had to say, or ever modified their own position or compromised. Anger and a raised voice were the only honourable response to disagreement. They were still Guelphs and Ghibellines, sensitive to every slight, determined to die rather than admit to a fault or forgive a wrong.

'Greece has no industry at all', Timo continued. I pointed out that Greece had shipbuilding, construction, steel, cement and many other industries, whereas Albania had completely destroyed what they once had.

'What Greek industry there is has been built entirely by the Italians, Italian money and brains', said Timo gamely. 'I myself will buy a Greek passport in a few years – they only cost $2,000 – to travel to see France and Germany. For tourism, not for work. To visit another country is to add to culture.'

No mention, though, of visiting Eastern Europe, home of all that strong industry.

A friend of Timo's had been trying to get to America for ages, he told me. After working illegally in Greece for several years he had saved $15,000. Then he had bought a false passport with a genuine US visa for $6,000. The first time he had got as far as Zurich before being turned back. He had procured another passport, and on the second attempt had got as far as Basle (those pesky Swiss!). The final try had been successful. He had entered the US on a visitor's visa and promptly joined the estimated 6 million illegal immigrants already in that country. Within a month he had bought a car on credit, rented a big house with a swimming pool, and got a job. He had phoned up his friends in Albania from the Bronx to let them know of his success.

Stories like this, true or apocryphal, fuelled the Albanian imagination. Edith Durham had encountered a similar quasi-mythic tale in 1908, when she toured the Gheg highlands on horseback. A dervish – always a cunning man in Albanian folk-tales – had shown the Turkish Vizier a spectacular trick. In a bowl of water he had conjured up a miniature steamship making way off the coast of Malta, heading for America. The dervish then asked the Vizier if he had that man's permission to get on the boat himself and go to America. The Vizier agreed, and to the amazement of the Albanian observers, the dervish had stepped into the bowl of water, got on to the steamship – and the boat had taken him to America! He had thus escaped from Albania and from the power of the Turks, by a magical trick.

But even paradise wasn't perfect: 'Many Albanians come back from America because they dislike it so much', claimed Timo, without much plausibility. 'Albania is treated like a zoo by the West. All the intelligent people joined the Communist Party in the past: either they volunteered from self-interest or they were forced. The intelligentsia comprises about 20% of the population, the rest are completely ignorant and know nothing at all.'

Dr Shkrelli didn't understand English, but this last he managed to grasp. 'Fifty per cent of the intelligentsia were Communist, the other fifty per cent were opposed to them. Most of the intelligentsia today support the Balli Kombetar', he said to me drily, in Italian, which Timo neither spoke nor understood. 'Albanians think Washington and Brussels sit up through the night discussing Albania because this is what Berisha has told them. The level of political culture is very low', he added.

Even when they understood, neither man ever contradicted what the other said. To do so would be to offend against honour. I could do so because I was a foreigner, though I knew they didn't like it. To be a friend was to agree or to remain silent.

Timo had a sister who was working as a nurse in England. 'She says the English are a people one must admire, and I agree', said Timo, somewhat surprisingly. 'Why?' I demanded.

'She says the English have roots and traditions. They build on the past. In Albania we uproot everything from the past and are

always having to start again from zero whenever a regime is over-
thrown.'

This was the most astute and penetrating self-judgement I ever
heard expressed by an Albanian.

The problem was compounded by the fact that Albanians only
knew the mythology, the propaganda of their own past. The most
ill-informed foreigner who had read one history book on Albania
knew more of the reality of the past than the most erudite Albanian,
because all the information inside Albania had either been suppressed or twisted into propaganda by one faction or another. Thus
the history of Albania was in the hands of foreigners abroad who
were not party to Albanian feuds and loyalties (though many
foreigners did adopt such feuds and loyalties). This was another
reason why foreigners were constantly called in by Albanian factions to try to add credence to their own claims.

'All the energetic Albanians have left the country or are leaving,
the lazy and the corrupt remain', Timo said without emotion. He
was at least without guile; he had already admitted to me that he
himself would be staying.

'The Communists made people work. At first there was idealism,
rebuilding the country after the war. Then there was just the endless
work. Now people don't want to work at all. They want to find
some way of getting money without working. Much hashish is produced in the villages and exported to Greece. Before the elections
the peasants said, "The government in Tirana should have sent us
cannabis seeds", and would not vote for Berisha because of this.'

Under Communism, growing marijuana had never been illegal;
it was grown as a garden herb by the villagers and used as an infu-
sion to help children sleep. I suggested opium and heroin would
soon be produced in the mountains, when Albanians could afford
the technology. Timo didn't disagree.

'Albania will become like Colombia', he added. 'If you are lucky',
I suggested, 'Tanzania, if you can't make the grade as South America.'

When I went round to Timo's house later, minus Dr Shkrelli, we
drank Greek Metaxa brandy together and smoked Assos Greek cigarettes. I had deliberately given Timo a hard time in our discussions,
to see if he could take it. Most foreigners, I knew, tended to baby the
Albanians, telling them only polite, nice things. I didn't think this
was either honest or fair to them.

Timo had a wide variety of Western drinks on display, including Red Label Scotch. His furniture was modern and comfortable, the house itself as large and attractive as a grand English manor house. I never again saw anyone who lived at this level of style in Albania. The only false note was a modern pine ceiling which Timo had installed 'because you could see the old, dirty bare beams'. Now hidden by this false ceiling was a pane of glass which had allowed light to shine directly down onto the fireplace hearth to illuminate the fire, he told me. This pane of glass had been brought especially from Constantinople in 1822 by mule when the house had been built – the nearest place to Gjirokastra such a luxury could be procured.

The house was frankly a fort, with massive walls and iron-covered front gates. There was a second line of defence actually inside the house on the first floor, with thick iron bars across the windows and a great barricaded door with loopholes for rifles, in case enemies got inside the courtyard and up the stairs. The ground floor had originally been the stables and store magazines. The water well and the bread oven were buried right inside the house to foil poisoners. You would need artillery to force your way inside this little stronghold.

Timo had found an early nineteenth-century sword hidden in the rafters when he had climbed up to install a coat-hanger aerial to try to get Macedonian TV back in Communist days. He had sold it in Athens in 1992, which he now regretted. The hiding of this sword surely dated from the mid-nineteenth century, when the Turks had forbidden arms to the Tosks after a rebellion. In Ghegeria I was to find evidence of British guns from the Second World War, which had been hidden away for forty-five years, then dug out and prepared for use once again. I had to smile back in England when, after the revolt of March 1997 and the looting of several million Kalashnikovs from the armouries, the serious papers wrote about 'the eventual problems the next government will have of disarming the Albanians'.

Hoxha had been a friend of Timo's family and had often visited their house. I sat in the chair he used to sit in, and drank my Greek brandy and reflected. In Moscow in 1990 I had spent an evening in an apartment just off Red Square which was occupied by the family of a celebrated Soviet film director from the 1930s, who had been a friend of Stalin. There too I had sat, drinking tea and eating sickly

East German kirsch-centred chocolates, watching the snow fall ceaselessly outside, as I discussed the possibilities of making a film about Lermontov in the Caucasus with the film-maker's grandson.

There I had sat in the large carved oak chair which Stalin used to sit in when he visited the apartment of his friend. How many Englishmen of my generation had sat in chairs occupied by Stalin and Enver Hoxha, I wondered. But again, perhaps this was like all those dubious beds in provincial English hotels in which Queen Elizabeth I was supposed to have slept.

Timo was the first Albanian I met who admitted freely that Albania was not a Western, a European country. 'We are an Eastern country pretending to be a Western country. We had the Turks for 500 years and the Communists for 50 years. Maybe in 550 years we could become Western. Maybe . . .'

He had been out all day on site supervising the building of a government school in a village. All the building materials now came from Greece: the tiles, the bricks and cement, even the sand. 'We used to make good cement, better than Greek', he told me defiantly. It had all ended with the end of Communism.

Timo insisted on taking me out for a drive in his car, an elderly BMW which he apologised for. Albania was awash with brand-new, expensive Mercedes. How could people afford them, I asked.

'In the beginning, when Albanians were allowed out to the West for the first time, they bought old wrecks for a few hundred dollars. Then they realised cars were so easy to steal in Europe, that the owners received insurance money and the police didn't care. So the mafia organises this now as big business. Owners of new Mercedes in Italy, Switzerland and Germany are contacted in person and told to leave the keys and the papers in the car. If they do this they are given a thousand dollars in cash. If they do not they are shot, their houses firebombed and the car stolen anyway. They always do as they are told. Who is going to risk dying to save the insurance premium from going up? The cars are then driven to Brindisi, the Italian police bribed, and the Albanian police bribed at Durrës and new papers issued. Albania has the lowest per capita income in Europe, comparable to the Central African Republic, and the highest per capita ownership of Mercedes Benzes. This is what the Democrats have done for us – given us a republic of thieves and brigands.'

Timo was a Communist, so his bitterness was understandable. Moreover, he hadn't got one of the new cars his enemies all now possessed, and for which he ached. Under Communism he would have had a Benz and the others donkeys.

He drove up to the very top of Gjirokastra, through winding lanes meant for mules. The houses became poorer and more ramshackle the higher we went.

'In the old days there was a bus service that came up here, because the Communist Party loved the working class', he said nostalgically.

'What do you think of Enver Hoxha now?' I asked. Timo lit another cigarette and thought hard.

'He was a dictator, but not like Mussolini or Perón. He was genuinely loved by the people.' No mention of the purges, the executions, the tortures, the ruined economy and the starvation.

We left the car and walked to the very edge of the town, which expired in a tumble of rock and scree. Below us an elegant old single-arched stone bridge spanned a stream, which in winter would spate into flood. Beyond, on the other side, three shepherds in boots and black sheepskin capotes, bolt-action rifles slung over their shoulders, whistled and ululated at a mob of goats and sheep which spread like large ants over the hillside.

'Is the bridge Turkish?' I asked.

'Older', said Timo, and asked a passing ancient, clad in a white fez and black baggy breeches.

'Ali Pasha', said the ancient, which meant the same as King Arthur or Old King Cole.

I discovered a small, ruinous stone pavilion from the Turkish period, which had been built in a pleasure garden of fruit trees. It overlooked the gorge and the high eagle-haunted mountains beyond. Here a poetic Ottoman gentleman had once sat and eaten peaches and smoked his *chibook*, admiring the view, possibly in the company of an attractive and compliant young Circassian slave girl, or else a rosy-cheeked, stoneless Ethiopian catamite. The trees were still looked after and fruiting, though the pavilion had fallen into disrepair. The whole orchard was surrounded by a high stone wall, itself pleasingly crumbled and holed, so that one could peer inside to descry the swaying mass of leaf and branch and fruit within.

'Let's look inside', I said to Timo, but his eyes were blind, and he was already walking back to the parked car. Albanians see nothing picturesque in the ruins of their past, only poverty, failure and shame.

The car had been showered with stones, though we had only left it a few minutes. A mob of chanting children ran round us excitedly, handfuls of gravel at the ready. 'Yiorgi! Yiorgi! Yiorgi!' they cried at me, recognising a Greek when they saw one. It was the glasses which gave me away, Egrem had told me in Tepelena: Albanian men were too vain to wear them.

On the way down we met a Chinese lorry staggering up with a monstrous load of hay aboard. Timo had to back up several hundred feet, slipping into a perilous ledge with a sheer drop to one side. He got out and stood between his car and the advancing lorry, to make sure it did not tip us over the cliff. I got out and stood well behind the car, not having Timo's confidence in his own stopping powers. The lorry creaked by him with an inch to spare.

At the one café in Gjirokastra with any pretensions to style, down by the main Greece-Tirana main road, Timo and I sat with a group of his cronies drinking imported Greek beer. The café was on the first floor, built over a supermarket, with a small veranda outside. We sat out there in the evening heat and drank and smoked.

In the group there was a grey-haired, middle-aged man in a patriotically striped blue and white shirt from the Greek minority, who looked just like a Greek from Greece, one younger Albanian with blond-brown hair who was billed as a 'very anti-Western Communist' for my benefit and discomfort, and two Albanian hangers-on who said little but sniggered on the sidelines from time to time. Although all were in their thirties and forties, the ambience was adolescent.

These men were all dying of boredom, and the conversation hovered around on football and coarse jokes in a long-drawn-out, desultory fashion. There was an attempt to irritate me with snide, grinning references to how wonderful Communism was, and how bad the West was by contrast, this from a group wearing blue jeans and sneakers, smoking American cigarettes and drinking Greek beer.

I took out a grey paper parcel containing a kilo of Tarabosh tobacco, which I had purchased from a Gheg gypsy I had met at Dhritero's little kiosk. I had been delighted to learn that this old, fine Turkish leaf was still being cultivated in the north, as it had been for forty years under Communism, and I was happy to pay the man the $2 he had asked for a kilo, with a thousand ungummed rice papers thrown into the bargain.

Now I rolled myself a cigarette slowly, and offered the tobacco round to the group in the café with a hospitable smile. They looked at me in horror, and refused with expressions of disgust on their faces. Albanian tobacco, even the finest Tarabosh leaf, was beneath their dignity as townee *effendim*: only imported American brands, or local forgeries of these, would do for their honour. I gave my little talk on supporting local industries to avoid becoming an African colony.

'Everything Albanian is *skata*', said the Greek-minority man crushingly, and no one contradicted him.

I tried to get the alleged Communist to discuss Marxism-Leninism, but he wasn't biting. 'It is a very beautiful philosophy', he said to me with a supercilious smile, 'too beautiful for Western people to understand.'

I understood enough of all this to realise I had been brought along merely to be insulted, but I didn't know why. Perhaps it was because I was passing through, and they were doomed to stay in this appalling place for the rest of their lives. I too, surely, would feel bitter in their place. Dr Shkrelli had been more philosophical when he learnt I was leaving the next day for Tirana.

'Ma che fa? Voi e pui fortunato che me, ma che fa?' ('What to do? You are more fortunate than I am, but what to do?') He shrugged hopelessly and puffed on his cigarette.

Cars raced up and down outside the café, burning rubber and squealing round corners, churning up dust. Below us, guarding the supermarket stacked with TVs and video machines, sat an elderly man with a bolt action Lee-Enfield .303 rifle of Second World War vintage. He was a private security guard in civilian clothes and he would sit there all night, in case of attempted armed robberies.

I had the feeling I was in some hot, dusty Iranian border town, a few kilometres from the Afghan border.

When we left, the pretend Communist told me he wasn't really a Communist at all: he grinned derisively, as if he had succeeded in playing a great trick on me. He drove away in a white painted ex-British army Land Rover ambulance, which he told me gleefully he had managed to steal from a British aid organisation he had worked for. He had friends in the police who had re-registered it for him.

'The West must help us', Dr Shkrelli had said to me as a parting word of advice before I left. 'You must send us all the things we need, of the first quality. You must do this because we are European and we are your friends.'

Dr Shkrelli had himself decided to abandon Albania for Skopje in Slavo-Macedonia, where he had been offered a post in a hospital. First he had to change his Albanian passport for a fresh one. His current issue was filled with hundreds of Greek entry and exit stamps. For Macedonia you had to have a passport with no Greek stamps in at all, or they wouldn't let you in. New Albanian passports cost $10 each, or you could buy the blanks already stamped up, and fill in your own details as you liked for $100. The only two crowds I ever saw in Gjirokastra were at the Greek Consulate and at the police office which issued passports.

Later, in Tirana, Carruthers of the British Embassy said to me: 'If they opened the US borders for ten days to allow all the Albanians who wanted to emigrate to get in, this whole country would be quite empty by the last day.'

The real price of the failure of colonialism, I now realised, was not paid by the colonisers, but by the colonised, who had been abandoned to a ruinous oppression by their native tyrants after tasting the sweets of European-enforced order and industry. Now the whole Third World was more or less like Albania, full of impoverished, desperate people in broken, bankrupt countries, whose only desire was to escape, to embrace the foreign thraldom that their grandparents had struggled to overthrow.

9

'We Need Culture'

Enter the Secret Police

EACH MAN WHO climbed aboard the bus had a Hoeckler and Koch sub-machine gun slung over his shoulder and a large calibre Colt automatic in a brown leather shoulder holster under his arm. They walked past us so slowly I could read the maker's name on the gun barrels.

Each man wore neatly pressed blue jeans, and a smart casual shirt with a packet of Dunhill King-size peeping out of the top pocket, brand new trainers on his feet and a walkie-talkie clipped to a leather belt. They all looked as if they had just strolled out of a Florida casting agency *en route* for an audition for a new TV cop series, Miami Vice Goes Balkan. They were all in their early twenties, slim, elegant and good-looking, with lustrous hair and clear skins. There seemed to be an endless stream of them racing up and down the Gjirokastra-Tirana road in brand new Japanese off-road vehicles, all provided of course by generous Western aid and soft loans to 'rebuild Albania after Communism'.

These men were SHIK, the élite of the Berisha forces. The ordinary roundel-wielding blue-uniformed cops earned $100 a month: these Dunhill-smoking men pulled in $400. They disdained to take bribes from bus passengers, but instead walked up and down the gangway with the easy arrogance of armed power, staring at everyone intently.

'Take off your dark glasses, look humble and stupid, and do not talk', Mimoza had instructed me, and so I did.

Foreigners rarely travelled by bus: with sun-glasses, sitting, I passed as a local. This experience of how ordinary southern

Albanians, unshielded by foreigners, were regarded by Berisha's SHIK was revealing.

They were on the look-out for known Socialists, were trying to stop them massing in Tirana to form the huge protest demonstration that the party was planning against the electoral fraud.

In theory all the *biographis* from the Communist era were supposed to remain sealed for twenty years to avoid political persecutions starting, but these secret policemen knew exactly who they were looking for.

The attentions of SHIK did not exempt us from the depredations of their low-life, uniformed brethren with the little hand-held roundels. We were waved in again and again, the driver having to pull yet another sheaf of lek notes from above his head each time, and get out for the pay-off by the rear inside wheel.

'This is why bus travel costs so much and takes so long', Mimoza told me.

I had planned on visiting Berat and Vlora first, but Dhritero had asked me to go with his wife, Mimoza, to Tirana, and besides doing him a favour this now seemed like a good idea for me too. Bus travel, any road travel, was becoming increasingly dangerous; buses and cars were being held up and robbed more and more often, and the women on board frequently raped.

Gjirokastra to Tirana was a particularly bad stretch. A British female aid worker travelling alone from Saranda had been taken off a Tirana-bound bus and raped at knifepoint by ten Albanian men only that week. The bus driver had been armed with a pistol, but he had done nothing to defend her.

'You have a black bag. This means you might have a pistol inside', Dhritero said to me. He thought that it would be unlikely that even a group of men would attempt to abduct and rape Mimoza if she were clearly protected by a man with a black bag on his lap, which might be holding a gun. At this stage in the decomposition of order in Albania there were still relatively few illicit guns and a heavy police presence. No Albanian man would be seen with a bag, unless it was holding something he needed to keep by him for protection or because it was precious: this meant money or guns or both. Black shoulder bags were becoming the trademark of men packing heat or carrying a wedge. All the currency traders in the town markets were tooled up, and they each had black bags similar to mine, for stashing all the dollar, D-Mark and lire bills. I realised there was also now a risk I was going to be held up for the bag of money I wasn't carrying. When I got to Tirana, I vowed to ditch all bags.

All this sounds very like paranoia, I know. But somehow, invisibly, like the static electricity growing in the air which presages a summer thunderstorm, the atmosphere of potential violence and destruction in Albania was building up, becoming oppressive. Before the elections everyone had hope: now the elections were over, and the Democrat Party had turned out to be just like the old Communists – corrupt and crooked, fixing the election and sending in their bully boys to break up demonstrations.

I had seen the intrepid Dutch cyclist Jan the day before I left for Tirana. 'Are you going to the Socialist protest demo?' I asked. He hadn't known there was one, but agreed that he'd be there when I'd told him the time and place.

'To get another beating?' I suggested.

He considered this for a moment, and then said 'Possibly'.

Angeliki was sorry to see me go. She made a packed lunch of goat's cheese sandwiches, a boiled egg and a woolly apple, all wrapped up in a greaseproof paper parcel: 'bread for the road', she said to me in Greek. My staying with her had been an unexpected treat, out of the blue: interesting neighbours like Timo and Dr Shkrelli had honoured her house as a result, and I had become a minor local personage. She was able to cook for me and pour me my morning glass of raki and light my cigarette, as an Albanian woman should.

On the day I left she was up at 4.30 a.m. making me Turkish coffee in a little copper *briki* boiler over a camping gas stove, 'ska sheker', as she knew I liked it, without sugar, and an unrequested supplementary cup of milky ultra-sweet cocoa. She waved me off from her doorstep in her slippers, and then slid back inside again to light up another ciggy and tune in to Italian TV.

*

Mimoza needed to go to Tirana to plead for a UK entry visa from the British Embassy for her son Egrem. She wanted him to enrol on some business course in England, under the kindly eye of Dr

Cider in Gloucester. The foreign friend would save her beloved son from going to the bad in Greece, or even worse, joining the local mafiosi in Albania. Egrem had been supposed to come with us, but at the last minute a translating job had come up with a group of Italian engineers called in to repair the new soft drink factory which made the local orange drink, called *Fresh*. Work was work.

We left at five in the morning, to get a good start in the short break between the night shift of freelance bandits coming off duty and the uniformed police and SHIK starting their own. A village idiot, crop-haired, bat-eared, cackling and drooling at the mouth, was placed beside the driver on the gearbox cover at the front. He waved his arms about and shrieked with demented glee every time a truck or bus passed us on the other side of the road. The passengers openly laughed and joked at his antics. I was glad to see Mimoza alone of all the other passengers did not join in this cruel fun.

The journey was terrible. The road was broken and ruined, the bus old and decrepit, dust pouring in through the cracked windows in billows, choking and blinding, covering us with a fine white coating like flour. The driver was anxious and drove nervously, foot hard down when he could manage it. We were thrown about from side to side to the staccato rhythm of Greek *rembetika* from the tape machine.

We passed through a landscape of abandoned fields and cut down trees, the road often following closely the deeply scored river gorge as it slipped through the mountains.

Mimoza had been formal and restrained with me in front of her family. Now we were alone she poured out her heart. First of all she asked me what I thought of her son Egrem.

'He seems rather, um, cynical', I said mildly. Mimoza took this badly.

'We were a poor family, the poorest,' she began in a rush. 'I had five brothers and sisters. "The Party loves you", they told us, but they did nothing for us. They took my brothers into the army for four years. When I got to Tirana University I went to the committee and asked for a grant. They said "when your sisters get married". By the time they got married I had finished my studies. My sisters and brothers had to support me. When I married Dhritero, he was a Communist and an army officer. But we hardly spent any time together. He was posted here and there all the time, living in barracks. I had to live with his family and they treated me like a domestic servant. Egrem was my only friend, my best friend. I had no money. I had to unravel old jumpers and knit new ones from the wool and sell them. I had no clothes, nothing – only what I stood up in. Dhritero knew nothing of all this and didn't care. We had a good *biographi* and we had no trouble from the Party. We got our flat in 1981, and when we moved in we had nothing, not a pot, a pan or even a bed. Just two rooms, eight walls. In 1990 Dhritero became a Democrat and the army persecuted him and sent him to a remote region. He wrote a letter to the Ministry of the Army but they ignored it. So he resigned and lost his pension and everything.'

She spoke in a low, insistent monotone, not looking at me. It was as though she were in Church, confessing to a priest. I nodded to show I was listening but did not interrupt her.

'I have never taken bribes. All the other teachers took bribes and gifts to pass the students. I refused. I taught poor people's children for nothing. When I wanted to get Egrem into a business course in Tirana I went to the director, whose children I had taught for nothing. "I didn't ask for money", I said to him. "You didn't need it", he replied. He wanted $500 to let Egrem into the course. I didn't have it and won't pay bribes anyway. This is to explain to you why Egrem is cynical.'

I said I understood entirely.

She continued with her confession as if I hadn't spoken. She could speak to me like this because I was a foreigner and would soon be leaving the country. So many Albanians I met made their confessions like this to me, alone, hurriedly, on buses or walking in the country where no one could overhear us. Albania was a land of desperate secrets locked up behind smiling masks.

'I have a cousin in Tepelena', she continued, 'a town full of thieves and liars who want a packet of money for doing no work, which is why they are still Communist. He came to me, this cousin, and said "Pass my son in his exams for me, he has failed in Tepelena." I refused. He said "What is the problem? We are one *fis*. If you say to me 'Go to Tirana and kill someone for me', I won't ask questions – I'll just do it for you." I wouldn't pass his son. Unless I get Egrem out of Albania, into England to do a business course I am worried for him, for his future. Maybe he will go to Greece and become a waiter. Maybe he will stay here and worse will happen. Before we found a sponsor for him in England, but that fell through. Now I must get Egrem another visa and find another sponsor. He means everything for me.'

She looked sick with anxiety and nerves.

While she was telling me all this, like part of a grim Greek chorus the village idiot at the front of the bus was roaring and shrieking senselessly, waving his arms about wildly, sound and fury signifying nothing.

We reached Ballsh but stopped only to drop two passengers, then raced on with no pause for coffee, soft drinks or the lavatories. The driver had a demon in him. Normally there were four stops on the way to Tirana; this man made none at all.

The houses now were small whitewashed cottages with red tiled roofs in the southern Italian style, with little kitchen gardens and well-tended vegetable patches, vines growing over trellises. It was a relief to see something being cultivated after the devastation of the south. In a five-and-a-half hour journey we had passed just two tractors, both towing trailers, one with a load of bricks, the other a load of hay. Mechanised agriculture in Albania was dead.

Around us now were the ruins of industry: stilled and rusting oil derricks; broken, abandoned plants and buildings; a huge glass factory with its courtyard a mountain of smashed crystal shards. The devastation was complete: everything had been destroyed. As an election platform the Socialists had said some of the old state enterprises should have money pumped back into them before they were privatised, but I could see this was an absurdity. The industrial world the Communist regime had created over forty-five years through oppression, exploitation and enforced discipline had been destroyed utterly.

At Fier there were signs of agriculture: maize and wheat growing, women hoeing fields of lettuces and tomatoes by hand, oxen pulling carts with wooden wheels, small boys on donkeys with wooden saddles.

In the small, ruinous towns of broken, filthy houses we passed through, crowds of listless people stood hanging round hopelessly in the streets; there were no shops, no kiosks, no cafés, nothing. A few mosques and medressehs were being built, each with a prominent sign outside, proclaiming that it was being paid for by either the Saudis or the Iranians. President Berisha had taken Albania into the Conference of Islamic States in a bid to get aid. 'We are a predominantly Islamic country, but with Christian morality', he had said to his Western friends, his tongue no doubt firmly in both his cheeks alternately. *Tek është khorde është besa* – 'The faith follows the sword' – was a traditional Albanian proverb.

We skirted the seashore at Durrës, sandy beaches fringed by pine trees. I saw long lines of brand-new Mercedes cars gleaming in the sun, guarded by civilians with machine-guns, the latest consignments from Italy awaiting their new owners. New mosques and stolen Mercedes in a country with little food, no work and no industry.

I was baffled. What could you do with a place like this? Even the usual authoritarian solutions that people on the extreme Left and Right advocate had been tried: dictatorship, compulsion, forced labour. I felt that not only had I passed through a landscape of fifty years ago, with its oxen and donkeys, hand-hoed fields and vegetable gardens, but also a terrible vision of the future, of an exhausted, broken, overpopulated world crammed with hungry, hopeless people with the ruins of failed industrial culture all round them. All of this within four hours' sailing distance from the coast of Italy.

I was shocked. I had known it was going to be bad, but I hadn't appreciated that anywhere was quite this bad. I felt I was in a vile dream which it was impossible to get out of. It was hopeless beyond anything.

There were people everywhere, mostly young, twenty-five or under, badly dressed and dejected, I didn't see one smile all day. What was there to smile about?

Mimoza was watching my reactions to all this now, her own confession done. She could not fail to see my spirits sinking. It was impossible to hide my depression at this landscape of ruin.

We got off the bus outside Tirana proper and crammed ourselves into a yellow Italian-made bus, creaking through streets thronged yet more densely with people, carts and horses, donkeys, ancient lorries, minibuses, new Mercedes.

Mimoza looked at me with pleading eyes. 'Is Albania as poor as England at its poorest?' she asked in a whisper.

She wanted some reassurance that all this wasn't as bad as she thought it was. But she had been to England herself for a week, the guest of Dr Cider. Perhaps she hoped they had deliberately kept the worst from her there, like a Communist-era tourist trip would have done in Albania.

It would have been so easy to lie. I couldn't do it. I had to be truthful and therefore almost unbearably brutal.

'No, Mimoza. Albania is as poor as Africa at its very poorest. Nowhere in Europe is this poor.'

She looked at me with small, hurt eyes, and said desperately: 'We need culture.'

'Do cultured, educated people in Albania take bribes?' I asked.

'Of course.'

'You need people who won't take bribes. If you have a bribery culture, everyone can be bought and nothing can be trusted – not doctors, not schools, not politicians, not the police, not justice, nor education – because they are all corrupt and therefore worthless.'

She looked utterly wretched and made no reply, but looked away from me and out of the window at the sea of swarming, pulsating people.

*

It was hot. We were both thirsty and tired. I suggested a drink at one of the pavement cafés near Skanderbeg Square. No, Mimoza wanted to find the *pallati* where I was to stay first, then she had to go to the British Embassy before it shut. On we trudged.

I had a hand-drawn map, another useless child's scrawl which showed where Alexei and his wife lived, no street name and no number as usual. I had a phone number for them, too, but all the phones were broken or crowded with massed, waiting Albanians. We circled round and round on foot, looking for an elusive alleyway which wasn't there.

There were police in flak jackets with machine-guns at every corner, almost as many police as civilians in the streets, it seemed. The pavements were crowded with people squatting on their haunches selling bananas, shoelaces, packs of cigarettes, old taps and washers, piles of rubbish.

I said 'Mimoza, please. Go to the Embassy. It closes soon for the day. I'll find Alexei's place myself.'

But no, she wouldn't leave me until she had seen me safely to the next person, by which time it was half past twelve, and we both knew the Embassy closed for the day at twelve. Mimoza had lost a whole day now because of me. That was what made me feel so terrible: amid such ruin, such kindness and decency.

10

Diplomatic Initiatives

The Discreet Charm of Our Man in Tirana

'TIRANA HAD BEEN to us what Damascus was to T. E. Lawrence', wrote Captain Julian Amery, originally a senior British military liaison officer in wartime Albania. Up in the hills with the partisans, living on fried goat and raki, paying their way with gold sovereigns and sten guns, suffering the constant theft by their hosts of mules, arms and gold, the British officers yearned for the fleshpots and the final prize of the capital, amid the slow general collapse of the Axis forces in the Balkans.

Thwarted in his attempts to organise a concerted rising against the Germans, Captain Amery smuggled himself into the Nazi-occupied capital in disguise in 1944, and went visiting various potentially pro-British allies: but no one would commit themselves to anything very much except vague hopes and wishes. The Italians had surrendered, and their soldiers had been sold in the markets by the Albanians as beasts of burden at one gold napoleon apiece, some of them even eaten in regions with food shortages. Colonel Smiley had himself supped on a meal of Italian soldier stew by accident, though he had the good manners to doubt that his hosts would have played such a rotten trick on him.

With Mussolini gone, surely Hitler would not be long following, agreed his cautious Albanian friends, but it did not do to rush things. What were Britain's intentions in the Balkans? And Russia's? In the meantime the Nazis were still *in situ*, the Allies a long way off.

'To have the Germans as friends is heavy on the shoulders', Count Ciano had said to King Zog in 1938, 'but to have them as enemies is terrible.' The Zogists and Balli Kombetar knew just what he meant:

and in the hills, waiting like jackals for the Germans to leave, were the forces of Enver Hoxha and his Communist brigands.

'You really must do something, my dear fellow', one elderly Tirana clubman had remarked to Captain Amery in the clipped accents of a cavalry officer, 'or we shall have a lot of trouble with these rotters up in the hills.' This was Jemaleddin Vlora Pasha, the last Albanian to hold the Ottoman title of Pasha, and son-in-law of the Khedive of Egypt, who had lived for many years in Cairo, where he had ridden to hounds in the desert and been an ornament to the Ghezira Club. His future under a Communist government would surely be problematic.

'Whom the Gods would destroy . . .' had been Amery's silent rejoinder. Nor had he been particularly impressed with either the partisans' or their nationalist rivals' military capacities: 'Gheg armies were nothing but the tribes on a war footing' had been his comment on the northerners, and on the Tosks: 'Ten out of every hundred bullets provided by the British to the partisans were used against the Germans and ninety against the Zogists and Balli Kombetar, who declined to fight the Germans, and more or less passively or actively collaborated and received supplies from the Germans.'

Kosovo had been subtracted from a defeated Yugoslavia and united with Albania by the Germans, and the Skanderbeg Division, a 10,000-strong SS force of Kosovar Albanians raised by them, was used to oppress the Serbs, paying back the hated Slavic enemy in their own coin of ethnic repression and persecution.

The Germans had attempted to set up an Albanian SS unit in Tirana, too. A captain of the reserve, Salami Chelai, was offered the command with the rank of colonel. The commander-in-chief of the collaborationist Albanian Army, General Prenk Previsi, was offended by this sudden advancement under independent command of one of his officers. He ordered him to refuse the post. On German advice SS Colonel-designate Chelai refused to obey this order, and one morning was seen by his enraged commanding officer entering German HQ dressed in full colonel's uniform.

Injured in his dignity, General Prenk Previsi decided to make an example of this disobedient minion, and ordered his immediate execution. His ADCs and orderlies sliced up the unsuspecting Salami with two hand grenades and machine-gun fire on the steps of the German HQ when he emerged after the first – and last –

meeting with his new masters. General Prenk savoured this dramatic spectacle from his office window while sipping his mid-morning cup of Turkish coffee.

The Germans were infuriated at the public assassination of their man, and demanded General Prenk's immediate dismissal and punishment. The Regent, Mehti Bey, who had learnt his politics under the Ottomans, called the errant general to his office in the presence of the German commanding officer.

'I must ask you to apologise to our German friend for the mess you have made on his doorstep. Next time you have to shoot an officer, see that is done in the barracks and not in the street' had been his emollient advice.

The Germans were not amused. They refused to give the Albanian Army any more guns or ammunition, which blackened General Prenk Previsi's face and made him hate his allies the more, though it did not stem his endless requests to them for further supplies of weapons.

*

Central Tirana had hardly changed in the fifty odd years since Captain Amery had prowled there incognito. The same wide colonial avenues with ochre-painted Italianate public buildings, fountains and palm trees stretched away from Skanderbeg Square, the mountains looming all around like an enclosing amphitheatre of stone.

There was the stately Parliament building, on the steps of which King Zog had survived an assassination attempt by a young student who had managed to hit the monarch with two bullets before being overpowered by gendarmes. Zog had entered the Parliament, still bleeding, and without any medical attention strode straight into the chamber to give a two-hour speech to a packed House, this regarded by many as one of his most eloquent. After the peroration the assembled parliamentarians had risen to give him a standing ovation. Only then had Zog deigned to go to hospital to have the bullets removed. The student, who had been disgruntled with his exam results, was given a three-year prison sentence.

Assassination attempts in this part of the Balkans appeared much like sporting events elsewhere, part of the risk, the rough and tumble of every day life.

The Parliament building now had armed guards outside who pushed me into the road when I tried to walk along the pavement beside it. In the road a white line had been painted, demarcating a sort of extra-curricular pavement, along which one had to walk, under armed surveillance. The idea was to give the guards a wide, clear field of fire at those who might throw bombs at the Parliament as they passed. According to the newspapers, this occurred with monotonous regularity. Often the guards missed in their own aim as the bomb-throwers ran away, adding to the sporting nature of the whole enterprise. It was to this Parliament building that King Zog has sent the bloodstained nightgown of his wife, Queen Geraldina, after their wedding night. This poignant garment then had been publicly displayed to the deputies in the chamber by the President of the Assembly, as evidence that the royal bride had been a bona fide virgin: this in *Anno Domini* 1938.

Zog had married Geraldina Appoyoni, an aristocratic Hungarian-American beauty, in a successful attempt to get an heir to the newly invented Kingdom of the Albanians. As a wedding gift, Hitler had sent a scarlet supercharged open Mercedes-Benz, the exact duplicate of his own car. Count Ciano was the official witness at the wedding. Zog himself had ordered his bride jewels from Bulgari and Cartier, clothes from Chanel and Worth. The clothes remained behind when the Zogs fled after the Italian invasion of 1939; but the jewels went with them, along with strong boxes containing gold napoleon coins to the value of £50,000, the loading of which Zog supervised himself.

King Zog, Queen Geraldina and the baby Crown Prince Leka then made a triumphal royal refugees' progress through eastern Europe with the white leather upholstered Mercedes which was loaded on and off the Orient Express. The fall of France found them fleeing Paris *en route* to Bordeaux. The convoy of refugees was dive-bombed by German planes, but Zog refused to quit the car, and admonished his less brave companions who fled that 'the pilot is not yet born who would fire on the Führer's car'.

Assured that the large royal party, now known to the British Foreign Office as 'King Zog's Circus', could support itself, the King and his entourage spent the war in England, initially at the Ritz Hotel in London where they received a royal discount. After the war they moved to Egypt, leaving a trail of bad debts, and spent several years as the guests of King Farouk, himself of Albanian descent.

Though in exile, Crown Prince Leka grew up in an authentically Albanian milieu. His English nanny asked what he was playing at one day, indicating his rows of lead toy soldiers. The five-year-old replied solemnly, 'firing squads'.

Zog, who had been brought up at the oriental court of Sultan Abdul Hamid in Istanbul before the First World War, and had later proved to be an exemplary dancer of the tango in the Vienna of the Emperor Franz Josef, died, still in exile, in Paris in the 1960s. 'The most intelligent man I ever met', said Captain Julian Amery of him.

Zog was reputed to have survived more than fifty-five assassination attempts. He always carried with him his personal automatic pistol, gold-plated for him by Cartier. When he married Geraldina, he had presented her with a miniaturised version of the same pistol, also gold-plated. He chain-smoked cigarettes through a holder and was something of a dandy. He spoke Arabic, Persian, German and French, as well as Albanian and Turkish – but he never regained his self-invented throne.

By the Parliament building was King Zog's Palace, armed Berisha guards outside to protect the large Italianate villa from the curious. Inside, it was said, nothing had been touched since Zog left. Even the glasses with Z engraved on them were still on the shelves, along with the monogrammed Sèvres chinaware and the royal chamberpots decorated with roses and gold leaf. It was said that neither Hoxha nor Berisha would use Zog's Palace for fear of the Evil Eye. It was widely believed that one of Zog's dervishes, an adept in the dark arts, had put a strong curse on the Palace, should anyone but a Zog try to use it. People claimed that Hoxha's former colleague in the partisans Mehmet Shehu had ignored this, scoffing at the dervish's hex as a bourgeois superstition. He had gone into the Palace and tried to steal some of the furniture, and had been found dead the next day, inexplicably shot in the head. Other people claimed that there was nothing whatsoever inside Zog's Palace, as the whole thing had been comprehensively looted by the Italians and that the business about the Evil Eye was simply a journalist's joke which the unsuspecting had swallowed and repeated.

Here, too, was the enormous, glittering black and white pyramid in which Enver Hoxha had been buried, built out of the finest imported marble from Greece and Italy, at a cost of $5 million, at a time when Albanians were dying of starvation in 1985. Now the Red Pharaoh was in disgrace, his body removed from its sepulchre and buried quietly elsewhere. The vast mausoleum was empty, the marble tiles already falling off the outside shell from where they were also prised off at night and then sold as souvenirs to foreign diplomatists by enterprising street vendors. The pyramid was to become a trade centre, but like every other public building in Tirana it was presently closed because of the political tensions.

The Palace of Culture, the central museum, a socialist realist monolith with a magnificent stone carving in the pediment of Hoxha being adored by his peons, was also closed until the whole Communist era could be comprehensively rewritten. As in ancient Egypt, doubtless Hoxha's face would be recarved to represent another ruler.

On the streets and at the corners, in the shady parks planned and built by the Italians, were police, and yet more police: in uniform and out, SHIK and *ordinaire,* in cars and off-roaders, perched up on the tops of building in machine-gun nests, driving to and fro in open trucks and armoured cars, patrolling in pairs, threes, fours and fives, lounging on street corners, carrying shot-guns and bazookas, AK-47s and anti-tank rockets, packing every conceivable kind of handgun and automatic – police, Special Forces, and yet more police. Central Tirana in the summer of 1996 was an arms salesman's wet dream.

But among all this uniformed might the people carried on doing what they were doing regardless, and this was having fun. For forty-five years they had slaved to no avail. Now the West and their relatives abroad had poured in foreign currency, aid, loans and goodies of all sorts; it was time to party.

A huge fun-fair had been set up in Skanderbeg Square with a children's carousel (much used by adults as well), a dodgem-car circuit, a big dipper, candyfloss stalls, peanut vendors, ice cream pedal-carts, blaring pop music from cassette machines, one-armed bandits, prize-grabbers, slottos, coconuts and bananas – all the fun of the fair. Tiny children pulled and tugged their bemused, delighted elders to and fro among the differing attractions with excited little cries of ecstacy.

Everyone was good-humoured and smiling, dressed up to the

nines in new summery clothes, a cigarette between every man's lips, the pavement cafés bursting with Albanian customers swigging down imported German and Italian beers, or sipping *cappuccini* and nibbling sticky cakes. A few brand-new Mercedes cruised up and down, and ragged beggars from the backcountry swarmed happily, some still tugging on bits of string the goats they had brought with them from the villages to supply fresh milk while they were on the razzle in the big city. From somewhere a tethered donkey brayed, and a dignified elderly Gheg highlander just down from the mountains sat on the pavement in his white fez and traditional white trews, with bathroom scales in front of him, on which you could weigh yourself for 10 lek.

This was the fun-fair capitalism which was to end in disaster in six months' time. 'How do you Albanians live, seeing as none of you do any work?' the Italian visitor had asked bemusedly, in the current Tirana joke that everyone was repeating. 'Well, half are in the cafés drinking and eating – and the other half are serving them' came the Albanian's reply.

In a darker vein was the joke which admitted to the self-destructive urge abroad: a farmer was being interviewed by Albanian TV about his miraculous pig, which had saved the family from burning to death by alerting them to a fire, and which had also pointed out a place where they had dug and found buried gold, and even saved the farmer's life by pushing a tractor off his body when it had turned over on him. 'Yes, okay, I understand all that', the TV interviewer had said, 'but tell me, why does this miraculous pig of yours only have three legs?' 'If you had a pig as intelligent as this one, would you eat it all at once?' came the farmer's reply.

To one side of the fun-fair was the open air, now legal, foreign exchange market which had once been the black market, positioned by a historical irony in the street right outside the Communist Party headquarters. Here intense-looking Albanian men in pale flared polyester trousers and fake Lacoste shirts wandered up and down calling out: 'Dollari! D-Marki! Lire!' and waved sheafs of folded lek notes to make their point. Customers were patrolling around, testing to see if they could shave a few cents off the rate with the next guy. On the pavements squatted the rate-makers, with their ears to small transistor radios on which they were listening to money market prices from the BBC World Service in Albanian. Here also sat the legendary Sheikh Dollar, an old blind man with a white beard and embroidered skull-cap, who could tell merely by touch whether a dollar was false or genuine. The US Treasury had apparently put five hidden raised serrations on each bill, which the expert could feel to detect forgeries. In *Zeri i Popullit*, the official former Communist Party, now Socialist, newspaper there had been a whole page article written by an expert on 'Getting to Know Your New Dollar', with a larger than life-size facsimile of the new issue, front and back, with arrows pointing to the salient features. Already the printing presses of Shkodra and Durrës were said to be turning out excellent imitations of these new dollars, which had only been in circulation a few months.

One of the few modern buildings was the Tirana International Hotel, a Sheraton-type tower block on Skanderbeg Square. There was to have been a genuine Sheraton, but the *émigré* Kosovo Albanian who had returned to build this had collected several million dollars in investment money locally, excavated a huge hole in the ground, and then vanished to Switzerland with the loot. His extradition was still being sought, and the hole, just behind the Tirana International, was now used by tramps and beggars to sleep in at night.

I wandered into the Tirana International in search of some action. The celebrated Daiti Hotel, Tirana's grand pre-war watering-hole, once an Eric Ambleresque Balkan hotbed, was as dead as the dodo.

In the lobby of the Tirana International I saw a sign in English: '2nd Floor: 6.30 p.m. British Embassy Reception, Queen's Birthday'.

It was 7.15 and I walked up two flights and breezed in, expecting either demands for an invitation or else a body search for hidden weapons. A questing lady asked in French if I had a pen but swept by, not staying for an answer.

In a crowded room of three or four hundred people, all smoking, drinking and eating canapés, it wasn't hard to spot Ms Sniff. She stood alone, pallid and depressive, emanating a coldly radiant glow of 100% British miserabilism. Flat-chested and spindly, shod in low-heeled shoes and clad in a pastel trouser suit, her spiky short hair glowed mousily in the rays of the sinking sun, which illuminated, indeed irradiated, the room from the huge west windows.

'Ms Sniff, I presume?' I said, proffering a hand. 'I have a letter of introduction to you from Dr Cider.'

Ignoring my hand, she allowed her pale, watery eyes to dwell on me with that frank distaste which has long been the prerogative of the British aid worker abroad towards lowly supplicants.

'Oh, really? Drop it by at the office. They'll send it up to me. I hardly know Cider, of course. Met him once I think . . .'

The dying fall spoke ungiving volumes. I mentally tore up Dr Cider's introductory letter and chucked the pieces in the bin. I was going to get precisely nowhere with Ms Sniff. British overseas aid staff seem to be chosen with uncanny precision for their low-voltage chill factor. I remembered a school matron who had run her surgery strictly from 10 a.m. to 11 a.m. Once, during a rugger match, a visiting player from another school had been taken to her suffering from concussion, a broken nose and a suspected broken ankle. 'Come back at surgery time!' she had screamed, and slammed the door in the carrying party's faces. The victim had to be taken, eventually in a taxi, to a nearby hospital still groaning and spouting blood. She missed her vocation in foreign aid I always felt, our matron.

'Do they have a press attaché I can talk to by any chance for a briefing?' I asked, turning to a lady who looked as if she belonged there. This was more or less true, as I had extracted a cautious commission to write several articles on a freelance basis on Albania and the elections for a derisory sum of money.

'Oh, they don't have one of those', she replied, as if of municipal rat-catchers, 'but it's Mr Carruthers you'll need to see. He's Our Man In Tirana for all that sort of thing.'

I edged my way towards the indicated Carruthers, who was chatting to a Swedish General in full dress uniform and a depressed-looking, copiously moustachioed Bulgarian naval officer in jackboots and Sam Browne belt.

Before I could introduce myself, a glass was resolutely tapped with a knife by a small, rugged-looking military man in a splendidly Balkan outfit, scarlet-striped white trousers, red and blue military jacket with epaulettes and gold frogging, highly polished black patent leather shoes and full dress sword in an ornate scabbard. He was the only genuinely Ruritanian figure in a room full of Albanian and other Balkan military officers still dowdy in their Soviet era drabs. The Albanian uniforms, at least, would surely return to geographical par when the new constitution was finally decreed.

A microphone was brought forward. A TV cameraman with a shoulderpod advanced into position and a distinguished-looking gent stepped up to the podium. The military man in the splendid uniform cleared his throat and announced in full cockney:

'Ladies and gentlemen, quiet if you will, please, for His Excellency the British Ambassador!'

The military dandy was, I realised, the major-domo of the British Embassy.

H.E. then gave a very creditable speech in Albanian for the TV camera, for which he was duly applauded by those Albanian-speakers present.

'If you would charge your glasses, ladies and gentlemen, I would like to propose the toast . . .' he continued in English.

Half the room, including myself, found our glasses were unaccountably empty, and in a flurry of activity white-coated and -gloved waiters circulated with yet more bottles of wine and mineral water.

'There is always a drought at this time of the year, I'm afraid', quipped H.E., and all the English speakers dutifully laughed.

'I give you His Excellency President Sali Berisha of Albania and Her Majesty Queen Elizabeth II of Great Britain,' proposed H.E. and raised his glass. A general chinking and slurping ensued.

Half hidden behind the podium, an Albanian string quintet in tailcoats and white ties now struck up the most moving and elegiac rendition of 'God Save the Queen' I have ever heard, like something by Schubert. It was a warm evening and the windows had all been flung open wide. As the quintet started to play, from across the other side of Skanderbeg Square came the evening call to prayer from the central mosque, the voice of the muezzin rising and falling in counterpoint with the national anthem. It was a beautiful and moving collision, surreal and elegant at the same time.

Before I could get to Carruthers, I met an unreconstructed public-school type from Price Waterhouse, with his small and perfectly groomed Albanian sidekick, who evinced immaculate English and a 100-watt smile.

Price Waterhouse offered me a King Edward VIII cigar which I accepted with alacrity. I crinkled it between my fingers, smelt it approvingly, and said to him '*Vero* or *falso*?'

He looked at me with blank incomprehension, but his Albanian sidekick burst into sudden, uncontrollable laughter. I explained about the fake-Marlboro factory at Pogradeç. Price Waterhouse was appalled.

'But that's piracy and theft!'

'I'm afraid so', I said. Then I told them a couple of Enver Hoxha jokes, which I often found good ice-breakers. Price Waterhouse hadn't heard them, but his sidekick had.

Finally, I managed to get to Carruthers, who was a slim, youth-ful-looking fellow with a luxuriant moustache and a double-breasted, diplomatically striped suit.

'Are you on expenses?' was his first question. I had to admit I was not.

'Well, we'll just have a sandwich for lunch, then, at the Rogner and I'll pay', he replied with practised *savoir-faire*. He flicked through his diary and said: 'Tomorrow? – 12.30?' Evidently his lun-cheon diary was as empty as my own. He gave me his card and I gave him mine and we parted, his arm already gently but firmly requisitioned by a Roumanian cultural lady of Junoesque propor-tions. Just before he vanished he said to me: 'Chap you want to meet is General Johnny, over there, talking to the Minister of Agriculture's wife and the Dutch Ambassador. He's got all the gen.'

What on earth was a British General doing in Tirana? I spent half an hour chasing him round the room and observing his style. He was a popular fellow with a big smile and a hearty handshake. He had in tow a tall, slim and extremely attractive blonde aide who I assumed was either French or Italian. She was in her early twenties, dressed in high fashion; I heard her speaking in at least six lan-guages with equal fluency, but could not place her accent.

I had obviously stumbled by accident into *le tout Tirane*.

I have always loved those travel books from the 1930s where the inevitably well-connected authors drift in to the capital from the Gobi Desert or the High Pamir, still suffering from beriberi, dressed in rags and reeking of yak's pee, only to launch immediately and effortlessly into diplomatic high life with borrowed dinner jackets, putting up at the Embassy and squiring bored young debs around in rickshaws from languorous tennis match to smart cocktail party.

Now was my chance: I too could attempt to gatecrash this charmed circle. I knew the British Embassy in Tirana was only three small rented rooms in an office building, so bunking down with His

Excellency was out of the question, but the high life clearly beckoned.

I'd had some extremely impressive visiting cards run up for myself for just such occasions as this. They stated in bold terms my credentials – 'Freelance BBC Broadcaster – author – film-maker' – in French, Spanish, Greek, Arabic, Russian and Amharic as well as English. The Amharic was for a proposed expedition to Ethiopia which had never come off. I had won countless drinks from people challenging them to guess what language the Amharic was: the nearest anyone had got was Armenian, and I had made a mental note to get Armenian added to the cards when I returned to London.

Finally, an undefended salient opened on the General's left flank and I rode in hard, card advanced at the ready like a galloper bringing urgent news of Blucher's advance.

'*The Caledonian* newspaper, Sir', I blurted out, 'hot-foot from Korça, Pogradeç and Gjirokastra in the south.'

The General's eye darted quickly between my card and myself. In his fifties, he was a small, wiry fellow with merry, dancing blue eyes and a clean-shaven face, with a thinning golden thatch. He was dressed in *mufti*, a conservative dark blue suit and regimental tie.

'He who dares wins', I added quickly. The General's tie was that of the Parachute Regiment, and I had a hunch he might be former SAS as well. His face gave nothing away. He slipped my card into his wallet and offered me his own.

'You know the Ambassador of the Netherlands, His Excellency Baron Gerhard van X?' he said. The Baron and I shook hands and smiled politely.

'And this is Natasha, my translator and aide', continued the General. I found myself gazing at an elegant apparition shimmering in what appeared to my untutored eye to be expensive *haute couture*. Prominent, unavoidably so, were also a pair of splendid, gauze-enveloped breasts which fully deserved to be declared national monuments in their own right. I didn't dare ask '*Falso* or *vero*?', although it did cross my mind. Natasha crinkled her nose at me and gave a big smile.

'Why isn't there a Scottish embassy in Tirana – it's just what we all need, surely?' she purred. 'All that wonderful malt whisky at the receptions.'

'We could start one', I suggested. 'I can be the Ambassador and you can be everything else, which you'd obviously do very well, and we'll make a fortune issuing Scottish passports for dollars.'

Natasha was in fact Albanian and the laugh she gave at my passport quip indicated the double irony of our exchange: she was the brightest and best qualified amongst us for all this badinage, but she was the only one without a Western passport. Her parents had both been high in the Communist *nomenklatura* and now were in deep disgrace.

One of those hectic, four-sided, impossible-to-reproduce conversations now took place between us, as we all shouted to be heard over the increasingly Balkan-volumed din. The Baron was asking me about Korça and telling me about Bajram Curri; the General wanted to know about the Greek minority in the south and was telling me about his military mission to protect Albania's borders; and Natasha and I were passing snippets of information to one another in code about altogether different things.

'I met a compatriot of yours cycling in Gjirokastra last week', I said to the Baron, *en passant*. He took this badly; indeed he looked as if I had just thrown a glass of Euro-plonk in his face.

All that time I didn't know about the Dutchman who had just been murdered in the north. Obviously the Baron and the General did. They gave each other micro-second glances redolent with inner knowledge from which I was excluded.

'Was he all right?' asked the Baron faintly. 'Where was he going?'

I was able to reassure the Baron that Jan had cycled off to Saranda to get the ferry to Corfu, and was by now almost certainly safely back in The Hague, proudly displaying his collection of authentic Balkan welts.

It quickly became clear that the diplomatic set in Tirana had little idea of what was going on in the rest of the country. The two envoys gently but firmly milked me for information for over half an hour.

'You are the first person we've actually met who has been able to travel around low on the ground on your own, staying with the locals, all that sort of thing', the Baron admitted. Tirana dips rarely left Tirana, and when they did it was in convoy and heavily guarded. Baron X himself lived in The Hague, and flew into Tirana and Skopje once a month to keep an eye on things Balkan. He had almost certainly just come down on account of his murdered compatriot, but of this, of course, I as yet knew nothing.

The General and I made a rendezvous for a fuller meeting at his office in two days time. He was due to go off to Slavo-Macedonia the day after that, then back to London to give the Cabinet – and no doubt other less high-profile committees – a full briefing.

*

Back at Alexei and Alicia's flat I showed them my crop of cards from the new Western *nomenklatura*: as old Communists who knew about these things they were highly impressed. Alicia made me a cup of Turkish coffee and served a home-made cake made out of maize flour and courgette, which was pleasingly unsweet. The electricity had come on after three days off, and the water would be on for an hour at midnight: we could all have showers at last.

I sat on the balcony of their apartment and smoked a cigarette of Tarabosh tobacco and watched the velvet night embrace the old red roof-tiled horizon of Ottoman Tirana, which stretched down below me. The centre of town with its triumphalist neo-Fascist buildings and broad avenues was but one block deep; after that the crumbling ruins of *palatti* and stone Turkish houses began again amid broken roads and cracked, pitted pavements. The white satellite TV dish on the wall beside me pointed up to the star-speckled, deep indigo skies above. In the distance loomed the deepening purple mass of Mount Daiti, within whose bowels slumbered a legendary Albanian hero and mystic who, like King Arthur, would sleep on until such time as his country's dire need awoke him to redemptive action.

From inside the flat I could hear the TV news in English from CNN telling of alleged fraud and ballot-rigging in the Albanian general election; according to the report, the Socialists had refused to enter the new parliament and their candidates had gone on a hunger strike. Of this we knew little, since the Berisha-controlled state TV spoke of nothing but victory and the triumph of Democracy.

11

Massage of the Candidates

Arrested by the Secret Police

WE ARE CONVINCED THAT WITH US IS THE MAJOR-
ITY OF THE ALBANIANS

Massage of the candidates for deputies of the Albania Socialist Party, indorsed in the hunger strike, addressed to the Albanian People.

Brothers and Sisters,

We, 55 candidates for the Albanian Socialist Party in the elections of May 26-th, were indorsed today in a hunger strike. We undertook such a step fully convinced that this is a form of our protest against the democracy seduction that the police state of Berisha did on May 26-th. That day was expected with great hopes by the Albanians, but Berisha's regime turned it into a morning day and the day of tears. The people of the executive power, uniformed police and civilians as ordinary band and vagabonds, inspired and preached by Berisha himself, with terror and violence and arbitrary actions, seduced the will of the Albanian people. Those, that during the four years time, stole the people's national property, on May 26-th stole the people's mandate, in order to use it for another term of four years.

Thus, the democracy, on May 26-th, received a hard blow. Berisha's people put in their pocket the unmerited mandate of the people.

Zeri i Popullit, official Albanian Socialist Party organ, English
page, Sunday June 2nd 1996

*

SEDUCED BY THE carnival atmosphere in Skanderbeg Square, my mistake was to risk taking a photograph of the giant equestrian statue of Skanderbeg.

Click went my camera. Within seconds I had two SHIK in plain clothes at my side, each of them with a drawn automatic pointing at my stomach.

'Anglisht turist', I said faintly, as handcuffs were slipped on my wrists. I was bundled away swiftly into a smart Italian-made Black Maria, which was gradually filling up with Albanian malcontents unhappy with the way the election had gone.

The SHIK made no attempt to take my camera from me. I had put it into my black bag, and when I was left in the bus to await developments I was able to wind the rest of the film forward, remove and replace it with a new, unused film. I didn't care about the photo of Skanderbeg but I did want to save some good shots of Gjirokastra I had taken. In the event I needn't have bothered. Nobody ever asked me for the film, or even showed any interest in the camera.

I tried to work out what I had done wrong. Obviously it wasn't snapping the national hero Skanderbeg. Albanians had a curious relationship with the pictorial image. When Edward Lear travelled through Albania in the middle of the nineteenth century he had to have an armed guard provided by each local *pasha* whenever he wanted to go outdoors to sketch. A hostile crowd of Albanians would always form and, often led by a dervish, would start to stone Lear and utter curses against him for his 'writing'. 'Shaitan!' they would cry. 'Shaitan! Scroo! Scroo!' 'The Devil! He writes and draws!'

To be 'written' in Albania, to be noted down in words or images, especially by a stranger, was almost always a bad thing. The Evil Eye, the Padishah's tax collectors, Hoxha's Sigurimi, the picking out of eyes from portrait photos, the amused contempt of foreign journalists or anthropologists at Albania's 'primitive' conditions: all these and many other complex results flowed from 'writing'.

When Lear was staying in Shkodra, he had been requested to sketch a portrait of his host, an Albanian merchant. Having done so, Lear was then requested by the merchant's brother to do the same for him too. Having no more paper, Lear added a miniature portrait of the brother on the side of the larger portrait he had just completed. Both brothers were outraged.

'Why do you make me so much smaller than my brother? You insult me and my blood! Am I a negligible person, so small as a mouse, compared to my brother?' said the second brother.

'Sancto Cielo! You insult me, too, by God, by insulting my brother in such a way. Do you hope to curry favour with me by appearing to make me so much bigger than him?' said the first.

It was all Lear could do to escape without a beating or worse from his infuriated hosts.

For Albanians the image defines the reality. A man in a smart Western car is a smart Western man; a big political parade in the streets means that the party in question is strong and popular. The quite other realities which might underlie these often very misleading images are ignored in favour of the visual impression that has been made.

As a result, making a show, making the correct impression, sustaining a series of illusions which disguise the reality of events, is of paramount importance in ordinary Albanian life and in national politics. No one looks below the surface: the image is the real. Hence the immense power for good and evil of the photograph and the filmed image.

Berisha's supporters had packed the streets celebrating after the election victory of May 1996. These filmed images had been relayed all over Albania by the Berisha-controlled TV to show the power and popularity of the Democrats and their alleged victory at the polls. The complaints by international observers about vote-rigging – with no accompanying images – were completely drowned by the triumphalist Berisha media circus. Subsequently, the Socialists had been attempting to make a mass demonstration, first in Skanderbeg Square, then in a Tirana sports stadium. The idea was to provide the Albanian people with images of a rival group, a protesting group and, inevitably, a group being beaten by Berisha's police and SHIK. Only thus would the Albanian people have visible evidence that there was not universal satisfaction with the Democrats.

So, of course, the Berisha forces had to prevent not only the Socialists forming into a demonstration, but also prevent any unauthorised persons not controlled by them from recording any images which might possibly be used against them. A Spanish photographer had been attacked and beaten by the Berisha police for taking photos outside the Socialist headquarters. The BBC in turn had filmed the beating, and this film sequence had been got out of the country and eventually shown on satellite TV back inside Albania – loss of face for the Democrats. It was foreign TV which had destroyed the Albanians' belief in Enver Hoxha's propaganda that Albania was the earthly paradise. It was foreign satellite TV which now showed the reality of Berisha's police brutality. Control of the image, and the use of violence to sustain the pictorial illusion of order, was at the heart of the Albanian political reality, now as then. To lose power was to lose control of the image-making. The Communists eventually fell when they could not stop Albanians massing angrily to demonstrate against them, and TV images of this defiance were shown across the world.

Being in control meant retaining your honour. To be shown to be weak, to be opposed violently in public and insulted was to be shamed, to have your face blackened. Anyone so shamed lost respect and therefore credibility in Albanian eyes. A leader had to be strong enough to shame his enemies and to prevent them shaming him.

The political graffiti in Tirana on the walls was so often shaming in its thrust, usually using sexual or scatological insults: 'PC – Mut' ('Socialist Party – Shit'), 'Fatos Nano – Pederaste'. Paradoxically, although riven with blood feuds and revenge killings, with family quarrels going back decades or even hundreds of years, public life in Albania normally proceeded on an extremely polite level, with much smiling, caressing words, charm and honeyed sentiments. To say nice things was to be nice; to be optimistic was to bring good things down from heaven. The whole grotesque tyranny of the Enver Hoxha years was projected publicly as a floral pageant where the united people came together to worship the Great Leader in a Socialist paradise of peace and plenty. There were many, many Albanians, probably the overwhelming majority of the population, who had believed all this, the continuously constructed image of the Communists' rule, against the evidence of their stomachs and their eyes.

Albanians were not pragmatic and did not analyse. What you were formally presented with was what was real, so controlling what was officially seen was of paramount importance. Similarly, the foreign friend, in order to remain a friend, had to remain uncritical and notice only that which gave honour to his Albanian friends, and which avoided shaming them, concentrating instead on that which shamed his enemies.

My remarking on dirt and squalor in Korça had been an insult to the Western aspirations of Gabriel, and thus I had shamed him, and so damaged our friendship. For Western journalists or photographers to report or record demonstrations opposed to the Democrats after the election was to shame the 'friends of the West', Dr Sali Berisha told his supporters. To do so was to 'betray' these Albanian friends, and so blacken their faces in the eyes of their enemies; after such betrayal and shame, how could beatings not follow?

*

The Black Maria filled up slowly, while I tried not to think of the beating I could expect back at headquarters. Like the Ottoman gendarmes from whom they had inherited their traditions, the Albanian police had a reputation for beating people first, and asking questions later.

I had been given the front seat in the Black Maria, as a mark of respect to the foreigner; and I had exchanged cigarettes with the guards, who smiled at me happily. The handcuffs had been taken off once I was in the van: they were needed outside for more arrests. Socialists were still managing to get inside the guarded perimeter around Skanderbeg Square, possibly through underground passageways which led to the Socialist HQ, and the police kept wading in to stop them forming to demonstrate.

It grew hotter and hotter in the van. In the end, almost full by now, we rumbled away to HQ. I was shown into a room with a middle-aged man in plain clothes who sat behind a quite unintimidating, small plastic veneer table, similar to – perhaps it actually was – a child's school desk. There was a sedate calendar on the wall advertising Coca-Cola, but no other decoration. The floor and walls alike were free of bloodstains, I was pleased to note. The man at the child's desk fingered my passport as if it were a pack of cards, flicking and riffling it as if about to deal me a poor hand at poker.

'British?' he inquired.

It seemed rather futile to deny this so I nodded and said hopefully: 'Arsenal – Totten'am 'Otspurs – West 'Am United.' Albanians are big soccer fans. The man frowned, burped and examined my passport photograph critically.

'Do you know of the Ealing School of Computer Science?' he insinuated cunningly.

'Not personally – but I know Ealing terribly well.'

'I am sending my son Ali Achmet there. I want to know that this is a tip-top academy. "Tip-top" is right, no?'

The Albanian mania for learning English clearly gripped even the secret police. The street sellers flogging soggy bananas by ones and twos often did a sideline in dog-eared English textbooks. America was the new nirvana, and the mantras all in the language of McDonald's.

'I think perhaps I could get you a discount', I hazarded. This was brushed aside: 'We have scholarships from the British secret police. We shall be learning to use Windows 95!' he exclaimed proudly. 'I myself have an IBM-compatible Pentium computer and also one for my son Ali. These we shall learn to use in Ealing.'

'I only photographed Skanderbeg's statue, you know', I threw in, while we were still at this chummy computer-buff level.

'Now is a bad time for people with cameras', said the interrogator dispassionately, closing my passport with finality. He spoke oracularly, as if of left-handed people, or dwarves. 'We have also just arrested a BBC cameraman who was trying to film the children's carousel in Skanderbeg Square', he added, professional pride inflecting his voice.

I was released, eventually, with no charge being made against me and with my camera and films all intact. The policeman who saw me on to the bus back to Alexei's gave me two Dunhill King-size to tide me over on the journey, as I'd smoked all my own cigarettes in detention.

'But what I was doing was not illegal', I complained to Natasha, when I was explaining the situation to her later at the Christ Restaurant and Pizza Parlour.

'It wasn't illegal – but it wasn't legal either', she replied evenly. This was a very Albanian response.

*

I trudged round Tirana in the baking heat and glaring sun of late June. The city which swam before my eyes was a blend of shabby-colonial, crumbling ex-Communist Third World slum and booty-capitalist modern. The combined effect was surreal. I kept noticing strange conjunctions which I noted down in my journal every day

Statue of Second World War partisan hero in Tepelena – the only town where the
Communist stars had not been defaced

The expedition horses and mules by Lake Gashit

Ali Pasha's castle, Gjirokastra,
with 'American spy plane'
from the Communist era

Mountain stream *en route* to
Lake Gashit

The Accursed Mountains
looking into Serbian Kosovo
from Valbona

Inside a Gheg highland *kula*,
looking to the mountains

Classical ruins at Butrint, with modern Albanian actor in fancy dress and make-up

Wealthy Moslem landowner's
fortified house, built in 1882,
Gjirokastra

Bajram Curri, from the
missionaries' *palatti*

Skanderbeg Square, central Tirana

Abandoned political prison,
Gjirokastra

Young boy, Tirana, with the
Flintstones Restaurant in old
Italian colonial building behind

Aryan, my demented driver,
with his sawn-off shot-gun
and jeep

Gheg highland hay mowers taking a coffee break, Radomirë

Gheg gentleman near Kosovo border

Nineteenth-century fortified house, Gjirokastra

Italian colonial era administrative building, central Tirana

The author (*left*) with Major-Doctor Muharrem Bajraktar and gun, resting on their wooden saddles at Sylvicës in front of the hut they slept in

Bajram Curri, *palatti* and mountains

Gheg children at harvest time, with their father's rifle

Lorelei, aged 19 – translator, armed guard and Michael Jackson fan

Traffic jam in central Bajram Curri during rush hour

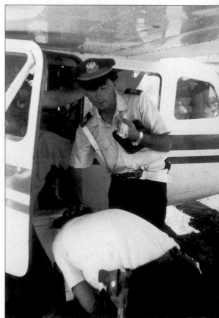

Policemen with guns and money by the missionary plane, Bajram Curri

Shepherd children with donkey, by the Serbian Kosovo border, *en route* to Lake Gashit

The author with his noble steed, killer saddle and rope stirrups at Sylvicës, *en route* to Lake Gashit

Communist-era apartment in central Tirana, with Democrat-era security cage additions and graffiti

under the heading 'Tirana Surrealismo' lest I forget them. Later I made a list of the most memorable:

1. A large, shaggy brown bear chained to a pillar outside the front door of an Italian gynaecological hospital.

2. A legless man perched on a cushion, who handles and closely examines with great concentration many, many different pairs of shoes which a woman is selling from the pavement.

3. A Scops owl perched on a white TV satellite dish which has been screwed to the outside of a Stalinist-era concrete tower block apartment, with a backdrop of wild Balkan mountains.

4. A donkey-cart built of wood with old tractor wheels and rubber tyres moves slowly down Mysylm Street, loaded with a pre-war Bechstein upright piano, the Gheg driver perched on top wearing a white fez.

5. A black American Air Force colonel in uniform and peaked cap sits at a table on the pavement outside the Christ Restaurant with his tiny Vietnamese wife, both of them sharing a 'Four Seasons' pizza. (I overheard the order, incidentally, hence the gastronomic precision.)

6. A yellow Fiat bus packed with commuters, 'Scuolabus Comune de Firenze' painted on the side, with an advertisement for Camel cigarettes on the front, whose destination above the driver now reads 'Mashallah'.

7. A gypsy hunchback cripple lies on the pavement outside the mosque of Etem Bey, begging; barefoot and bare-backed, his only clothing is a Royal Stewart kilt.

8. Gleaming white Land Rovers belonging to the BALFORCE Nato border patrol parked in the villa gardens of King Zog's prime minister, this subsequently the Communist Party of Albania's social club – now guarded by an Albanian with a machine-gun sitting in a white plastic chair wearing blue jeans and a Snoopy baseball cap.

9. On a pavement bookstall, next to each other in line: Petrarch's *Laura* in Italian, Nabokov's *Lolita* in Albanian, *A Hundred Most*

Usual Mistakes in English, and a Baha'i book of faith – all forbidden books under the Communists.

10. At the station, a Chinese locomotive pulls Italian coaches – but the railway line never leaves Albania.

11. The wrought-iron gates from King Zog's Palace with a 'Z' motif in the centre lie dismantled against a wall at AlbaFilm Studios, grass growing through them. But they are fakes, built for a movie: Count Ciano allegedly stole the originals and had them shipped to Italy as booty.

12. A bearded Albanian Orthodox cleric in black robes and tall hat sits on a park bench eating an Italian ice cream, engrossed in reading an English-language brochure produced by the US Embassy entitled *Notes On Applying For A US Greencard*.

13. Ali Pasha's Disco-Boogie Klub, advertised by a winking neon sign at night, the 'l' of 'Ali' having fused and now invisible.

14. A wandering gypsy youth with long hair and bare feet leads his blind elderly mother through the streets, she gripping his arm. Very beautifully, he is playing a French *chanson* tune from the 1930s on an accordion slung from his shoulders. Both of them seem oblivious to the world; neither is begging.

15. A large sign advertising a soft drink called Alba-Cola on the road in from the airport, which reads in English 'Drink Alba-Cola – You're Always Welcome to Albania.'

16. An Albanian restaurant salad: Greek olives, Italian lettuce, French olive oil, German tomatoes, Spanish onions, Danish feta cheese, and all served in a Chinese bowl with cutlery from Japan.

17. A thin, large dog trots slowly through the market bearing in its mouth a substantial piece of meat it has stolen, on which one can easily read the stamped words in English: 'Gift of USA – Not For Sale'.

18. At 6 p.m. sharp all the blind beggars near Skanderbeg Square make their way to the pavement from where the pirate music tape sellers operate. The chimes of Big Ben ring out from

London, as the beggars stare sightlessly at the sky, the radio-cassette player having been tuned to the BBC World Service in Albanian for the news.

Some of these apparently bizarre situations were easily explicable for those in the know. I told Natasha about the bear chained to the gynaecological hospital. 'A gypsy woman was having a baby inside, so she chained the bear up', she told me, as if it was the most obvious thing in the world. As in Turkey, the gypsies often used bears in their begging routines.

It was hard to put a finger on Tirana, but it seemed to me like that apparent contradiction in terms, a Moslem country in Central America, a sort of Balkan Guatemala.

Misha Glenny wrote in 1990 that 'Albania was a collage of fantasies', and in 1993 T. Barber in *The Independent* wrote that 'it was the sort of place that made surrealists weep for joy'. In 1993 M. Milivojevic considered the place to be 'Europe's Bangladesh'. All of these judgements seemed to me completely accurate still in 1996.

I found I could walk around the city with ease and in safety during daylight. There were a few foreigners on the streets, and even Albanian men in glasses carrying attaché cases. I didn't stand out, though the police could still tell I was a Westerner and so let me through the cordon round Skanderbeg Square which was still in place to stop the Socialists massing.

*

I met Carruthers in the Europark Hotel, better known as the Rogner, after the Austrian company that had built it.

A new, clean, efficient post-Communist concrete palace, this was surrounded by neat, flowering gardens, with a swimming pool to the rear, and an arcade of offices, boutiques and coffee shops on the ground floor. Air-conditioned, isolated by order and money from the poverty-stricken Albanian chaos outside, it was an oasis of Teutonic calm and efficiency. Western newspapers could be read, faxes sent and received; here all the phones worked and the lavatories were spotless.

All the building materials for the hotel and even all the workers needed to put the place up had been brought in from abroad:

Albanian workers would have stolen the bricks, cement and tiles for their own houses. All the capital was foreign, too, provided by an international loan of several million dollars to 'develop Albania's tourist infrastructure'. As there was no tourism in Albania, the Rogner formed part of the post-Communist Block, the enclave of comfort for the Western *nomenklatura* and the new Albanian élite of Democrat politicos and free-enterprise mafiosi who could afford its Western prices. There were two uniformed, intimidating Albanian security guards by the front entrance to inspect visitors closely, and discourage or even prevent the wrong sort of people – poor or merely ordinary Albanians – from coming inside. Even expensively dressed Albanians quailed slightly on approaching, I noticed, as if they might be refused entry and thrown back on to the pavement again by the bruisers. Like so much 'foreign aid', the Rogner merely reinforced the existing status quo, providing a convenience for Western businessmen and diplomatists. There was always electric light and clean water here: the Rogner had its own diesel generators and water well and purifier. It was like a self-supporting spaceship on a hostile planet, virtually independent of the outside atmosphere.

Carruthers was on time. We met in the cool, quiet foyer and adjourned to the even quieter dining-room, a vastness of plate glass and pastel drapes conceived for corporate jamborees which would never take place. A group of eight young Albanian mafiosi in sharp Italian jackets, each with an automatic in a shoulder holster bulging underneath, sat conspiratorially at a table in the corner, evidently at the cigarettes and coffee stage of some lucrative scam. Otherwise the restaurant was empty.

'The garlic soup is very good', said Carruthers, adjusting his tie, 'and then I usually just have a club sandwich.' I said this was fine by me, too. After all, Carruthers, or rather the FO, was paying.

Brimming with *Gemütlichkeit*, the uniformed waiter, Albanian but evidently Austrian-trained, hovered with pen and pad sympathetically at the ready. Carruthers ordered in fluent Albanian. The waiter looked pained.

'I'm sorry, sir', he said, 'Could you repeat that in English, please? I didn't understand.' Suddenly I discovered my shoelace needed tying up.

The garlic soup was off, it seemed, so we decided on asparagus instead, with mineral water and *cappuccini* to drink: a sober working luncheon.

Both Carruthers' parents had been diplomatists. 'I was genetically bred for this job, you might say', he told me. He was in his late twenties, I suppose, and had a degree in political science from a Welsh university. Before coming to Tirana he had studied Albanian for several months. He wanted to know about the south, and about what I had discovered. He was very interested in the black-market cost of visas and passports, and particularly interested in the fact that, allegedly, American visas could be bought. I began to see that what I was telling him was going to form part of a memo to his superiors, a reversal of the usual state of affairs where diplomatists brief writers.

I asked him about the many allegations of ballot-rigging in the recent election.

'I was an official observer near Kruja, with a Bulgarian lady. She was convinced all Albanians had horns and tails, so she refused even to contemplate staying the night outside Tirana. As a result we had to leave before the count was finalised.'

'Didn't that rather defeat the object of having international observers?' I suggested.

'Well, when the Socialists pulled out officially at 6 p.m. with their observers, it was all decided anyway as the Democrats then simply stuffed the ballot boxes with their own slips. They made no secret of it, either – I sat there watching them do it. So it was better really to head back to town and be able to say one had left early.'

Did the EU and American governments realise the election had been rigged?

'Well, we've been telling them so until we are blue in the face, but when a government has decided something at policy level – and our own government has decided to back Berisha – there's little we can do to change their minds. Now if you were French, for instance, I wouldn't even be talking to you. It's policy from London. We've had strict instructions not to co-operate with the French at any level.'

This was either because of the British beef scandal or the French fishing policy, or perhaps both. In spite of all the rhetoric of a European 'union', very little had changed in international affairs in the last hundred years. I might have been a late Victorian traveller talking to a British envoy in the Near East at the time of Anglo-French rivalry over Fashoda.

I told Carruthers I was going into the wilds of the north, and that I would be relying on the missionaries.

'Rather you than me. They are a pretty wacky bunch – the mishes, I mean. You'll meet some genuine screwballs. Do give me a ring if you get back – I mean when you get back – and tell me what the bandits of the north are up to. Oh, and if you hear of any Allied planes with bodies of our chaps buried nearby, do make a note for our War Graves Commission.'

So tight had Enver Hoxha locked Albania since the Second World War that big bombers which had crashed into the mountains in 1943–4 on their way to or back from Germany were still being discovered in 1996, and their crews brought down to be buried in the British War Cemetery in Tirana. This was an especially poignant matter for me as my Aunt Barbara, whom I never met, had been in the Royal Air Force in the war. She had disappeared on just such a flight over the Alps in 1944. Neither the plane nor her body had ever been found.

Carruthers paid for our lunch, which had been extremely poor: the bill came to $30, the price I had paid for the delicious fish dinner at Lake Ochrid, a poor swing balancing an excellent roundabout.

On the way out we met two young international bureaucrats on their way in. Carruthers stopped for five minutes or so to discuss with great passion the next meeting of the Tirana Hash Hound Harriers, while I waited to one side, feeling spiritually as well as conversationally excluded.

'We've just managed to get the Albanians to take three Dennis fire-engines', Carruthers said to me proudly outside on the pavement, as we were about to part. He was busy fiddling with his walkie-talkie to tell the office he was coming back. He had to keep checking in every hour so they knew he hadn't been kidnapped. He carried a heavy black leather briefcase with him all the time, which he never opened. I had noticed at luncheon that he had placed it within easy reach by his side. I wondered idly if it had a 9 mm automatic inside, or rather a Hoeckler and Koch sub-machine gun. The abduction of diplomatists in Tirana was by no means uncommon.

'Amazing', I replied, apropos the fire-engines. 'You mean they actually agreed to buy them from us?'

Carruthers gave me a very old-fashioned look.

'Old boy, one doesn't sell Albanians these things. One tries to get them to accept them as gifts.'

It was scarcely surprising that Albanians, and by extension most countries in Africa and Latin America, had developed into corrupt beggar states in the last fifty years. There was a whole foreign aid industry which ran on reverse economics. You bribed people to take aid gifts which somehow helped the donor country: food from unusable mountains already paid for, dud industrial gear unsaleable in the real market, out-of-date or dangerous medicines and drugs, gigantic public works buildings which would rot away unused. You filled unfillable courses and packed sparsely attended universities in your own country with students from these republics without even bananas, giving them 'scholarships' which always taught them a dependency on the West and on Western technology and solutions. And all of this taught incapacity, this promotion of a subsidised dependency culture was puffed as so wonderfully altruistic and progressive. Yet in these countries the corrupt élites continued to starve and brutalise their own people without compunction, between shopping trips to London or New York. In the old colonial days there had at least been some recourse to the metropolis, the centres of ultimate power. Now these places had their 'independence', criticism was stifled in the name of national pride and political correctness; the colossal theft, corruption and oppression went on unchecked and unreformed. The robber-élites in these countries were far more ruthless and rapacious than their colonial predecessors had ever dared be: their only fear was being toppled by rival local gangsters who wanted to get their snouts in the trough. The West no longer got involved in the day-to-day running of these barracoons of disorder. They had tried to regulate them for centuries and failed. It was too expensive and too unpopular. Now small, starving islands in the Indian Ocean begged France to take them back once again as colonies. France, of course, refused. While professors and savants of Third World origin safely established in America or Europe continued to denounce white racism, imperialism and colonialism, their less fortunate compatriots left behind in the abandoned colonies, without either education or capital, tried in desperation to smuggle themselves out of their fate and into the West, often by any means possible: stowing away on ships, hiding in aircraft landing gear, skulking in refrigerated meat trucks.

I remembered a charity concert I had attended in Oxfordshire at the time of the famines in Ethiopia in the 1980s. The local gentry were raising money in a self-congratulatory fashion to send bags of wheat to the starving.

However, in the London *Times* it had just been reported that the Ethiopian harbour master at the only port open on the coast had been turning away Western ships bringing grain for the last three months. There was still a mountain of unshifted grain in sacks lying exposed on his docks, he complained. It had started to sprout and was now useless. The wheat could not be stored as there was nowhere to put it, and could not be transported inland to the famine areas because of a local dispute *en route* which involved the clan which controlled the truck-driving concession. These drivers were being castrated if they attempted to cross the battle lines: naturally, they declined to do so. Thus, the wheat lay where it had been unloaded and rotted.

I told the organiser of the charity bash in Oxfordshire all this, and he gave me in return one of those holier-than-thou smiles of the professional do-gooder.

'Up here we believe in helping people, not in being negative like London journalists.'

'Would it not be more useful to provide either storage depots for the wheat at the port, or trucks, petrol and armed guards to ship the wheat through to the areas suffering starvation?' I suggested.

'We are farmers', he said. 'This is a farming community. Starving people need wheat for bread – it's as simple as that.'

He might as well have said: 'My tribe here need to keep their CAP subsidies to enable them to drive their Range Rovers and buy new Agas and send their children on skiing holidays at Christmas.'

They were giving wheat from Oxfordshire because giving wheat helped them: that it never reached the starving in Ethiopia was not their business. Nor that if it did, then it so depressed the price of locally produced grain that the Ethiopian farmers could not sell their own with any margin of profit, and so did not bother to plant next season, and thus the cycle of dependency was made worse.

Yet to point out this simple equation was to be that worst of people, the cynical London journalist. Better – in Oxfordshire as in

Albania – better, far better to think nice thoughts, do well-intentioned, useless things, say honeyed words, and so bring down great gifts from heaven, *inshallah*.

After her long and emotionally gruelling trip through AIDS-stricken Central Africa by bike in 1991, Dervla Murphy came to the inescapable conclusion that foreign aid was a disaster for Africa and should be stopped for the ultimate benefit of the continent itself.

With much less experience or evidence I had concluded exactly the same about Albania. 'Communism' had been rejected for 'capitalism', but in fact little had changed: the people were still locked into a psychology of dependency on foreign patrons, and a feudal subordination to a domestic élite which lined its own pockets at the people's expense: what fuelled all this was foreign aid.

The only thing which could ever save Albania would be to break this cycle permanently; and for a complete revolution in consciousness to take place in people's minds, where hard work, independence, honesty and fair dealing replaced the clan-based honour and revenge of tribal law. It was just such a revolution of consciousness that Enver Hoxha had tried to impose by force but in this, like everything else, he had ultimately failed. In the end, when Communism was collapsing, senior Communist Party officials openly spoke of the inadequacy of the human material they'd had to work with. The Albanians had failed them. As Brecht put it so accurately: the people had failed, so the government would have to elect a new one.

But could these remote mountain peoples ever change or be changed? The Kurds, the Afghans, the Albanians, lived now much as they had two thousand years ago, plus guns, coffee, tobacco and the internal combustion engine to aid their tribal squabbles. Could you have a consort of foxes, a democracy of wolves?

12

The New *Nomenklatura*

Natasha and the General

'IF YOU DO go to see Colonel Jean-Luc, make sure it's not after dark. He's surrounded his villa with mines and booby traps. He has a perfect mania for what the French call *pièges à feu*, or fire traps, with petards, fougasses, loaded shot-guns behind doors and so forth. It's all due to the Froggy Dien Bien Phu complex, I think. All they are ever taught about at St-Cyr, it seems – being ambushed in the night by small Communist chappies wearing big hats and black jim-jams.'

General Johnny leaned back in his large leather armchair and sipped his *cappuccino* appreciatively. He was wearing his smart civvy suit trousers with a striped shirt and plain tie.

His office at BALFORCE HQ was in the Block, in the villa which had originally been King Zog's prime minister's, then the social club of Hoxha's Politburo. The original furniture from the 1930s was still in place, including a fine Persian carpet, a carved wooden desk of Mussolini-esque proportions, a French eighteenth-century-style cabinet displaying ornate glassware, and a large triumphalist gilt mirror over the marble fireplace, decorated with Imperial Italian eagles and *fasces*.

The only hint of the 1990s in this Fascist-era museum was a delicate coral-pink Japanese fax machine on the General's paperless desk.

The General himself was in high spirits. His tour of duty as O/C BALFORCE in Albania was coming to an end, and he was shortly due to go to Macedonia, where the ex-Communists had just been voted back into power, and bread was once again being rationed.

'Skopje is like Paris after Tirana, I can tell you', he commented.

General Johnny had been a sharp-end soldier for much of his

career – in the Falklands as a Major, and later in the Gulf War as a Colonel on General de la Billière's staff. He had subsequently developed into a sort of international military civil servant, heading up peace-keeping forces in various war-torn parts of the world. As a result he had become very good at smiling and pressing flesh.

The task of BALFORCE in Albania was to prevent the Serb, Montenegrin and Macedonian army patrols from coming across the border. The Albanian army itself, unwilling conscripts led by demoralised officers, had more or less collapsed, apart from the Special Forces, which were deployed in Tirana to prevent the Socialists from attempting a *putsch*.

The General's team motored around the frontiers in smart white Land Rovers with EU flags waving on high. Were they allowed to shoot, I asked.

'Well, not really, no. But we are armed. So we might, if we were attacked. And then, of course, if some of us were killed by the Serbs, then NATO might start bombing them again. We're seen as being considerably less wet than the UN, whom I'm afraid were rather pissed upon from a great height by everyone.'

I hadn't realised the extent to which NATO had become the military arm of the EU since the collapse of the Soviet Union. In effect it was a return to the days before the First World War when 'the Powers' intervened collectively whenever and wherever they wanted to. I imagined my late father's goggle-eyed disbelief if I'd been able to tell him before he died nine years earlier that in 1996 I would be sitting in a British General's office in post-Communist Tirana.

General Johnny was very matey indeed, and alarmingly frank about conditions in Albania.

'The corruption goes right up to the highest levels, including the President. Nothing can be done without bribes at every point. It's entirely oriental – no one tells you the truth by design. Everything you do or say is observed, recorded and interpreted. I scraped a car last week in my official Land Rover. A mob formed immediately, the policeman with me vanished into the crowd never to reappear, and several hundred dollars were demanded as compensation by obvious mobsters. The car I'd scratched was evidently owned by a mafia capo. I had no dollars on me. Gave the mobsters my card through a crack in the window and drove away, pushing the bodies aside as I went. Angry mob. Had I stopped, they'd have smashed the windows. What a mess, I'd have had to shoot my way out. Not what NATO pays me for at all, no. Next day a group of thugs came to the front door here demanding cash. Had to buy 'em off with $200 via the armed guard out front. Even in the Congo you don't get that.'

What did the General think of the recent election results?

'They were fixed, obviously, by the Democrats, no doubt. There was police intimidation, vote-rigging and the stuffing of ballots. I saw it and so did every other foreign observer.'

I said that in Korça I hadn't seen anything untoward. The General gave me an old-fashioned look.

'Dear chappie, they didn't need to rig Korça. It's 100% Democrat as it is.'

I was starting to get a bit alarmed at the General's *glasnost*.

'Ought you to be telling me all this, sir? I mean I am a journalist and writer . . .'

The General gave a great smile of satisfaction, put his hands behind his neck and stretched.

'Three more days and I'm finished, laddy. Greek Brigs who play tennis all day and run up phone bills of $3,000 a month ringing Mummy in Athens, Dutch Captains with smelly socks, paranoid French Colonels with mined villas, Scandinavian subbies with long hair and drink problems who come and cry on my shoulder at midnight, Italian Generals in Armani uniforms and designer stubble – these and other *Euro-problemi* will all be a thing of the past and the subject of humorous reminiscence only, DV. After Macedonia I retire – definitively.'

'So you're "demob happy" then, sir?' I suggested. The General looked at me queerly.

'How do you come to know these archaic pongo expressions? Are you one of Carruthers' young men from the Firm, by any chance, come to check me out?'

'Is Carruthers the local Passport Officer, then?' I asked, my eyebrows inadvertently raised.

'So it's assumed. So they say. This is the Balkans: anything could be true.'

In the Near and Middle East, traditionally, the head of station of SIS, the British secret service, is known at the Embassy as the Passport Officer.

I was even more certain than ever that General Johnny was ex-SAS, and was probably now working for MI6 in the Balkans. In between his own disclosures he had been pumping me for information very gently for over an hour.

From time to time Natasha would dainty in with more *cappuccino* from the Italian machine in her office. One thing I had to admit: you got a better cup of coffee in Albania than anywhere outside Italy.

'It can't really be true that Italian Generals wear Armani uniforms and designer stubble', I asserted.

'Natasha, tell him about Capodimonte', ordered the General jovially.

Natasha wrinkled up her nose with distaste. She'd had her hair done since the Embassy party. A lock of formerly blonde curls resting on her forehead had been dyed punkishly pink. Her fingernails were very long, I noticed, and newly varnished scarlet. She wore a thin summery Italian dress, quite short, to show off her legs, the material of which swished as she swayed. She smelt delicious. I was close enough to her arm to savour an odour of mingled scent and young female flesh. The General and I both examined her with frank enjoyment and admiration: she basked in the attention.

'Capodimonte is a pig, you can say, truthfully', she replied in a balanced tone of voice. 'He is short, bald and has a pot belly. He smokes little black cheroots like Clint Eastwood, though there the resemblance ends. He made a pass at me within half an hour of arriving.'

'Yes – but his uniform – and his shaving habits . . .?' insisted General Johnny.

'He has watched too many spaghetti westerns as a boy. He has stubble but you cannot really call it designer unless the designer is an Albanian. But his uniform is definitely Armani – I have seen the label.'

'What an admission, Natasha! And from next week he will be your new boss. You'll have to drive him all over Albania, down those lonely lanes, late at night', teased General Johnny.

'If he touches me I will stab him with my flick knife', said Natasha, granting a prim smile before leaving us to our coffee.

'Heard about the Greek Second Secretary at the Embassy here?' the General asked me blithely.

'I did hear some rumour about his diplomatic car being solen.'

'Well, he would try and drive up here from Greece without an armed guard, against all advice. He walked into the Embassy two days later in his underpants and socks. He'd had everything stolen – suit, tie, shoes, shirt, watch, diplomatic passport, car, the lot.'

'Still, not as bad as the Bulgarian Military Attaché', I suggested.

'What happened to him?'

'He was abducted by bandits from his diplomatic car in Tirana back in '91, taken away somewhere quiet, and then serially raped by the whole gang. Apparently he wasn't even particularly attractive.'

'Some mafia deal that went awry no doubt, like the bombing of the Vefa supermarket here before the election this spring. Berisha said it was the old Sigurimi, but I heard the owners hadn't been paying their protection money, and that was the warning', said the General.

'They say it was the Albanian refugees in Sicily and Calabria who started the mafia in the Middle Ages.'

'It wouldn't surprise me at all. Still, you'll get your fill of bandits up in the north.'

This was the only slip the General made in a very polished, even bravura, performance over several hours.

I hadn't told him I was going into the north. So who had?

'What's Bajram Curri like?' I asked.

'The Dodge City of Albania. We drove up there in a look-see convoy fronted by an armoured car. It was very quiet that day though, we only saw three dead bodies in the streets. Oh, and someone blew up a bar with a bundle of dynamite – clan revenge. Otherwise all very calm. It can get rough, though, they tell me. You're taking your body armour I suppose. No? Well, I would lend you mine, but I still need it for Skopje.'

*

Natasha had a sign in English over her desk made by computer printout. It read: 'When she was good she was very, very good, but when she was bad she was horrid.'

I said to her: 'We have another way of saying that in England: "When she was good she was very, very good – but when she was bad she was better"'.

She paused for only a fraction of a second before giving a lovely peal of laughter. A beautiful young Albanian girl, unmarried, with her own flat, and a sense of humour to boot.

We agreed to meet after work at 4.30 p.m. for a drink and a pizza. In the summer of 1996 in Tirana the last word in gastronomic sophistication was a pizza eaten *al fresco* at The Flintstones, the Christ Restaurant or the American Pizza Forum.

I walked slowly home through the dazzling heat on glowing pavements to collapse on my bed and sleep for several hours, drifting into a lurid, sweaty dream-world of mingled erotica and nightmare.

*

Later, refreshed and calm, I walked slowly down the broad central avenue from Skanderbeg Square towards the Parliament and the park where I was to meet Natasha. It was still hot and the soldiers on duty were stiff and dazed with fatigue.

Memory lies so often. I went back just now to my travel-stained journal to check what I'd written about that day, of that precise afternoon in June 1996, to see if I wasn't being wise after the event.

'Tirana has the air of a South American republic on the eve of a coup – armed, nervous soldiers guarding every public building', was what I'd recorded; and that is what it was like, hot and nervy, summer thunder threatening like distant gunfire from the mountains.

Natasha was waiting for me at the pizza restaurant with a chaperone, a pudgy girl of about her own age who spoke English with a marked US accent. This was Lisa, who was Natasha's best friend and confidante. We drank Coca-Colas through plastic straws and chatted, the two girls weighing me up.

Lisa was the daughter of an Italian father and an Albanian mother, and as a result had been able to get an Italian passport after Democracy came. This meant she could leave at any time and get work abroad, but she had no relatives or friends in Italy. Her late father had been the manager of a mine in colonial days and had simply been kept on by the Communist regime, which had refused ever to allow him back to Italy, much as in the early nineteenth century Ali Pasha had refused ever to let his own French and Italian experts leave.

Both of the girls were in their early twenties, but young in manner, like English girls of sixteen or seventeen, though with an overt and unembarrassed southern sexuality. Both were well educated and intelligent, if necessarily provincial.

Lisa was an enthusiast for all things American, whereas Natasha had decided to be an Anglophile, which made for no boyfriend competition. Lisa had had a serious American boyfriend already, a Peace Corps guy from Kentucky; she was obviously much keener on marrying an American than on going to Italy to work. They both spoke remarkably good colloquial English, and were openly scathing about Albanian men: 'primitive', 'brutish', 'violent', 'jealous' were their comments. Both of them would only consider older, foreign – Western – men.

What was 'older' for 24-year-old Tirana girls, I enquired. Natasha volunteered that her last boyfriend had been thirty-eight, and that anyone below thirty was impossible. Lisa seemed a bit more flexible. It would depend. 'Every forest has its pigs', she said, enigmatically. She was good on Albanian proverbs. 'You chew it every day with your meal', was another, apropos absorbing influences slowly and unconsciously. 'Ashes and bread – stay at home' was yet a third, on the dismal fate of those who did not emigrate.

After half an hour Lisa made an excuse and left. She was meeting someone, giggle giggle. The two girls exchanged happy-hunting smiles, and I was left with Natasha.

Within minutes she was pouring out her life, loves and *problemi* to me in what I recognised as the confessional Albanian monologue. Her parents were high Communist Party *nomenklatura*. Her father had been dean of a university, her mother director of a research institute, both in Tirana. Natasha had gone to an élite *nomenklatura* school with foreign equipment, books, the best available teachers and the very highest standards. Even here it wasn't entirely safe. She remembered a bright girl of fifteen in her class who disappeared one day, never to return. This was Mehmet Shehu's niece, and after Shehu was murdered by Hoxha the whole clan was banished to a remote mountain village in the north. Hoxha always exiled the whole family of enemies, to avoid leaving anyone behind to attempt revenge. It should be remembered that Hoxha himself died of natural causes in his own bed in Albania, the first Albanian national leader since Skanderbeg to do so.

'That was the end of her life', commented Natasha, 'a bright, confident clever girl, exiled for ever. Bad *biographi* – destined to marry a shepherd and die in childbirth in her thirties in some mountain hut.'

With the coming of Democrat rule Natasha's family fortunes had been reversed. Her parents were thrown out of their good jobs and were currently employed in junior positions, lying doggo at home much of the time. Her grandfather was dying of cancer, and could not get a place in a hospital because of their bad *biographi*. He was dying at home in the family flat by inches, in all a grim post-Communist *Cherry Orchard*.

Natasha was the only one with a good job, earning the fabulous, incredible salary of $500 a month in a land where a teacher got $75 and a policeman $95 a month. She earned more than a SHIK. This was because she was working for foreigners, where *biographi* didn't matter, and because she had so many languages: Greek, Macedonian, Italian, German, English, Albanian. She had worked for AlbTurism originally as a guide, and had been all over Albania, including the north, which was she said 'unbelievably poor and deprived, but the people noble and kind in an old-fashioned way'.

Natasha had her own flat in the same block as her parents – heaven knows how. This for a 24-year-old in Tirana was like a young Kensington girl having her own Lear jet. She was the most advanced and independent Albanian I ever met, female or male. She'd had a long relationship, over a year, with a university lecturer, the Albanian of thirty-eight. He could not handle her independence, the fact that she mixed with rich foreigners all the time, and that she earned far more than him.

'He used to beat me too much. I would go into work with black eyes', she commented.

In the end she'd had to ask General Johnny to intervene, but the boyfriend had ignored his representations and continued beating her just the same, and hanging round outside BALFORCE HQ waiting for her. So she'd 'had a word with some Sigurimi people, old family friends', who had in turn had a word with lover-boy. The beatings had stopped and the lecturer had left her alone. She never saw him now, though they knew people in common.

'What did the Sigurimi say to him?'

'That if he touched me again, or even tried to see me, then he would be disappeared', she replied coolly.

A shiver of apprehension ran through me. Natasha sipped her Coke decorously and smiled coquettishly. She had lovely eyes, brown and liquid. You could drown in them.

'Do all Albanian men beat their women?' I asked.

'All is difficult to say. It is normal you can say. Albanian men are violent and repressed. They cannot express their violence in public. They must smile, and smile, and eat shit from people they hate, day after day. So they let go in private and usually this is on the wife, yes. I will never go out with an Albanian man again.' She paused and then said: 'You have to learn to smile a lot in Albania.'

After some humming and hawing we ordered a Four Seasons pizza between us, and two beers. A young woman dressed in old clothes, a scarf over her head, approached across the grass of the park, and held out her hand, a beggar's whine on her lips. She thought we were both foreigners. Natasha replied to her very politely in Albanian.

'Why don't you get a job? You are young and strong, there is plenty of work.'

The woman smiled and straightened up. 'I know', she said disarmingly, 'but this begging is easier.' She had a plastic sack, which she was slowly filling with empty aluminium drink cans. For every ten of these the soft drink company in Tirana paid $1. There were empty drink cans chucked on the streets all over town, hundreds of them. It would not be difficult to earn ten to twenty dollars a day collecting them – to earn the monthly wage of a policeman in a week, say.

'Why don't they all collect cans, the poor?' I asked Natasha, after she had translated all this into English for me.

'Albanians are both proud and lazy. Manual work is from the Communist time and is for uncultured people. To wear a uniform, to have a gun, to frown and give that "I am looking at you! Be careful!" expression to people – that is what the Albanian wants. We have more police than any other country in the world, and they are useless. They run away if there is trouble.' This was the first intimation I had that the massed and apparently mighty forces the Berisha regime had concentrated in the capital would not stay and defend their masters when real trouble came.

Natasha had been out of Albania several times. First she had been to East Germany in the Communist era. Her father had been owed a favour by a visiting German academic, and had refused a present or money. 'Invite my daughter to Berlin to study', he said, and that's what had happened.

'I loved Germany. So ordered, so clean, so modern, so friendly, so open', she gushed. This was a new take on the East German regime, but coming from Albania it did make sense.

'At first I was shocked. They said I was staying with an academic, a middle-aged man, in his house. He was not married, there were no women. I protested: "I cannot stay in a house with a man alone. I cannot share a bathroom with a man." Because you see in Albania this man would rape a woman in this position, any man. They said, "He is a nice guy – you'll see – no problems." And it was true. He was wonderful. He never touched me, he allowed me my privacy, respected me, never interfered. We sat and drank hot wine in the evenings and listened to classical music and talked about philosophy and poetry. He was so wise and so kind and rather sad. He'd had no luck with women. He treated me like a daughter. I thought I had died and gone to heaven. Oh, how I loved the GDR! It was so, so free and open and liberal.'

Then, after Democracy had come, she had been to England. That wasn't such a success: 'I dreamt of England, I had such a romantic idea from the films and novels and poetry. But the reality! It was terrible. These fat, ugly people, this dirty town, London, this conversation about nothing. I fled and came back here after five days.'

She had stayed in Twickenham with a man of fifty. The arrangement was she would look after his children, 'but he wanted me to marry him, of course'. She didn't think much of Twickenham. She wanted to live in either Mayfair or Kensington; after all, she had lived in the Tirana equivalent all her life.

'I couldn't believe how boring the English were. I stayed at General Johnny's house in Wimbledon. Wimbledon! Have you ever been there! He is a serial husband, Johnny, and completely dominated by both his wives, the ex- as well as the current. They hated me, of course, I was the Scarlet Woman from Tirana. They talked about nothing all day long – double-glazing, the lawnmower, the mortgage, tennis, the lawnmower, on and on. I couldn't believe it. Double-glazing! A General's wife! No culture at all!'

'You met the wrong people. There are plenty of cultured people in London', I said, leaping in to defend the Old Country.

'Not in Wimbledon. And 99.9% of England is Wimbledon – I have seen it from the train!' she said vehemently.

I felt vaguely affronted that the GDR had won out over dear old Blighty, but I had to admit she had a point. The impression of England you gain from the BBC World Service, from the writings of Shelley, Blake and Byron, bears no relationship to the contemporary reality. In many ways even India is, today, rather more like traditional Britain than Britain itself; you are certainly far more likely to meet a courteous, civilised, old-fashioned English gentleman in Delhi than you are in London, a city now dominated by rapacious egoists with bad manners.

'Do you know what he does at the weekend and in the evenings at home, the General? He walks his dog! No Albanian man would ever walk a dog, it is so demeaning!' Natasha said with utter contempt. As in all Moslem countries, dogs were the lowest of the low, next to pigs. Packs of stray dogs roamed the streets of Tirana by night, howling and baying as they went. So bold and ferocious had these beasts become that they were reputed to have combined to attack and kill sheep from flocks grazing just outside the city.

Natasha's original idea had been to meet a suitable Englishman, marry him and stay in England. However, on close inspection the product hadn't lived up to her expectations.

'Most Englishmen are total wimps', she avowed, delicately nibbling on a slice of pizza. Albanian men were too macho and violent, the Brits too feeble and wet. What was a girl to do?

'English women are nothing to write home about either', I countered.

Natasha gave me grin: 'I know. I've met them! Life's a bitch – and then you marry one!'

I laughed and drank some more beer. How had her English got this good so quickly, I asked myself. Was she this good in German and Macedonian, too?

'Why not give up on the Brits and go back to Germany?' I suggested.

But no, she had decided on England. It was the most civilised country in Europe and only Europe would do. 'The Americans are very full of themselves with very little reason. They are only a jumped-up colony, full of second-hand Italians and Greeks, after all. The Brits have their feet on the ground. They are more realistic. And there is culture, too. Germany is too materialistic.'

So she was going to try again in London, this time in the centre, and no more 50-year-olds with kids. 'I want a flat right in Mayfair and a good job, a proper serious job.'

'Natasha, English people spend all their lives trying to get these things and don't succeed. You can't just expect to go in and get them like that, as an illegal immigrant from a Third World ex-Communist state.'

Her face set hard and she gave me that 'the-Albanian-knows-best' look. A sheep on a long tether was cropping the grass in the park and had by now manoeuvred itself right next to us. It raised its head, bleating from time to time, particularly when a passing Mercedes from the avenue sounded its horn.

'Tomorrow's shish kebab?' I suggested, trying to lighten the mood.

'Albanian lawnmower', she replied with a smile.

I ordered more beer.

Natasha had also been to Turkey, the first Albanian I'd met who had. Her mother had been there on holiday and Natasha went to visit her in Istanbul and Ankara.

'What did you think of it?'

She gave a broad, fulsome smile. 'I loved it! They are just like us, the Turks! I felt so much at home.'

This was the first time I had heard an Albanian admit to any similarity between themselves and the Turks. Normally, the very mention of them brought forth scowls and denials of any influence or similarity. But Natasha was right. Albania was as close to Turkey as, well, closer than Italy and Provence, closer than England and Scotland even. Albania was like a province of Turkey, cut off for fifty years, now desperately looking westward, away from its roots.

Natasha claimed she 'loved reading at school'. I pressed her on what her tastes were. French poetry, she said, Baudelaire, Rimbaud, Verlaine. And now? She wrinkled up her nose. She didn't read so much. She had tried a novel by Stephen Fry in English, but hadn't liked it, and had given up: Communism to Democracy, the triumphant ascent from Baudelaire to Stephen Fry.

'Perhaps because he is gay?' I asked.

She looked frankly disgusted. 'I did not know this. I hate these people. Thankfully there are very few in Albania.'

'And lesbians?' I enquired. 'Even fewer', she replied.

She told me she had been separated from her boyfriend for eight months now, and really missed having a lover. She was frank enough to admit she missed the sex.

All over Eastern Europe I had met girls and women like Natasha: too Westernised for their own men, not Western enough to accept the limitations of the modern, streamlined, economy-model Euro-male, necessarily feeble as this article had to be to pass muster on home territory.

Over the last thirty years the gradual feminisation of society in Britain, and most of the formerly macho northern European democracies such as Holland and Germany, had blanded men down to an acceptably low-testosterone product, suitable only for occasional use by the quasi-liberated woman, as and when required. These use-and-chuck, Kleenex-style Euro-wimps were of no use to Natasha and her ilk: they wanted real, old-fashioned Western males, authentic gas-guzzling pre-feminist models.

'Have you thought of going to Africa?' I hazarded. You still got red-blooded white men in Africa. It was like a game reserve, a refuge of the unreconstructed, pipe-smoking, shorts-wearing *bwana*, the last few white rhinos of an otherwise extinct species.

'Yes', she said immediately. 'I have thought of working there for Save The Children. With my languages this would be an easy job to get. But I have to have a Western passport.'

She looked me straight in the eyes.

*

Although the centre of town was still crowded and there were many heavily armed police about, Natasha asked me to walk her back to near her block of flats.

It was so nice to be on the streets with such a tall, beautiful young woman, so well dressed, feminine and clever, who smiled and laughed at my jokes, and made her own too, tit for tat, a woman unaggressive and confident in her own feminity and sexuality. This is how I remembered bright English girls in the '60s and early '70s, when I had been young, before miserabilism and feminism had become so fashionable. You never saw young women revelling in their own sexuality like this anywhere in the West now, not even in Paris or Aix-en-Provence. Now they all had hard, brittle features, with career scowls.

That was the appeal of Eastern Europe, and why I liked it so much, in spite of all the discomfort and danger. In Moscow and Warsaw, Prague and Tirana, you got a taste – more than a taste even – of a world that had finished decades ago in the West. I recalled that I had thought of buying a flat in Leningrad, Prague or Kraków years ago, had even enquired in Gjirokastra recently what an old house would cost. I had been offered many jobs in Eastern Europe and it was tempting: the low-cost, low-pressure life, full of regrets and sighs, poverty and dreams of escape never to be achieved. It would be like emigrating back to the England of 1968 – few cars, no stereo, a cold flat in a cold, snowy northern city, where the girls bravely made the most of what little they had and love trembled in the air with the blue cigarette smoke in night-clubs thick with the reek of alcohol, testosterone and poverty.

But I was middle-aged and sensible and had a hollow life in rich, shiny '90s Britain which I despised and clung too. There was no going back, surely.

We shook hands and parted, Natasha and I, a few hundred yards from her *palatti* so the neighbours wouldn't see us and start to gossip. We had both hoped we might be right for each other, and we nearly were. So nearly.

'Make sure you come and see me when you get back from the north', she said, meaning it. And she smiled, and turned, and tripped away, my past vanishing from our present into her own future.

13

Missionary Positions

Death in the North

'THE DUTCHMAN WAS murdered in broad daylight last week in the streets of a village near Bajram Curri. He was held up and robbed of his camera and wallet by a gang of thieves at knifepoint. He had made the mistake of following them to try to get his stuff back. They turned on him and stabbed him to death.'

Peter Dobson, who told me this in the flat, unexpressive accent of an Englishman from the Midlands, was a civil engineer and evangelical missionary, currently working on a road construction project to link remote villages in the northern mountains near Burrel.

I questioned him closely about the killing, though it was not something I particularly wanted to hear about – the risks involved in travelling deep into Ghegeria. Nothing like this was ever mentioned in the local or foreign newspapers; there, all was still sweetness, light and the dawning day of Democracy and capitalism.

That Albanians were once again murdering each other in blood feuds, revenge killings and robberies was not news. But foreigners were supposed to be sacrosanct. The code of the *besa*, the high honour with which the Albanian defended the guest, was popularly supposed to make foreigners protected persons.

I had been introduced to the Dobsons by Paul Quiller, a young American evangelical missionary who was staying at their villa, which was itself a sort of informal guest house for Western Baptist visitors in Tirana. The evangelical Christians had an administrative centre in Tirana called the Albania Encouragement Project. Lodged in a mundane suburban house, surrounded by a walled garden and unadvertised by any sign, it was discreetly guarded by an Albanian watchman who lounged in plain clothes outside the gate.

The Protestant missionaries were not popular with the authorities in Albania. The Jehovah's Witnesses had preached disobedience to the state, it was said, and encouraged their converts to refuse military service. To their dismay the evangelicals were lumped in with the Witnesses by the government, and denied the status of churches. Almost the first thing the missionaries explained to me, at some length, was that they were genuine Christians, subscribing to all the requisite articles of the faith, that they were not sects of New Age heretics.

Albania had been declared the world's first officially atheist state by Enver Hoxha in 1967. Priests, imams and babas had been imprisoned and executed. As a result, when the country finally opened up after 1991, it became an immediate magnet for all the world's proselytisers from the Baha'i to the Plymouth Brethren.

I needed the Christian missionaries badly. They were spread out right across the wild, mountainous north. They spoke the language, lived close to the people, travelled about and knew the terrain and the dangers. They had their own short-wave VHF radio link, 4-wheel-drive jeeps, even a small plane service which dropped down into roughly hacked airfields in remote valleys. No one else had this sort of network in the north. The ordinary Protestant missionary in the field knew more about the real conditions in the Albanian countryside than all the foreign diplomatists of Tirana put together.

These two worlds, missionaries and envoys, rarely came into contact, each having a certain contempt for the other. At first I'd had a difficult time of it with the missionaries. Secular writers and journalists, invariably sceptics and often left-wing, were not their favourite people. Apparently the BBC World Service in Albanian had recently done a hatchet job on Christian missionaries in Albania, which still rankled. They were not a bunch of ignorant fanatics, I was told. They were doing vital work no one else was even attempting.

'Write a reasoned letter of protest to the BBC, citing evidence that the report was biased, and send it to the Director-General, c/o Bush House, Strand, London, UK, and politely request that a balanced reply be given by one of your own Albanian speakers to redress the bias', I advised David Trimble, the current co-ordinator of the Albania Encouragement Project, who had told me this. 'The BBC is a government-funded body. It tries to avoid bias and takes these sorts of complaints very seriously. Write in and make your point. Don't fume in silence. Insist on your voice being heard in reply.'

Trimble began to relax, seeing I was not immediately hostile to the missionary standpoint. He was a pleasant, open Texan from Dallas, in his thirties, dressed in jeans and a short-sleeved shirt. He had taught at an evangelical college in the States before serving abroad in various administration posts. He had a private aeroplane pilot's licence and had been instrumental in setting up the Albanian branch of MAF, the world-wide airstrip organisation established by evangelical missionaries after the Second World War. This cut the jeep journeys of two and three days over impossible mountain tracks to the far north down to forty-five minutes by air. These flights were used to get people with chronic maladies out, as well as to get missionaries and their supplies in.

Neither the Communists nor the Democrats had ever done anything like this for the remote north. All the money they had ever got from foreign aid was spent on themselves and their cronies in the cities. The evidence of this was before my eyes: Tirana had everything, the villages had nothing. Anyone trying to understand the revolt of March 1997 should use that simple fact as a starting-point.

I wrote out the BBC World Service's address for David Trimble on a piece of paper, and insisted he take it, repeating that he should write in to them. He had continued to relax visibly as I was doing all this; he could see that I was taking him seriously.

We talked about Albania for fifteen minutes or so, and didn't disagree once. I explained what I was doing:

'I meet people, talk to them, write down what they say, observe, make my own comments, analysis and judgement, then pass on. It will be a serious book, I hope, and quite unpartisan. I have no axe to grind. If I see good, I will report it. When I see bad, that is what I will put down.'

I managed to convince him of my sincerity. As a result, David decided to swing the powerful forces of the missionaries' organisation behind me.

'OK, Robert, we'll help you all we can. I'll radio up our guys in the field and tell them you are coming. They'll help you all they can. You can use our plane service, though you'll have to pay the commercial rate. Our people will try to find you some place to sleep. It'll be rough, have no doubt.'

I thanked him and said I was used to sleeping rough. This offer of help was a great boon. Without it I simply would not have been able to travel in the north, short of a large armed guard, for which I did not have the resources.

The Protestant missionaries were all from different sects, but they co-operated, and they had some things in common. One was a profound respect for the Word. Anyone writing a book which aimed to reveal the truth was someone they were obliged to take seriously. The Bible, knowledge, revelation, light, dispelling ignorance, helping people, spreading the Word – these were what they were in Albania for. They were Christians: unless there was good reason not to, they felt obliged to aid people who came to them sincerely who asked for help, as I had done, even though I was not a believer.

And so my journey began to take on a completely new colour and tone. Until now I had been meeting and staying with secular people, unequivocal dwellers in St Augustine's City of Man. Now I was to meet people who had devoted themselves to the spiritual and the metaphysical, people who lived by a strict code and upon whose word I learnt I could depend.

The evangelicals in Albania took their Christianity very seriously; they would not have been there otherwise. It was moving and humbling to meet highly intelligent, well-educated young Midwesterners in their 'twenties like Paul Quiller, who had decided to live in one of the poorest and most lawless countries in the world, in conditions of discomfort and danger, to spread what they believed to be the truth. They could have had comfortable, privileged lives in the States, good jobs in corporations or even in local churches. I was just passing through Albania for a few months, a tourist with a notebook. They lived and worked here year in and year out, in the remotest places, among the most abandoned people; they had studied the language and dedicated themselves to these people, who lived in such terrible misery and darkness. I couldn't have stuck the missionaries' lives for six months. I had to admire them.

I'd had a Christian upbringing myself, though like many I lost my faith in my teens, becoming a skeptic and a secular person. I had devoted myself to books, rather than the Book, but I found it impressive and moving to find people like Paul, who was patiently learning Greek in his spare time, verb by verb, so he could read the New Testament in the original.

I learnt from Paul, whom I'd met at the Stephen Centre – a sort of campus cafeteria where the missionaries ate and socialised when in Tirana – that in the south and west of the USA there were many correspondence courses for people living in the remote countryside, to enable them to learn Ancient Greek or Hebrew: that you could take exams in Greek or Hebrew in the Texas panhandle or Arizona or New Mexico; that there were Protestant theological colleges with summer courses where the ancient tongues of the Middle East were still taught and studied.

I found this both extraordinary and touching. In England or Germany in the seventeenth or eighteenth century, even into the nineteenth, knowledge of Greek and Hebrew was an accomplishment possessed by many scholars and divines. But who now in Europe knew anything of these tongues or the rich literatures and histories they spoke of?

With the widespread loss of Christian faith in Europe had come the inevitable result: a loss of interest in classical and Christian knowledge itself. How could you understand Milton or Shakespeare without a grounding in the Bible and the Book of Common Prayer, not to mention classical mythology, Judaeo-Christian ethics, divinity and iconography? Now, outside the specialist departments of the old universities, almost no one under fifty knew anything of these things, never mind being able to read or write Latin, Greek or Hebrew.

Paul and his friends and colleagues were bright, eager and learned. They were skilled in debate and their business was talking and convincing people. They knew about the histories of all the Churches, the Reformation and the varieties of Christian faith, Roman Law, something even of Islam and more of the ancient Jews. And, of course, they knew the Scriptures themselves, old and new, and about the origins of Judaism, ancient Egypt, Mesopotamia, and even sects such as the Essenes. Many had been on pilgrimages on foot throughout Palestine and the Holy Land. Some of the more sophisticated had even studied Darwin and evolution, the better to counter scientific criticisms of the faith.

It was also a relief not to be talking about politics for a change; to be among people who weighed evidence, listened to argument and did not take recourse in vituperation, naked propaganda and out-right, blatant lies. Christianity depended upon faith, but its defence and explication rested on argument and logic, the twin pillars of all developed Western theology.

The missionaries were not hypocrites. They did not pretend that people in the Third World had some kind of moral superiority to decadent Westerners, as aid workers often protested. There was no pretence that Albania was anything other than a place sunk in ignorance, evil, corruption and sin.

These strongly judgemental words have all but been erased from the enlightened liberal's vocabulary. Cultural relativism, seeing the other person's point of view, bending over backwards not to impose one's own cultural values on other's equally valid experience have all become the contemporary cant, spouted by all.

But what could you say about a culture where outside the *fis* everyone stole and was proud of it; where girls were kidnapped at fifteen and sold into prostitution; where lying was normal and the government stole more than anyone else? Where people trafficked in guns, drugs and false identity papers, and went to richer countries deliberately to rob and pillage? Where wife-beating was normal, rape and buggery the fate meted out to anyone not protected by either guns or their family? Where sadistic torture by the secret police was routine and everything from a school certificate to a doctor's degree could be bought for cash? Where the blood feud and revenge killings paralysed whole swathes of the land, drenching them in the gore even of innocent children of seven and eight?

The missionaries said these were sinners, benighted heathens who were living in a land of darkness and ignorance, and that they had to be converted to true Christianity, the Protestant evangelical variety, before there could be any hope for them. For myself I didn't feel confident enough to believe this could or would work, but I could not fault the missionaries' moral judgement of the Albanians. How relativistic can you get about heroin-smuggling and child prostitution?

The evangelical missionaries still believed they were right and the heathens wrong – and were out there in the field proving their point. They also knew that just providing aid was no answer. Giving money and food to places like Albania would only encourage the dependency and corruption.

Peter Dobson's engineering project was up in the high mountains of Ghegeria. The conditions in the villages were primitive in the extreme, 'far more so than either India or Bangladesh'. He and his wife had spent the last ten years in Assam and northern Bangladesh, so they knew what they were talking about.

One village to which they were taking the road had no school-teacher, doctor or nurse. Here the peasants grew maize, potatoes, onions, green tomatoes (it was too high for them ever to ripen) and raised sheep, goats and cows. That was it. There was nothing else – no shop, café, school or clinic. There had been a telephone link installed by the Communists, but with the coming of Democracy someone had cut the cable down and sold it for scrap copper value. The village was split in two over the road link. The old man hated it, fearing they would lose their power; the young men all wanted it; the women, as ever, were mute. At present it took the best part of a day to get to this place on mule or donkey from the nearest dirt road. There was no electricity that worked and no one had money for oil lamps. At dusk everyone locked their doors and went to bed. The birth rate was very high, but so was the death rate. The doctor never came up there: they had no money to pay him.

The Dobsons had been involved in the case of a gypsy girl of four-teen from this village, who had never been outdoors because of the risk of her being kidnapped by men and sold into prostitution. Eventually, she had murdered her own father, stabbing him to death with a kitchen knife, in revenge for his having sexually abused her and a younger sister of eight. She had been sentenced to fifteen years in gaol, but this had been reduced by seven years after the missionaries in the area had arranged for a bribe of $500 to be paid to the judge, the money collected from well-wishers in UK. The girl had served seven years of her eight-year sentence so far. Her mother and sister lived barricaded inside their house. They had been attacked several times by gangs of village men, bent on raping them. Up there, apparently, a household without a man to protect it immediately attracted the raping classes.

Peter Dobson told me all this unemotionally. It was just another story of darkness. He saw himself as being in the business of light-bringing.

'The road and the Gospel go together. We have to connect the villages with the rest of the world, and with the Word', he said.

I might have been listening to a character from a short story by Rudyard Kipling, a progressively inclined jungle wallah temporarily down in Peshawar from duties up-country. But then rural highland Albania in 1996 differed not so very much from the north-west frontier of Hindustan of 1887.

*

It was in the Stephen Centre that I met Tybalt. Round-faced, serious, bearded, he looked like an intellectual theatre director in his black polo-neck shirt and jeans. But he was an Albanian evangelical, originally from the Greek minority in the south.

I had seen him reading a book in English entitled *Captured by Brigands*, by Gjerasim Qiriazi, and had fallen into conversation with him. He was in his late twenties and spoke good English.

'Qiriazi was a Protestant missionary from the British and Foreign Bible Society', he told me. 'He was an Albanian who was captured near Korça in 1884 by Albanian brigands and held to ransom for six months. He was treated very cruelly and died shortly after the ransom was paid by the British Bible Society. It's well worth reading. It is very contemporary, I'm afraid – it could have happened last week. The brigands themselves are soaked in self-pity as well as pride, a very Albanian mixture. They hate being bandits but cannot and will not become anything else. It is a study in self-hatred – also very Albanian.'

I asked Tybalt if he had heard of George Borrow, author of *The Bible in Spain*, that superb nineteenth-century picaresque travel book. He had not, but he noted down the title. Another reader. We fell into conversation and he told me his story.

With the coming of Democracy he had gone to Greece, not to work so much as to study. He was already a Christian, but he wanted to learn more. He stayed with the Jehovah's Witnesses and the Roman Catholics, but rejected both as being 'unscriptural'. His own Orthodox communion he found 'too hidebound and obsessed with nationalism and empty ritual'. He had worked for a while, and then travelled in Western Europe, in Italy, France, and England. He had already learnt ancient Greek to read the New Testament; now he learnt English to read the Authorised Version. He had visited Canterbury and Westminster Abbey.

It would have been easy for him to get a Greek passport and so escape Albania for ever. He could not do so, since it would involve him lying, which was a sin. He was an Albanian, and so had returned to Albania to spread the gospel. He was a Baptist and belonged to an Albanian Baptist Church. They had American preachers who visited them sometimes, 'good men, sincere and helpful'. They received no money from foreigners, nor would they take any.

'The only people who can rescue Albania are Albanians. We must return to honesty, truth, justice and a belief in the word of God', he told me quietly.

'How likely is this to ever happen?' I asked.

'We must make it happen. No aid, no investment, no reform can do anything until we have remade ourselves and admitted our sins and become new people.'

He invited me to meet his pastor. In a small room in a rundown tenement the group were preparing themselves for a prayer meeting. The congregation was mainly women with young children. The pastor was a lean, bearded man in his thirties. He was tuning his guitar, which he would play to accompany the hymns.

Two Albanian men with beards, in a land where men rarely now grew these. In the old, pre-Communist days, in the folk-tales it had always been the bare-faced man who had been the villain. Hoxha had turned all Albanian men into bare-faced men. In his day to have a beard was to be suspected of being religious , to a have moustache was to be a Royalist: both were outlawed.

The pastor greeted me politely, but with reserve. He, too, had been, as he put it 'on a pilgrimage to England'. For these Baptists England was the home of the great evangelical missionary endeavours of the nineteenth century which had spread the gospel in Africa and Asia. Like Tybalt, the pastor had been to St Paul's and Westminster Abbey. 'I had to pay three pounds', he remarked mildly, 'for entering the house of God.'

Did he prefer the New English Bible or the King James' Version, I asked.

'King James – though it is harder to understand for us. It is closer to the original.' Both men had had Greek Testaments and King James' Bibles in English. The New Testament had only been translated into Albanian in 1991, and then 'very badly, with many errors'.

The New and Old Testaments had been published together in Albanian in 1994, 'but still badly translated', they said. They still depended on the Greek and English versions.

Outside, corruption and gunfire in the streets, crooked politicians, theft, murder, rape and mayhem; in here, two young Christians ministering to a small congregation of the most downtrodden, the women and children, and depending on foreign bibles. No wonder evangelical Christianity had taken such a hold so quickly in post-Communist Albania. Conditions here were so like those in the late Roman Empire in which the original Christians had flourished – the City of Man outside visibly corrupt and unworthy.

As in much of Central and South America, the most intelligent and moral of the young Albanian élite were clearly turning to evangelical Christianity, for Orthodoxy, Catholicism, Islam and Marxism had each failed them successively. In a place of dishonesty and deceit, where none could be trusted, Christians banded together, because they told the truth and dealt honestly while the others lied and cheated. It was why Christianity had been so successful originally in the corrupt late pagan world.

They invited me to stay for their prayer meeting, but I made an excuse and left. I wished them well, but theirs was not a world I could enter, though I recognised it as a hopeful sign in an otherwise hopeless land.

*

Back at the apartment I heard on the news that the Minister of the Interior had banned all demonstrations. The Socialists were still trying to mass near their HQ and then move on Parliament and make a *putsch*.

'Berisha is the new dictator now', Alexei said to me as we watched Euronews on satellite, which they still called 'the BBC' out of habit. The Voice of America and CNN both reported that 'all was quiet in Albania' and that 'the elections had been generally free and fair'.

'American capitalists', commented Alicia. 'What would you expect them to say? They have Berisha in their pockets.'

PART 2

What are these mountains thinking about?

Into Ghegeria

'What are these lofty mountains thinking about
These enigmas of ridges stretching north and south?
I continue on my way
In the shadow of the long rifle:
Your Archimedes' lever, Albania.'

Through the sight of his rifle
The Albanian observed the horizons and the times,
The solitary whistling of his musket
Forced the centuries to duck.

This rifle barrel
On the Albanian's back
Has grown there like a long sharp bone,
Transplanted into his spine a difficult destiny.

This land which has brought forth
More heroism than grain through the ages . . .
That is what these lofty mountains are thinking about,
As evening falls in the distance beyond the highway.

What are these mountains thinking about?
Ismail Kadare (b.1936)
[written 1962-4, and published in Albania
during the years of Hoxha's dictatorship]

14

Strong Colours

The Night Belongs to the Djinn

I SAT CROSS-LEGGED on the ground sipping raki and Turkish coffee, eating dark red cherries which, a bare-footed clamberer, I'd just picked from the spreading tree in the Frasheris' mudbrick-walled garden. Old Mehmet Frasheri, the head of the household, sat cross-legged next to me, also partaking of his early morning coffee, raki and cigarette. We smiled at each other wordlessly, tranquil and happy to be alive for another day, another beautiful, fragrant day just starting. Simple early morning pleasures – light, warmth, silent companionship, black coffee and the first draw of aromatic smoke in the mouth.

The sun filtered through the leaves of the trees which shaded us on the porch of the old stone Ottoman-style house. In front of us lay the enclosed garden, green with herbs and vegetables; then the land sloped away gradually to the south. Beyond and below the far garden wall lay the valley, green and bright in sun, and framed with lines of tall poplar trees silvering in the breeze.

To my left, at the side of the Frasheris' hidden orchard, was a gate set into the wall, this woven wicker and sticks, through which I could see the faint blur of donkeys passing in the stone paved lane, their hooves sharp on granite. The clay-yellow mudbrick garden walls were laced and garnished with grapevines, fruit canes running up too, frothing and tumbling over the top. Water channels had been cut in the red soil of the vegetable garden to succour the onions and beans, tomatoes and radishes. The ground was still stained dark from their early morning douche. In the far distance, beyond the valley and trees, lay the mountains of Macedonia, rising in hummocked layers, drifting into cloud and mist and obscurity.

The air was cool and fresh up here after Tirana. It was so pleasant to be sitting cross-legged on the ground in the early sun, basking like a cat, the rustle of leaves from the trees soft all around me, shut inside this oriental garden of seclusion, privacy and ease. No sound of the town outside, of the people, the chaos.

I had a spacious, peaceful, pale-green painted, wood-walled room upstairs with a view out over the garden and the valley. There was a narrow, spartan bed and a hard wooden chair; and a great pile of mattresses, quilts and bedsheets wrapped up on a disused double bed in a corner. All of these were marked clearly Turism Hotel. In the days of Communism the Frasheri clan had controlled Peshkopi's one hotel. Democracy had come and they had lost the place, but had clearly managed to loot all the furniture and linen before being dispossessed. Off the landing next to my bedroom was a covered balcony with two tables and four chairs. Here I would sit and contemplate the valley and the distant hills. On the landing stood another table; on it a Chinese-made thermos, small decorative coffee cups on saucers and framed black and white photographs of the family as children neat in old-fashioned French-style school uniforms.

The Frasheris spoke no language apart from Albanian, though one grandchild, a girl of seven or eight, was learning English. She would solemnly ask me 'How are you?' every day, but that was all. They were a strong Communist *fis* still, fervent Hoxhaists; strong Moslems, also, and, I later learnt, believers in traditional superstitions as well, these three worlds co-existing without any apparent contradiction.

They had not been keen on feeding me at first. A group of American students had stayed with them the summer before, and had gone down before the proffered fare. I assured them I ate all Albanian dishes, which I did. They gave me goat in tomato-soup sauce, sticky macaroni topped with tiny songbirds, salads and sweet white vermouth, rice and roast potatoes, green onions, raw, and furry apples. To cherries I was welcome to help myself from the garden. With coffee and raki, it was enough

Their household was traditional. The men occupied the right side of the building, the women and children the left. Mehmet Frasheri dined alone, sitting cross-legged on the floor, served by his wife, who withdrew to the kitchen while her master ate. As fitting for a Frank and a *giaour*, they served me alone and in state in the room with the television, and gave me a wooden chair to sit on, and a small side-table for my plate, as they knew *giaours* required. Two daughters of the house, perhaps ten and twelve, would serve me, waiting at my side until I had finished each dish, carrying away the big, white ex-hotel plates, or pouring me more water from a plastic jug. In front of me, sole concession to modernity, the TV babbled away in an Italian that none of the family understood. Each room in their house had beds, as if they were still inhabiting a hotel.

For the Frasheris, Europe and the West were distant and only dimly recognised entities. They switched and surfed TV channels endlessly, attracted by colour, pattern and music more than anything else. They had no notion of the difference between the channels or the programmes, or the places from whence they came. When I was not in the TV room – and sometimes when I was – they often watched the Turkish satellite channel, 'because we love the music', I was eventually told when Elaine from the missionaries passed by to translate for me.

With the end of Communism I sensed the Frasheris had gone to ground. Mehmet and his wife, Engelushjia, rarely went out of their own walled garden, save to shop or visit kin in the neighbouring houses. Their clan occupied most of the quarter, which was right on the outskirts of Peshkopi. You could walk into open hilly countryside five minutes from their house; yet the lanes all around were narrowly urban, medieval almost, threading between large Ottoman houses with overhanging second storeys, each dwelling closed and inward-looking, with walled gardens all round. There were no cars or trucks in this part of town, only donkeys and silent, light-footed people.

In Peshkopi the muezzin called out with a strident confidence I had not as yet heard in Albania, and there were young, bearded Iranian clerics, missionaries, walking the lanes in their robes. I felt as if I was on the far borders of Persia, as if Afghanistan, not Macedonia, lay just beyond the near mountains.

Peshkopi was in the Dibra region, in the east of the country; it had always been a byword for its traditionalism and conservatism. In the streets there were no Mercedes and few cars even. Not many people dressed in modern clothes. Communist drab still prevailed, and here for the first time among the older people I saw a few men in the traditional *cheleshë*, or white fez, with homespun black waist-coats and traditional white breeches, these with a black stripe down either side – mourning for the death of Skanderbeg, so the romantics said.

The pace of life was slow. There was a broad central avenue, lined with linden trees, on which stood the Soviet-era Turism Hotel; further on there were a few small restaurants and the *bashkir*, or prefecture. Off the main avenue spread low blocks of *palatti*, then two-storey traditional stone houses with red tiled roofs. People walked about slowly by day, pausing to talk with much animation in the middle of the road. A few minibuses were parked with the ancient, once Greek country buses at the far end of the avenue by the open market, which was frankly a peasants' souk. Here were exchanged honey, yoghurt, cheese, raki and fruit for cloth, salt, needles and metal tools. The short dark men from the high mountain villages sat all but motionless on their heels, watching the passing throng, a pile of produce by their side. Great mounds of loose shredded tobacco lay like brown vermicelli on trestle tables; passers-by, prospective purchasers, turned it over with their hands, rubbing strands between their fingers and smelling it. Wicker baskets full of fruit – apricots and cherries, apples and strawberries – lay in profusion.

You could peel away the layers in Peshkopi: the Soviet-era hotel, the Hoxhaist *palatti*, the Italian *bashkir* – and underneath, quite near the surface, was a traditional Turkish market town which lived by and from the surrounding countryside. Fruit, meat, local cloth, tobacco and raki were all here in plenty. The gardens and orchards of Dibra were rich and fertile; no one had destroyed them in the frenzy of 1991. Somehow these people had survived Fascism and Communism alike, smiling, doubtless agreeing with every passing regime, and carrying on regardless, growing and producing.

That Albania had gone back to the pre-industrial era scarcely mattered in Peshkopi. It was clear they had preserved what they needed to survive from the old ways. When the electricity failed , they had lamps which burnt their own oil; they made their own clothes and ate their own food. They could still build their houses in the old way, with stone and mortar and wooden beams and planks. If there were no tiles, then they made do with wooden shingles; if there were no fired bricks, then they used mud and straw.

There was a sense of quiet purpose I had not seen before in Albania. People were getting on with their lives, growing things and selling them, coming in to market and going back again. The hopelessness of the south was not apparent, nor was the obsession with either politics or emigration. They were good-humoured people who smiled and even laughed. I was able to relax in Peshkopi for the first time.

Here people still used a few Turkish words and phrases: 'tammam' for 'okay,' and the bus drivers saying 'Haide! Haide!' to the passengers – 'Come on! Get in!' In Tirana I had heard nothing but Italian music and American blues in the cafés and buses; on the minibus to Peshkopi, five hours through a mountain wilderness of broken industry, constant police road blocks and impoverished countryside, the inevitable Greek *rembetika* accompanied us. In Peshkopi people played the music of Dibra, churning, ancient wedding songs, high-pitched women's voices and a syncopated rhythm of drums, violins, *oud* and lutes. It sounded like the oldest of music, repetitive, driving tunes which curled back on themselves, twin voices circling round each other in chorus and counterpoint. What Pasolini would have given to have discovered these songs for his films of ancient Greece and Asia Minor! They were sung for days on end, apparently, in the elaborate wedding ceremonies that took place in the villages in the autumn, always in the autumn, so that the first child would be born early the next summer, to allow for a stronger chance of survival.

Peshkopi represented the old Albania I had hoped against hope to find amidst the ruins of the south. Traditions lived on up here, and life itself still had some meaning for people. But I was still not content: I wanted to get right up into the villages of the high mountains of the north, where things surely had changed even less.

Ted Armstrong, Elaine's husband, had arranged for a cousin of the Frasheris to go with me up to Radomirë. Apparently the cousin worked at the *bashkir* and spoke some English, which he had taught himself from the BBC World Service in Communist days.

The Armstrongs were Midwesterners, in their thirties, with a teenage family. They both spoke good Albanian and knew everyone in Peshkopi, where they'd been stationed for the last two years. Their lives were lonely. It was an eight-hour drive to Salonika for them when they wanted to shop or see other Westerners. They rarely went to Tirana. They were Plymouth Brethren ('liberal, not legalistic'), and organised a Sunday school, Bible classes, a service once a week and various other activities in the town. They had a small congregation and had made a few converts. They were renting a separate house from the Frasheri clan, and it was they who had arranged for me to stay.

The Armstrongs had been studying the Albanian language for years before the country opened up, in Kosovo, which was then part of undivided Yugoslavia. It was their mission in life, Albania, literally their God-given vocation. 'Oh Lord', they said during grace before meals, 'we thank you for the Albanians', as if speaking of a special type of personalised club sandwich. They were very open and friendly, Tom even managing to look like an Albanian with his reddish fair hair and broad cheekbones. They had been told I was coming on the missionary short-wave radio.

Getting to Peshkopi had not been easy. Alicia had taken me to a bus depot on the outskirts of Tirana, where we had waited for several hours. It was a seedy place, full of gypsies, small children hawking drinks and men in dark glasses mooching round aimlessly. There had been a minibus, whose driver claimed it was going to Peshkopi. But in the end not enough people had appeared, so he roared off to Shkodra instead. That was the Albanian free market – everyone just did exactly what they wanted. We had trudged back to the apartment, and the next day tried again, much earlier, at another bus depot. There were no schedules, no timetables – you just had to turn up and hope for the best. This time I was in luck. The minibus filled with young men newly returned from Greece and Italy – almost the only people with money to pay for bus travel – and off we went.

'Be very careful in Peshkopi. The people are very bad. Put your money down here', I was told by Igor as he indicated his crotch. 'They will murder you for your money.' Igor had been in Greece and spoke some Greek. He got off at a turn-off to a village in the middle of nowhere, and shook my hand, wishing me luck. 'Come and visit me next week in my village.'

'*Inshallah*', I replied, and waved him goodbye.

In Peshkopi I had trudged round with André, a young student from Tirana home for the holidays who spoke some Italian. Everyone had heard about the Christian missionaries I was looking for, but no one knew where they were. Some said they were Italian, some Austrian, some American or even Greek. On our peregrinations they became as figures from mythology; yet Peshkopi was a tiny place, an overgrown village the size of Shaftesbury. We had been deflected into the Turism Hotel at one point, where a room for which Albanians paid $2 had been offered to me for $15. I offered $10, but the new owner hadn't grasped the idea of market forces. Every room was vacant – a complete row of keys was on display above the pigeon-holes – but the manager refused to budge. I was a foreigner, and $15 was what foreigners paid. Not this one, however, so on we trudged.

Eventually we found the missionaries' Sunday School and meeting place. A beautiful Albanian girl of about sixteen, voluptuously curved, with enormous breasts and a lovely smile, directed me to the Armstrongs' house in American-accented English.

'I'll look forward to meeting you again later', she promised me, fluttering her eyelashes. I trudged on in a happier frame of mind. Western missionaries in Albania attracted the same calibre of girls who in England became successful groupies servicing major pop bands. To marry a Westerner was to get out of Albania for ever, eventually, which was the most successful career move any Albanian family could make. It was slightly alarming, if ego-boosting, to be subjected to such blatant come-ons from such young, pretty girls. 'He is Western. He is not married', I heard said of me in whispers a dozen times by young Albanian girls. If I had been in the market for an under-age child bride, I would have been spoilt for choice. Marriage is still a matter of clan alliance in Albania, and as such personal preference had little to do with the process of mate selection. What the clan thinks is good is what the girls think is good. So they were directed at Westerners like little heat-seeking missiles; almost every missionary I met who had arrived in Albania a bachelor had married a stunningly good-looking Albanian girl within a year. One winter in the country and I know I'd have done the same myself.

*

Elaine Armstrong and I got on well. She was pleased to see a new face, someone who spoke English. I made her and the teenage daughters Earl Grey tea with lemon and sat in their little house talking. They had become semi-Albanianised. You kicked your shoes off in their lobby and slipped into wood and canvas or plastic indoor shoes. They offered you bon-bons in little glass dishes, and Coca-Cola, and smiled, smilingly, all the time. Ted was always elsewhere, out in the field, with his portable radio and 4-wheel-drive jeep.

There were several other American missionaries in town, all families, all Midwesterners. I could see now the appeal of provincial Albania for these people. In many ways they fitted in here much better than in modern America: strong, united, patriarchal families, no drugs or discos, sex only within marriage, masses of children, a simple rural economy, no diversionary seductions from an established East Coast liberal élite. Only the Protestant Christian faith was missing here, and they were on site to provide that. In some ways the Albanians were more like them than their fellow secular Americans.

Elaine knew a great deal about the Albanians amongst whom she lived, and for the first time I heard a Western woman's insights. These were quite different from any others I'd heard.

Curiously, Elaine would only tell me these things when we were alone together, when her husband and her daughters were not there. The night before I left for Kukes she poured everything out, like an Albanian, making her confession. I had to go away and write it all down immediately lest I forget.

Because they were Christians and because they wanted to convert the Albanians, the missionaries had to do a certain amount of research and analysis into what Albanians believed. From what Elaine told me, I realised that among women a whole realm of superstitious knowledge still existed in Albania which was closed off to men.

In the traditional Albanian family child-rearing and domestic management were exclusively female activities. Children of both sexes were taught a complete cosmos of knowledge by the women which stayed with them, at least in their subconscious, for the rest of their lives. The basis of this was magical, superstitious and essentially pre-Islamic pagan.

Beyond the northern Albanian walled fortress-house lay a dark and terrible supernatural world which was dangerous and had to be placated. The night in particular was feared. 'The night belongs to the djinn' was a common woman's saying, and terror of these malevolent roaming spirits was passed on to the children. No one would sleep alone for fear of djinns. Going outside in the dark was highly dangerous and avoided. The doors and windows of a house must be shut and barred before the sun set to prevent them getting inside.

Averting *Syy Kec*, the Evil Eye, was a major concern of the women: a blue brooch would be pinned to the lapels of children's clothes so the attacking djinns would be deflected from their eyes. *Mashallah* ('What God wills') was exclaimed to avert the Eye whenever there was thought to be risk. Boys would be dressed as girls when young, to confuse the djinns. 'Half of everybody dies from the Evil Eye and the other half die from not taking precautions against it' was a Jordanian proverb widely quoted by Albanian women. *Marrim syte* meant 'to catch the Eye' through envy; thus the Eye was drawn down upon those not content with their lot.

There were many superstitions concerning bread. To take a piece of bread from the table when a pregnant women was present who might possibly have wanted it was bound to draw the Eye. Bread itself had sacred and symbolic qualities; to trample bread underfoot was a sacrilege and an insult, as was letting any bread go to waste. Women were careful never to throw bread away; it had to be given to a shepherd or, *in extremis*, to animals. In the Communist times an Albanian had made a public speech saying, 'The Americans can eat their bread and crush it under their feet for all we care'. This, to an Albanian audience, was a very terrible insult to America, and in Albanian eyes deeply shameful for Americans.

Women, especially pregnant women, were known to have occult powers, and these were feared by men, although women themselves were despised. Occult knowledge was preserved and passed on by women secretly, without their men knowing anything about either the process or the people involved. The unseen world of the supernatural was thought to be able to be controlled, at least in part, by these powers which women alone could possess. Women also passed on the culture of shame to children in secret in the nursery; the culture of honour was learnt from men in public. Thus in Albania there was a constant conflict between what was honourable and could be spoken about, and what was shameful and secret. To remain silent about the shameful was the only honourable course.

The insistence on 'truth', 'consistency' and 'honesty' among Westerners imbued with the Protestant-secular tradition posed immense problems for Albanians, since to admit to the 'truth', if it was shameful, dishonoured them and was thus always avoided. This led to disappointed Westerners, angry at having been 'lied to'. The Albanians resented this anger and became angry themselves. Honourable men avoided shaming other honourable men; shame was reserved only for their enemies. Albanian conversation between friends was thus largely a ritual of agreement and face-saving. What you thought and what you said bore no relation to each other.

Elaine had herself only become privy to secret women's knowledge slowly, and only because she spoke good Albanian. Engelushjia had been going through Elaine's clothing with her one day, and had remarked on the 'strong colours' of her underwear, some of which was black, and some red.

'Why do you need such strong colours to hold Ted?' she had demanded three times. In highland Ghegeria a serious question which demanded a serious answer was always asked three times. Once only was merely politeness.

A woman could hold a straying man to her by wearing strong colours, it was revealed. Red was a strong colour, black even stronger; blue was the weakest of colours. Engelushjia regarded it as a matter of puzzlement and shame for Elaine that she needed such strong colours to 'keep' her husband.

Elaine admitted to me that she had never told Ted about any of this. She only told me because I was English – a foreigner to her – and would be leaving the next day for ever. Also, I was, in a sense, like a female Western confidante to Elaine, for we had talked together about 'women's matters', which Anglo-Saxon men rarely feel comfortable discussing with females. In America or England we probably wouldn't have done so, but here she was deprived of suitable female English-speaking company. She didn't feel she could talk about such things with the other missionary wives.

Elaine also told me that Engelushjia was a 'wise woman' in the Western sense, a moral leader and repository of occult and herbal lore that she passed on to a group of other women in various secret initiation ceremonies about which their the men knew nothing. It was beneath Albanian male pride to enquire or even show any interest in female activities or areas of competence.

In Albanian thinking the Tree of Blood, from which a man made his descent, and the Tree of Milk, from which women made theirs, were entirely separate. Only the killing of men could result in blood feuds, unless the woman killed was found to be carrying a male foetus. Thus in villages stricken with endemic blood feuds, where most of the males over seven were armed and in hiding, many of the day-to-day decisions about running the community, as well as the manual work, devolved to the women, who could move about freely without being shot. It would be an interesting, if dangerous, assignment for an anthropologist to live for an extended period in one of these villages. The seclusion of so many breeding-age males in enforced celibacy in the stone towers of refuge must also surely contribute to keeping down the birth rate. The blood feud could even be seen as a positive, perhaps even vital, mechanism for preventing over-population in a subsistence farming economy with finite available land: in effect it was an extreme form of community self-culling.

The Frasheris' house, which I thought dated back to Ottoman times, had in fact been built in 1962. That is to say, a large, private house had been constructed on private land during the ostensibly extreme collectivist-Stalinist period when even sheep and chickens had been nationalised. A Moslem *hodja*, or sage, had come to bless the foundations, and had sacrificed a ram: the blood had been poured on the ground and the head of the ram buried under the east-facing corner-stone of the foundations, to 'help make the building strong'. In antiquity the Romans and others buried slaves alive under their houses' foundation corners for the same purpose. As late as the 1890s Edith Durham reported local fears that virgin girls were still being abducted and buried alive inside river bridges to protect them from being washed away in both northern Albania and southern Montenegro.

There was a great deal of lore concerning animals, Elaine told me. Ants were never poisoned or driven from a house: 'All good people have ants in their houses', she had been told. Cats, too, had a semi-sacred character, whereas dogs contained evil spirits. Birds could speak sometimes, and often carried messages from the dead and from the spirit world.

None of this secret cosmos was ever spoken about to adult males. It was the preserve of women and used by them to control and influence each other and their children. When boys grew up into men, they never talked of these things with other men because they were shameful, yet these influenced their behaviour and beliefs. In Ghegeria no man I ever met felt comfortable out of doors after sunset; the night was a dangerous time, and belonged to the djinn.

I later asked people in Tirana about all this, secular people brought up in the city, both men and women. They were genuinely astonished and amazed. They had heard of none of this lore and had no idea people in the highlands of the north still believed these things. 'It is like something from the time of Edith Durham', Alexei told me.

Enver Hoxha, who hated and feared the British because of their part in his rise, always made an exception for Edith Durham, who had streets named after her all over the country throughout the Communist period. She more than any other Western writer on Albania has caught fragments of the secret world of Albanian female knowledge, which still lies buried inside the women's rooms of northern Gheg households. Some skilled female Albanian-speaking Western anthropologist must surely one day devote herself to charting this unknown mental universe. Much that remains puzzling about Albanians' attitudes and behaviour can, I suspect, be traced back to superstitions imbibed with their mothers' milk, and which may go back deep into the pagan pre-history of the Balkans.

*

I was able to watch the Frasheris' grandchildren at play in the garden as I sat and smoked and ate cherries with their grand-father. They had no toys at all, and their game always revolved around the older boys chasing, catching and beating the younger boys, while the girls watched; then the younger boys escaping, and in turn chasing the girls, catching them and then beating them and making them squeal. The beatings were sometimes quite hard, often with sticks and even stones. None of the adults interfered or mediated in these exchanges, which were regarded as play, normal and quite unremarkable. This catch-and-beat play was confined to the garden. Girls never chased or beat, but were purely passive. Once in the house this play ceased, and the girls had to wait upon the adult males as they were bidden, while the boys were cossetted and fondled by their female adult relatives. Girls were never cossetted or fondled by either adult males or females; their role was to wait upon the men inside the house, and to be chased and beaten in the garden. Beyond the garden the girls were not allowed to go, though the boys could play in the lane outside.

'Engelushjia keeps coming round and borrowing all my electrical things, and then breaks them', Elaine told me once. 'I don't criticise or complain. I just leave her to work out a learning curve, that if she breaks it, then it's not around anymore for her to use.'

'Allah gives and Allah takes away', I suggested. 'Factories, research, capital, labour, import and distribution don't come into it. This electrical machinery is Allah's gift, not yours, here for Engelushjia to use, break, and then forget until Allah provides the next lot. This is surely why historically the West won out against the Islamic world: cause and effect versus fatalistic determinism.'

'Maybe you're right', Elaine commented, not entirely convinced. 'The hardest thing we have to convince Albanians of is that stealing, lying and murder, even in the interest of the *fis*, are neither good nor honourable. They can't see it. For them the end always justifies the means. And the Christian symbols don't work for them either. All the references to shepherds in the Bible just draw scorn. For them the shepherd is the stupidest of people. You know their Communist shepherd joke?' I didn't, so she told me.

'The Communist Party decided to politicise the shepherds in the north, so the local officials called them all in for some propaganda. "You", an official said to one shepherd, "What is the Communist Party to you?" "Dunno", replied the shepherd moronically. "Idiot!" shouted the Party worker, "It's your mother and your father and all source of authority for you! Now get out and tell that other shepherd to come in here." At the doorway the waiting shepherd asks the departing shepherd what the official wanted to know before stepping inside. "Right. You, shepherd", said the official to the second man, "What's the Communist Party to you?" "Oh that's easy. I know that one, it's his mother", he replied, indicating the departing first shepherd with his thumb.'

15

Mountain Fastnesses

Wolves, Bears and the High Passes to Serbia

'ASK YOUR UNCLE if he has much trouble with wolves', I said to my guide, Rafiq.

The three of us were sprawled out upon sheepskin rugs on the floor inside a fortified stone farmhouse, or *kula*, in the village of Radomirë, the last inhabited place before the Serbian-Macedonian border. In theory you could walk up the valley on foot, snow permitting, and over the high mountain passes into former Yugoslavia. It was only three hours away. In practice the border had been closed since just after the Second World War; it was a sore point with the villagers. They all had *bjeshkë*, alpine pastures, on the other side. Sometimes they went to them anyway and risked the Serbian and Macedonian border patrols. 'They do not dare attack us', said Rafiq proudly, if optimistically. But they did attack, and had killed Albanian shepherds in the past.

This was a corner of remote, roadless high mountain territory where Serbia, Albania and Macedonia marched, and according to my map there were no villages or farms on the other side for dozens of miles, so wild and austere was the terrain. As we had walked up the valley towards Radomirë the bulk of Mount Korabit towered above us all the way, the peak rising to 2,753 metres, snow-covered still in mid-June.

Radomirë was a scattered collection of stone houses with wooden shingle roofs. There was one mosque with a pencil-slim minaret, but no shops or café: this was the last village of mountain Albania before the frontier, perched at an altitude of 1,750 metres.

Our host, Rafiq's uncle, was called Rustem. A small, tightly knit man in his forties, he was both lithe and muscular from a hard outdoor life. He wore a homespun black jerkin, black breeches and a round black hat like a beret. His face was creased and tanned from the sun, but he was fair-haired and had blue-grey eyes; he could have been a Cornishman or a Breton. Rustem and his family lived in the village, farming a hectare of fertile valley land and herding sheep in the alpine pastures during the summer months. He had thirty hectares of *bjeshkë*, and more on the other side of the border. He was married with three children. His wife was even smaller than he. She wore a homespun dress and Turkish-style trousers, with a scarf over her head. When she spoke to her husband she bowed low and muttered in almost a whisper, staring at his feet. Neither she nor the children came into the guest room where we, the three men, lay on rugs and sheepskins – except to serve us food and coffee.

Without even translating my question, Rafiq replied: 'No trouble with wolves in summer. Only winter.'

'Ask him anyway', I insisted. The two men conferred in Albanian together.

'He says they have a lot of trouble with wolves', Rafiq told me with equanimity. 'Last week a mare was eaten during the night in a neighbour's paddock just behind this house. In the winter they come right down into the village during the day and move about through the streets.'

Radomirë lay under snow for at least three months of the year, sometimes more. I asked when Rustem had last seen a wolf.

'Last week', came the reply. 'He saw four of them, two adults and two cubs, quite near, less than two hundred metres from the village. Wolves are not very afraid of men these days. There were also bears – more bears then wolves.'

Rustem carried an old breech-loading rifle with him every time he went out with his flock of sheep. Sometimes he stayed up on the alpine pastures for days at a time. He had built sheepfolds of stone up there, and a tiny hut for himself to sleep in, or to shelter when it snowed; sometimes it snowed even in June. At the end of September the *bjeshkë* had to be abandoned for the winter. By then the hay had been cut and brought down by mule and stored in the farm barn. The sheep lived in the barn all winter and the upland pastures remained snow-covered and unvisited until the next summer. It took three hours of steep climbing to get up to Rustem's *bjeshkë*. He had a large hound to protect the flock from wolves, bears

– and men; this beast had flung itself, snarling and slavering, at Rafiq and me when we entered the farm courtyard. Fortunately it was chained with iron rings to the outside wall.

We had come up by village bus, very slowly, from Peshkopi as far as Kallë Dodes. It was Sunday and the bus was full of peasants from the high mountain villages returning from market. Most of the men over forty were dressed in traditional costume: rough linen shirts, homespun jerkins, *opinga* sandals of leather, and the white, flat-topped *cheleshë*, or fez. For the first time in Albania I saw men with moustaches. Once upon a time Gheg men had been great moustach-wearers. In the old days even the Franciscan Catholic priests had to grow them when they arrived from Italy; a man was not a man without whiskers. 'You must have courage to grow a moustache in Albania', Rafiq had told me as we walked up the mountain track. 'The first thing an enemy will say is, "Shame on your moustache!"'

On the bus the young men had looked at me curiously: the small children were timid, some evidently even frightened. Their elders explained to them quietly that I was a Frank, a *giaour*, a man from the West. They had obviously never seen such a specimen before in the flesh.

The bus rumbled on, and we rose through the mountains on winding dirt roads, past fields of ripening maize, then terraced fields of cherries and plums and on into spectacular alpine scenery: streams crashing down through ravines, white gypsum rock cliffs, jagged peaks, pines leaning out at jaunty angles, the odd goat sil-houetted against the skyline. There were no police or roadblocks up here, no concrete bunkers even, just men in white fezzes on donkeys, and women in bloomers and headscarves hoeing in tiny fields.

As the bus clambered and wheezed its way up towards the distant peaks, the mudbrick houses gave way to small stone forts, these without windows on the ground floor, instead with loopholes for rifles set into the walls above.

For the first time in Albania I was entering the heartland of the northern highlands, where traditional law – and the blood feud – had held sway until Communism. The *Kanun of Lek Dukagjin* was the ancient code which had been the only law recognised by the tribes to the north of Dibra: but the influence of this *kanun* had stretched down to include much of Catholic Mirdita and Moslem

Dibra as well, these highland regions though not strictly Dukagjin tribes.

Under the Turks the Dukagjin mountain tribes had been left to administer traditional justice themselves in their *medjlis*, or assemblies, under village elders and chiefs, just as the British had left the tribes of the North-West Frontier of India to do the same. How much of the old system, the old values, had survived Communism, I wondered. President Berisha, a Gheg and Dukagjin highlander himself, had often praised the *kanun* publicly. Under Hoxha it had been strictly forbidden as a remnant of feudalism.

The passengers on the bus were frankly curious about me; Westerners rarely penetrated this far into the mountains. There were no Mercedes or minibuses up here, no smart young men just back from Greece or Italy. This was traditional Albania. Apart from the bus itself, there was nothing at all from the landscape or the people that would have been out of place a hundred years ago. I was passing through a region as locked in the remote past as any in the world today.

At Kallë Dodes, a scattered mountain hamlet in the middle of nowhere, the ancient bus came to a halt. Rafiq and I got down and started to walk. The bus driver would stay here overnight and the bus would creep back down the mountain at 6 a.m. the next day. This was the end of the road; the next was somewhere dozens of miles over the peaks in Serbia. From here onwards man travelled by foot or on mules, up narrow defiles through the mountain passes. Here any two men with rifles – bandits or soldiers, Communists or Democrats – were equal. Here no wheel had ever passed in all history; here, no police patrolled, no army marched: neither NATO nor the EU ever penetrated these rocky defiles. This was high Albania, home of the wolf and the bear, and of the mountain men who had clung so tenaciously to this savage, magnificent land for thousands of years. I was both proud and humbled to be here at last, in this place where almost no Westerners had ever trodden.

The air was sharp and clean, the silence broken only by the click of our boots on the rocks under our feet. Thus we walked, clambered, gasped our way up the narrowing valley, Rafiq and I, and talked – or rather Rafiq talked, subjecting me to a virulent dose of Albanian nationalist propaganda. In Tirana and the south the Serbs had never been mentioned, were considered an irrelevance: in the

Dibra region one heard nothing but diatribes against them. Across the border lay traditional Albanian lands, Kosovo and western Macedonia, where a majority of Albanians were ruled over, or rather, as one heard it, tyrannised and oppressed by brutal, wicked, murderous Serbs – who were all cowardly and like women.

'When is the West going to come and help us throw out these vile Serbs who have stolen our ancestral lands and robbed us of our flocks?' Rafiq asked me rhetorically. 'Don't hold your breath', I felt like telling him, but I smiled on sympathetically instead, and nodded encouragement. I was myself becoming quite Albanian by now.

Rafiq was a civil engineer who worked at the *bashkir* in Peshkopi. He was probably in his early fifties, I thought, small and stooped, white-haired, with bad teeth and a paunch. He had learnt English from the radio and by reading books: he was able to quote great chunks of poetry in English by Lord Byron and even Robert Burns, for heaven's sake. The mimetic talent of Albanians was extraordinary. As well as poetry, Rafiq had memorised whole football commentaries in English from 'Sports Round-Up' on the BBC from the 1960s, Bobby Charlton being a particular favourite player of his. He could remember these commentaries word for word, and recited the long-forgotten goals, penalties and free kicks in the clipped tones of the sports commentator of yesteryear – all in English, mind, which echoed bizarrely in the rocky canyons of highland Albania all round us. Eventually I could take no more and instructed him to shut up and tell me something of the folklore of the region. But instead he switched into his monologue about the wicked Serbs again. Like a doctored, Communist-era radio set, you had a limited choice of three channels with Rafiq: romantic poetry, 1960s football commentaries or the wickedness of the Serbs.

We strode along a whisper of a footpath up the ever shadowing valley, the high snow-capped peaks of Serbia looming ahead of us. Rafiq had now switched channels again and was chanting Robert Burns in English, or rather, Albanian-accented Scots. Burns, like Byron, was a favourite poet under Hoxha, studied and memorised by every Albanian schoolchild. Lord Byron had been to Albania and had written noble, flattering verse about the Albanian people, and Burns, of course, was a Man of the People.

To our right now, in a sloping field, a group of women in Turkish trousers and shawls were stooped, hoeing a field. They looked up and waved, calling out to us and asking where we were going. Rafiq replied, and told me to repeat a short phrase in Albanian, which I did.

'What does that mean?' I asked, half-expecting it to be more Robbie Burns, an incantation of wee sleekit Albanian beasties.

'May Allah lighten your ploughing', he replied. It reminded me of Lin, the village near Lake Ochrid, where the peasants had said to Gabriel: 'Sali Berisha should have lightened our ploughing.' But neither Allah nor the Tirana politicians had ever concerned them-selves overmuch with lightening the Albanian peasants' work.

We came to an open plateau of grassland, where new-cut hay lay bronzing in the bright late afternoon sun. Two men, the mowers, sat cross-legged, taking their ease beside a large shady bush, drinking coffee from a thermos and smoking. Their long-handled scythes lay on the ground near by.

Below and beyond them the valley opened out away to the west, sweeping down towards the plain. We were on a superb natural balcony, even if the view was obscured in mist below. One of the men hailed us and we strode across to them. He turned out to be a cousin of Rafiq's, a man in his sixties dressed in homespun waist-coat and white *cheleshë*.

We shook hands and sat down with them. The younger man was sent away to wash two small porcelain cups in the stream, and bring us back cold, slightly muddy water in glasses to quench our thirst. The cousin, the elder man, was called Ali Rashid, and the younger was one of his nephews. Ali Rashid poured sweet, scalding black coffee from the Chinese-made thermos for us, and offered his silver tobacco box to roll cigarettes. In the mountains there were few shops and most men carried their own home-cured tobacco for rolling, with little packets of rice papers without gum. Rafiq didn't nor-mally smoke, but he made a cigarette for himself inexpertly and puffed it to be polite. I offered Ali Rashid my loose Tarabosh: he saw the name printed on the grey package and smiled at me happily.

'Tarabosh is the best of tobaccos', he told Rafiq, and helped himself to a generous cigarette-full. His eyes twinkled at me: I was obviously a connoisseur. His own home-cured leaf was as hot as chillies and scorched my mouth.

It was almost impossible to be a male adult and not smoke cigarettes in the mountains of Albania. The giving and receiving of tobacco and fire was one of the very basic ice-breaking and bond-creating social rituals. Later, in the *Kanun of Lek*, I read that in the olden days the giving of a coal to light a man's pipe had automatically granted a man *besa*, or protection.

Had any other British ever been up this valley, I asked Ali Rashid via Rafiq.

'Oh yes', came the reply, 'We had a *kapitan* here during the war, with another English soldier, a sergeant. They came from Cairo, by parachute, and later planes came over to drop things for them – articles of the very first quality which we'd never seen before. The *kapitan* had a bicycle to make electricity, this to talk on his radio set to Cairo. His uniform was very fine, made of the best wool. My first shirt was made by my mother out of one of his blue silk parachutes – very good material. And he had gold British pounds, too, and excellent guns with heaps of ammunition. The Germans tried to come up here to chase him, but of course we knew they were coming days before they got here, so we smuggled the *kapitan* away over the border safely into Serbia. It was winter but he had a fine thick coat, made of wool, too. I was young but I remember him well. He was very tall.'

When I got back to Britain I checked through the records of the British liaison officers in the Dibra region during the war. From Ali Rashid's description this officer sounded like Captain Seymour, whom Captain Julian Amery mentions several times in his book. It was only just over fifty years ago, after all, and Ali Rashid would have been ten or so, quite old enough to remember such details.

'When did the next Englishman come up here?' I asked.

'You are he', Ali Rashid replied without hesitation.

Neither England nor Cairo seemed remote to Ali Rashid, although he himself had never left the Radomirë valley. His two sons had escaped over the border, and were now in America. One was a lawyer in Washington and the other a college lecturer in Brooklyn.

'When did the Communists come up?'

Ali Rashid's face clouded for the first time and his smile went abruptly. 'They came up in 1944, Allah curse them in Gehenna. They killed eighteen of our clan, including my father. We were all Balli Kombetar.'

We finished our coffee, made our farewells, and left. When quite out of sight of the two men, Rafiq vanished completely into the dense bushes near the stream, obviously for a pee. I found a separate patch of shrubbery for myself, and did likewise.

After he and I had emerged, and continued on our way together, Rafiq asked me suddenly: 'Tell me, is it true that the French men will do this thing, pissing, in public, in full view of everyone, standing openly without shame?'

I replied that they did indeed; and that other Europeans too, including the English – though not as flagrant as the French – didn't feel it necessary to hide the body completely.

'The shame!' Rafiq exclaimed. 'And I had thought the French a cultured people. To stand openly and piss . . . ' For the first time that day words failed him. I pressed home my conversational advantage. At last I had discovered a way to silence Rafiq's broadcasts: shock tactics.

'In India the men, and women, go out into the parks and streets every morning and openly squat down to crap in full view of the world. Some of them throw their robes over their head so no one can see their faces. Thus the shame belongs to the one who sees them, not to them.'

Rafiq looked first astonished, then frankly horrified at this. He gaped at me and exclaimed: 'Wah!'

We walked on, climbing ever higher. He was now beginning to look very seedy, Rafiq, and was obviously suffering.

'What's the matter?' I asked.

'I have bad pain from my teeth', he said. I sympathised, and asked if there was good dentist in Peshkopi.

'This hurts very much I think, going to the dentist, no?'

'They give you an injection to kill the pain. It doesn't hurt', I told him reassuringly.

'In Albania I don't think they give you this injection. I think they just drill or pull, and sell the injections over the border into Serbia for *dollari*.'

I wasn't able to contradict him on this with any real feeling of confidence. I asked Rafiq how old he was and he told me he was forty-one – and I had thought him fifty-five or more. He had never been to a dentist in his life.

We came to a small shop, or rather a wooden shack, staffed by two tousled girls. This sold packets of biscuits, cigarettes and chocolates.

I bought some of each of these as a present for Rustem and his family. There was an elaborate charade where Rafiq tried to pay, and we stood thrusting lek notes into each other's pockets like silent-movie comedians. Rafiq earned almost nothing as a civil servant: $45 a month. He had refused to take any money for guiding me up to the mountains, and had even tried to pay for our bus tickets, one dollar each. I had insisted on paying, however, and in the end he had acquiesced. 'You are my guest', he kept saying. Nor was there going to be any question of paying Rustem for my food or overnight stay. Hence the presents.

After accepting these tokens in silence, without thanks, as was etiquette, I noticed that Rustem tucked two of the chocolate bars into his own pockets, passing on the others to his wife and children later. The cigarettes went on the mantelpiece for guests, as no one in the household smoked, though every highland house had to have tobacco and raki for guests: that was the sacred tradition. 'Sacred' was not putting it too strongly. 'The Albanian house belongs to God and the guest', said the *Kanun of Lek*, and the iron tradition of hospitality still existed in northern Albania as it had a thousand years and more before.

Rustem was very pleased to see us, though he was clearly dog-tired after a day out watching his flocks. 'You honour my house', he told me, very seriously via Rafiq, and he meant it. A guest was always an honour, one from the West even more so.

Rustem was a strong anti-Communist and fierce partisan of Dr Sali Berisha and the Democrat Party. His family lands and flocks had been nationalised by Hoxha in 1967 and for him life under Communism had been bitter and loathsome.

'There was never enough food to eat and we had to do exactly what the head of the commune said. We even had to ask permission to kill a sheep or lamb. We almost never ate meat. All our produce went away to Tirana and we never saw anything in exchange for it except a bit of maize flour and oil. We were always hungry. We used to eat cooked grasses and herbs in the summer. In the winter we were just cold and hungry all the time. We got nothing – no produce, no industrial goods – we were slaves.'

His family, like the rest of the village, had been given their lands back in the privatisations of 1993. But the farm was too poor to support a large household. His eldest son had just gone off to try his luck in Italy. He had caught an illegal motorboat from Durrës with other boys from the village. It had cost Rustem $600 for his son's passage-money. He was still worried, though: it had been several weeks and there was still no word from Italy. His son had promised to phone the doctor in Kallë Dodes, but so far there had been nothing. Some of these *scafi*, or motorboats, had foundered, drowning all on board. It was rumoured that the Italian navy sometimes sank them deliberately, *pour encourager les autres*.

Rustem was by no means an ignorant or an uneducated man. He said of Enver Hoxha, 'He was a tyrant worse than Ali Pasha of Tepelena', a comparison no member of the intelligentsia had yet made to me, but which was certainly apt. Indeed, Rafiq had tried to convince me earlier that Ali Pasha – who had roasted his enemies alive and poured the blood from the slit throats of others over his mother's grave, a ruler who cut off French prisoners' heads (these his former allies) and sent them to Constantinople in their comrades' chained hands – this monster, Rafiq claimed, had 'never attacked anyone except foreign invaders'. Ali Pasha, like Skanderbeg, had been recruited by the Communists as a nationalist hero, and so largely sanitised. Albanians found it hard to admit that any Albanian had ever done anything wrong throughout history: it was always someone else's fault. Rafiq strenuously denied that Albanians had volunteered to serve as soldiers under the Ottomans: 'They were all forced, all conscripted!' he shouted at me. But it wasn't true, and I told him so. Albanians had been mercenaries all over the Ottoman Empire. In Egypt they had founded a dynasty in the early nineteenth century; by the 1850s in Khartoum in the Sudan, then an Albanian-Egyptian slave colony, Sir Samuel Baker had been told by the British Consul that the worst punishment available to the Ottoman Governor was to put an offender in gaol with the Albanian soldiers, who would bugger the unfortunate wretch half to death. I didn't tell Rafiq that: I didn't think his constitution would be able to take it. But forcible rape of men, women and children was a constant in Albanian history; every sacking of a town, every defeat of an enemy, was followed as night followed day by the mass buggery of the survivors by the victorious Albanian soldiery.

Rustem was the first Albanian I had spoken to who dealt with the concrete, without a confusing conversational cloud of rhetoric or woolly abstraction. When I asked him how many animals he owned he told me exactly: 100 sheep, 4 cows and his hound. His herd produced between 100 and 110 lambs a year, most of which he sold, except those which replaced the dead in his own flock. He grew beans, maize, potatoes, and plums for raki. It was too high for grapes. What about onions, I asked. Rustem looked disgusted: 'Those things are for Germans', he replied with contempt.

The guest room in which we lay had a large dowry kilim on the floor, which his wife had made in six weeks, by hand. There was a traditional fireplace in the far wall with a thin white gauze sheet hanging down over it to hide the fire-blacked rear. The rough stone walls of the room were whitewashed with lime. Apart from embroidered cushions and sheepskins there was no furniture. In one corner stood a large fridge, and there was a single electric bulb overhead, but the electric current very rarely got up as far as Radomirë. 'They all steal it on the way and there is none for us', Rustem told me. People connected themselves up to the pylons nearest their homes – you saw the wires dangling down everywhere.

Rustem's own house was an almost exact replica of the Ethnographic Museum I'd visited in Gjirokastra, complete with work implements outside, sheepskins, rugs and kilim inside. In 1908 Edith Durham had called northern alpine Albania 'the museum of the living past'. Nothing had changed in almost ninety years. Apart from the dead light bulb and fridge we could have been in the eighteenth century, or the eighth. The Communist interregnum had done nothing to change this timeless way of life. What indeed, could ever be done to alter it? No wheeled transport could ever get up here – why should it ever alter?

Rustem did have a transistor radio, though, which he used to take out with him and listen to while guarding his herds. He was an avid follower of the BBC World Service in Albanian, and asked me detailed questions about English political life. Was the vote of no confidence moved against Mr Major in the House of Commons serious? Why was Diana, Princess of Wales, behaving so shamefully? Why did Prince Charles not give her a sound thrashing? Would the British and the Americans invade Serb-controlled Bosnia in strength, now they had small military forces there?

The constant flow of reliable information in Albanian from the BBC in London, together with Britain's active role in the resistance campaign against the Italo-German occupation in the Second World War, lent England a prestige and prominence in Albanian eyes that in reality she no longer deserved.

It was extraordinary to think of this Albanian shepherd with his rifle and flock, sitting up on a hillside on the Serbian-Macedonian border, tuning in to the chimes of Big Ben every day; but all over the world there were millions and millions like him, poor, isolated and otherwise ill informed, their own radio stations known to produce mere government propaganda. Even though Rustem supported the Democrats, he didn't believe the news on Democrat-controlled Albanian radio.

Both Rafiq and Rustem asked me to explain the British and American system of democracy. I told them about freedom of speech, parliamentary privilege, a free press, the right of assembly, the rule of law, an independent judiciary, and the theory of checks and balances. They were frankly baffled.

'What is your idea of democracy for Albania?' I asked Rustem.

He grew animated. 'We will have true democracy only when every deputy in our parliament is from the Democratic Party!' he shouted. Rafiq said nothing. I had a feeling he was still a crypto-Communist: besides, he was a guest in his uncle's house.

Rustem's wife had brewed us Turkish coffee on a small Greek camping-gaz stove when we arrived. Naturally, she had taken no part in our discussions. After several hours, she reappeared carrying a small, round low-legged dining wooden table, the *sofra*, and the three of us manoeuvred ourselves about it, leaning on our elbows. Rustem and Rafiq both clucked over me like mother hens, stuffing cushions under my shoulder to make me comfortable.

Rustem's wife – I never learnt her name and it would not have been polite to ask it – served us a large dish of sticky rice, a bowl of thick, very sour yoghurt, unleavened maize bread flaps, fried potatoes and cold fried eggs, and to drink glasses of thin yoghurt diluted in cold water, called *ayran* in Turkey and *thali* in highland Albania. There was far too much food for the three of us, but then the wife and children would eat what we left after we had finished.

We ate slowly and talked. Rafiq said to me in English: 'Eat something from every plate, even if it is a mouthful.' Neither of them would touch anything until I had first tasted it – that was etiquette. I made sure I did not point the soles of my feet at either of them, this being considered an ill-mannered solecism. Our shoes had been discarded when we had entered the house. The only really serious insult a guest could offer his host was to look inside the cooking pot while it was still on the fire. If you did this, the host went to the window, threw open the shutters and shouted out to the village: 'I have been insulted by my guest!' The protection of the *besa* was thus removed, and the host might and could shoot you. I had read all this in Edith Durham with fascination, not realising for a minute that I would ever find myself in a situation where the information was of practical use; but here I was.

Rustem only had one book in his house. It was a paperback copy in Albanian of the *Kanun of Lek Dukagjin*, printed in Tirana in 1993. He had read 'some of it', he told me. He seemed very surprised when I quoted laws from the *kanun* in English, and Rafiq translated them into Albanian for him. 'Do you know of the *kanuni* in England then?' Rustem asked me, genuinely curious. Those who know about Albania know about *kanuni*', I replied, which was true. He was evidently very bucked at this. It became clear as we talked that Rafiq knew nothing at all about the *kanun*, had never read it, or heard anyone quote it.

I found it highly significant that this key book which had been absolutely banned during the Communist era had been reprinted under the Berisha regime, and was now to be found in an ordinary highland household in the remote mountains – the very first I'd visited in fact. The obvious implication was that in spite of fifty years of Marxism-Leninism the Gheg highlands had retained their centuries-old, perhaps even millennial, allegiance to this traditional tribal code of laws.

'My uncle from Mirdita is a great expert of *kanuni*. People come from miles around to get his opinion on their disputes', Rustem told me. I asked if his uncle demanded a fee of gold, as in days of yore. 'No, only a cup of coffee', he replied.

I sat glancing through this thin, badly printed paperback which looked like a cheap school textbook, trying to understand the Albanian; it was deeply frustrating. The *kanun* was translated into Italian in the 1930s and into English in America in 1991 – but neither the British Library nor the London Library had copies of either. This was the first time I'd actually had the *kanun* in my hands – and I could read no more than a fraction of it.

I was not the first Westerner to have come up to stay with Rustem. An American anthropologist called Terry Cooper from New York had lived here for five weeks with his female Albanian translator, whom he'd later married. He was studying the language and customs in the villages all around and had also done some mountaineering, climbing the local peaks. He had turned a corner down a track one day only to come face to face with a large brown bear on its hind legs, standing taller than himself. He stood stock still, and the bear eventually retreated. Rustem had seen a bear recently, in the distance. They seemed to be increasing in numbers, he thought. I asked him why his hound did not have the traditional collar with sharp iron spikes, to protect it from wolf and bear attacks.

'Because sometimes the dogs get into fights with each other, and if the spikes kill the other man's dog, that is the start of a feud.'

Were there many blood feuds in the area, I asked.

There were some, he admitted uncomfortably, but nothing like in Tropoja. Bajram Curri was the centre of the blood feuds: down here they read the parts of the *kanun* which applied to reconciliation; up in Tropoja they only read the parts about *gjak*. *Gjak* meant blood, and *gjakmaria* was the blood feud, terms I was to become increasingly familiar with as I progressed north.

It was only ten o'clock, but we had to be up at 4.30 a.m. for an hour's walk down the mountain to catch the early bus. Rustem's wife, who had cleared away the food and *sofra*, now brought in a mound of embroidered quilts with coarse linen sheets buttoned to them, which she laid out over the sheepskins on the floor.

After she left, the three of us removed a token garment each, and wriggled down under the quilts, lying in a line like olden-day travellers in a caravanserai. The women and children would sleep in the family room next door.

I was the only person to employ a toothbrush before clambering into the collective bed. I had brushed my teeth on the steps of the front door. The low growlings of the wolfhound prowling outside kept me from venturing any further into the night.

The night belongs to the djinn, says the Hadith in the Koran, but according to the *kanun* the night belongs to the dog. After sunset guard dogs are loosed from their chains and allowed to roam the walled courtyards of the highland farmsteads. Anyone, friend or foe, who is attacked by such a beast can claim no revenge or blood money: he or she should not have been out of doors. Edith Durham had written about just such a test case, where a woman had been killed in her own backyard after dark by a neighbour's dog, which had sprung across the dividing wall. The elders' ruling was that she should not have been out of doors, even in her own yard, and that the night belonged to the dog, so no compensation was allowed for her death.

Outside, from the doorstep, I could see the moon was high and full, silver and ghostly, a necromancer's orb redolent of werewolves and madness. The air tasted cool and clean, with a tang of pine and a taste of dew. Was there a more remote, a more untouched place in all Europe than this, I wondered. I was deeply content. I had found what I had hoped against hope I might find: a traditional Albanian world still intact.

I went back indoors and clambered underneath my quilt. The floor was hard under my hip, but what did I care?

*

At 4.30 a.m. it was still dark and cold. Starlight twinkled through shutter-cracks in the glassless windows. Rustem's wife came in and shook us awake. We rose, and the two Albanian men wiped a thimble of cold water into their eyes. Quilts and bedding were rolled up by Rustem's wife, and sweet black Turkish coffee brewed on the camping gaz.

Rafiq was in a lather to be away. He was terrified of missing his nine o'clock start at the *bashkir*. Punctuality was one habit the Albanians had not lost from the Communist years. 'You were shot if you were late more than twice', I had been told, laconically, about time-keeping under Enver Hoxha.

The dog had been rechained; I made my way across the courtyard through the twilight in rubber clogs to the medieval outhouse, to a chorus of canine baying with accompaniment of grinding iron against stone: how he would just love to rend my pallid *giaour* flesh!

At the last instant Rustem concluded that he couldn't bear to be left alone with the sheep for another day. On the spur of the moment he decided to come down to Peshkopi with us to sell some raki and goat's cheese. He was a countryman, though, and moved at a rustic pace in his preparations. Rafiq stumped about, fuming impatiently.

I said to Rustem's wife 'Frësk!' and rubbed my hands to illustrate the chill. She looked at me as if I was completely crazy. For her this was a hot midsummer's morning, I realised. I lost face completely, too, for having deigned to speak to a woman. The look she gave me expressed the abyss of her contempt.

Finally, Rafiq said we could wait no longer, and away we strode. Rustem rushed after us, carrying two flagons of raki and a bundle of cheese. It took him several hundred yards to catch us up. Rafiq's watch had stopped – panic, confusion. The race down the mountain path became a Keystone Cops affair, sliding, slipping, raki spilling, shouting, mayhem.

We took a perilous short cut down a goat track and nearly all tripped over a precipice into a ravine. Finally, panting and heaving, we arrived at a cut-off below Kallë Dodes where we would waylay the bus. We waited with a mounting sense of anti-climax. Nothing happened for half an hour, except a slow accretion of peasants in homespun and white fezzes carrying market-bound sacks, each of whom looked at me with frank amazement.

It was our turn to look amazed when a smart new Mercedes minibus with 'Tirana' emblazoned on the front as its destination now rolled down the hill from Kallë Dodes, the driver shouting at us to make ready. It had arrived the night before from the capital with a group of young men just returned from Italy. Now it was heading back empty, though not via Peshkopi. We waited on.

Finally our ancient bus arrived. I paid for all three of us – it was the least I could do. In his own house Rustem had been a self-confident, self-possessed patriarch, but as we ground down the mountain slowly, signs of approaching civilisation appearing one by one – the first bridge, the first car, the first food aid truck with flour sacks, the first shop, policeman, 4-wheel-drive jeep – at each of these Rustem shrank into himself more and more, and seemed to grow humble as well as silent. He had been happy to talk to me boldly up in his own *kula*, and tell me about everything in his village. Down here in the valley he was a tongue-tied mountain man.

In Peshkopi he waved goodbye shyly, and without waiting to shake hands, slipped away into the morning market crowds with his flagons of raki and cotton-bundled goat's cheese under his arm.

16

Pistol Practice in the Dust

'Let us see how well an English can shoot . . .'

THE DRIVER REACHED into his waistband at the small of his back and pulled out an automatic pistol. He removed the magazine and slipped one bullet into the chamber.

Flashing me a smile of broken, yellowing teeth, he held out the pistol to me, butt first.

'Let's see how well an English can shoot', he said.

The Mercedes 309 had broken down for the third time. Already two of the young men from the minibus were levering a rock into place twenty metres away by the side of the road as a target. We were high in the mountains, on the dirt track road from Peshkopi to Kukes, miles from anywhere. Apart from the wind there was no sound. Dust covered the vehicle like a shroud; dust whirled about our feet like cloud; dust caked our eyes, our lips, our throats.

Three small children had been sent down to the river bed with plastic buckets to find water for the overheated engine. I was supposed to have been in Kukes two hours ago to catch the MAF light plane to Bajram Curri. It was four o'clock already and the plane left in half an hour; I wasn't going to make it. There wasn't another plane for a week. I was going to have to continue like this, crawling through bandit country – if I ever even got as far as Kukes.

I examined the driver's pistol with feigned admiration.

'Amerikanski?'

'Sovietski!' he replied, and indicated with much grinning and waving that I should take a pot-shot at the target.

The gun had a Soviet star on the hand grip. It was a Markarov 7.5 mm automatic, the standard Eastern-block side-arm, perhaps looted from the state armouries in 1991, or else bought or stolen from a policeman or army officer.

To my right, under the shade of the cliff face, stood a group of Gheg men in their twenties, my fellow passengers, each of them dressed in '70s Oxfam style, with longish hair and sideburns. They weren't smiling and grinning. Their faces were pinched and hostile. For the last three hours they had been passing sarcastic comments in Albanian among themselves about 'rich foreigners' and *Shen Dollar* ('Saint Dollar'). I was wearing my oldest clothes, had only a plastic bag as luggage and wore no wristwatch: nevertheless, I was foreign – and therefore rich. I suspected that the young men were trying to work out how they could kill and rob me and get away with it.

The road from Peshkopi to Kukes had one of the worst reputations in all Albania, being remote and subject to frequent hold-ups, murders and robberies. There was no regular bus service, merely occasional minibuses, often driven by ex-Special Forces drivers, always armed. Most Albanians had told me there was no way of getting from Peshkopi to Kukes, other than going back to Tirana and up the coast road via Shkodra. I had spent a day asking in the market, and at the two minibus stations. No one had known anything definite, though everyone had an opinion. The consensus was that I should go back to Tirana and start again.

One taxi driver had offered to take me to Kukes for $120: this I declined. Another minibus driver said he was starting in five minutes, and that I should get aboard his Mercedes, which still had one wheel off and was nowhere in evidence; ten hours later he was still there, asleep in his cab, the wheel nowhere to be seen.

I was told by both an evangelical Christian Albanian family and the Frasheris that there was a minibus which left at either 6 a.m. or 8.30 a.m. every day, *inshallah*. So I got up at half-past five and waited at the depot, just in case. No one from the Frasheri clan offered to come with me to the bus – the first and last time this ever happened in Albania. Normally, the guest is accompanied as far he wants, or at least until the edge of the village. They probably considered me a guest of the Armstrongs.

I was still waiting there at twelve noon, tense, exhausted and dry-mouthed from too many cigarettes. The police had taken me under their wing, installing me in a small café where I was no longer pestered by small boys, hucksters and more sinister types who offered to take me to Kukes in private cars they obviously didn't have.

In June 1996 Peshkopi was still under the firm rule of law: armed police in uniform patrolled the streets and were shown every respect. Out in the country it was a different matter. There was no police presence at all. For the first time in Albania, no road blocks, no police patrolling the villages, no SHIK, nothing. I was in Ghegeria, Berisha's home territory. North of Kukes, Berisha's personal tribal territory started. Nothing underlined the intensely political nature of the country's policing more than this absence. The bulk of the armed forces were in the Tosk south, and in the capital, Tirana, to prevent the Socialists from massing and openly rebelling. The rural north was Gheg and pro-Berisha, and so could largely be left to its own devices. In spite of nearly fifty years of Communist rule, Toskeria and Ghegeria were still different countries. Hoxha had been a Tosk, Zog a Gheg: that was how it went, a Tosk ruling the whole country until a Gheg managed to defeat him and seize control. When Berisha fell, I realised, it would be to the forces of the Tosks.

Finally, at one o'clock, a Kukes-bound minibus did appear and we had left Peshkopi, the driver having been briefed by the police as to who I was and where I was going. Did I have a *shocku* ('friend') I was meeting in Kukes, I was asked insistently by both police and driver. Yes, I replied. The chief of police in Kukes – a keen evangelical Christian – was expecting me, as were my good friends the German Lutheran missionaries. No one now spoke anything but Albanian. I was having to communicate in what little pidgin I'd managed to scrape up. The invention about the chief of police I had blatantly cribbed from Dr Shkrelli in Gjirokastra. It had worked then and it worked now. I could see they were impressed. I reasoned that it was going to be that bit harder for them to risk murdering a pal of the Kukes chief of police.

My invention soon became common knowledge in the minibus, as did my putative occupation. I had to be something, obviously; there were no tourists here, and I wasn't a missionary, so a BBC journalist was easiest. I was not just the only foreign passenger on board, I was also the only foreign passenger anyone could ever remember having made this journey. On this road even the missionaries went in pairs, in their own 4-wheel-drive jeeps, leaving at odd, unpredictable times, and not stopping at all *en route*. It was, they had told me, a truly terrible road, perhaps the worst in Albania – but the scenery was sublime.

The pretence at tarmac, pocked and old though it was, disappeared after few kilometres from Peshkopi. We wrapped cloths round our faces like Arabs in the desert and tried to avoid eating too much dust. The road had degenerated into a one-lane cart track, deeply rutted and rolling in light grey dust which boiled up under our wheels like pulverised volcanic ash.

We passed through a pastoral landscape untouched since the days of antiquity, fitting subject for the palette of David Roberts, Edward Lear or even Claude Lorraine; small rectangular grey stone houses, unwhitewashed, stood baking and shimmering in the heat, their terracotta roofs glowing like fire, each dwelling surrounded by a mud-walled garden full of grapevines trellised high to give shade. In the fields stood apricot and cherry trees, laden with fruit. Oxen browsed in the fields and small, lone donkeys gazed at us with curiosity. Below, to our right, the River Drin glistened like a thin silver-blue ribbon winding through a white bouldered bed, which in spring would fill with torrents from the mountain snow melt. Along the banks by the side of the river a file of tall Asiatic plane trees rose shivering in the heat haze. I could see a mule train in the distance, led by a man in a white turban, which was crossing the river at a ford, each beast piled high with roped sacks. Beyond, across the river, rose the mountains of Serbia, a stepped mass of grey-silver rising to snow-capped peaks, a range majestic in its form and stillness. In the thermals over the valleys circled prey-questing eagles in wide, slow-motion gyre.

It might have been 1896, or a thousand years before that, or two thousand even. This was the timeless East, which was supposed to be a malevolent invention of Western orientalists, and it lay in the heart of continental Europe, in a land populated by blue-eyed, blonde-haired mountain men, a land little more than two hundred miles from Italy as the crow flies.

We passed no cars, no trucks, no villages, only mules and donkeys with old men in turbans and homespun costume or small boys in rags. The cassette machine on the minibus played Dibra wedding songs, endlessly, the churning music orientalising the landscape into something Persian. As in Peshkopi, I felt a thousand, even two thousand, miles further east than I was.

*

We rose and rose, and continued to rise, crawling on switchback turnings and hairpin bends, the dirt squealing under our slipping wheels as we ground up in whining first gear. At first I had sat next to the driver in the front, in the place of honour and most danger in the event of bandits or a crash. From here I could see the temperature gauge rising steadily until it went into the red and then stuck at the top. The driver ground on regardless, pushing the Mercedes diesel as hard as it would go.

The orchards finished. The only houses we now saw were like red, shimmering miniature shields hundreds of feet below us in the valleys, guarded by tiny silver spears of poplar.

We were mummified in dust. The windows had to be left full open or we would have roasted with the heat. After the first breakdown, the engine boiling over, we drove on with the cowling propped open to allow the air inside, to cool the motor directly. We stopped only when we broke down. No one apart from me had brought water. Everyone became thirsty, tired and sullen.

We entered a desolate upland zone, treeless and unpopulated, where great river valleys, now dry, had scoured through the scrub-covered mountains.

Though we saw no houses now or villages, from time to time we came across groups of mute, waiting Ghegs: a man and wife, a woman and two children, an old man in a turban and green skull-cap. How long had they been waiting by the roadside? How long would they have had to go on waiting, had we not turned up? One man told the driver he had been waiting for three days for a vehicle. Each morning at dawn he walked from his village in the remote mountains to the road, there to wait all day; each evening at dusk he walked back to sleep, and then to try again the next day. What was time to these people? It was all they had – and it was free.

I had moved into the back to allow these village newcomers to sit next to the driver and talk, which they did without cease, after hours or days of silent waiting. He knew them all and their families and he often refused payment, after much chaff and attempts to pay.

These Ghegs were the poorest of poor: if they had an old sack with a few vegetables in, that was wealth. They had no shoes, merely *opinga*, tied leather-and-thong sandals, or else roughly hewn clogs fashioned out of wood and cast-off car tyre rubber. Their clothes were a mixture of homespun and ancient Western Oxfam donations.

All the time I could feel a groundswell of hostility against me rising from the young Gheg men in the minibus. How could they kill and rob me, and get away with it, that was the question. They could smell the dollars in my money belt and the passport in my jacket pocket. It was as though the plumpest, the rarest of partridges had fallen into their hands.

The driver thrust his pistol at me again insistently. I bowed, hand on heart, and said 'Falerminderit, shumë, shumë, shumë' ('Thank you very, very, very much'), which was the politest way there was of saying 'No'; and turned on my heel, forcing myself to walk slowly towards the small group of women and children who stood watching us from behind the back of the minibus.

What worried me about the pistol I had been offered was the single bullet the driver had slid into the chamber. If I took it and shot at the target, the pistol would have been fired and have my finger-prints on it, but would then be empty. If I were subsequently to be shot down and robbed it could be plausibly claimed that I had pulled a pistol on a Gheg first, and then been shot in self-defence.

There were no banks outside the cities in Albania: it was necessary to carry what money you needed in cash, in dollars, in a money belt. Westerners were all rumoured to be fabulously rich. Fifty dollars would procure an assassination in highland Ghegeria, I had been told. My passport alone was worth $4,000 on the black market. Poor as I looked, I was a tempting target.

Apart from failing a local test of machismo, there was no advantage in my getting involved with pistol play in the mountains. I determined not to touch the driver's pistol at any price.

It was midsummer and hot. All the young men on the minibus were in short-sleeved shirts. The fashion in Albania was firm: men's shirts were tucked inside trousers. The only exception to this sartorial rule was that men carrying pistols in their back waistbands wore their shirts outside their trousers, for ease of access to their firearms.

I had thought hard about buying a pistol for myself on the black market in Tirana before I left for the north. It would have cost around $600 and could easily have been resold when I got back. I decided against it, in the end. It would complicate what was going to be a complicated expedition already, and might give me a false sense of security. Against automatic weapons a pistol is fairly useless, except at close quarters. I might well interpret a situation incorrectly and shoot someone by mistake. On the whole, I thought, I would be safer without a weapon.

However, I did have a small pocket camera in a black leather case. This I had strapped to my belt, in the small of my back. I left my shirt outside my trousers from Tirana onwards. The slight bulge of my camera against my shirt, and the very fact of my shirt being outside my trousers was, I estimated, almost as good as actually having a pistol. Albanians are not good at dissimulating what they think about you: it was obvious that everyone I met thought I was, in fact, carrying a pistol. Before I got to the Armstrongs' house I'd removed this *falso*, and put it in my bag; I did not want to give the missionaries the idea I was some kind of undercover agent or gunslinger.

So when I turned on my heels and walked through the late afternoon heat and dust towards the women and children by the rear of the minibus, leaving my back exposed to the driver's pistol, it was not entirely uncalculated. He, and all the young Ghegs, could surely see quite clearly the dark bulge under my shirt, right at my waistband.

I walked on in silence, my skin prickling, beads of sweat dripping from my forehead. I wanted to light up a cigarette quite badly, in spite of my parched mouth.

The silence grated on endlessly.

There was another element at play here, too. In Albania the killing of a woman does not involve *gjak*, or blood. Killing a boy-child, however young, does. Right in the line of fire were several small boys, standing with the women in front of me. If the driver or any of the young Ghegs decided to gun me down they might well hit an Albanian boy and kill him. At this range their bullets would go right through my body, even if they did get a direct hit: killing a boy, even by accident, would start a blood feud.

I made sure I was walking directly towards the oldest, largest little boy, who must have been seven or eight. I smiled at him insincerely, and kept my arms quite still and my hands well away from my waistband. I wanted to give the Ghegs behind me as many reasons as possible for not shooting me.

When I was just a few paces from the women and children, I heard the clicking of half a dozen safety catches behind me. I had obviously calculated wrongly. They were going to shoot me anyway. I kept walking.

Six pistol shots suddenly crashed and echoed all around us, waves of noise bouncing off the canyon opposite and the cliffs behind us.

I walked on unharmed, circling the women and children closely until I was quite behind them.

I turned and looked the Ghegs and the driver. They stood, their backs to me, facing the target stone, each with a smoking pistol in his hand. I'd no idea that modern – well, relatively modern – Communist-era automatic pistols still emitted such clouds of smoke. Perhaps the shells had been reloaded with home-made powder?

The men cocked again and aimed up their pieces once more. Not one of them had hit the quite large rock a mere twenty metres away. I lit a cigarette, and tried to avoid drenching it with my sweat, which seemed to be pouring off me as though I were under a shower.

*

The German Lutherans' base was a fortified apartment in a crumbling *palatti* block on the outskirts of Kukes, barred and bolted against thieves and bandits. There was neither water nor electricity when I arrived, but that I was beginning to take for granted.

No one had known where the German missionaries lived. I had been followed by three of the young Gheg men from the minibus when we finally rolled down into Kukes; they obviously still had the idea of robbing me if the opportunity arose.

Having hardly been out of sight of Albanian policemen for the last two months, it was alarming to be in a largish town where none were to be seen at all. The central streets of Kukes were all in the process of being remade, gaping trenches running down them like preparations for a war. It was the hour of the *volta* and the pavements and streets were full of people, poorly dressed and stony-faced. The *palatti* blocks were dirtier and shabbier than any I'd yet seen. There were hardly any cars.

I kept in full view of the crowds, walking down the central avenue purposefully, the three young men from the bus trailing me at about thirty yards. Where the hell were all the police? There appeared to be no Turism Hotel, no *bashkir*, no police station, nowhere into which I could dive to escape my pursuers.

Then, at a café, I saw a uniformed policeman with two crowns on his epaulettes, sitting with friends, eating ice cream and drinking coffee. I hailed him from afar as a long-lost friend, and almost ran across to him. He, of course, didn't know me from Adam. I shook his hand vigorously and knelt down beside him, there being no free chair to slump into. Immediately I pointed out the three young men from the minibus, who were wavering on the other side of the road.

'Tre banditti communisti, Signor Commandante! Uno, due, tre, la – la. Tutti con pistoli automatici – uomini tanti pericolosi', I gabbled, pointing out the three Ghegs with my outstretched arm.

The policeman was remarkably stupid: he gaped at me as if I was a madman.

'Io sono un amico personale di Presidente-Dottore Sali Berisha', I lied desperately, 'Guarda, Signor Commandante, guarda i tre banditti communisti di Peshkopia!'

I mimed the firing of pistols and indicated the three young Ghegs yet again: but they were no longer there. Wisely, they had backed away and vanished into the swirling early evening crowds.

The policeman gaped on at me: he understood not a word of Italian, French, Greek, Turkish or English.

'Turista', I croaked, 'Turista Anglisht', pointing at my own heaving, perspiration-drenched chest.

He grinned at me and waggled his head from side to side, which in Albania, like India, meant polite agreement.

'Missionari evangelici tedeschi? Il centro Cristiani?' I asked, 'Dove ci sono?'

He had no idea. Useless as he was, though, I was reluctant to leave him. He was at least a policeman and he did have a gun.

It was getting dark. There were no street lamps in Kukes that worked. I was going to have to find the missionaries soon. Waving goodbye to the useless cop, I dived into the café on whose terrace he and his pals were sitting. Inside, behind the bar, was a youngish

Albanian man, more smartly dressed than most in the streets of Kukes. In order to open a café or bar in Albania it was necessary to have saved some capital, usually in Greece or Italy. As a result, the proprietors were usually get-up-and-go types who had actually been abroad, and who therefore spoke fragments of foreign languages. The police were men of no education, from the villages.

This man understood me and spoke Italian. He immediately grasped who I wanted to find. He did not know the German Lutherans himself, but he left his bar and, taking me firmly by the sleeve and leading me as if I was a child at risk (which of course I was), he accompanied me through the crumbling, empurpled streets of night-time Kukes.

I relaxed. I had *besa* now, and no one would harm me. Paradoxically, while for the stranger in Albania danger is ever-present, for the man with *besa* there is little risk. In Gjirokastra I had been sent across the worst part of town by Dhritero with his five-year-old niece to defend me; she and his *fis* were known to all.

We wandered round for almost an hour, asking person after person. All I had to go on was 'Gunter – tedesco grande, un missionario evangelico, con barba rossa'.

Everyone had heard of Gunter. Some had even seen him. No one knew where he lived. Kukes was about the same size as Peshkopi, a small country town. Of course, there were no street signs or house numbers.

Finally, we were led down an alleyway and up the broken concrete steps of a *palatti*. I knocked on the door of the first floor, and was gratified to hear German being spoken as the door was unbolted from within.

'Welcome', a shaggy-bearded young man in white T-shirt and blue jeans said to me in English. 'We were expecting you hours ago at the airstrip. You missed the plane.'

This was Gunter. I thanked the café owner profusely in Albanian and Italian and shook his hand with heartfelt gratitude. He smiled and waved me goodbye.

Inside the apartment a group of young German and Austrian missionaries, men and women, all in their twenties, were washing up after their evening meal. They looked like students at summer camp: long hair and shorts, plastic flip-flops and tennis shoes.

I sat on the small balcony of their flat and looked down into the patch of garden below, which they were trying to get to flower. A new cement block wall ten foot high, with barbed wire on top, kept the world beyond at bay. The apartment was very small, the smallest I'd been in yet.

Gunter offered me Bulgarian mineral water and bread and cheese, which I picked at. I drank deeply of the water, though, and smoked cigarette after cigarette, trying to drain the adrenalin from my system. I told Gunter of my adventures. He was not surprised.

'It's a bad road. We guessed you'd had problems. I'll radio ahead to Bajram Curri to let them know you got here okay.'

Gunter was a muscular Christian, six foot or more, with big shoulders and bare feet. He had dark hair and a reddish-brown beard; he looked like a hippy. He was, in fact, a carpenter from Düsseldorf. He'd been in Albania three years, spoke the language and was training young Albanians to make things in wood. He had a complete workshop, with tools imported from Germany. The apartment had been largely rebuilt by him. There was a characteristically German-looking solid pinewood table on the balcony where we sat, his own work.

He was soberly realistic about the task ahead of them.

'There has been a complete breakdown of everything. No one can do anything at all any more. Anyone with a skill gets out, either to Tirana or abroad. Under Hoxha no one could move without authorisation, but now everyone can do as they like. Who would want to stay here if they could leave?'

He had trained several generations of Albanian carpenters already: they had all left Kukes for Tirana and Italy. I asked him about blood feuds.

'There have been at least thirty-eight deaths by shooting here this year so far, that we know about. In the countryside many more of course. The police don't interfere with revenge killings. Theft of anything not locked up is automatic, even a half-empty bag of cement left outside for the night.'

The missionaries had two Benz jeeps which they had to keep locked up, night and day, when not in use. You couldn't park on the streets, ever.

Inside the apartment there was a football match between Italy and Germany showing on a small black-and-white portable TV, which operated by car battery. The missionaries hospitably offered me a seat, but I couldn't concentrate on football. I just wanted to sit on the balcony and drink cold water and smoke cigarettes.

The good news was that the ferry from Kukes to Fierzë, which was only a few kilometres from Bajram Curri, was due to leave at six o'clock the next morning. It had been supposed to go the day before but had broken down. Now it was fixed. A young, rather sweet Albanian Christian convert called Peter offered to take me to the ferry point the next morning. I took up this offer with alacrity.

The water came back on again later in the evening for an hour, and I was able to get under a hot shower, which was a relief. The Germans, with characteristic thoroughness, had completely rewired and replumbed the whole apartment. There was even an imported Teutonic lavatory, complete with mid-level inspection trough. I sank onto a sprung mattress for the first time in two months and fell instantly asleep.

After what seemed like five minutes I was awoken by Peter. It was 5.30 a.m. I jumped out of bed, instantly awake, and dressed in two minutes. We drank coffee and ate rolls and jam in the hallway, which had been turned into a sort of kitchen, with stainless steel sink, taps, a worktop and fridge. The Lutherans' domestic set-up was the most professional and well organised I'd seen since I'd been in Albania.

None of them was married, and all had practical skills of one sort or another: they were plumbers, carpenters, engineers, nurses, teachers and so forth. The women lived in a separate apartment across the hallway. They lived apart, like monks and nuns, but worked and socialised together.

I realised I had slept very well, but at first couldn't work out why. Then it came to me: there had been no nocturnal gunfire. In Tirana, every night had been accompanied by random shots of pistol and rifle fire, repeated bursts from machine-guns, and the occasional crump of hand grenades. In the mornings there was never any sign of dead bodies or even blood in the streets; the buildings were so pocked with bullet-holes already that it was impossible to tell if more had been added during the night. Whether the fighting was political or merely mafiosi turf wars no one knew.

And then there was another thing; in Kukes there had been no all-night chorus of dogs howling wildly as they roamed the streets scavenging for rubbish. I asked what had happened to the Kukes dog packs.

'The police went round in trucks a few nights ago shooting them all with rifles. A few escaped, creeping away wounded, and hid until morning. Then when they crawled out, the small children chased them and stoned them to death with rocks.'

This last detail about the children with the rocks gave Peter's account its authentically piquant, Albanian flavour.

*

We walked through the silent and empty streets of Kukes as the sun came up. Peter had originally come from Tirana, where he had been converted, to work as a missionary in the north 'where the need was greatest'. He was nineteen and had absolutely no trace of Albanian arrogance, chauvinism or puffed up pride. I tested him with some terrible truths about Albania, and he happily agreed to the very worst of my analyses, which would have had Gabriel or Dr Shkrelli foaming at the mouth with outraged national honour. Christianity had converted Peter from Albanianism, a genuine triumph and the most hopeful sign I'd yet seen in this benighted land.

The miracle of Christianity, I realised, especially evangelical Protestantism, was that it sometimes – only sometimes, of course – actually managed to restrain the all too human and universal urges to pride, vanity, selfishness, and destructive family- or tribe-first loyalty. Of course, there were many, many Christians, evangelicals included, who had these faults buttressed rather than diluted by their faith, but nevertheless, in its purest form Christianity insisted on humility, and a personal reconstruction based on a higher social ethic than that of naked self-interest.

The repaired ferry boat was nowhere to be seen at the landing point. Instead there was a worn-out old wreck of a motor launch which had obviously been pensioned off decades ago, its paint peeling, now a useless rusted hulk moored with a hoary rope to an iron spike rammed in the ground.

There was no kiosk, ticket office or landing stage, just a grassy bank and the pale blue of the tranquil water.

'When does the boat arrive?' I asked Peter.

'That's it', he said, indicating the hulk.

There seemed to be no one on board. We slid down the steep banks and tried to see if there was any sign of life. A single, thin wooden plank stretched between the bank and the boat. I couldn't believe this ruin was going up the lake, or anywhere else for that matter.

'You'd better get on board', Peter said. 'It's due to leave in five minutes.'

'Please wait for me here', I begged. 'Wait to see if it actually goes.'

I walked the plank aboard. There was still no one in sight. Peter stood and looked at me from the shore.

Then, with two minutes to go, a man appeared from the bowels of the hulk, wiping his hands on a grease-stained rag.

'Fierzë – Bajram Curri?' he enquired of me. I shook my head, agreeing.

He descended into the lower depths again, started the engine and came upon deck again and told Peter to cast us off, which he did. The man pulled back the plank and off we chugged, right on time: the amazing Albanian punctuality once again.

I was the only passenger, which was a relief, for I had visions of the three young Ghegs from the minibus turning up and clambering aboard at the last minute. As if by remote control, the launch – it could hardly be called more – slid away through the utterly still waters of the lake.

I waved goodbye to Peter from the deck: 'Thank you very much for coming with me', I told him with great sincerity.

He nodded, and said: 'I will pray for you.'

17

Bandit Country

In the Footsteps of Death

'PLEASE DON'T MENTION the deceased gentleman from the Low Countries. That guy sitting there is head honcho of the clandestine goon squad in B.C. . . . The official story is that the victim in question fell off a cliff while out for a ramble in the country', muttered Karl as we approached the jeep.

The secret policeman was a dapper young man in his twenties, smartly dressed in bright-coloured casual shirt, blue jeans and trainers, with a silver-nickel Colt automatic in a brown leather shoulder holster on open display, and a new Hoeckler and Koch sub-machine gun slung over his other shoulder. He had a brown paper bag full of white cherries in one hand, which he offered me with a smile. I put my hand on heart and took a small bunch, thanking him profusely. As he bent forward, I noticed he had a packet of Dunhill King-size in his shirt top-pocket, proof positive.

Karl was in his late twenties, though with his short fair hair, clean-shaven, boyish face and bright Midwestern smile he looked younger. From Minnesota, he was the senior Lutheran missionary in Bajram Curri. I had been astonished to see him, lone gringo, standing waiting for me on the shore when the ferry docked at Fierzë.

He came down the gangplank and seized my hand and shook it vigorously. 'Great to see you safe, Robert', he said, with evident relief.

During the boat journey we had picked up half a dozen Gheg villagers: these now scrambled off and headed for a battered minibus which waited to take them the few miles up the road to Bajram Curri.

Karl had led me to a newish Japanese jeep, in which sat another young American missionary, who was introduced as Thomas – and the SHIK in the front passenger seat. Thomas had been guarding the jeep against theft, and the secret policeman had decided to grab a more comfortable ride back to town than the minibus could provide.

I thanked Karl profusely for his kindness in coming down to meet me, something I'd not expected.

'It is nothing, Robert', he replied. 'We cannot afford to risk any more, ah, accidents up here.'

Karl drove with caution up a winding road that had once been tarmac, but which now had all but returned to dirt track. I sat in the back with Thomas, who engaged the secret policeman in animated conversation in fluent Albanian. Occasionally Karl would interject as well: both missionaries wore radiant, full-time diplomatic smiles, and their Albanian was larded with elaborate politenesses and compliments. The young policeman ate cherries stolidly and kept offering the bag to Thomas and myself.

'Don't say anything at all about anything serious until we get in the apartment', Thomas managed to convey to me at one point, *sotto voce*, while Karl distracted the policeman. Underneath their bluff manner the missionaries were tense and edgy, evidently worried I might say something undiplomatic, or even dangerous. I was a completely unknown quantity to them, after all.

'Is that the Light of the Party Dam down there?' I asked, indicating the grey concrete retaining wall below us, behind which lay the dammed-up lake along which the ferry had come from Kukes. This, surely, was an uncontroversial subject. Karl confirmed my conjecture. The controlling of the River Drin to provide hydroelectric power, and to regulate flooding lower down the valley, had been one of the undeniable achievements of the Communist regime. It had been started by the Chinese, and finished, with great acrimony, by the Albanians after the split with Peking. The Albanians claimed that the Chinese had left them without even the plans to finish off the construction when the split occurred. There were dark rumours about slave labour, with many hundreds of deaths, the corpses simply slung into the concrete walls to save time and trouble. Most of the electricity generated was exported to neighbouring countries for foreign exchange.

The mountains rose steeply all around us now. Fierzë itself was nothing, merely the dam and an electrical substation. Although pitifully small and old-fashioned by Western standards, this hydro complex was impressive in the Albanian context; it was the largest industrial enterprise I'd seen that was still functioning.

The small lake steamer had provided an eye-opener of a similar sort. Although itself of great age and dilapidation, reminding me of Humphrey Bogart's *African Queen*, on the walls in the saloon there were framed black-and-white photographs of the shipyard in Durrës where the boat had originally been constructed. These spoke of an Albanian industrial world, which although only ten years or less in the past, might as well have been a century ago. Here hundreds of disciplined workers in boiler suits were hard at work welding, riveting and drilling; cranes hoisted steel segments on high, trucks delivered components, completed ships on slipways slid down into the sea. It was quite incredible amid the devastation of the country in the summer of 1996 that any of this had ever gone on. Yet the evidence was there before my eyes, and in the trembling of the diesel engine beneath my feet: once upon a time Albanians had built all this.

My attitude towards Enver Hoxha and the Communists had been changing throughout my journeys in Albania; the simplicities of Left versus Right, oppression versus freedom, simply didn't work. Albanians were very difficult to rule, perhaps incorrigible. To organise them into even the simulacrum of an industrialised society, making and producing complex machinery, was a staggering achievement. That it had been done at the cost of great, even barbaric cruelty and suffering was not in doubt; that it had been done at all was some sort of miracle. Enver Hoxha was the only man in history who had ever managed to master this unruly and anarchic people to this extent. Gabriel had told me of a supposed secret speech given by the now gaoled Communist leader Fatos Nano, delivered to Albanians from Kosovo and Macedonia in Switzerland in 1992. 'Everyone has a father good or bad, and Albania had a father and his name was Enver Hoxha', Nano was alleged to have said. Gabriel took this as evidence of great wickedness and bad faith, that Nano was an unreconstructed authoritarian Communist instead of the Democratic Socialist he now claimed to be. But if you had lived through the brutal, forced industrialisation of the country, seen its achievements and then seen the collapse, you might well consider there to be some truth in the statement. There was no law that fathers had to be good, or kind. I thought of Peter the Great, beating his Russian peasant workmen with his fists to get them to hurry, having the Winter Palace built during the winter, with huge fires made inside the ground-floor rooms to dry the plaster and stop it from freezing, of the deaths and tortures, the ferocious punishments. It was appalling, but then the present state of Albania and Eastern Europe was also appalling in other ways. There were cultures, continents even, I now suspected, that could not be run with any degree of order without strict discipline and terrible brutality. Democratic Western liberalism claimed, with little evidence, that these places could all be converted to sweetness and prosperity by embracing Enlightenment principles: the evidence was that instead they simply fell apart into anarchy when dictatorship collapsed. I couldn't bring myself to approve of Hoxha, but I began to understand what he had been up against. It was already obvious that Berisha's brand of corrupt, *laissez-faire* cronyism was going to lead to disaster sooner rather than later.

The *African Queen* steamer, once state-owned, had been given to cousins of the President, relatives from his clan. That was what 'privatisation' meant in Albania. I had been invited into the captain's cabin, up on the top deck. His whole family was there in residence: wife, brother, three children, plus a policeman cousin in uniform with gun. All of them were Berishas, passing through Berisha clan territory all day, as we zigzagged to and fro across the narrow lake – merely a dammed river valley after all – collecting peasants with goats, sheep or piles of fish from one side and depositing them on the other a few miles further down. This ferry was the only means they had of getting across, apart from primitive canoe-type wooden boats which we passed from time to time, manned by despondent fishermen in rags.

There were no villages or towns on either side of the lake, just Mediterranean scrub bush, low trees and bare beige-grey cliff faces of jagged rock. The mountains reared up thousands of feet, impenetrable and desolate. I expected to see giraffes or monkeys coming down through the gulleys to drink at the clearings, so African was the sense of virgin bush sweltering in heat. The cicadas kept up an insistent shriek all the time.

There were only two steamers on the lake, this one and another derelict moored at Fierzë which had broken down and was awaiting spares. Most of the peasants being ferried across had to pay in kind, with fish or vegetables: they had no money at all. This journey through pristine desolation made the River Congo look like the Seine.

What sort of living could this ferry bring in for the President's cousins? Surely almost nothing. I had paid 180 lek for the full distance fare – $1.80. The diesel fuel alone would have cost them $10-$20 and most of the peasants had no cash. Where was the profit? It made no sense at all. Perhaps they got the diesel free?

The policeman got off in the middle of nowhere, but there was no trouble with any of the passengers afterwards – this was their lifeline, the boat.

The scenery we passed through was magnificent though monotonous, even senseless; great fiords leading nowhere, empty, pointless beaches, unscalable peaks and cliffs. With no men or animals, no buildings or history, the banks on either side were like explorers' illustrations of the nineteenth-century Australian bush: grand but meaningless. This lake trip would be a tourist sensation if anyone knew about it, or could get to it: as it was, I enjoyed its peace and calm alone, high up above the bow, feeling like an explorer but knowing I wasn't, a highly satisfactory sensation.

*

After a drive of twenty minutes or so in Karl's jeep we came to B.C. – Bajram Curri. There were police road blocks on the way in, painted oil barrels across the road, through which one had to filter, and small sun-darkened police in blue uniforms with pistols, who were checking papers and taking bribes.There was no *pudeur* about going behind the back offside wheel up here. The cash was simply handed over and counted in full view of everyone. We were waved through untaxed, perhaps because we had the secret policeman on board.

Bajram Curri revealed itself as a small, dusty township surrounded by high, austere mountains, these treeless and grey-green with scrub and bare rock; this was the start of the *Bjeshkët e Namuna*, the Accursed Mountains, so called because it was through this chain

that the Turkish invaders had first penetrated the Albanian highlands, or else, more prosaically, because they were such an awful
range of peaks. That day these Albanian Alps were shrouded in
grey belts of thick cloud, but their bulk and immensity were impressive.

The town of Bajram Curri lay on the plain in the valley; it was
entirely a Communist invention, a planned workers' town of
Stalinist tower blocks built to be the regional capital of the Tropoja
region in place of Tropoja town itself, this thought by Hoxha to be a
nest of feudal reactionaries. Bajram Curri himself had been a local
warlord, brigand and *soi-disant* nationalist, an enemy of Zog and his
clan, who had finally been gunned down by Zog's gendarmes in a
cave just outside town in the late 1920s. On the principle that my
enemy's enemy is my friend, Hoxha had promoted the safely dead
Bajram Curri into a national hero, and named the new town after
him.

The sun shone brightly but the air was cool; we were high up in
the mountains after all. There were few people on the streets; those
that there were did not smile or look up as we passed. There were
few cars; those we passed were old and battered. This was the
poorest place I had yet seen in a poor land, worse than Leskoviku
even. The *palatti* looked as if they had been fought over many
times, and were now inhabited by refugees from a distant war
made bitter and angry. The streets were pocked and dusty, and
there was rubbish blowing everywhere, goats and sheep wandering between the tower blocks chewing discarded plastic. If it had
been smarter and less tawdry, it might have resembled a quarter of
Beirut which had been fought over and largely destroyed; but there
was not that degree of prosperity or chic. Bajram Curri resembled
a failed Soviet township from an oppressed Central Asian satrapy,
whipped and then ignored by Moscow for fifty years – a sort of
small-scale Dushanbe, though without any of that city's charm or
amenities.

There was nothing in B.C.: no proper shops, only little *dukas*, no
buses, no taxis, no garages or petrol stations – just a dusty, wide
main street two hundred yards long, with crumbling concrete
blocks leading off, fading away into vegetable gardens and sheep
pens, before the parched, crop-grassed plain commenced, where
shepherds in turbans, cloaks and ragged pantaloons walked their

spindly herds. The Communist-era museum, one of the largest and most modern buildings, was closed for ideological cleansing. The Kosovo Cinema had metamorphosed into a bingo parlour.

Karl drove off the road into a large compound surrounded by twelve-foot-high reinforced concrete segments, the whole topped with barbed wire. In the centre of this laager stood a four-legged high metal tower with a small wooden hut on the platform at the top. On a chair outside this hut sat a man with a Kalashnikov across his knees, the parking-compound guard. He raised his arm in slow-motion recognition of Karl's jeep. Karl waved back vigorously.

The three of us walked slowly through the mid-afternoon heat down the main street, for the secret policeman had got out before we entered the compound and vanished without a word.

Ringed with individual fan clubs of flies, donkeys and mules stood tethered to iron spikes embedded in the walls of the buildings; *merde*-bespattered cows wandered around the street untended. We strode along the middle of the main street akimbo, like three liberal, yet puissant Marshals confronted with the task of cleaning up a bad-ass, black-hat cowtown.

Bajram Curri evidently was the Dodge City of northern Albania. The atmosphere of imminent violence and death was palpable, of gunfights, dynamite and blood feuds. The three of us turned off the main street and waded through piles of banked up trash, picking our way over shards of broken glass and rusted cans. We passed a small state bank guarded by two fatigued-looking policemen in uniform with machine-guns at the ready. Next to the bank stood a small, empty Communist-era tin shed, a sort of cone-roofed kiosk with glassless windows. I thought this was probably a defunct tobacco shop. I asked Karl, pointing it out.

'It's for sheltering the cops, when it rains. They have to be on duty twenty-four hours a day against armed robberies', he told me.

'Not that their presence stops the thieves', Thomas added. 'The raids are running at about two a month now. The cops just throw down their guns and run away when they attack. Who is going to die for $75 a month, after all? The last raid the hoods used a bull-dozer with welded steel protection plates.'

'When was the last robbery?' I asked.

'Two weeks ago', replied Thomas. 'But that time they didn't even manage to get the money up here from Tirana. The bandits ambushed the car on the road. They got away with $25,000 in lek. The government salaries here are sometimes six months in arrears.'

'Why don't they fly the cash up in helicopters?' I asked.

'They'd shoot 'em down with stingers', replied Thomas laconically.

Karl and Thomas were not like any missionaries I'd yet met, but then Bajram Curri was not like any town I'd been in before. The missionaries in Albania all found their own level, somehow. In easygoing, relaxed Peshkopi it was families with kids, happy, jolly singalong-type church services with guitars and Hammond organ, including my first ever experience of the DIY, self-service, smorgasbord Holy Communion. In besieged, gun-happy, dog-hunting Kukes it was muscular German counter-cultural types with power tools and beards. Here in Bajram Curri were the hip young missionary gunslingers – cowboys for Christ I ended up calling them. They were fit and smart as paint, sharp of eye and tongue, bright but laidback, with highly polished smiles and much practised banter in Albanian – Jesus's cool dudes, in fact. There was an undercurrent of *humour noir* to both Karl and Thomas which grew as I got to know them better.

They were a highly intelligent duo who had worked out a sort of double act: Karl was the enthusiastic, dominant one, the team leader with pep and vim. Thomas was his smiling sidekick, more cynical and diffuse, a natural second in command. You could have based a TV series round them, a missionary Starsky and Hutch.

They walked on either side of me, as if I was under escort – which of course I was. It was obvious that nothing could or should be said in the streets and alleys of Bajram Curri, so we remained silent.

The atmosphere was bright with sunlight and closely oppressive. I felt tense and prickly, as if I was being examined by many hidden eyes. We were surrounded by high *palatti* all round us. Into one of these we now entered, climbing the concrete stairs quickly. On every floor was an open window-hole, glassless, frameless, looking down on the litter-strewn waste ground below. Each of the apartments had great welded steel iron cage doors in front of its front doors, bolted and padlocked for security.

We came to Karl's apartment and pushed the bell: inside, a twittering bird call sounded, a South-East Asian style announcement of arrival. Bolts and locks were undone, and the door opened. We went inside, to be greeted by Sally, Karl's English wife, an attractive, dark-haired girl in her late twenties, originally from Bath. Her accent had taken up North American cadences from close proximity to her husband and his colleagues.

We kicked off our shoes and went into the living room. There was a big electric fan, a large TV, a settee and easy chairs, carpets. The place was neat, orderly, clean and freshly painted. We sat down and Sally brought us soft drinks, coffee, fruit and bon-bons wrapped in paper foil. Although I was a Westerner, as they were, we had all been with Albanians for so long that we responded to each other according to Albanian etiquette: much smiling, bowing, offering and accepting of sweets, compliments and head-shaking of sympathetic agreement. Karl and Thomas often spoke to each other in Albanian, or else in a mixture of American and Albanian. They had been in Bajram Curri for almost three years.

It took a while for the aura of the now absent secret policeman fully to evaporate. Neither Karl nor Thomas wanted to talk about the murdered Dutchman. Instead they told me about the situation in the region generally.

'Tropoja people are regarded in the rest of Albania as being stupid, aggressive, lazy and macho, all of which is true', Thomas told me. There was no employment and no chance of any ever coming to the region. All the Communist enterprises had collapsed and basic subsistence shepherding was all that was left. A steady drift of young people to Tirana had been in progress since 1991. There was no tradition of emigration to America or Italy up here: this was the heartland of old mountain Illyria, to where the ancient Albanians had retreated to escape the Slavic invasions of Kosovo and Montenegro, and later that of the Turks. They bore the grudges of centuries of dispossession: their mountain land was poor and hard but, until Communism, they had at least been free. Hoxha had disarmed them and reduced the resistance of the tribes by terror. 'He hanged one man in every *fis* from the family doorpost', Gabriel had told me.

Now Communism was over and all the men in Djakova had weapons again, either pistols or machine-guns. You simply weren't a man without a weapon. Rocket launchers and landmines were freely available for cash, looted – like the guns – from the Communist armouries in 1991.

The whole region was once again gripped by blood feuds and revenge killings, some over land, some over ancestral quarrels. There was no knowing how many were killed every week, but it was certainly many hundreds. Whole valleys now had no men in evidence at all: they were hiding in the tall stone towers of refuge because of clan vendettas. In the five years since the fall of Communism the region had gone right back to the state of endemic lawlessness described by Edith Durham in 1908. The Communists had not abolished the blood feud, merely nationalised it. Everyone had owed the state blood if they transgressed. As the land had been privatised under Berisha, so had the revenge killings. SHIK was not Sigurimi; they would not avenge blood; that the *fis* now had to do for themselves, as in the days of Zog and the Ottomans. Hoxha had tried to abolish feudalism by creating an industrial economy and a modern, industrial mentality. It hadn't worked. The economy had been feudalism in modern disguise, a Potemkin industrial village. Like so many Third World countries, all Albania's apparent ideological volte-faces and revolutions were merely mimicry, grotesque reflections of what was happening for real in the larger world outside. Albania had been Stalinist in the same way that Paraguay under Stroessner had been Fascist.

Now there was shooting every night on the streets of Bajram Curri. No one went out of doors at night unless they had armed business to conclude. The town's last dentist had been shot dead at 9 a.m. on the steps of his surgery the week before I arrived: a blood feud. The town's best doctor had just left for new post in Vlora; the day before he went he blew up the apartment of a family with which his *fis* was in blood; using landmines to blow up apartments was a recent innovation. The whole family, eight adults and twelve children had all been killed. On coming out of Karl's apartment early one morning he and Thomas had seen three men engaged in a complicated shoot-out by the entrance: one man had been on the ground, fighting with another, *mano a mano*, each of them with a pistol in his hand, while a third had danced around trying to get a clear field of fire with his machine-gun, aiming at one of the two figures rolling in the trash before him. Eventually he had loosed off a burst, which had killed the intended victim, but also wounded his friend. The wounded friend, now in agony from the stray bullets, had shot dead the man with the machine-gun, and thereby started yet another blood feud. Karl and Thomas had watched all this, appalled, from the doorway of their *palatti*. They never allowed their wives to go out of the apartment unaccompanied, ever.

Thomas had married an Albanian girl from Tirana, who was now expecting their first child. The two missionaries usually drove together, in one of their two jeeps, and never on a predictable route or at the same time of day. They had not yet been ambushed but they regarded it as inevitable, eventually.

In the winter the town was under snow for several months at a time, and often without food, electricity, heating or water. People just went to bed to keep warm and stayed there.

There was, as it happened, neither water nor electricity when I arrived – this in a town right next to a vast reservoir of fresh water which generated massive amounts of hydro-power. The electricity sub-station was controlled by a Democrat *fis*, the water pumping station by a Communist *fis*. As they were locked in a blood feud neither would agree to supply their enemies with either power or water. Each *fis* despatched furious telegrams to Tirana blaming the other. Meanwhile the town operated on candles and water brought up in buckets from polluted wells. Typhoid had already broken out, and cholera could not be far behind. The missionaries used bottled mineral water, trucked in from Shkodra, a day's combined ferry journey and drive away. The border with Serbia was only a few kilometres from B.C., but had been closed for years, due to the arms smuggling, violence and general lawlessness of the Albanians from Tropoja, who had robbed and raped extensively when allowed into Kosovo.

Few of the police in Bajram Curri bothered with holsters for their pistols – they just stuck them in their belts for ease of access. Although they never got involved in blood feuds, they did shoot to kill on the least provocation and then 'disappeared' the bodies to avoid any investigation or revenge killing from the victims' *fis*.

After a long struggle, the town had only just changed hands from Communist rule. The recent election victory by the Democrats had been celebrated by night-long volleys from Kalashnikovs in the streets. The police had rumbled up in a truck from their barracks, not to close down the celebrations, as Thomas had at first thought, but to add to the *feux de joie* with their own automatic rifles.

In the midst of this litany of woe, it slipped out that two

Hungarian doctors had recently been held up by bandits just outside the village of Valbona, a noted beauty spot a few kilometres north of Bajram Curri. Unwisely, they had two large cameras on open display and these had excited the cupidity of the local brigands, who had robbed them of everything they possessed and then shot one of the doctors in the knee with a Kalashnikov to prevent them following the thieves. The Berisha government in Tirana, whose guests the doctors were, had sent a helicopter up to Bajram Curri to evacuate them. The wounded doctor had refused to be treated in the hospital in Bajram Curri, which he knew well. It was regarded as sentence of death even to enter this place, which was the last repository of people dying of everything from syphilis to bubonic plague, and which had neither drugs nor equipment. Everything of any value, including the beds, had been sold into Serbia years ago.

'If you remember seeing the Turkish hospital scene in the movie *Lawrence of Arabia*, that is what the Bajram Curri hospital looked like in its glory days under Communism, when things were all ticketyboo up here', Thomas had told me. 'And it's been downhill all the way since then . . .'

In this unpromising environment Thomas and Karl had opened an office on the main street which they called a 'Tourist Agency'. There was a carved wooden sign outside advertising the place, which creaked in the wind with a melancholy, authentically Wild West note. Inside lay brochures in English and Albanian which the optimistic missionaries had had printed up, these lauding the undeniable physical beauty of the region. But where were the tourists going to come from? Afghanistan? Somalia? Iraq? What jaded palate would be titillated by the blood feuds and verminous *palatti* of Tropoja? Bajram Curri made Haiti and Liberia look like the Côte d'Azure. Perhaps one could start a specialist travel agency for such places, Dystopian Tours Inc., which would specialise in Graham Greene-style Third World disaster areas. Every client could be guaranteed at least dysentery and gunshot wounds, with a no-quibble money-back guarantee. B.C. would certainly qualify.

'We were trying to get some sort of legal activity going that puts money directly into the pockets of the locals', Karl explained. 'And also we try to ensure that the few visitors who do come up here have an armed guard and so are not robbed and killed.'

Neither the Dutchman nor the Hungarians had had an armed guard. I asked how many tourists actually did come here. There was an embarrassed pause.

'Well, in the winter none, of course, because we're cut off by snow. And in the summer, well, maybe one a week – or perhaps one a month . . . '

The aura of the dead Dutchman's fate still hung over us like a miasma. Gradually I managed to coax some of the elements of the drama out of the missionaries, bit by bit.

The Dutchman had met his end in the village of Curri i Siperm, the site of many fine fortified *kulas* some kilometres to the south of Bajram Curri, in the region of Lekbibaj. This rugged tribal territory of the Nikaj had always been a nest of hardened villains and men on the run from blood feuds elsewhere, even in Turkish times. It was extremely mountainous and difficult to get into. Now it was home to a gang of about 200 desperados who, owing blood in their own villages, had nothing to lose and so had formed themselves into a traditional Albanian corps of brigands. They were well armed with jeeps, heavy machine-guns, mortars, bazookas, landmines and grenades. They used to descend on the villages in the region *en masse*, assaulting the fortified *kulas* with rockets and mortars. If the police had not already run away, they were caught and killed, as were all the men they could seize. The women and children were raped, and everything portable was stolen. No one risked going up into Lekbibaj now – except the Dutchman, who had been after adventure.

His end was clouded in mystery and rumour. Some said the family he had been staying with had turned on him, others that the bandits had done away with him for his money and wristwatch. What was certain was that his battered body had been found at the foot of a cliff near Curri i Siperm, his hands tied together and his body showing signs of having been tortured before death. His head had not been cut off, but in the mortuary the police had not allowed anyone to examine him below the waist. The suspicion that he had been castrated was therefore not allayed. Karl had been called to the mortuary to identify the body. He had been given to understand very clearly that if he spoke about the incident to anyone his residence permit would be revoked. The Dutchman's father had spent a week in B.C., staying with Karl and his wife. He had just left, the day before I arrived. The official story that the lad had had a climbing accident was accepted by his father, 'who had not wanted to know the truth', according to Thomas. The assumption they had all made when they heard I was coming up – me advertised from Tirana as 'a journalist from the BBC' – was that I was hot on the heels of the story. This put the missionaries in a quandary – to help me and get the truth out to the world – or to remain silent and protect their own position? I made it quite clear I was not going to report on the allegedly murdered Dutchman, except in the context of my book, which would not appear for a year or more, and then only in England. This cleared their minds a good deal.

There were four policemen in Curri i Siperm but they could do nothing, it seemed. They were poorly armed, and if the bandits came they simply ran away. They had been replaced by others several times to no avail: the bandits were stronger and more ruthless than the Democrat police could ever be. All this explained why Enver Hoxha had been so successful: he was a more brutal and better organised bandit than the bandits who had opposed him.

These Nikaj outlaws were all Catholics, not Moslems, but just to show they didn't care for convention, they had raided a Catholic mission and raped all the nuns, so there, yah-boo. The Italian Franciscans hardly came up into the highlands any more, as they had in Edith Durham's days. They couldn't get the volunteers. The Roman Catholic Church had been reduced to importing Brazilian priests into Mirdita, I'd heard – but Mirdita was relatively civilised compared to Djakova. The evangelicals knew of some Catholic missionaries near Shkodra, but not in Tropoja.

I queried the rumours I had heard of young girls of fifteen being kidnapped from school for sale as prostitutes in Italy.

'Not only are they kidnapped', Karl added, 'but many of them volunteer rather than marry the men their fathers have sold them to.'

In the highlands of Albania young girls of twelve or so have always been frankly sold as wives from one tribe to another, often having been betrothed at four or five, the money changing hands then. Many revenge killings between men occurred because girls refused to go to the man they had been sold to and instead ran away with another, her family refusing to return the money. Sometimes a substitute wife was forcibly abducted from the tribe by the bilked clan, which often caused resentment and eventually feud and then revenge killings, which once started went on tit-for-tat for ever. The central tenet of the *kanun*, that women should be obedient to their fathers and their husbands, was very important; the whole process of exogamous arranged marriages outside the tribe depended on the acceptance by the women of their fate. The development to cash-economy prostitution in Italy from arranged tribal marriages was only a logical extension of this system, after all. It was said that there was still a great deal of venereal disease in the mountains, especially syphilis, which the Communists had never managed to eradicate in spite of continued attempts. Incest was so common as to be unremarkable. Sisters-in-law were taken in common-law concubinage by a man when his brother died, her children becoming his. To anyone familiar with the domestic arrangements of the Old Testament there was nothing unusual to be discovered in highland Albania in 1996.

'The only place Tropoja can be compared to is Afghanistan', Karl told me. He had missionary friends there and they had swapped notes. 'Or Tajikistan', added Thomas, pouring me more mineral water.

Personally, I doubted if there was anywhere left in Afghanistan still as pre-Islamically pagan as the Accursed Mountains. Rather, rural Djakova resembled Kafiristan before its conquest and conversion into Nuristan by a proselytising Moslem army from Kabul in the 1890s. Communism might have briefly nationalised the Tropojans' sheep and goats, but it didn't appear to have changed their belief system or customs a whit.

The evangelical organisations had registers for the most dangerous places for their missionaries: Tropoja was rated as second only to Afghanistan, where the Christian proselytisers were beheaded if caught.

At the time it seemed to me that the anarchy of Lekbibaj was probably an aberration, but it was later to reveal itself as the first outbreak of the disease which was to engulf the whole country in March 1997. Even in my most pessimistic moods I could not have predicted such a collapse so quickly.

Thomas left us as dusk started to fall. He had to get back to his wife in their apartment before the unofficial curfew, and the gunfire, started.

I had asked the missionaries about the local Turism Hotel, but they had been vehement in their condemnation.

'It is dangerous. The locks don't work, there have been thefts, rapes and violence there committed by the owner and his family.'

'You will stay here with us as our guest', Karl had insisted.

They had a spare bedroom and small library of books in English on Albania, including the first – and last – copy I ever saw of the *Kanun of Lek Dukagjin* in English. I did not protest very hard in my token attempt to refuse their offer of hospitality.

Sally prepared a light supper of boloney sausage, salad, cheese, yoghurt and bread with honey. Karl and I had a couple of beers each, and watched satellite TV, the power having come on again for a few hours, as it sometimes did in the early evening.

While the gunfire started outside as a light fugue and distant pizzicato, we watched in lurid reds and greens a tennis match beamed from the Wimbledon championship. The plump, prosperous crowds, the tanned players in neat white sports clothes, the order and applause, the voice of the umpire, clipped and British, all flickered and echoed unreally in this Stalinist apartment in a ruined town lost in the mountains on the edge of the world. The slow, liturgical ceremony spoke of a world of order and civilisation which I had almost forgotten. I gaped at the spectacle in amazement. Where were the goats chewing rubbish, the police with machine guns, the ragamuffin children with snot dribbling down their noses?

In Tirana I had sat with Alexei in his living room watching a TV programme on the European Union. There had been clips of Brussels, big buildings, conferences, then a sudden shot of a car plant in Germany, thousands of brand-new automobiles rolling out of an assembly line like robot soldiers, filmed grandiosely, as if by Leni Riefenstahl. Alexei's jaw had dropped with amazement.

'Wah!' he had exclaimed, at the brute force of the image: technology, science, capital, organisation, power, order, industry and a high conceptual civilisation all combined as one crushing juggernaut which could not be denied.

Confronted with two tennis players and the serried ranks of smartly dressed spectators in faraway London, I now felt that same force of shock. It was so ordered, so formal, so regulated and well behaved, so improbable. How could you ever get human beings to comport themselves in such an impeccable fashion? It didn't speak of money, but of rules voluntarily obeyed, reasonable laws formulated by intelligent, civilised people with the good of the community at heart, of trust, compromise, safety and peaceful co-existence. Everything Albania wasn't, in fact.

No wonder there was such a slow, vast march of desperate people from the Third World to Europe and North America! If you lived in Bajram Curri and could see this on TV every night, of course you would just get up and walk towards it, if you possibly could. How wise Enver Hoxha had been to keep foreign TV out of Albania!

As W. B. Yeats so clairvoyantly prophesied, the slow beast, whose time had come, was slouching towards Bethlehem to be born, this not Communism or Fascism or fundamentalism – but simply a mass of poor, desperate people from ruined countries; nightly we were watching the beast's universal dreams and hearing its anthems and siren songs on our TV sets, this beast which would in time overwhelm us and destroy us in its desire to become like us.

18

Cowboys for Christ

Teething Trouble with My Bodyguards

THE POLICE STATION in Bajram Curri was an armed fortress, with loopholes for rifles and metal-covered slits instead of windows. There was no one outside on duty. Karl and I walked through the entrance and into the lobby. There, behind a defensive concrete breastwork we could just see the eyes and mouth of the man on duty.

Karl spoke to the man fervently and ingratiatingly in Albanian. Two dark eyes looked at Karl impassively, the mouth saying nothing, merely grunting from to time.

Our plan was to hire a detachment of armed police, and then for the two of us to go up together with a mule train into Lekbibaj, to Curri i Siperm. Writing this now, in the light of subsequent events, I think we both must have been mad. The Dutchman had just been murdered in Curri i Siperm, two Hungarians had been held up and one shot, and we were proposing an expedition into the heart of bandit country with police we knew would simply throw down their Kalashnikovs and flee at the first sign of trouble.

What were we thinking of? I suppose a sense of *fin d'époque* was starting to grip both Karl and me, that unless we did what we wanted to do now, immediately, we would never be able to. Democrat Albania was crumbling around us. There would never be another chance for an expedition like this. Karl had been in B.C. for three years and never managed to get into the wilds; now he could leave his wife in the care of Thomas, and go up into the Accursed Mountains with me. While Karl could not in conscience take up firearms himself, he knew that I had no such qualms: when I went into the badlands, if I managed to get there at all, I was certainly going to be part of a well-armed expedition.

The money was not a problem. It only cost $10 a day to hire a guard. The problem was the arrant cowardice of the Albanian police, who shivered and trembled behind their fortified walls in town, rather than going out on patrol and taking on the bandits, whose raids were weekly growing ever closer to Bajram Curri.

After long confabulations with the police chief, via the eyes and mouth of the desk officer, we were told that we were quite at liberty to go up into Lekbibaj ourselves, but that under no circumstances would any police be allowed to go with us, pay as much as we might.

Karl and I went back to his apartment to think again. Sally was visibly relieved that we had failed in this obviously unwise plan. Curri i Siperm was one of the places I had always intended to get to. The other was the alpine range right on the border of Montenegro and Serbia, off limits for over fifty years to all foreigners. This was simply the remotest and most difficult place to get to in the Albanian mountains, perhaps in all Europe. There were no roads and no villages. The passes were only clear of snow for three months a year or less. Apart from the summer shepherds in the high alpine *bjeshkë*, the only inhabitants were wolves, bears, eagles and bandits on the run. The frontier was not patrolled regularly; it was too high and too rugged. There were frequent raids across the border by Serbs, Montenegrins and Albanians on each others' flocks when the weather permitted. Even the British liaison officers in the Second World War had never managed to get up into this region.

The Moslem tribes of Djakova, which included the Tropoja region and across the border into Serbian Kosovo, were traditionally the most xenophobic in Albania, and the most difficult to travel among. In 1908 Edith Durham, though well armed, well guarded and herself speaking fluent Albanian, had the greatest difficulty even getting into Djakova at all, and had found out little from the people about their customs. Virtually no Westerners had been up into this part of the Accursed Mountains since.

It was now or never. Soon the summer would be waning, the passes closed again. I was determined to strain every nerve to mount an expedition into this forbidden region, and luckily Karl felt the same.

While intense negotiations were set afoot with a reliable *fis* from the mountains not currently at blood, who might provide me with an armed escort, Karl introduced me to a potential translator. He was called Jules, and was billed as 'having a degree in English from Tirana University'.

Jules turned out to be a weedy youth in his early twenties with round granny glasses, his bee-sting mouth decorated with wispy moustache and goatee. He looked like a decadent, absinthe-drenched French poet from the late nineteenth century, droopy and emaciated from profligate over-indulgence in nameless vices. On investigation he proved to have a certificate in TV repair mechanics from a Tirana college, rather than a degree in English, and was currently employed calling the numbers in the town's electronic bingo parlour which had once been the Kosovo Cinema. The proprietor of this establishment was a local boy made good who had escaped into Serbia over the mountains in Communist days, got to Italy and eventually saved some capital. With the fall of the old regime he had returned and set up the electronic bingo, which facility was popular with the bored male *jeunesse dorée* of B.C. and its outstations. Festooned in illegally held automatic rifles and machine-guns, their belts drooping with grenades, these young sprigs sat in front of their electronic modules all day, while Jules, the local intellectual, did the 'Legs Eleven' for them from the illuminated podium. This was all B.C. now had to offer in the way of culture. Irate losers would fire off volleys of machine-gun bullets through the ceiling, but an attempt to threaten Jules personally with a pistol for an alleged unfair call had met with an instant response from the owner, who had shot the threatener through the heart with a German hunting rifle, thereby starting yet another of the town's innumerable blood feuds. The owner had not been in the slightest bit worried about his employee's personal safety; rather, he was concerned for his own precious electronic equipment, which Jules was standing in front of, and which the owner could neither get repaired nor replace in Albania.

Jules doubled as the in-house sparks, hence the relevance of his TV-repairing diploma. He had learnt serviceable, if painstaking, English from various aid workers who, from time to time, descended on B.C. to distribute clothes, food or goodwill, before being driven out by the town's frontier lawlessness and violence.

The plan now was for the *fis* of the Engels-Mustaphas to send down an armed guard with a Kalashnikov from the high mountain pastures, and then to accompany Jules and me up there on foot and by mule, if mules could be procured. Once in the mountains we would be regaled with tribal hospitality; lambs would be slaughtered in our honour and seethed in their mothers' milk. We would go wolf-hunting on horseback with antique breech-loaders, drink home-distilled whortleberry raki, carousing the night away with plaintive mountain ballads, and generally living the life of Balkan Reilly.

I detected a silent expression of skepticism about this alluring fantasy on the face of Thomas – Doubting Thomas, as I'd already privately dubbed him – while the scheme was being woven into theatrical existence. The scheme suited Jules, on the other hand, because he was dying to get out of the bingo parlour; it suited me because I wanted to get up to mountain *bjeshkë*; it suited Karl because he had to go off to Tirana on business with his wife, and he wanted to see my mission afoot before he left. The problem, as I saw it, was that the Engels-Mustapha clan had very little to gain by it.

Karl and I had gone to negotiate with the representative of the *fis* in B.C., Abdullah Engels-Mustapha, who was none other than the man with the Kalashnikov who sat on the top of the metal tower all day, guarding the town's complement of cars. This service came pricey – Karl paid almost $50 a week for his jeep to be corralled – but it was essential. Cars parked on the streets, even by day, were stolen, vandalised or had limpet bombs attached underneath them. The compound was one of the few businesses in B.C., apart from the bingo, that was obviously thriving.

We climbed up the metal ladder and squatted down beside Abdullah, who was a slight, tubercular-looking man perhaps in his late forties, with many gold teeth and a radiant, insincere smile. He and I plied each other with L & M cigarettes, accompanied by much bowing and waggling of heads and exaggeratedly polite lighting of each other's smokes.

Karl did the talking in Albanian. The sun beat down on us through the thin mountain air, and I felt beads of sweat running down my ribs like shards of melting ice.

I was unhappy that Karl was not to be coming with me. I had no faith in Jules at all. I had very little faith in Abdullah, who struck me as too much like a stage villain not in fact to be a real one. As for the brother with the Kalashnikov, who knows? Nevertheless, it was all settled: terms, times of departure, payment on safe delivery of myself back in town and so forth. We shook hands and departed.

'Are they a trustworthy *fis*?' I asked Karl.

He was vehement: 'They are the most trustworthy *fis* in the region. I'd stake my life on their honour. They will look after you, Robert.'

I trusted Karl, and I respected his judgement. Perhaps it would be okay. We went back to his apartment for lunch. There was, in fact, a small restaurant in town, and every evening I took Karl and his wife, Sally, and Thomas and his wife, Valbona, for a meal as my treat. They wouldn't hear of me paying for my accommodation with them, so this was a fair compromise. We used to have thinly beaten steaks with yoghurt and *garniture* – that is, chips, salad and mayonnaise, plus bottles of Italian or sometimes Tirana beer to drink, depending on what had arrived on the ferry from Shkodra. So I didn't feel bad about eating a light lunch *chez* Sally and Karl every day, quid pro quo.

After lunch we were all having our siesta when the bird twitter at the door announced unseasonal visitors. I was deep in Edith Durham's *Tribal Customs of the Balkans* – another book I'd not managed to get hold of in London – and so was only gradually drawn out into the living room by my growing curiosity about the newcomers.

A gaggle of Albanian males in their early twenties had delivered an exotic cargo to Karl's threshold, not knowing what else to do with it. This turned out to be two female American hikers strapped to rucksacks almost as big as themselves. The girls were in their early twenties, and dressed in lumberjack shirts and jeans, with chunky ankle boots. They looked tired, hot, confused and worried.

Karl and his wife simply gaped, then invited them in, gently shooing away the Albanian escort party with great politeness. I watched all this from my half-opened door, and could not resist quickly dressing and coming out to hear their tale.

One was a postgraduate student, and the other had a job as a *speakerine* on Blue Danube Radio, a station in Vienna I'd never heard of. I suppose they were twenty-two or twenty-three. They did mumble their names, which were reminiscent of artificial fibres: Raylene, Shirlene, Lurleen, something like that. But as one was small and dumpy and the other tall and lanky, I thought of them immediately as Stan and Ollie; and that, I regret to say, is how I continued to think of them from then onwards.

They had hitched a ride on a food aid truck bringing up sacks of flour from Shkodra as far as Theth; then they had gone on foot to Valbona, and so down to Bajram Curri. Sally, Karl and I were shocked into silence by the banal recitation of this information.

The track – and it was a footpath only – which led from Theth to Valbona, was reckoned to be one of the most dangerous in northern Albania. No police dared patrol it, and there were frequent robberies, rapes and murders in the region through which it passed. No one, not even the boldest Albanian, used this track unless armed and accompanied by armed friends. It was impassable to either motor vehicles or mules. Just outside Valbona only the week before, it was on this Theth track that the Hungarians had been ambushed, robbed and one of them shot.

Stan and Ollie knew nothing of any of this and cared even less. They had been begged by their Albanian friends in Theth not to walk to Valbona – a good day's tramp – but they had ignored their pleas. In the end the *fis* had sent a youth with an old shotgun with them as a guard, and it was this, surely, which had saved them from assault. The youth would have been given instructions to get himself killed rather than let the guests of the *fis* be attacked. The bandits would have known this, and known that by killing the Albanian guard they would get themselves in a blood feud with a possibly powerful *fis* in Theth, an unattractive proposition. The Dutchman and the Hungarians had no local kin to revenge them, hence their extreme vulnerability without an Albanian guard. The Hungarians had refused to pay $10 a day for an armed guard, as had the Dutchman.

The two girls represented a staggering prize for the local bandits: two American passports, worth $6,000 each, great rucksacks full of still and video cameras, Walkman stereos, new Western clothes, make-up, hiking boots and money belts with thousands of dollars inside. And this in a region where people were regularly murdered for their old boots by those who had none.

Sally made instant coffee for the girls, while Karl and I gently tried to point out, as tactfully as we could, that their safe arrival in B.C. was something of a miracle, that perhaps they should be more careful in future. It was obvious from the hardening of their eyes and facial muscles that this well-meant advice was taken in quite a different spirit.

Stan and Ollie were professional feminists. Karl and I were evidently traditional patriarchal males, up to our old tricks of attempting to disempower liberated women by playing the protective-detention, false chivalry card.

Stan and Ollie were determined to do Albania, and that meant the mountains of the bandit north. They reminded me of young American travellers I'd met who claimed it would be 'real neat' to catch malaria in Africa. That cerebral malaria could and did kill you they decried as 'bullshit, man'. Karl was a practising Christian and felt obliged to help his fellow man, even if incorrigible. I didn't. I let him take the strain of trying to convince Stan and Ollie. Their small, frightened eyes told me they were out of their depth, but their pride and their ideals meant they couldn't admit they needed help.

They had no idea of what was going on in Albania. They did not believe, I could see, Karl's talk of blood feuds and vengeance killing, rapes and shootings. This was all sheer sensationalism. They had been in the country three days.

We took them out for an ice cream and a walk round the silent late afternoon town. We walked with them as far as the limits of B.C., where the broken *palatti* finished in a rubble of trash, broken stones and wandering goats.

'This is as far as it's safe to go', said Karl; and I could see Stan and Ollie's eyes saying, 'Bullshit, you faker!'

As if on cue, a stretch Mercedes bounced slowly down the track towards town from the hills. Inside, in the front passenger seat sat a corpulent local mafioso in dark glasses with a machine-gun in his lap. His bodyguards sat all round him front and back, each armed to the teeth. In the back, between two guards, was a thin and miserable-looking policeman in uniform, disarmed and dejected, who had obviously been found doing something the boss didn't like. It was obvious he was being taken to his place of torture or execution, or both.

The car slowed to halt. A window wound down. The capo was well known to Karl, and he leaned out to chat. The policeman-prisoner stared straight ahead like a man already dead. The bodyguards looked hungrily at the two American girls, lowering their dark glasses the better to ogle them. The capo indicated the girls and laughed, and made a suggestion to Karl. Then the window wound up and the car bounced on, leaving us in a cloud of dust.

There was no way you could put any but the most sinister interpretation on this dreadful cortège.

'That was one of the Democrat party bosses, the local Mister Big', said Karl.

'What did he say about us?' Stan asked Karl, her voice hard and angry.

Karl avoided her gaze, instead leading us back at a smart pace towards the centre of town, eyes to the ground.

'Go on. What did he say?' insisted Ollie.

'He said: "How much for both of them?" I think it was only a joke', Karl added, as lightly as he could.

The ice creams were eaten outside, at a café which had tables under an awning on a terrace. Karl and I insisted on paying for Stan and Ollie, in my case more in the spirit of a last meal for the condemned before execution. I didn't give them more than a fifty-fifty chance of getting to Tirana, their next destination, unviolated.

The girls accepted our hospitality without thanks or any lessening of hostility. Nothing we could say or do would be any use to them.

'Gee, you two have become just like Albanian men already', Ollie said to me, as Karl was paying inside the café. This wasn't meant as a compliment.

At first they said they were going to stay for a week and aimed to go trekking in the mountains; but then they heard that an empty food lorry was heading down to the ferry the next day early, and on to Tirana. The next day we heard on the grapevine that they'd left at 6 a.m. on that, without telling anyone. They'd said to their Albanian hosts, who had been persuaded to take them in for the night by Karl, that 'they had hated Bajram Curri – so unfriendly'. I never heard if they ever got to Tirana, but when I enquired at the various aid agencies no one had ever heard of them. Perhaps they got through, perhaps they didn't. All sorts of people were disappearing without trace in Albania that summer.

Ollie, the one who worked in Vienna, told me *en passant* that she had a boyfriend, a half-Serbian, half-Iraqi guy. He was 'having some problems' with Austrian immigration about his residence permit, she added. I can't say I was surprised. Where had they met, I wondered. On top of a food aid truck in Kurdistan, perhaps? After all, she was obviously the type to live dangerously.

When Thomas was told about the visitors, he groaned and shut his eyes: 'My worst nightmare has always been an American TV info-babe in heels, miniskirt and attitude getting out of the MAF plane from Tirana.'

That day was surely getting ever closer.

*

Karl did manage to get me into the closed museum. He knew the woman who had the key, or one of the keys. The building was well designed in a functional, modernistic style. The quality of construction and finish was up to Western standards. When the Communists in Albania had wanted to put up good buildings they had done so.

The museum was shut for an ideological *remont*, but the official line was by no means clear up in Bajram Curri; no one had yet been sent from Tirana to effect the purge, so the place stayed closed. There had been a number of robberies recently, a window having been broken and thieves having clambered inside. An old Martini-Henry .45 rifle had been stolen, together with several *yataghans*, Turkish-era stabbing dirks. Only weapons had been taken.

The museum exhibits were a hymn to hatred of the Serbs, who, just across the border in Kosovo, dominated and suppressed millions of ethnic Albanians. There were exaggerated maps claiming vast swathes of territory for Greater Albania, patriotic paintings in the heroic style showing Albanian *çetas* fending off the Slavic hordes with rifle and sword, and heaped ethnological praise for the noble Illyrian throughout history. Alexander the Great was an Illyrian, and so was Aristotle. I searched in vain for evidence that Mozart, Descartes and Charles Darwin also were Illyrians. Perhaps those exhibits had been stolen. Albanian museums made no pretence to scientific objectivity, but rather represented the rant of the government of the day.

In a far corner, partially hidden behind a barricade of plywood to pen the monster in, sat a huge plaster model of Enver Hoxha, thrice life-size. This was possibly the last such Pharaonic statue anywhere in the country. I peeked round the plywood purdah and gazed upon the chalky features of the great dictator. He looked costive and unhealthy, which was probably accurate. He'd had diabetes since 1948 and was overweight for years.

As we left I slipped the woman with the keys the equivalent of five dollars in lek. She shut up the museum again with a chain and padlock. When would it ever open again to the public, I wondered. What would happen to the statue of Hoxha?

Karl also managed to organise a mini-expedition to test out Jules as translator-cum-guide. This was not Karl's description of the trip, but was how I thought of it. We decided to go up on the bus as far as Valbona, unarmed and without an escort. I took literally nothing with me but my camera, strapped to the back of my belt. The idea was that we would try to meet some villagers to whom I could ask some questions about the *Kanun of Lek*, through Jules.

Valbona was a Communist-era beauty spot, a hamlet in the foot-hills of the Albanian Alps which had been developed into a sort of Marxist micro-resort. An Austrian-style guest house with wooden shingle roof had been built and 'foreign friends' were invited up there for hiking trips and skiing in the halcyon days of Hoxha's *raj*.

Buses left B.C. at 6, 7, 8 and 9 a.m., we were told. In fact only one bus actually went up to Valbona, a complete wreck with half the seats missing, which eventually left at 1.30 p.m. Jules and I spent the morning waiting at a café, watching flocks of sheep being driven through Bajram Curri on their way up to the *bjeshkë*.

Jules' father was a vet, currently earning a pittance in government service. Jules himself had recently finished school and was trying to decide what he should do with his life.

'I would like to go to America', he told me, 'if someone would organise it all for me and pay.'

As this seemed unlikely, the international drugs trade was his next career choice. Many of his school pals had already gone across the border into Serbian Kosovo illegally, bought false Yugoslav papers and thence departed to Germany and Switzerland, there to traffic in heroin. It seemed quite easy to get into these countries, and Jules was merely waiting until he could get enough money together before taking off on the same route.

I suggested that dealers of heroin rarely lived to a ripe old age, all ethical considerations apart. Jules brushed that aside; it was a way out which paid good money quickly; that was enough for him.

He had a local girlfriend, he told me, who was seventeen, whom he'd met at school; but he had to rendezvous with her in secret: neither his parents nor hers knew of the connection, nor would they approve. All marriages in Tropoja were still arranged by the two families concerned, Jules told me. He was utterly astonished, even dumbfounded, to learn that I had no girlfriend, no wife, no children and that my parents and grandparents were dead. I had no *fis*! It was inconceivable.

'Have you ever had a girlfriend?' he asked naïvely.

'Yes, I have', I told him, 'but in the West we don't put the same value on a strong family and *fis* as you do in Albania. Many of us live alone from choice.'

He nodded his head with incomprehension.

The bus eventually whirled us away in a cloud of dust. We passed through mountain scenery of great beauty; jagged peaks of grey rock reared up to white-ice glaciers locked in high valleys, quite visible to the naked eye. By the side of the dirt road a river babbled and rushed over boulder and scree. Pine trees grew in craggy eminences, and in small fields cows and sheep were at pasture. The sky was a bright, cloudless blue. Grand, savage, apparently impenetrable, the Accursed Mountains presented an unbroken chain stretching into Serbia and Montenegro. We were only a few kilometres from the frontier.

We whirled through Dragobi, a few houses merely, where the famous caves in which Bajram Curri had been gunned to death were to be found, and on up the valley to Valbona itself, where the bus terminated. There were half a dozen stone and shingle houses, a few goats, the mountains – and the burnt-out ruin of the Communist-era guest lodge. A partisans' memorial stone had its red star in place but the names had been defaced. The few locals on the bus, men returning to their mountain villages, waved us goodbye and trudged off with sacks over their shoulders. One fellow insisted we come with him to Rogem, three hours down the Theth track, to meet his aunt, who he claimed was a hundred and six and knew all about the *Kanun*. Jules was all for it.

'How will we get back?' I asked. And how did we know, I didn't ask, who or what lay in wait further up the track? It was up here that the Hungarians had been ambushed, I finally pointed out. Jules had thought it was in Shoshan. Anyway, Allah would provide.

Jules was a typical modern Albanian youth in that he knew

nothing about either the history or the culture of his country. He had read nothing and so understood nothing, not even Communist propaganda. Instead he was saturated in the lowest common denominator of Western pop culture. He told me the names of his favourite bands – Guns 'n' Roses, Led Zeppelin, Saxon – as if of impossibly arcane incunabula, certainly quite impenetrable to someone of my antiquity and background. Why was it that Rambo and thrash-metal rock were what appealed to Third World youth the world over?

After we'd looked round Valbona on foot, we – or rather I, since I was paying – decided to walk back down the track as far as Dragobi, and then catch a minibus to B.C., if one was to be caught. Perhaps there would be people to talk to *en route*. There was no one in Valbona except some small children herding goats.

Jules didn't mind; it was better than bingo. Up in the high pastures there was a type of wild bilberry, he told me, which sold for $15 a kilo. The Germans bought them. If this was a hint, I didn't take it. Before we left I took a photo of the children. This went down well with Jules.

'You have pleased them', he said happily.

'Why?' I asked. I thought they'd looked shy rather than pleased.

'Because you have honoured them', said Jules. Some people claimed that northern highlanders feared the camera for casting the Evil Eye. As elsewhere in Albania, I found that in the mountains photography was bound up with shame and honour. The portrait snap of happy, smiling people in pleasant surroundings always bestowed honour. Photographing 'bad things' – primitive squalor, dirt, burnt-out buildings, old, shabby or disfigured people – was considered shameful, and therefore bad. I'd found exactly the same dichotomy in Turkey.

The day was hot in spite of the altitude. I felt as if I was in a sort of Austrian alpine zone which had somehow slipped down the map of Europe as far as Greece. Coming up the track towards us as we descended were flocks of sheep, pairs of cows and lithe men with turbans wrapped round their necks and heads against the sun. They were leading mules laden with sacks of flour, heading for the *bjeshkë*, where they would live for months. Their rifles were wrapped in cloth against the dust. They raised their hands and called out 'Mirdita' ('Good-day') as they trudged by. No motor vehicles passed us. This was the Albanian Alps exactly as Edith Durham had known them ninety years ago.

We stopped at regular intervals to drink from the river. The water was snow melt and tooth-numbingly cold. There were meadows with thick green grass and buttercups and daisies lying in deep tree shade by the river where it would have been pleasant to lie and look up at the mountains and the sky. But we couldn't. We had to be back before dark and the unofficial curfew. I had promised Thomas we'd be back before nightfall. If we weren't, he'd have to motor out with a posse to look for our bodies.

For defensive reasons, few of the houses in Dragobi had doors or windows on the ground floor, I'd noticed. As we passed, the women outside these stone forts went inside immediately, and bolted up their doors and shutters. No one replied to our greetings. We were strangers, two men with no accompanying women or children; and one of us with his shirt outside his trousers. This was serious bandit territory.

I had doubts that a minibus would ever appear. There was no coffee shop in Dragobi, nothing. So we kept walking down the sun-blistered track towards Bajram Curri. We would not get there before nightfall unless a motor came by.

But after an hour one did turn up, a green Mercedes van crudely converted for passengers with bench seats in the back. The driver had welded iron bars down along the aperture between the passengers in the back and the front cabin where his vulnerable neck was on display.

'Look – ', I pointed out to Jules, 'to prevent robbers.'

He frowned and looked offended. 'I think you do not like the Albanian people', he replied sadly.

I had said a shaming thing, a bad thing, though obviously true. This was why Albanians could not analyse things for themselves: they were trained not to notice, or talk about 'bad things', if they reflected badly on their own people or interests.

Jules had not done any translating for me all day; everywhere we had gone people had avoided us like the plague. It was ironic: for fear of attracting bandits we had given the impression we might be bandits ourselves. There was a whole tribe in the Accursed Mountains called Dushman. In the Farsi language of Persia and Afghanistan *dushman* meant 'brigand' or 'enemy', and also the same sometimes in eastern Turkish. Geographically and culturally, we were at the far end of a line of mountains soaked in brigandry and blood which started at the Hindu Kush, the killer of Hindus. I had come here as a traveller, as a tourist, but I now appeared as a *dushman* myself. Folklore was simply not on offer. There were sheep and wolves, nothing in between.

Back in town, Jules suggested he come back later and bring me to his aunt – another aunt – who was apparently a mine of information about the region's strangely elusive folklore. I agreed and we parted. It was still only early evening. Several hours passed. Jules reappeared eventually to say his aunt was dying of cancer – another relative dying of cancer, and so quickly stricken down! – so could not see me.

Wearily I paid Jules his $10 for a day's work, and away he scuttled. 'Dying of cancer' was what Natasha's grandfather had been doing in Tirana, of course. Perhaps this was a Communist-era evasion that had survived; in the purges in Russia, or at times of political crisis, people would suddenly develop these symptoms in Moscow and stay at home 'ill' until the storm had blown over.

*

The next day Thomas came round and asked me if I was busy. I said I wasn't. Could I help him, then? He gave a cute lop-sided grin. I said I could. He was dressed in blue jeans and neat beige short-sleeved shirt: he looked like a ski instructor on summer sabbatical.

We drove out of town to the airstrip, which had been bulldozed flat by bearded Gunter of the German Lutherans from Kukes. A flock of sheep now grazed on the site. As Thomas put out the concrete holders and metal poles for the windsock and half-way markers, I cruised down the sides of the grass runway looking for 'anything unusual', as Thomas had put it.

'What sort of unusual things am I looking for?' I asked.

Thomas gave me another grin: 'Well, kind of disturbed earth, recently dug, bumps and lumps, that kinda stuff.'

'Why might these bumps and things be there?' I enquired.

'Well, there are about ten different families who claim to own this land and they are all demanding thousands of dollars for letting us use it. We've already paid the government, who say they will settle the claims. That doesn't satisfy 'em. So they've threatened they are going to put landmines down and blow up the plane when it comes in to land.'

'But don't the local Albanians use the plane to get to Tirana for emergencies?'

'Sure, but that won't stop 'em.'

So I looked for hidden landmines while the shepherd cleared his flock off the landing strip with whoops and hollers. 'Robert Carver, traveller and writer, killed by a landmine, Albanian Highlands, 1996': I could see the carved gravestone in the English cemetery so clearly. Then I got realistic: no one would ever bother to ship my mangled carcass back. I'd just lie forgotten in a hole in B.C.

Karl and Sally arrived with the owner of the electronic bingo parlour and his bodyguard: the patron had decided to fly down to Tirana to buy a new Mercedes. Two hayseed policemen in uniform had followed, either as escort or in the hope of bribes. They hung about and hit each other on the back, grinning like loons.

A faint mist obscured the mountains in the distance. A line of trees shivered in the breeze. A group of small boys appeared from nowhere and gazed at us blankly.

There was no radio contact with the light plane after it left Kukes. We all stood and listened to the wind, trying to hear the plane's engine, gazing down the valley in the direction of Tirana.

I had a strange sense of *déjà vu*; and then I realised – this was how it had been in the Papua New Guinea of my youth back in the '60s.

The plane was late. Tension mounted. If a one-engined light plane crashed in these mountains, the chances of ever finding it were remote. There were still bombers up here missing since 1943. Then it came; a low, distant hum on the air, relaxing us all.

The plane looked tiny. It waggled its wings to indicate it was coming in. The policemen stopped hitting each other and stared at this apparition with their mouths half open. The MAF light plane had only been coming into B.C. in the last few months. Before that, no air transport had ever been seen in this remote upland valley.

The plane bumped down, once, twice, and taxied on up the strip past us as Karl and Thomas physically held the two policemen by the sleeves of their shirts to stop them rushing out into the path of the propeller.

Karl and Sally got aboard. The electronic bingo man and his guard could not decide whether to get on board or not. They havered and chaffered outside the small cockpit, shouting over the engine, which turned on low revs. They had obviously never been in a plane before and were nervous.

In the end they decided to risk it, and clambered aboard as the plane was starting to taxi away. Within seconds the pilot was taking off again. He had been on the ground less than five minutes.

We watched them lumber up, then soar away, back towards Tirana and civilisation. The sheep trickled back on to the runway and the engine faded to a hum. Thomas and I packed the concrete blocks and poles and windsock into the jeep with a sense of anti-climax. All the gear had to be taken away every time: even the concrete holding blocks were stolen if left behind.

As we started to drive back to town, the two policemen waved us into the side of the road. They had been kidding with Thomas for the last hour, and now they wanted to get some money out of him. He laughed and joked with them and said he had 'ska deutschmarki' – 'no Deutschmarks'. They wouldn't give up. They inspected his car papers over and over again, claiming they were out of order. It was evident from the way they looked at them that they couldn't read. They jabbed their peasant fingers at the print and bent and twisted the documents as if they were a newspaper. Until the Democrats came to power these lads had been simple mountain shepherds; now they had guns and uniforms, but they were still poor. They had old broken leather shoes on their feet.

Thomas smiled on and joked with them endlessly. I sat silent, tense, and increasingly irritated. The two cops had automatics in their belts. Their faces were deeply tanned from standing outdoors at road-blocks taxing cars all day.

Thomas wouldn't budge: no bribes. We sat there for an hour before one of the police weakened and became bored. But the other wouldn't give in; he was determined to extract some baksheesh. The documents were ignored now: 'D-marki!, D-marki!' he chanted, getting angrier and angrier.

We were just across the border from Serbia, and in there the foreign currency of preference was the D-Mark rather than the dollar, because so many Yugoslavs went to Germany as 'guest workers'. That Thomas and the missionaries never went to Serbia and had no D-marks was irrelevant; they were foreigners and all foreigners had D-marks.

In the end the obstinate policeman pretended to take down the number of Thomas's jeep with a pen on a slip of old newspaper, and promised to report Thomas 'the very next day'. Then we were allowed to drive on. Thomas was still smiling and waving as we pulled away. I lit a cigarette with trembling hands.

'How can you sit there and take that stuff, Thomas?' I asked.

He smiled and shrugged: 'We get that every day, from all of them, always. They've got no dough – they think we've got plenty.'

Back in town I bought Thomas a beer at one of the small Italian-style bars. The owner looked at me with unashamed distaste and said something in Albanian to Thomas, who laughed.

'What was that?'

'Oh, he asked if you were the brother of the Dutchman come up to revenge his blood. He said if so I'd be seeing you in the morgue pretty soon, too.'

It turned out that the café owner had a son studying in Afghanistan. He'd had a letter from him recently, saying it was very peaceful and nice there, after Bajram Curri.

When we left, this unpleasant character tried to charge me triple price for the beers. Thomas laughed and told him not to be so fresh.

'Let the foreigner pay – they have plenty of money', said the bar owner with a sneer. Thomas was evidently no longer considered a foreigner. As we walked back to the apartment the first crackle of early evening gunfire was starting up from the other side of town.

'You know', said Thomas, 'if Karl could run for mayor in this town he'd win by a landslide.'

It was true. The missionaries exerted a moral influence out of all proportion to their age or experience. They were honest, they treated people equally, and they weren't involved in any blood feuds. People came to them all the time to try to sort out their problems. There was always a queue of people waiting for them at the Tourist Office.

They were very subtle and discreet. They held no church services, no rallies, no Billy Graham style meetings. Their Lutheran mission had worked out a system called 'buddy evangelism'. The missionaries simply met people in bars and cafés and became their friends, and then tried to help them. Christian doctrine followed practice, not vice versa. They didn't compete with the locals at all; they wouldn't pay bribes or use their influence dishonestly. They wouldn't even teach English classes, to avoid putting the local teachers out of work.

It was impressive. But the two young men were Americans. They had jeeps, a plane, nice clothes, money, all the good things Albanians dreamt of. What if they had had nothing, like the Iranian Shia missionaries? How much influence would they have had then?

'They think you've got the *grincardis* hidden away in there', I'd said to Karl about the gaggle of local lads hanging round the Tourist Office. He'd laughed and agreed.

'They think we're CIA as it is', added Thomas.

The thought had crossed my mind already that indeed CIA was precisely what they both probably were. They had VHF radios in their apartments, a light plane, jeeps, and contacts all along one of the most sensitive frontiers in the Balkans. They were right next to Kosovo, which could one day become the next Bosnia; Bajram Curri was an excellent listening post. They spoke suspiciously fluent Albanian and were politically *au fait* in a way that was surprising to me, at least, in men of the cloth. My picture of American evangelical missionaries was based on Norman Lewis's pudgy suburban Babbitts sweltering in compounds in the Amazonian rain forest. Karl and Thomas were much more like the men from U.N.C.L.E.

Who knows what they were in reality?

I know they certainly had their doubts about me and my alleged book. I could catch their eyes sliding across to one another with skepticism from time to time as I was talking. From their point of view, I too would surely seem to know far too much about the local political set-up to be the innocent travel writer I claimed to be.

After all, this was the Balkans, where after a while a man begins to suspect his own shadow of following him with ill intent.

19

The Accursed Mountains

Trail of Blood to the Forbidden North

OUR HORSES AND mules skittered, shying and whinnying with fear; they stumbled then reared, making to break away from the narrow, stony trail through the mountain pass. They could smell the spoor of some large beast that had crossed this way recently – wolf or bear. Our own wolfhound had vanished ahead of us into silence and mist above the cloud line, in pursuit of the mysterious animal. We waited in silence for yelps of discovery.

Grey clouds loomed up ahead; delicate traceries of snow began to fall, mantling our shoulders. The light fled and the landscape reduced to monotones of grey and white – moss and lichen, scree, rock and ice, glacier and moraine, the translucent stream beside us gushing over polished bald boulders.

Major-Doctor Muharrem Bajraktar reined in his horse hard and reloaded his sawn-off pump-action shot-gun one-handed, replacing the yellow cartridges of grape with the bright red ones of ball. Without having to ask him, I knew he thought the unknown beast was a bear. We had left the rifles with the shepherds in the *bjeshkë* thousands of feet below in the valley. A pump shot-gun was lighter, shorter and more versatile at close range than a rifle: fifteen shots as quick as you could lever the action. Lower down the risk was wolves rather than bear; there he'd charged up with the heavy grape cartridges.

The Major-Doctor had experience of all this. With a cousin of his he had waited in ambush the year before for a bear that had been raiding a maize field belonging to their *fis* in the foothills several kilometres outside Tropoja town. Then he'd been armed with a Kalashnikov; but although he had hit the bear several times – it was a large male, over six feet on its hind legs – the enraged beast had kept on coming at them. His cousin had been badly mauled at close quarters, and Muharrem had been forced to pump bullets into the bear's head and chest at almost point-blank range. In its dying spasms, the bear had turned its attention to the Major-Doctor and mauled him too. With the predator finally dead, staggering under the burden, himself bleeding and badly shocked, he had carried his unconscious cousin on his back for several miles down the valley to the nearest village. The man had lived, though he was badly crippled. Muharrem was terribly scarred from this encounter, his legs, arms and chest a mass of thick lacerations encrusted with new skin. These had been impossible not to notice when, lower down the valley, in the almost subtropical heat, he had stripped off his shirt. For nearly fifty years this border region of highland Albania had been forbidden to all but army patrols, the peasants cleared off the land. As a result, the bears, wolves and eagles had inherited their ancient territory once again, and with no human competition had flourished accordingly.

Since 1993 the peasants had reclaimed their mountain fields after the privatisations, and had ploughed and replanted; but no one had told the bears and wolves. A constant war, reminiscent of the early European penetration of North America, was now going on as men, bears and wolves competed for food and territory. The higher *bjeshkë* were only accessible to men for three months of the year; where we now were, several thousand feet higher in a frankly alpine zone above the tree line, snow lay all the year, and neither men nor horses ever came. It was only natural that our little party would be a magnet, a target for the region's self-confident beasts of prey.

There were three of us: Major Muharrem Bajraktar, myself, and the Major's nineteen-year-old, six-foot-tall, blonde daughter Lorelei. The Major spoke no English, only Albanian and German. Lorelei spoke English and German, so she had come along as our translator. The Major was in his mid-fifties, though still tough and light on his feet. It was strange for two middle-aged men to have to communicate with each other through the medium of a teenager who was far more interested in Michael Jackson than politics, ethnography or the *Kanun of Lek*.

We dismounted and tightened the horses' and mules' blinkers, stuffing peppermint-scented bunches of grass over the nervous animals' nostrils to mask the smell of bear or wolf. Taking the reins in our hands and looping an arm round our mounts' necks, we tugged, cajoled and virtually frog-marched them up the track, talking to them soothingly all the time right in their ears.

The falling snow turned to icy sleet, which soon drenched us to the skin. It was bitterly cold and the wind whipped us sharply when we made the crests of the rocky defiles.We were all tired, and I certainly felt close to exhaustion, though I tried not to show it. The Major and his daughter were tough Gheg mountaineers who displayed neither fear nor any other signs of emotion; they were stoics by philosophy and in practice.

There was still no sign of Lake Gashit, though it surely could not be much farther ahead of us now. We had passed no one all day, no sign even of human presence. We were in one of the remotest mountain ranges in Europe; no shepherds ever came up here, no army patrols, no bandits even. The last foreigners who had been on this mountain track, so the Major-Doctor told me, were two Italian explorers in 1933, who had gone with a full mule-train expedition to Lake Gashit. Under Communism the borders with Serbia and Montenegro had been off limits to all but the Special Forces patrols. Muharrem had been a major in Hoxha's commandos. As well as being a physician, he was also a trained alpinist. He was one of the very few Albanians who had ever been to Lake Gashit: in the 1960s he had led a team of mountain troops there as a young officer. They had camped by the waters of the lake for one night before returning. He had not been back since, but he remembered the way. There were no maps for this region, other than the large-scale general map of the whole of Albania I had managed to get in London before I left.

The planned expedition to the *bjeshkë* with Jules and the brother of Abdullah Engels-Mustapha had never come off. On the appointed day, at the appointed hour, there had been no sign of the promised brother or his Kalashnikov. Jules had turned up in a thin T-shirt and a pair of plastic flip-flops, with no sweater or jacket, this for an expedition into the heart of the Accursed Mountains. Thomas had translated for me, as Jules would take no part in any dispute between the Engels-Mustaphas and myself. Abdullah Engels-Mustapha suggested a new plan as his brother hadn't arrived: we would hire a car, from him of course, for $60, to take us to the trail-head. There we could hire mules, *inshallah*. His brother? Oh, well, his brother would probably be down some time or other.

'What do you think of this deal?' I'd asked Thomas. 'Do you trust this *fis*?'

'It stinks', said Thomas pithily. 'And I wouldn't trust these guys as far as I could chuck 'em. They may get you up there to the *bjeshkë*, Robert, but will you ever get down again?'

The same thought had occurred to me. The two of us retired to Thomas's flat to mull things over. Taxed with his unpreparedness, Jules claimed he'd known nothing about our plans, nor where we were going.

'I heard Karl explaining everything to him yesterday in slow, easy Albanian', I told Thomas. The trip to Valbona had convinced me that Jules was incapable of taking responsibility for anything. If an accident or a crisis occurred, I knew he would simply evaporate. I decided I wasn't going up to the *bjeshkë* with either Jules or the Engels-Mustaphas.

Major-Doctor Bajraktar was a different kettle of fish. He was a stern Communist of the old school, educated in East Germany, a believer in culture, science, discipline and order. In Albania the old brigade, the middle-aged huffers and puffers at youthful degeneracy and modern decadence were all the Communists. The flash-Harry wide boys with dodgy Italian clothes and false Marlboro cigarettes were the Democrat supporters.

Karl knew the Bajraktar *fis* well. The two of us went round to their apartment in Bajram Curri, where the Major-Doctor and I looked each other over. He was not overkeen on the expedition, which was a point in his favour. He was a former senior officer and a physician; I was a decadent Western tourist and possibly a spy as well, proposing to go along a sensitive international border for no apparent reason. I was an 'ethnographer' by now, 'journalist' being too frankly political in Albania. Edith Durham had been an ethnographer, interested in folklore; well, so was I. 'Ethnologue', Karl called me in his persuasive Albanian; I wondered if this was a genuine Albanian word or whether he'd made it up.

The Major's womenfolk had served us bowls of sour milk, yoghurt, flaps of bread, and thyme honey in small dishes, with raki and coffee. They gazed at us with smiling curiosity from the kitchen. As a modern girl and an English-speaker, Lorelei was allowed to sit with the men in the guest room. Karl did all the negotiations in his admirable Albanian.

The Major loved the mountains. There was little for him to do at the hospital in B.C., as there were no drugs or medicines and no equipment. He was earning $45 a month. By escorting me on a short stroll in the mountains he would be getting several months' salary for a few days of pure pleasure. We eyed each other up and came to the conclusion that we could more or less trust one another. He was reluctant to talk about things as primitive and feudal as tribes, but his *fis* came from the Hoti, who had members scattered all round the border region, and in Kosovo too. The Major was another red-hot Serbophobe. More to the point, he had relatives actually up in the *bjeshkë* with their flocks in the valley on the way to Lake Gashit.

It was all agreed and the next day we set off in a borrowed 4-wheel-drive Japanese jeep driven by his son Aryan. A Communist with a daughter called Lorelei and a son called Aryan might have caused raised eyebrows in other countries, but not in Albania. German culture was strong culture and the Albanians were of ancient European, Aryan stock. I never met one Albanian who could give me even the vaguest outline of a Marxist-Leninist idea, after forty-five years of indoctrination. Like Jules, they just hadn't been listening. Hoxha's Communism seemed to have been about 75% Albanian nationalism, anyway. And after all, 'Communism is the poor man's Fascism', as the Cuban writer Cabrera Infante so accurately remarked.

The Major was fond of both Wagner and Goethe; he would sing choruses from the operas of the former and chant the poetry of the latter while springing from high peak to high peak in the Accursed Mountains, like some two-legged chamois auditioning for a part as a Nazi in a Julie Andrews movie.

Aryan seemed to think that the way to drive a Japanese jeep was as fast as possible without actually turning it over. Every rut and pot-hole was a challenge for him to see if he couldn't get one of us up through the roof. We left B.C. at five in the morning, to get a good start before either the Engels-Mustaphas or the bandits were abroad. The Bajraktars weren't exactly in blood with the Engels-Mustaphas, but they weren't exactly friends with them either. If one of the E-M's Krasnichi tribesmen saw me with the Major-Doctor heading for the *bjeshkë* they would put two and two together and probably try to ambush us.

I left my travel journal, passport and most of my money behind with Karl, together with a copy of my last will and testament and a letter to my London publisher, just in case I didn't get back. I took with me my camera, film, toothbrush and cigarettes, with a jumper round my waist for the chilly nights in high peaks. The Major would only get paid if he managed to bring me back alive and in one piece. All this was explained at great length to him by Karl.

We ran out of dirt track half an hour the other side of Tropoja town. Out we got and Aryan turned the jeep round and bounced away again at full speed. The three of us started to walk uphill past fields of ripening maize and dense beech woods.

Unlike any other Albanians I'd been with, Bajraktar *père et fille* made no attempt to ingratiate themselves with me. There was no bowing and scraping, no smiling even. Rather, they gave off waves of *froideur*, as if I was some delicate species of low life they had been lumbered with that had to be protected from the wood-sprites.

There were two ways of getting to Lake Gashit: one was to follow the river valley upstream, which was how all the peasants at the *bjeshkë* with their flocks got there; the other was to clamber across a jagged mountain range right along the hostile Serbian Kosovo border at 9,000 feet with no climbing equipment, ropes or boots. Without consulting me or even discussing the matter the Major had decided on the latter.

I only realised this when we were actually up in the mountains, jammed in a crevasse, and it was too late to do anything about it. There were probably several reasons for the Major's choosing to take this route. The first was that he was a trained mountaineer; simply strolling up the valley held no appeal for him at all. As ever, when the foreigner was paying for an expedition the Albanians organising it did everything to suit themselves and nothing to suit the person paying. Secondly, it was possible that the Major had doubts about the legality of what he was doing. No one really knew what the laws were any more. Could it really be allowed to take a Western foreigner right along such a sensitive border, especially for a former member of the Special Forces? If no one saw me go up with him, then no one could ever accuse him of having taken me there, should the political climate change. Thirdly, and perhaps most important, he may have wanted to test and, if possible, even humiliate me by taking the hard way, which both he and his daughter had considerable experience of. He was a proud man, and I felt he thought escorting a Western tourist up into the mountains for money was beneath his dignity. He kept up a punishing pace, never pausing or resting. I refused to be hurried, however. I ambled along at my own speed, taking photographs and pausing to look at the view and examine wild flowers: it was what I was there for, after all. The military mentality is similar in all countries: bash on regardless, as quickly as possible. Lorelei took her cue from Dad and kept passing cute remarks down the trail to me in English: 'There is a pothole! Be careful!' she would admonish. 'There is a crack! Beware!'

She was so busy patronising me that she missed her footing and slipped down a slope of loose shale, starting a small avalanche, her loaded shot-gun dragging on the ground beside her. More Albanians were killed in shooting accidents than in blood feuds, I'd been told, and I could believe it. Both the Major and Lorelei were dangerously sloppy in their weapons handling. I spent a great deal of time making sure I was not in the line of fire of their guns.

When Lorelei managed to clamber up on to the path again, red-faced and dishevelled, I said to her in a schoolmasterly voice, 'Be careful! The path is slippery!' After that she shut up and left me in peace.

More or less as soon as we'd started from the trail-head we came to a large, lone, whitewashed stone *kula* with a wood shingle roof – and stopped. We hadn't been walking for more than an hour and the sun was hardly up.

Inside, a curious sight met my eyes. Sitting cross-legged on the floor in the living room were several elderly and middle-aged Albanian highland men in homespun clothes, white *cheleshës* on their heads. They were bent over intricate piles of steel and wood; these they were assembling, filing, cleaning, buffing and polishing. Other men were using primitive mechanical contraptions with long levers to pack grey powder into small round brass cylinders sealed with pointed slivers of lead, which were moulded individually in little purpose-built metal clamps.

The three of us were ushered in and seated by the fireside, though there was no fire burning, which was just as well. The Major-Doctor and his daughter kissed the cheeks of the head of the household four times, and elaborate welcomes and enquiries of health were exchanged. The cross-legged workers smiled and bowed at us, and returned to their labours.

This was a *kula* whose owners had only been allowed back since 1993. Before that it had been used as a forward post by the Albanian army. The border with Serbia was no further than a kilometre away.

I could not take my eyes off the activities of the men on the floor. They were cleaning and putting together ancient, even antique firearms which had obviously been stored away for the whole of the Communist period. I recognised Sten guns and Lee-Enfield .303 rifles from the Second World War, Turkish Mausers and short Italian carbines, and the traditional rifle of the old Albanian highlands, the breech-loading Martini-Henry .45, with which the blood feud had been pursued in Ottoman times. I was intrigued to see one man breaking down school pencils, crushing the graphite core in a pestle and using this dust to lubricate the loading mechanism of the 'Martina'. At the time I took this to be some quaint local custom, but when I got back to England I read that using graphite as a lubricant for breech-loaders was an old wrinkle of the Victorian British Army, used in such places as the Sudan and Egypt where dust might adhere to oil or grease and cause jamming. It was jammed breechloader rifles, fresh from the armoury and unstripped of all grease, which had done for Colonel Custer at Little Big Horn; his troops had not been made to test-fire their new weapons or to clean off the storage grease properly. With repeated use in hot action the rifles had jammed, and the Sioux closed in for the kill.

We were served coffee and raki; my American L & M cigarettes were eagerly consumed by all, not least by the men funnelling gunpowder into the brass cartridges. After all, it was an Albanian Khedive of Egypt in the nineteenth century who, as an after-dinner entertainment, used to take his guests for a barefoot stroll by candlelight through his personal gunpowder magazine – which had been strewn ankle-deep in loose powder for that added *frisson*.

Numerous weapons were inspected, aimed and clicked by the Major-Doctor and myself. The Lee-Enfield and the 'Martina' – both British rifles – were much approved of by all those present. 'All honour to England!' they said of them, 'Roftë Anglia!' These weapons had been broken down forty years ago and wrapped in oilskin cloth, coated in grease and hidden in hollowed-out tree trunks deep in the beech forest, buried under domestic hearth and cloaca, or secreted actually inside hollowed-out roof timbers. Now their time had come again. The Albanian army had abandoned this border zone and the Serbs came across regularly to raid and kill. Then again, the blood feud had returned and every *fis* needed protection. What I was seeing must have been going on, more or less in secret, all over Albania; as Democrat control was breaking down, so the old pre-Second World War feudal Albania was re-emerging – a whole society going back to the law of the rifle. When the rebellion of March 1997 finally erupted, all these old guns came out into the daylight again, from Thompson sub-machine guns and Brens to these antiques from the days of Gordon of Khartoum, for the 'Martina' was the weapon the British Army had used in the Sudanese campaigns of the 1880s. A hundred years and more later they were still giving sterling service in the Gheg highlands. Some of these old rifles had been 'fed' silver groschen coins, hammered in between stock and steel as a 'reward' given to honour the rifle by the owner when it had just shot someone dead in a revenge killing; this was a very ancient custom.

The Major-Doctor and I were equipped with a 'Martina' each from the cache and a home-made leather bandolier with brass cartridges which went over our necks, balancing the rifle on the other side. On the trail, to start with, this burden seemed light, even negligible; by the end of the day, after trudging, slipping, grappling and scrambling over the Accursed Mountains it seemed to have become a leaden cross scarcely to be born. No wonder that in the Army abandoning a rifle was made a capital offence in the old days; only the fear of death would stop you leaving the brute behind when the going got tough.

The Major-Doctor and Lorelei ate yoghurt and thick goat's meat soup with maize gruel before we left; I stuck to coffee, raki and cigarettes. Shortly before midday, after a long but fascinating interlude, we shouldered our rifles, whose muzzles and breeches were shrouded in cloth, and waved our host goodbye.

Up a narrow path through the beech woods we wound, towards the Serbian border.

'What do we do if a Serb patrol sees us?' I asked Lorelei nervously. She looked at me with undisguised contempt.

'Nothing. They will shoot us with their machine-guns.'

We came to the border within minutes. You couldn't mistake it. A *cordon sanitaire* about a hundred yards wide had been ploughed through the woods by the Albanian Communists and flattened to give a clear field of fire; this long strip of now grass-covered earth had been, and still was, mined. There were no border guards or fences, no towers on wooden stilts with machine-guns. You could just stroll across, if you wanted to risk the mines and the Serbs on the other side.

We walked on the very edge of the beech forest, a few metres from the start of the cleared border zone. If we saw a Serb patrol, we were to run back into the forest on the Albanian side. It was hard to say how high we were, but we were still below the tree line, though rising all the time. Gradually the clumps of beeches grew thinner and the mist seemed to be turning into fog and even cloud.

Surreally, all around us we could now hear the sound of cow bells and goat bleatings, though we could see nothing of these ghostly beings. We had come to the start of the *bjeshkë* and the herds were all about us, right up to the frontier.

Looming up like mythological creatures out of the mist ahead came a flock of shaggy goats and sheep. They swarmed past us slowly, hairy phantoms. Two women in black dresses and head-scarves came out of a stone shack and smiled at us; they obviously knew Doctor Muharrem well. He was in his element up here, of course. He hardly spoke, but kept ahead of Lorelei and me, some invisible compass guiding him through the swirling mist.

Apart from guns and ammunition, we were not exactly over-equipped. All three of us were wearing soft shoes and lightweight clothing. Apart from an extra jumper each, nothing. I'd had no idea what the terrain was going to be like. Up to the frontier and along the border it was fine – easy mountain hiking. After several hours, though, we had veered off back down the range into Albania again, away from the frontier zone. The next five hours I would rather not recall in detail. We progressed very slowly across ridgeback after ridgeback, traversing the mountains by going down deep into the tributary valleys then climbing the steep, rocky cliffs on the other side – to slide down again into the next valley on the other side, on and on, down and up and down. Even without the guns it would have been hard work; with them it was like some exercise dreamt up by the SAS to show how tough you were, or in my case how tough you weren't.

By now we were mountaineering, but without any crampons, picks or rope. We were all falling, and it was only a matter of time before one of us shot either themselves or the next in line. After two bad slips in which we all nearly went sliding and tumbling over a sheer cliff together I forced Lorelei and the Major to unload their guns before I would agree to continue. The insanity was that there was no need for us to be traversing the range like this; below us, thousands of feet below, I could see the mule track snaking up the valley beside the river which everyone else took to the *bjeshkë*.

On the bare, rocky peaks it was chill and damp with cloud and mist; when we plunged down to the valley below the heat and vegetation grew to summer Afghan proportions, cicadas loud in the shrubbery. I became very thirsty. There were small trickles of water running off the high peaks, but these were few and far between. Even the imperturbable Major got himself into difficulties several times: lodging himself far up a chimney and having to retreat backwards like some foiled giant sloth; slipping down the track and skidding on his rear end for dozens of yards before he could get purchase on the slippery shale; falling heavily on his side as a rock gave way under him.

I grew very tired. Finally, searching out a slim track straight down to the riverbed, I told the Major that was where we were going, right now. He didn't disagree. It took us about an hour to lever our way down into the valley over a half-overgrown goat track about a kilometre in length. My heart was pounding in my ribcage and I cursed the rifle on my back like some old Kitchener–era sweat.

We sat on a granite slab by the river for fifteen minutes, recovering. The temperature was twenty degrees hotter than above, high summer again after the damp spring of the peaks. We were not far from the *bjeshkë* where the Bajraktar clan were camped with their flocks; earlier in the day it would have taken us an hour to get up there, but our legs had turned to lead and our feet to stone. On we slogged slowly, but at least on a mule-trodden track and a gentle slope.

We arrived after two hours, as the sun was waning. The *stanë* were dry stone wall hutments built shoulder high, with wood shingle roofs, one large room in which the whole family ate, slept and scratched. There was a wood fire at one end, with a hole in the ceiling for the smoke; the floor was packed earth and the beds were made of tree branches lashed together. This was life at one level above neolithic cave-dwelling. Outside, the sheep were gathered each night inside a ten-foot-high fold made of dry stone topped with thorns – protection against the wolves. The mastiffs were chained to great logs and kept semi-starved, forever on guard at the sheepfold entrance.

Başkim Bajraktar was the Major's cousin, a thin man in his late twenties, wild-haired and smelling of woodsmoke, wearing old Oxfam flared jeans and a windcheater over a sweater. His wife and sister and three children were in the *stanë*, the women making yoghurt and cheese by the open fire. Baskim's eyes grew wide when it was explained who I was; he welcomed me to his highland world with great courtesy and kindness.

After coffee, a glass of water and a cigarette, I lay down on the bed beside the fire and slept for several hours. When I awoke it was dark and the wolves were howling outside; they sounded as if they were about ten yards away; perhaps they were. The *stanë* doors had spring-loaded logs inside, which shut and locked them automatically. The wolves were very bold, and used to lurk about at dusk in shadow, sometimes coming actually inside the *stanë* on the heels of a man back from the *bjeshkë*, as if a dog. Orphaned lambs being suckled indoors were often taken like this, and even a small child had been seized and eaten the week before from a *stanë* on the other side of the valley, in just such an opportunistic raid. There was no light inside the huts save the low glow of the wood fire. The mastiffs looked like wolves themselves.

We ate yoghurt, unleavened maize bread, cheese and raw milk by a very small fire; all the fuel had to be brought up by mule from the beech woods thousands of feet below. This place was called Sylvicës, but the trees the Romans evidently knew had long been cut down. The whole valley was full of people and their herds from the lower regions of Tropoja; as ever in Albania, the different *fis* had nothing to do with one another. In even this most hostile region man was still predator to man.

The *stanë* was smoky and cold, the wind blowing through the roof as if through a sieve. After supper the Major and I took ourselves off to the cheese storage *stanë* and rolled ourselves fully dressed into thick quilts next to each other on the large beech-branch bed. The only light was the glimmering of the tiny fire on the floor under a skillet of thick milk which slowly simmered away. I fell asleep to the creak and groan of the wooden roof, as if afloat on some antique vessel on the storm-tossed seas.

*

The mist cleared, the sleet stopped, the sun came out. We were in a lunar landscape, low eroded hills scraped clean by glaciers, thick moss and lichen underfoot. The horses and mules ceased to skitter, and we mounted up again. As we crested the next hill I saw in front of us, dead ahead, a smear of a gunmetal grey-blue against the horizon – Lake Gashit. I let out a whoop and holler of triumph, and digging my heels into the flanks of my mount, standing up in my rope stirrups, descended in a slow, ungainly canter of triumph towards the distant flash of water.

The weather held. There was an eerie silence now the wind had dropped.

'Seven men decided to stay the whole winter up here in a cave', Major Muharrem had told me. 'They laid in enough food and fuel – but when their friends came the following summer they were all dead. They had killed themselves. They had left a message which read: "We have seen such terrible things which no man could imagine or describe."'

That day in July we had the luck with us; over the peaks to the left a pair of eagles glided nonchalantly; behind us lay the twisted cone of the valley and somewhere far below, Sylvicës. The air distilled to an absolute of pureness and clarity. We were as high and as remote as it was possible to go in this part of the Balkans. Underfoot was marshy earth which oozed and gurgled, alpine wild flowers dappled bright against the Irish green of the bog grass. No trees, no bushes, only swatches and troughs of clean unmelted snow amid the watery, rock-strewn hills.

We picked our way slowly down towards the lake, making wide zigzags across the slope to prevent our mounts slipping and foundering. Snow lay in patches and drifts all around.

The lake was very small and the water very clear. Earlier I had asked the Major if there were any fish. 'No fish', he had replied decisively. We got down, and hobbled our mounts with rope; they cropped the lush lakeside grass voraciously.

We sat on grey, eroded stones, the three of us, and ate a little picnic – boiled eggs, flat bread, salami, cheese, apples – and drank the icy water from the lake. As the Major and I were scooping up water in our plastic cups, shoals of tiny fish darted away from us into deeper water.

'Look', I said, and pointed, 'Fish.' The Major said nothing but gave me a blank Albanian stare.

I supposed that this lake was connected with other underground aquifers which snaked under the mountain ranges, the fish moving to and fro, up and down thousands of metres in their peregrinations. Could a trout from Lake Baikal in Siberia get here, underground, I wondered. What a map that would make, if we could but chart it, the immense underground lakes, rivers and seas hidden beneath our feet!

There was still no sign of the wolfhound, which had evidently found some intriguing trail of his own to follow. The Major examined the rocks around the lake for signs of useful minerals. He was the only truly focused Albanian I'd met; his mind was always working and he was constantly doing things of a practical nature.

My legs were stiff and my bottom extremely sore. The wooden slatted saddles were padded with cushions, but these always slipped out from under me, ensuring a constant buffeting and chafing by raw, sharp timber.

I strolled over beyond the lake and looked down across a wild and broken moorland indented by jagged mountain peaks, rolling on into Serbia and Montenegro. We were right on the border, which, though unmarked, was only yards away from us. The view was clear for twenty miles or more. There was no trace of any human endeavour: this was authentic, untouched wilderness.

After half an hour we began to feel the cold; cloud swirled up from below us and it began to snow again. We unhobbled the mules and horses and set off back towards Sylvicës. The Major was convinced there was a bear near by; he kept his gun at the ready the whole time. After half an hour the wolfhound reappeared, wagging its tail happily. Perhaps it had been chasing a rabbit. The little foal which had been following closely its mother with us all day now felt confident enough to gambol freely.

Once we got below the cloud line the air cleared and the snow stopped, weak sun gradually drying us out. The valley down to Tropoja spread out before us now, a labyrinth of folds, curves and impromptu peaks. The way down was easy.

As we came to the outskirts of the hutments of Sylvicës in late afternoon sunlight, we passed two highlanders flaying a dead wolf with their knives. It looked small and insignificant, mangled thus on the ground, like a spindly collie. They had trapped it outside their *stanë* and killed it with rocks; they had no guns.

By now I was feeling distinctly seedy. I had brought no aspirin nor indeed any other medicines with me. I tried to get warm and dry by the small, flickering fire in the *stanë*, but continued to shiver and shake. I was bleeding intermittently from my rear end, and I hoped this was merely normal wear and tear from the mule saddle rather than evidence of any internal injury. The Major and Lorelei tucked into another great meal of meat, soup, yoghurt and maize bread. I went to bed and tried to sleep or at least stay motionless. When I didn't move the pain was almost bearable.

The Major was alarmed that I wasn't eating. He came into the cheese *stanë* and tried to question me in German about my ailments, these being of too delicate a nature to employ his daughter as translator. It is a delusion widely held by some foreigners that the English can understand German if they really want to. By repeating 'Ich kann nicht Deutsch verstehen' in what was obviously, to the Major's ears, a perfect German accent, I did not advance my case much.

'Komm, komm mein Mensch, kannst du die doo-die die doo?' he asked me, or words to that effect. 'Wo ist die Schlumpf-blicker in sein Zeitgeist-schadlerungen Kreig-streicher? Mit Nacht und Nebel ein-zwei ausaugen in die grosse-spektacle Quatsch-Qualitäten galgenhumor Kombinatizion?' he added, or words to that effect.

'Kein Deutsch spracht', I repeated like a Zen mantra, 'Kein Deutsch verstehen.' Also sprach Zarathustra, and also sprach I.

It was now dark outside and the wolves were howling once again. By the fireside one of Başkim Bajraktar's womenfolk was crouched like a witch from Macbeth, stirring the skillet of steaming milk, her head snooded, fronds of fair hair gleaming gold in the firelight. It only wanted Wright of Derby to paint this moving scene – *The Pathetic Death of an English Tourist in a Picturesque Hut in the Albanian Highlands*.

I noticed the Major had removed my rifle from the *stanë*; perhaps he thought I might shoot myself and he would end up not getting paid. Having embarked on an attempt at communication in dog-Italian and foundered, we finally fell back on wolf-Latin, with addments from the lexicon of James Joyce.

'Intestinum exteriore est?' the Major-Doctor enquired. 'Dolendum malus est? Quid? Hic? Haec? Quod?'

He poked me experimentally in several places and was gratified by an instant stream of non-Latin exclamations expressing pure Anglo-Saxon agony.

'Majoritam intestines interiore sunt', I gasped, 'Fragmentum minusculus exteriore temporarium – spero – est, eheu, fluidus sanguinus copius fluvia. Dolendum maximus intestorum aggravatus par equitem in montanum est. Hic, haec, hoc', I indicated, with more feeling than grammar.

'Caecae normalorum?' he enquired. 'Excrementalis durum est? Opera gravitas?'

'Durissimus – opera maximum gravitas', I replied, between whimpers of agony. 'Cago, ergo sum', I then quipped in Cartesian vein, tears pricking my eyes, in a vain attempt to lighten up the mood.

The firelight flickered. The doctor prodded me with sober intent. The wolves kept howling away outside. Perhaps this was actually part of Dante's *Inferno* he'd unaccountably forgotten to describe: the Circle of Hell for the Travel Writers.

What was 'Ouch!' in Latin, I wondered. The shades of my late Latin master were spinning in the Elysian Fields by this time at my ludicrous attempts to recall the rudiments of Caesar's *De Bello Gallico* after forty years. Moreover, as I recalled it, intestinal ailments had not loomed large in the vocab tests of our school curriculum.

'Nutritia necessitus est', the Major-Doctor declared. 'Supremum necessitum – fortitudus augmentum importantissimus est.'

'Maximus necessitam ego dormus tranquilus est', I countered. 'Necessitam pax, tempus, puellae voluptuae [this couldn't be right, surely?] et abstencia absolutus centum per centum de lupus Albinesus, glaucus yoghurtus, pane maizum, carne caprum brutum et fromagus crapulus acidulus. Natura simplex doctorus maximus effectivus est. Quod veritas est, credo ego, in hoc signo vinces,

Centurion-Doctorus illustrissimus', I concluded, with more hope than belief. But he didn't look convinced.

After this taxing *viva voce* with the Major-Doctor I was at least let alone for several hours. I slept and dreamt of large wolves which tore at my innards in between quoting from Virgil, or perhaps it was Horace.

'Audentis Fortuna iuvat!' snarled one ravening wolf: 'Fortune favours the brave!'

'Dis aliter visum!' slavered another: 'Heaven's thought was otherwise!'

'Forsan et haec olim meminisse iuvabit', I riposted, as my liver was slowly devoured: 'The day may dawn when this plight shall be sweet to remember.'

I awoke later in sweat and confusion, with Major Muharrem shaking my shoulder. He had made up a bowl of spinach and herb posset seethed in fresh cream for my troubled intestines. He insisted I eat it all, and spooned it into my mouth. As soon as I had finished this, I fell back on the beech-branch bed again, and returned to the arms of Morpheus.

*

The next day I awoke much refreshed, and the three of us strolled down the valley on foot after breakfast, back along the stony mule track towards Tropoja.

Lorelei had waited on her father like a medieval page before breakfast, bringing him water in a tin bowl for his toilette outside the *stanë*, holding a glass of warmed milk for him, presenting his comb, a mirror, and his jacket. I left twenty dollars in lek and a packet of sweets for the children pinned inside the bed quilt before we departed; I knew Başkim would refuse these if they were offered.

The Major-Doctor was in a more expansive mood: I had not died on him after all, the sun was shining, and he'd had a nice little ramble in the mountains. Sporting a flower in his mouth, he ambled at a sedate pace ahead of me, Lorelei bringing up the rear. We had left the Martini-Henry rifles and bandoliers behind at the *stanë* and were walking light as air downhill with only the shot-guns. Our expedition had merely been a convenient method of transporting the rifles to where they were needed, rather than as any protection for ourselves.

The track followed the river all the way, winding and twisting over rock and through narrow single-file passage. It was just like Afghanistan. From time to time we had to wade or jump over the river, when the track continued on the other side because of a sheer cliff face. Sometimes the shepherds had built primitive, rickety bridges of timber and rock, as in the North-West Frontier of India; in other places we had to jump from stone to stone.

All day, coming up the trail, were pack mules loaded with sacks of provisions or bundles of timber, flocks of sheep, and sun-drenched men in old clothes. They often stopped to pass the time of day.

'Tungjatjeta!' I would say, 'A je mirë? A je shëndosh? A je burrë forte?' – each of these three times: 'Long may you live!' 'Are you well?' 'Are you in good heart?' 'Are you a strong man?'

This went down a treat. 'Does the foreigner speak Shqiptar then?' they would ask the Major-Doctor.

'No he doesn't, not at all. That is all he can say', the Major would reply sourly in Albanian. His failure to communicate with me in German still rankled; he was convinced I could understand him really.

We were passing through magnificent pine- and beech-clad slopes with grey rocky peaks, mountain scenery of the utmost romantic aspect, which was soaked in a history of human blood. Every kilometre or so we would pause and the Major-Doctor would point out some fresh scene of tragedy, infamy or carnage.

Here was where just last year a five-year-old boy had been playing with a Kalashnikov and had shot dead his father by acci-dent; there was a carved wooden sign to this effect written in Albanian attached to a tree which marked the spot. Further on were the stones marking the graves of four celebrated brigands, all shot in Turkish times. There, by that rough bridge over the river, a shep-herd had been held up by two men with knives three years ago and had fought with them, killing one; the shepherd had escaped into the mountains and lived as a fugitive for two years, then was cap-tured during a visit to his home. Now he was in gaol. Up in that cave high in the rock face was the secret hideout of Shah Achmet, a cele-brated brigand leader who had put to flight a company of Austro-

Hungarian cavalry which had come up here in search of him and his gang in 1916. At this point, just here, two robbers had engaged shepherds taking their flocks up to the *bjeshkë* in polite conversation, while a confederate hidden behind them had seized lambs and hurled them through a gap in the rocks to another partner hundreds of feet below, who had cut the lambs' throats immediately. This scam had been going on for years – it was the Major-Doctor who had discovered it and told the shepherds. They had formed a posse and caught the thieves red-handed; they cut the robbers' throats, all three of them, and then hurled the bodies down through the gap to the man waiting below for the lambs. He had been finished off later, when he emerged, shaken, from the river bed, drenched in his partners' gore. Then the shepherds had broken up the gap so it couldn't be used any more. This had all happened just the year before, in 1995.

All the valleys round about in this region of Djakova were full of tall stone towers of refuge populated by men hiding from blood feuds. Everyone whom we met on the trail was overwhelmingly polite, and smiled us half to death; everyone was terrified of everyone else. Here arguments or umbrage alike led to bullets within minutes.

The Major-Doctor was still raving on about the Serbs, between recounting this doleful litany of blood and revenge, theft and murder, as we strolled through the sublimest mountain scenery I'd seen anywhere in the world.

'Listen', I said, finally, via Lorelei, 'No more politics. I'm sick to death of hearing about the Serbs. Tell me some folklore, for heaven's sake.' But he wouldn't: old customs were primitive and uncultured, shame-making.

'What do you think Albania must do then?' he asked me. I was a foreign expert of sorts, so I must have a 'plan'.

'Albania needs national unity, an end to *hakmarre*, and hard work by all. If everyone worked hard and honestly, all the problems would be solved.'

He looked at me earnestly, took my hand and shook it forcefully.

'You are a friend of Albania', he declared. But of course it wasn't true: I wasn't a 'friend' of any country. I was an anti-nationalist, a partisan of common sense, moderation and goodwill, qualities held of no value at all in Albania.

'Do you believe in God?' he continued. 'I am an atheist', he added provocatively. I had come to him through the missionaries, so he obviously thought I was some sort of Christian.

'We know religion and God exist as social ideas: every time we see a church, a mosque or a man praying we see evidence of this, it is scientifically observable. Whether religion and God exist on a metaphysical plane we do not know. Belief in them is an act of faith. Much that was considered to be of God two hundred years ago can now be explained by science. What will we learn from science in another two hundred years? Very many extraordinary things, to be sure. It is possible that a belief in God is some sort of evolutionary necessity. It is conceivable that the spark of divinity lies within each of us as a possibility, like learning a difficult foreign language. Mystics have believed this for millennia. As yet we know very little about the human brain.'

This was translated slowly and haltingly by poor Lorelei, who was right out of her depth. The Major-Doctor chewed on his flower stem and pondered. It wasn't quite what he'd been expecting.

'What about Communism?' he demanded.

'Like Christianity, it has never really been tried, so how can we say? They both exist only as failed prototypes.' Lorelei chuckled at this; she was no supporter of Hoxha, that was for sure.

'There were no bandits, no *hakmarre* under Communism', the Major avowed.

'No, all the bandits were in Tirana and robbed the country from there', I countered. This was an old joke, from the Zog era. Lorelei hadn't heard it and laughed out loud.

Dad didn't say anything for a while, then: 'We need more people. The birth rate is dropping terribly. This happened to France after the First World War, and they lost to the Germans because of it.'

'Albania has too many people to feed as it is', I riposted. 'Your food is mostly imported, free foreign-aid wheat keeps you alive. You cannot defend what you have as it is. The army has collapsed and the whole country is demoralised. You need moral regeneration, and fewer people.'

'We need more people', he declared, 'to fight the Serbs and recapture Kosovo.' It was an article of faith – but futile. Albania could never defeat Serbia in battle. They could hardly get enough to eat every day, never mind fighting wars.

Everything the Major had worked for all his life had collapsed, and he was left impotent with just the ideology, all that remained. He was a decent man, as far as I could tell; he had examined everyone in the *stanë* for TB, pulling up their shirts, tapping their ribs and backs, making them cough. He was a doctor with no medicine in a country with no real government any more.

Hoxha's regime, for all its appalling brutality, had educated men like the Major-Doctor and turned them into useful citizens who helped their fellow men. How did it feel for him to see young spivs selling cigarettes earn ten times his salary? He was the only Albanian male I ever met, apart from Alexei – another Communist – who didn't smoke.

Lorelei now felt emboldened to ask a question off her own bat.

'How much do mules cost in London?'

'We have cars, not mules', I replied. She gave me a hard, unbelieving Eastern European stare. I'd seen it in Russia in 1990, when I explained about fax machines to the intelligentsia in Leningrad; they'd thought I was lying, capitalist propaganda.

'I know the rich have cars, but what about the poor?' she added. 'What about donkeys? Do you have those?'

'Some children have them as pets', I replied. She simply didn't believe me. She had never been outside Djakova, after all.

The hills flattened out and the river bed widened. We were nearing Tropoja. Fig trees and grapevines could be seen now in small fields. We passed the grave of a celebrated Bektashi dervish whose photographs I'd seen all over Bajram Curri in cafés and small corner shops. He had died ten years ago, but was still revered. Somehow he has managed to stay out of gaol throughout the Communist period.

In Tropoja, a town virtually untouched by the Hoxha era, we rested in the house of the Major-Doctor's widowed mother. There was a black-and-white pre-war photo of her late husband on the wall, dressed in full traditional highland costume, his everyday wear.

We lay on couches in the pre-war furnished living room, resting our legs, and Muharrem was fed yoghurt with bread broken up into it by his mother, this confection covered with white sugar. In the Gulf States of Arabia this dish is favoured by expectant mothers and is thought to be both soothing and nourishing. I ate nothing: my innards were still in a parlous condition.

The Major was astounded and horrified at my fasting. I had eaten no breakfast and now refused any food in mid-afternoon.

'Are you a man or a robot?' he demanded.

'A robot', I replied. The word – Czech originally – was the same in Albanian. Lorelei laughed, but the Major shook his head.

There was an ancient telephone in the house with a crank handle that you would turn to try to get the person at the other end. I had never actually seen one of these before except in silent movies. Muharrem cranked and turned to no effect, trying to reach Aryan in B.C. to instruct him to come and collect us in the jeep.

'Problema di infrastructura in Albania', the Major said to me sadly.

It was pleasing to see this upright old Communist patriarch being waited on hand and foot in such a biblical manner by his mother and daughter, who obviously both adored him and loved looking after his domestic needs. It was extraordinary to be in a culture where women simply didn't feel the need to compete with men; but almost certainly it was this feminine adoration which fuelled the men's ferocious machismo.

Aryan turned up anyway after a couple of hours, unbidden. He had figured we'd be back about now. My punctured posterior took a savage pummelling from his manic driving as we bucketed back to B.C.

'Go slower! Go slower!' I screamed, and he would reduce speed by five miles an hour for five minutes. Behind us the Major-Doctor was teaching Lorelei 'The Earl-King' in German: high culture in the back seat while I was being lacerated in the front. I could feel the blood start to drip down my legs again. A loaded sawn-off shot-gun bounced around between Aryan and me by the gear-shift. Perhaps with luck it might just go off and shoot him in the balls, and then he'd slow down, the moron.

'Go slower, you bastard!' I screamed again, and he made his token deceleration once again for five minutes.

I was in bad shape when we got back to Karl's flat, barely able to walk up the stairs. Muharrem could see no cause and effect between his son's driving and my condition. Karl and Sally were relieved to see me back again in one piece, if the worse for wear. I paid off the Major-Doctor between gritted teeth. He smiled broadly and gave me a whiskery four-cheek kiss. I don't think he'd believed he was actually going to get more than a month's pay for such a holiday jaunt, but there it was, cash in hand. Perhaps capitalism wasn't so bad after all . . .

'They were happy with you. Were you happy with them?' Karl translated.

'Very happy', said I: apart from Aryan's demented driving, the futile mountaineering and the portage of the Martini-Henry rifles, I didn't say. But, as Lord Byron so accurately observed, 'those who would a-pleasuring go cannot expect comfort'.

I bade them farewell and retreated to the bathroom to inspect my wounded fundament in a shaving mirror, ramming up a suppository of damp loo paper to staunch the bleeding at least. Then I went to lie down and die quietly in Karl's spare bedroom.

'A twenty-year-old Bavarian girl arrived while you were away, on her own. She is a mountain lover. She wants Muharrem and Lorelei to take her up to Lake Gashit tomorrow, and they've just agreed, but she can only spare one day, not three', Karl told me as I hobbled 'twixt bathroom and bedroom like some crippled crustacean.

'Does she have lederhosen, two long blonde plaits, and big, chunky guy-kicking walking boots?' I asked.

Karl looked at me dumbfounded. 'How did you know?'

'Elementary, my dear Watson. Tell her to insist on being taken up there by the mountain route, not the valley route. All the way, mind', I stated sadistically. 'She'll get the full flavour that way.'

I had been hoping to stay with Karl and Sally for several days more to let my bum heal up a bit. No such luck.

'Seven Macedonian evangelical missionaries are coming over the mountain passes tomorrow by mule', Karl told me. 'We'll need your bedroom I'm afraid.'

I wondered how he was going to stash them: lengthways on the floor like sardines, or hanging from the walls like vampire bats. Where were the mules staying? Seven mules for seven Macedonian missionaries – what a movie that would make.

'How do you know they are coming tomorrow, precisely?' I asked. Karl looked at me as if I was crazy.

'Because they told us on the short-wave radio before they left.'

But of course. Next year, Karl had already informed me, their mission was going on the Internet with its own website. 'Christ-gjak

@ B.C. hakmarre ska problema.co.Albania', I thought: that can be
your site address.

*

The next day at noon Karl drove me to Fierzë to catch the ferry
downstream towards Shkodra. On my heels, oblivious beside a
stinking open sewer, squatting crouched in the shade of a burnt-out
building, ragged plastic Marlboro bag at my side, dark glasses covering my eyes, lighted *falso* ciggy drooping from my lips, I saw
myself as others must now see me. I excited absolutely no comment
or attention from any of the waiting Albanian passengers.

In two and half months I had become a ragged, scrawny, tousled
Albanian myself, clad in shabby jeans and filthy shoes, the whole
ensemble crowned by a mop of unkempt hair and a badly shaved,
hollow-cheeked face. I'd weighed myself at Karl's; I'd lost a stone
since I left England.

The ferry was three hours late and broke down twice *en route*,
making the journey eight hours instead of five. There was nothing
to eat or drink and it was blisteringly hot. So what? I had been to
Lake Gashit by mule and survived the Accursed Mountains.

20

Hakmarre and *Gjakmaria*

Honour, Feuds and the Code of Blood

'I WAS THE first man arrested in Albania by the Communists, on 5th May 1945. I was fifteen years old. I spent twenty-seven months in prison under investigation. I was condemned to death at the age of eighteen. I was tortured and beaten. I was a member of the Balli Kombetar, and the Communists found weapons, radio sets, typewriters, documents, medicines, food and other supplies in our house, all of which had been supplied by UNRRA and which were *en route* to our fighters in the mountains. I refused to tell my interrogators anything. They used electrodes on my legs, stomach, genitals, ears, face and tongue. I was beaten with whips, steel rods, sticks and fists. My head was put under water until I half-drowned. I still bear the scars today.'

Here Pjetri Ndrek, director of the Blood Feud Reconciliation Committee in Shkodra, pulled down his socks and indicated his deeply flayed and scarred flesh. He had pale skin, thin white hair and watery blue eyes set in a lined face with a prominent, beaky nose. He spoke very slowly, as if under sedation. It was useless to question him; he merely replied 'Later, later', and continued in his droning monologue.

'They never got a confession out of me. The judge said "You've wasted enough of our time" and condemned me to be shot. I was finally taken to a cemetery by the firing squad and a bandage put over my eyes. I looked at the sky for the last time as they were putting it on and shouted out: "Roftë Shqipëria! Long Live Albania!" Some people shouted "Death to Hoxha!" or "Down with Communism", but I didn't. The rifles all fired but I wasn't killed or even harmed. All the others with me were killed. "You are to go back to prison", the leader of the firing squad said to me and gave me a cigarette. I didn't care. I wasn't happy at being spared. It meant more suffering. And so I was escorted back to gaol.'

'I spent seven years in prison in three different camps. In the first, at Maliq, there were 2,000 of us. Twelve hundred were worked to death, the remaining 800 were transferred to another camp after a few months. We worked from 5 a.m. to 6 p.m. digging a canal, which was never used even when finished. We had to run five kilometres to and from work every morning and evening. The healthiest prisoner weighed 55 kilos – you can imagine the rest. We had to dig four metres per day each; if we didn't, we got no food. We were given 350 grammes of maize bread, a few green peppers and a few drops of oil. If you didn't complete your four metres you got nothing and had to work again as normal the next day after a night without food. Many people killed themselves. An engineer and his wife hanged themselves in front of my eyes. They had been highly educated in the West. They were accused of being British spies and were going to be tortured. All the occupants in the camp were educated people, many with high qualifications from the West. Hoxha and the Communists deliberately set out to exterminate all the pre-war bourgeoisie. One of the the reasons Albania is in such a demoralised state today is that most of the educated leaders of society were murdered or worked to death by the Communists.'

Pjetri Ndrek paused, blinked several times and took a sip of black coffee and then a spoonful of ice cream. It seemed that recounting all this was both painful and necessary for him. We were sitting in an Italian-style café, almost empty, the overhead fans churning the air slowly. It was mid-afternoon. From outside there was a dull rumble of traffic. My translator, Mehmet Yezidi, spoke in low tones, as if wishing to avoid being overheard.

'We were beaten by the guards when we went out to work', Ndrek continued, 'and when we came back. Four or five people died every day at work – starvation, lack of vitamins, overwork, infected bites from leeches, exhaustion. We had dysentery, aggravated by the diet of maize and green peppers. We were allowed one glass of water a day. There were many priests in this camp. They all died. After six months we survivors were sent home for a month, then on to another camp. We were sent home to be fattened up again, and to show our families how we had been treated to make them frightened. We were walking skeletons. You can say that conditions were worse than Matthausen and the Nazi labour camps. The second camp was at Beden, near Kavajë: a dry, stony place. We were digging drainage canals for new fields. Here there were fewer deaths – three or four a day only. The weakest had died already, but the food was worse. We had to dig three metres a day. Also there were old landmines to be blown up with dynamite. Many prisoners were wounded – legs and arms blown off – they were simply shot by the guards then. I was the fattest in this camp: I weighed 46 kilos. The authorities allowed food to be sent to us by our families after they realised how many were dying. Then every three to four months we were sent back home to be fattened for a month. It was simply slave labour. New prisoners kept being sent in. Most died very quickly. Only the exceptionally tough lived. If you survived a year you were in the élite.'

'There were epochs of arrests. From 1945 to 1953 the intellectuals, men of high culture and foreign education, priests and politicians of the Zog regime were all sent to the camps. From 1953 to 1956 there were no arrests. From 1956 to 1964 the children of parents already arrested were sent to the camps – those with bad *biographi*. From 1964 to 1967 there were again no arrests. From 1967 onwards came the arrests of the high military, generals and colonels, Communist deputies, senior officials – people from the clans of Mehmet Shehu and Qemal Stafa. This was the Chinese period, the Cultural Revolution. The Sigurimi had quotas of production like everyone else. They were told: "Supply so many traitors to fulfil your norm." They tortured people to get confessions; just to be sent to the camps without a confession wasn't good enough. They became very angry when you didn't confess. The only reason I was not shot, I feel sure, is that I didn't confess. I tried to kill myself while under investigation, but failed. I suffered under seventeen different investigators. One even broke his own finger torturing me. My ribs were broken and my tongue was electrocuted so many times I could not taste anything. "I accept the sentence with pleasure", I said when I knew I was going to be shot. For months, when not being tortured I was chained up to a post, standing with my hands manacled behind my back. I did not betray any of our fighters. The resistance to the Communists by Balli Kombetar in the mountains survived until 1958, then gradually our people left through Yugoslavia. If the West had supplied us with arms by parachute we could have fought on for ever.'

I tried to get a question in, this time as a statement: 'The Communists nationalised *hakmarre*, then, all revenge killings were to be carried out by the Party . . . Everyone owed them blood.'

'Yes, of course, they nationalised *hakmarre*', he said dismissively, as if this were blindingly obvious. But it wasn't obvious at all for an outsider; it was something I had worked out very slowly for myself.

'You are the thirty-fourth person to whom I have given an audience', he told me. 'I have met the Pope and Mother Teresa – both of them blessed me and my work. I met President Ramiz Alia, the Communist president after Hoxha, a man of high education and culture. He denied all my accusations. He said "I am a persecuted man, too." The Communists forged the partisan legacy as well. There are 28,000 "partisan graves", they claim, but in fact there were only 2,000 partisan deaths. Yet 35,000 prisoners who were murdered in the camps have no graves at all. Four hundred thousand people were sent to Hoxha's gulag, which was far, far worse than either Stalin's or Hitler's. The only regime with which it can be compared is Pol Pot's in Cambodia. That is why the Communists are accused now of genocide and crimes against humanity by this government.'

So even in death the Albanians faked the record, claiming more for one side, denying the actuality, the reality of the others' deaths. This was what the Nazis had done with the Jews: 'liquidate' them and pretend nothing had happened, destroying the camps afterwards where they could, planting trees and pretend-farms on the site.

I asked Ndrek whether he was Moslem, Catholic or Orthodox. This started another wave of monologue.

'I have studied all religious systems – Christianity, Islam, Hinduism, Buddhism, Judaism and Marxism – not atheism or capitalism. They all have an axis called God. I love peace. I adore Christ. I am allergic to my past.'

But what had he been born, I insisted. 'I was born a Christian', he replied.

'He is a Catholic', added Mehmet Yezidi, who was himself from a Moslem family.

Ndrek came from one of the highland Dukagjini tribes but

wouldn't tell me which. No one liked using the word 'tribe' in Albania although there were still tribes; it was now a shame word, signifying 'primitive'.

All this took about two hours. It was gruelling: the heat, the concentration, the relentless piling up of suffering and pain, the slow drip of Ndrek's Albanian translated into hushed English by a nervous, anxious Mehmet Yezidi, himself only twenty-three years old and for whom all these horrors were both ancient history and hideous news.

But what of the Blood Feud Reconciliation Committee, of which Ndrek was head? Set up with Democrat government support, it attempted to get *fis* in blood to settle without resort to killing. How successful were they? How many feuds had been reconciled out of how many?

'Two hundred and forty-five families have been reconciled', he told me. 'We have twenty families still unreconciled on our books.' This sounded impressive.

'How many feuds are not recorded with you? Two hundred and sixty-five feuds altogether doesn't sound very many. In Bajram Curri and Kukes alone the killings are running at several a week. What about the rest of the mountains?' I asked.

'We have no camorra or mafia in Albania', he told me. 'Blood feuds are reducing. Democracy was a gift from God. If all work together for peace, God will help us.'

'How many deaths from *hakmarre* in the Dukagjini tribes since the fall of Communism in 1991?' I insisted. He didn't want to tell me. He hummed and hawed and waffled about peace and God and love. I insisted again.

'It is a state secret, the number', he finally told me. 'Three days ago there was a conference where all the figures were available. But not today. When are you next coming to Albania? Perhaps then the figures will be available. We have forty-three workers in Shkodra and eighty-three in all Albania, all unpaid. Can you raise some money for us in England?' he asked hopefully.

I told him I could not, but that I was here in Albania now. Why couldn't he tell me the figures?

The only people who came to his committee were families that wanted to settle. The others just killed their enemies as before; the committee had no powers of compulsion. It was, in effect a modern bureaucratic equivalent of the tribal *medjlis* which had arbitrated between different *fis* on the basis of the *Kanun of Lek*.

'Are you sure you can't tell me the total number of deaths by *hakmarre*?' I insisted. 'You have Democracy now. All information must be free.'

'I have the number, but I cannot tell you. My figures might not agree with the figures the police have.'

I had already got figures from England which suggested that several thousand people a year had been killed in feuds since 1992, and that the figure was rising steeply. To have reconciled 245 families was nothing; there were thousands, perhaps tens of thousands, of feuds; the committee was window-dressing.

'May God bless you and your family if you write good things about us – and if you don't it doesn't matter', was his parting benediction. The audience was over. I called for the bill but none came.

'This table has been paid for', I was told quietly by Mehmet. It seemed I had been the guest of the Blood Feud Reconciliation Committee, rather than the other way round.

*

As so often in Albania, I had gone to get information about one thing and been frustrated, but had learnt a great deal about something entirely different. The Blood Feud Reconciliation Committee was obviously another Potemkin village; but the appalling reality of Hoxha's camps had been exposed to me by a surviving victim.

But what of the blood feud, honour and vengeance?

'It was our experience that, like other codes of chivalry and the laws of war, the *Kanun of Lek* was honoured more in the breach than in the observance', Captain Julian Amery had remarked during the Second World War, before Hoxha had outlawed the old feudal code.

Hakmarre, *gjakmaria* and the *Kanun of Lek* were crucial to the understanding of all Albania, not just the Gheg north. The *kanun* represented the ancient values of all the Albanian peoples, Illyrian and Epirote. Under pressure and influence from the Greeks and Turks in the south, of Westernisation and modern ideas, the Tosks had modified their ways, but underneath a superficial adoptive veneer of Islam or Orthodoxy or French culture one could still perceive the old Albania. In March 1997 the revenge killings and blood murders were not limited to Ghegeria, but spread right throughout the whole land, as if the changes of the last two centuries had never taken place. The heart of Albania was in the *Kanun of Lek*.

Lek Dukagjini was a Catholic Gheg nobleman of the fifteenth century, a contemporary of Skanderbeg. His name – Alexander, Duke John – reflects the Roman and imperial past of medieval Albania. He was a political and clan opponent of Skanderbeg and had never allied himself with that paladin. Lek's word and honour, his fairness and sense of justice made him a byword; the *kanun* attributed to him codified the traditional rules of honour and shame. It is almost certain that Lek did not originate this code, however, and that it represents an extremely ancient set of rules dating back to pre-Homeric days. The closest resemblance to it is the *puktunwali* of the North-West Frontier of India, another clan-based, tribal, highland culture ruled by honour, shame and blood feud.

Reading the *kanun* explains much of the individuality of Albanians, and why dealing with them leads to problems for those not versed in the feudal ethos.

According to the *kanun* (entry 801), a man is dishonoured by a broad range of offences. These include being called a liar in front of others, or his wife being insulted, but they also include a whole host of offences against hospitality, such as someone removing the cover of a cooking pot in his hearth.

While not all of these would necessarily result directly in a blood feud, they are grounds for one if mediation is not sought or agreed. Once a feud starts, only blood can wipe out dishonour. Hence the endemic, the perpetual, nature of Albania's violence and disorder. Feuds are inherited over the generations. In Ottoman times in Ghegeria they were formally recorded by the state in a ledger, each killing noted and taxed.

'Every man's honour is his personal affair and no one may interfere with or constrain the defence of that honour in any way. Almighty God has touched the centre of our forehead with two fingers of honour.' (*Kanun of Lek*, entry 596). But if no one may interfere with the right of another to redress his offended honour, how can there be effective police, courts, armies or laws?

'Plundering is avenged by plundering' (entry 782): was there a simpler explanation of the apparently senseless destruction and looting of public buildings and goods when enforced order broke down? Property did not belong to the state, but rather to individual *fis*, which held it by right of their alliance with the ruling clique. When that clique lost power, the enemies of the holding *fis* looted and destroyed in revenge for past wrongs. However much aid and money were poured into Albania, they would always end up being plundered whenever order collapsed. Everyone was at war with everyone else.

In June 1997 food aid was being distributed by a Greek Orthodox charity in the Tosk south to needy, hungry families, the aid workers being protected by the Italian Army. While this food was being given out, Albanian snipers were firing from hidden vantage points at the aid workers, the recipients and the soldiers guarding them. This apparently insane activity – the starving firing on those bringing them food – is easily explained: those doing the firing belonged to *fis* at odds with those receiving the food, so of course they would shoot at their enemies, and those helping them, if there was no imposed autocratic order preventing them doing so. To help one Albanian family was to dishonour their enemies: to invest in one industry or support one government was to heap shame on those helped by their enemies.

In October 1997 Fatos Nano, appearing as Albania's prime minister now rather than as a man convicted and sentenced to gaol for embezzlement of foreign aid, turned up in Rome at the Council of European Ministers with the familiar Albanian begging bowl. He needed money, he claimed: loans, aid, grants. His first priority would be 'to restart employment in Albania'. Translated, this meant that without money for his supporters, the old Communist Party *fis* who were now the new Socialists, nothing could be done. He needed to give his supporters, his clients, booty to balance the booty that had been given to their enemies, all those Democrat *fis* which had been given the 'privatised' state property by Berisha. Europe would thus end up subsidising both sides in the Albanian morass.

How was life possible in Albania at all, then, in such anarchy? Because enough Albanians had in the past accepted the need for autocratic rule by a strong man; from him flowed power and privilege, goods and benefits. But there were always enemy *fis* who got nothing, and these waited their turn until the time was ripe and then overthrew the regime. All Albanian history was simply a variation on this theme.

*

In spite of the see-saw between anarchy and autocracy, there always remained the iron rules of hospitality laid out in the *Kanun*. For example:

602. The house of the Albanian belongs to God and the guest.

603. The guest must be honoured with bread and salt and heart.

609. At any time of the day or night, one must be ready to receive a guest with bread and salt and an open heart, with fire, a log of wood, and a bed.

610. A weary guest must be surrounded with honour. The feet of a guest are washed.

612. A special guest must be given coffee, raki, and food in addition to that eaten ordinarily.

620. If a guest enters your house, even though he may be in blood with you, you must say to him 'Welcome!'

621. The guest must be accompanied as far as he requests to be accompanied (when he leaves your house).

625. You must expend your labour and your food on a guest, in order not to be ruined and disgraced.

634. Hospitality honours you but also creates problems for you. 'Hospitality discloses the devil', some have said.

629. If your guest commits some evil while under your protection, you are responsible for it.

626. If you accompany your guest on his way, you are responsible for any dishonour that someone may cause him.

641. If someone comes to your door and asks for an ember to light his pipe, and you give it him, anyone who bothers him violates your hospitality.

The extremes to which these laws of responsibility extend, according to the *kanun*, are shown by the test case of The Traveller and the Bell-wether: A man from a *fis* in blood was making his way through a rocky ravine, *en route* to his home. He had a feeling, a prickling at the back of neck, that he was about to be ambushed. He was making for the house of a particular shepherd along the way, with whom he intended to claim the sacred right of hospitality and protection. He kept looking out for this shepherd, but could not see him. He did see, however, the bell-wether of the man's flock. 'Oh bell-wether!' the man cried in a loud voice, 'I put myself under the protection of your master as his guest, through you as his deputy!'

No sooner had these words been uttered than a shot was fired from the rocks high above and the traveller fell dead, a bullet between his eyes. His instincts had been right: his enemies had ambushed and killed him.

Now the shepherd had not heard the traveller place himself under his protection via the bell-wether; but two small boys herding goats in the mountain had, and they reported the man's last words to the tribal elders, who informed the shepherd, and called a *medjlis* to discuss this case. Was the shepherd obliged to take up the blood feud of the traveller or not? By placing himself under the protection of the shepherd by the proxy of the bell-wether, it could be argued there was this obligation. On the other hand, the bell-wether was not a person, and the shepherd could not be told of this matter by the bell-wether. Perhaps, therefore, he had incurred no obligation. Opinion was deeply divided.

The *medjlis* debated this case for days and could come to no conclusion. An expert on *kanuni* was called in from another tribe to deliver a judgement. He heard all the evidence on both sides and then pronounced that the traveller had placed himself under the protection of the shepherd legitimately via the bell-wether; this claim of protection had been reported to him by the two boys; and he was therefore obliged to revenge the dead man's honour with blood. Uncomplaining, the shepherd shouldered his rifle and bandolier, put provisions in his satchel and set out to search for and kill a male over eight years old from the *fis* of the traveller's enemies, to wipe out the dishonour to this guest he had never met or spoken to.

Such are the lengths to which Albanians will go both to defend their own honour and that of others. This code would have been quite understandable to Hector or Achilles: all across the ancient world feuds and revenge killings based on such strict notions of honour were normal for thousands of years.

The *kanun* also states that the man is undisputed head of the household; that he has the power of life and death over his wife and children. After three warnings he can beat, bind and whip his wife if she refuses to do what he tells her. He can also send his children out to work for him and keep the money they bring in. When a woman marries, her family give her husband a bullet, so that if he has cause to kill her for dishonouring him they have no right to any claim on him – she has been killed by her own parents' bullet. A man who has been dishonoured is considered as dead by the *kanun*. The blood-stained shirt of a murdered man will be preserved and hung out of the upper window of the family house, until such time as the killing has been avenged; and it is considered dishonourable to cut off the head or steal the weapons of a man killed in a blood feud.

The *kanun*, in fact, is a great fund of lore and even poetry concerning the old Albania: 'roads are the veins of the earth, water the blood of the earth'; 'the wolf licks its own flesh, but eats that of others'; 'soul for soul, all are equal before God'.

It is also a practical guide to explaining much that is obscure: 'If my spoken words enter the ears of another, and a third person uses them to ruin someone, I remain unaffected' (entry 521). This explains exactly how the Sigurimi operated in Hoxha's era. To those who denounced others nothing ever happened, and no feuds were started by such action when the third person, the Sigurimi, took up the dispute. According to the *kanun*, 'words do not cause death; a witch does not fall into blood.' 'You are free to be faithful to your word; you are free to be faithless to it.' 'Wash your dirty face, or if you like, make it blacker.' And 'There is no fine for an offence to honour. An offence to honour is never forgiven.'

When I finally managed to get hold of the *kanun* and study it thoroughly, the scales suddenly fell from my eyes. Much that I had found incomprehensible in Albania suddenly became entirely clear. I had read that the *Kanun of Lek* represented an archaic feudal code of the mountain tribes relating to past ages. What I discovered was a profound psychological portrait of contemporary Albania. It was not that Albanians 'followed' the *kanun*, as if a rule book or book of laws; rather, the *kanun* represented what Albanians, in their deepest essence, believed was right and wrong.

In all my travels, apart from Karl, I never met a foreigner, diplomatist, aid worker or soldier who had read the *Kanun of Lek*. In my view no official should be allowed to negotiate with Albanians, or even visit Albania, who has not mastered this quintessential code, which lays bare the very soul of an ancient, proud and much misunderstood people.

21

Albania Adrift

Mountains in the Soul

THE BULGARIAN MILITARY attaché had been taken by his kidnappers to the room above mine in the Hotel Kara Mustafa in Shkodra, and there had met his unsavoury fate. As I lay groaning gently on my narrow pallet I could see the terrible evidence: ancient blood now furred with green slime, brown, yellow and even purple organic stains, once grim liquids, which had crept through the floor to decorate the ceiling and upper wall of my cell-like room. When I closed my eyes I could almost hear the poor fellow's shrieks and moans as he was repeatedly sodomised by his captors.

Then his face would fade, and the Latin-quoting wolves would start up, gnawing away, often accompanied by a smiling Natasha egging them on, dressed in a sort of *Penthouse* version of Red Riding Hood's kit. Then the gunfire from outside in the streets would wake me, and bathed in my own sweat I would know night had fallen without having to open my eyes.

I was the only person staying at the Hotel Kara Mustafa, another factory-like Soviet-built concrete monstrosity in the centre of Shkodra, or Scutari as it had once been known. It was from Scutari that Edith Durham set off on muleback in 1908 to tour the Gheg highlands.

There was little Ottoman charm left now. The centre was peeling, shabby, pastel-coloured, colonial Italian public buildings and cafés, the rest Hoxha-era Stalinist blocks. Shkodra was bigger than Korça, smaller than Tirana, and contained echoes of both places. There were cafés and a few restaurants at least, and a *volta* in the afternoon. But I wasn't up to any of this.

I was in a bad way.

Sultan Murad had a specialist impaler from the Caucasus attached to his army who was known as 'the shashlikji'. By dint of long, careful practice on thousands of Christian prisoners, this cunning artificer had mastered the craft of inserting a sharpened stake into the fundament of his victim, and by wiggling and tapping it gently with a mallet, could manage to get the sharp end to come out eventually, after many a subtle twist and turn, through and between the *giaour*'s shoulder blades without touching any of the vital organs *en route* – bravo! This carefully skewered Christian would then be gently set upright, and the base of the stake firmly buried in the earth: some of these living shashliks managed to survive in this fashion for three or four days before expiring. The Sultan used to have great lines and avenues of these kebabs made for his entertainment, each one flopping about languidly on his own personal skewer.

Evidently the *shashlikji* had managed to infiltrate the Hotel Kara Mustafa and work his malevolent worst on me. As an added refinement, he had saturated the stake in chilli powder before inserting it. The whole of my entrails were on fire.

So I lay on the bed and groaned. Night followed day and day followed night. In the sharp sunlight the stains of the buggered Bulgarian on the ceiling and wall grew as lurid as a drug-induced, hallucinogenic light show.

There was no electricity for much of the time, and the mains water was erratic. I had a cold tap in my room, which sometimes ran for as much as one hour in every twenty-four, but never at the same time of day. I left the tap open, and when the gush or trickle awoke me, I hobbled over to the basin and doused myself all over, bathed my wounds, filled my water bottle and drank deeply.

I didn't eat or drink anything but water for three days and three nights. Then I felt much better. Fasting really does work. Part of the high spirits of the Middle Ages in Christendom was due to the regular fasts, I feel sure. We are all grumpy with over-feeding. Then I went out into hot July sunshine and ate an Italian ice cream, drank a litre of peach nectar from a cardboard box through a straw, and went to find Mehmet Yezidi's house.

No one knew where it was. I wandered up and down the hot, dusty streets thronged with people, asking, asking, asking. It took about two hours, though I had the address. Then someone said he knew the *fis*, and led me off the main road down a rabbit warren of lanes, through rows of *palatti*, and there it was: an old, crumbling Ottoman-era stone house with a red tiled roof, bizarrely cut in two and joined up to a modern *palatti*.

I knocked and called up to the wooden balcony. Voices came from within. It was the right place. Mehmet was out but his mother and grandmother were there. They welcomed me and I slipped off my shoes and went into their upstairs parlour, a faded, shabby-genteel temple to fallen prosperity. The Yezidis had been senior civil servants under the Ottomans and had lived in some style; it had been downhill all the way since then. This was *The Cherry Orchard* eighty years on. Everything had gone: the money, the land surrounding the fine old house, even half the house itself, knocked down in the Hoxha era. All around them were ugly tower-block monstrosities which had crept up, full of urbanised peasants. In the Yezidi house there was still a pretence at old-fashioned civilised living, with doilies on the table, flowers in vases, ragged and worn rugs on the floor, decorated mirrors, books on the shelves and a formal courtesy. But there was no money and no hope – there had been none for almost a century. The family had hung on and hung on and hung on, until hanging on was all they had left. Mrs Yezidi showed me Mehmet's pile of English books proudly, his classic novels and thumbed dictionaries and text books, his typewriter, his notebooks, all provided by 'English friends'.

He had got a place at the Tirana Art School when it wasn't necessary to bribe your way in. But now, a graduate, in order to qualify as a teacher of art and get a state job, he would have to pay a large bribe. He didn't have the money. His English patrons didn't approve of bribery and wouldn't help. He was trapped between two contradictory ethics.

His parents were very proud of him. He had learnt good English off his own bat; he had got '10 out of 10' at his art school exams, his father told me later, when he came back from his job at a factory – the first man I met who still had an industrial job.

Nothing good from the Democrat bonanza had come to the Yezidis. They had an old black-and-white TV and no new furniture, car or machinery. The atmosphere was distinctly Russian; it was like a Leningrad poet's house-in-exile in Alma-Ata or Bukhara, a place to which he had been evacuated during the Second World War, and from which he had never managed to escape. There were families like this all over the old Ottoman and Russian empires, left high and dry by the cataclysmic changes which had destroyed their world.

I was given Turkish coffee, bon-bons and cigarettes – Karelia brand from Greece – and cold water in thick, old-fashioned glasses. And then little home-made cakes and candied vegetable slices. From outside came the cries of children playing in the dust of the main road, and from time to time a slow rumble of old buses. If I hadn't seen so many of these heartbreak houses, lived the cramped, hopeless lives of their occupants with them, I might have found it exotic, romantic even. It wasn't any of that. It was failure and loss and poverty and just grimly hanging on because there was nowhere to go.

None of the older Yezidis spoke anything but Albanian. Mehmet was the only one who had mastered the new Latin of the late twentieth century, English. He was young – twenty-three – and well educated. He could get out. But where to? And what to do? How could he leave his family? How could he take them with him? Like Jules in Bajram Curri, Mehmet said to me on one occasion 'I would like to go to America, if someone would organise it for me.' He had no will, no drive of his own. Already he had given up the struggle. Vaclav Havel spoke of the 'post-prison psychosis' affecting the Czechs after the fall of Communism, this explaining their dazed passivity and confused inertia. Mehmet had it in spades; the weight of Albanian history had crushed the life out of him.

After an our or so of my waiting and being waited on, he appeared. He was overjoyed to see me, though we'd never met. He had heard I was coming from his 'friends' in England. He was a good-looking young man with a round eastern Anatolian face, dark hair and dark eyes. He could have been Armenian. He was running to fat already. He mother doted on him, bringing him roly-poly sweetmeats and virtually stuffing them down his throat. I asked him where he had been.

'Oh, out, walking round town slowly, seeing my friends. Killing time.'

None of them had any work or anything to do. The great hopelessness of provincial ennui! It spread out like a stain from the Balkans, across Anatolia and into Central Asia and over Russia – towns, villages, whole provinces where no one had anything to do, ever, where everything had been crumbling and falling down forever.

I told Mehmet I needed his services as translator for my interview with the head of the Blood Feud Reconciliation Committee. That at least would be some dollars in his pocket. But he didn't care about that. He wanted to talk, in English.

He was an authentic provincial intellectual from a nineteenth-century Russian novel, lost, confused and depressed. No one he knew read or was interested in foreign ideas. Money and goods were their gods. Mehmet actually thought for himself.

We sat and smoked my L & M cigarettes and his Karelia, and talked. His loneliness poured out of him in gushes, silences filling the gaps, until another spout.

'Skanderbeg, Ali Pasha, King Zog, Enver Hoxha – they are all the same person', he said, 'the Albanian character remains unchanged and unchangeable. It is a hopeless country with a hopeless people. This "democracy" is a temporary holiday from the killing and looting, then another dictatorship will come. You know, in the 1920s the death rate among young men was 20% per annum, due to the blood feud. It is an endemic disease, like malaria. There are feuds in Shkodra that have been going centuries. There are killings every week, in broad daylight. In the hotel you are staying at, in 1994, a man who was sitting in the lobby reading a paper had his head cut off while still alive by another man who came in with an axe. Revenge killing. They never found the head or the killer. I have seen people gunned down before my eyes while I sat at a café in the centre of town – *gjakmaria*. The killer comes up on a bicycle, pulls out a pistol or sawn-off shot-gun and boom! – shoots the guy at the table next to you and then slowly peddles away. No one sees it. No police arrive until the killer is far away. No one is ever charged. *Hakmarre*! This country is not Shqiperia but Hakmarria, Republica Hakmarria, the republic of revenge killings. Everyone blames someone else in the past: the Turks, the Serbs, the Italians, the Communists, the West, the Democrats, whatever. No one sees they are to blame.'

This was the most radical critique I had heard from any Albanian, and the most accurate. The depths of Mehmet's pessimism were only a reflection of the reality. The difference between him and others was he recognised the reality that they shut their eyes to.

We went out later in the cool of the early evening, sat at a pavement café, drank half-litres of imported draught beer, and smoked more cigarettes. We were the only two patrons. I had to pay for the beers, of course, because Mehmet had no money. He felt bad about this: 'You are my guest', he kept saying, but he could do nothing about it.

The café had a fixed awning for shade and plastic tables with wooden chairs. It was positioned on a roundabout. Next to it was a pizza truck which sold slices of thinly decorated dough to the few who could afford them. Across the way was a dusty open space which reminded me of a *maidan* in India, the province of dusty crows, organic litter and small, listless boys. On top of the disused chimney of a crumbling factory building beyond, two storks had made a nest; they stood there in full proprietorial dignity, each perched on one leg like a fakir. I had the impression of being in another geographical oxymoron, this time a former Italian colony somewhere in the foothills of the Himalayas; for behind us in purple shadow the Accursed Mountains rose magnificent in serried ranks.

The traffic ambling round the roundabout was mainly men on old Chinese-made bicycles, interspersed with the occasional jeep or Mercedes. There wasn't nearly as much money up here as in Tirana. Shkodra was reputed to have made fortunes in sanctions-breaking, supplying neighbouring Montenegro with petrol during the UN embargo in the late 1990s. Now that was finished. There was little industry and no tourism. What was the future for Shkodra?

'I pity Shkodra', Dr Shkrelli had told me, 'they are finished up there.' He meant that Gjirokastra wasn't, because it was near a 'better' border – with Greece, from where good things would flow. What could ever flow from Montenegro? Across the border were the descendants of the Albanians who had fled there during various wars. Albanians had this passive view of their country as a place into which things – goods, money, machinery – inevitably flowed from other places. They had been acted upon for so many centuries that they thought like catamites.

'The English invest in England!' the owner of the half-built fish restaurant near Butrint had said to me, wonder in his voice. Few Albanians who could do otherwise were foolish enough to invest in Albania; that was for gullible foreigners. They took what money they had managed to amass and fled with it abroad. King Zog was in this grand national stereotype.

So many Albanians had left Albania, over the centuries. Mehmet Yezidi would eventually leave, too, forced out by the events of March 1997.

'There is no chance and never will be for work or any occupation in Albania. This is the reality. Here in Greece Albanians have a very bad reputation and they are not seen equal to others. But I do not intend to be in touch, contact or make friends with any of them. They are risky people', he wrote from Salonika. Mehmet had abandoned not just Albania but the idea of himself being Albanian.

Mehmet's great advantage over the rest of the Albanians I had met was that he could see things as they actually were, without viewing them through the distorting optic of nationalist pride and grievance. But the cost of this clarity was exhaustion, a spiritual pessimism which showed in his lassitude and lack of initiative.

At the café we talked about Albania and about England. Mehmet had been to England for two weeks as a guest of his English friends in the West Country. They had shown him around, taken him to pubs, introduced him to people, gone on country walks, rambles round cathedral towns. He had even attended a summer school of some sort at Winchester College. What had he thought of England, then?

He was diffident. He didn't want to be seen to be begging for another invitation, a visa support letter.

'It was very clean, very well ordered – a high civilisation. People working together and co-operating. Compromise and common sense. The opposite of Albania', he concluded mildly.

He didn't mention how wealthy it was; he wasn't interested in that; it was the order and co-operation he noticed. All other Albanians talked about money and goods all the time, about how they could batten on to the wealth of the West.

How had Mehmet seen Albania when he returned from England, I asked him: did it look different to his eyes? He gave a grimace and took a puff on his cigarette.

'Very different. I noticed for the first time the dirt, the disorder, the lack of any sort of responsibility in the people. Albania looked to me like a giant rubbish tip, filthy, run down, ruined – a great ruin full of ruined people, people who had ruined themselves.'

I was shocked. Not because it wasn't true – it was – but because an Albanian had expressed it so frankly, without feeling shame. In this land of the proud Sons of the Eagle, heirs to the noble traditions of Skanderbeg, people always tried to persuade you of their great qualities, not to highlight their shortcomings. This frankness made Mehmet highly unusual: only Tybalt, the Protestant convert in Tirana, had been as bleak, but he had his faith to support him. Mehmet had nothing but his nihilism.

When you are travelling in a remote and difficult country where your life may be at risk, you often wonder if you have in fact got the whole thing entirely wrong. Perhaps the place has turned you doolally, and those men with machine-guns are not actually brigands but jovial Rotarians just doing a bit of weekend target practice. Mehmet Yezidi convinced me that I hadn't got it wrong about Albania.

He said to me once, while we were drinking beer one evening: 'The problem with the Albanians is that they have got mountains in the soul.'

22

Live Vests under Your Seat

Flying Dada Airways

A HIGHLAND GHEG wedding celebration was in full swing, crowding the reception rooms of the Hotel Kara Mustafa. Three generations were present: the old folks in tribal costume, the Communist-era apparatchiks in drab suitings and floral dresses, and the young sprigs in their pseudo-Italian finery. A pop group was grinding out old '60s numbers and the young set were sedately dancing. Small children ran around playing. The windows had been left open so the *feux de joie* could be directed outside; the concrete ceiling ricocheted the bullets dangerously. Rifles, automatic pistols and shot-guns were more in evidence than machine-guns. The noise of revelry, music and gunfire went on all night and into the next day. When I enquired how much longer the party would last, the hotel manager, who spoke some Italian, told me, 'Sempre tre giorni per i sposati – allora – due giorni piu'.

I paid my bill and was out within ten minutes. There were buses to Tirana every hour. I went round to say goodbye to Mehmet. He was sad to see me go.

'We could make a party, go to the beach, talk some more', he suggested hopefully.

But I was overwhelmed with talk and did not want to lie on any beaches. I needed to think and take notes and reflect on what I had seen and heard. Travellers as well as gastronomes can suffer from indigestion. Albania had presented an over-rich menu; I felt I had gulped down almost too much for one trip. I was exhausted and becoming bad-tempered.

We had a last coffee together in the café of the Hotel Kara Mustafa, strong and black.

'Can I do anything for you in England?' I asked.

'Books', Mehmet replied, 'send me some books, please, in English. They are impossible to find.'

'What sort of books?'

'On the English language. Colloquial expressions, slang, that sort of thing. Complicated stuff.' I promised I would, and when I got back I did my best, sending off a parcel with no real hope it would ever get to him, so many packets from abroad were stolen by the Albanian postal workers. But it did. He sent me a card thanking me.

He saw me on to the bus and waved goodbye forlornly. When would his next English visitor from Mars arrive? The last I saw of him was as he plodded off round the town again, the endless circuit, nothing to do, nowhere to go.

The journey to Tirana was bad, though the road was quite reasonable for Albania. My sore bottom made sitting painful and so I stood most of the way. There were police everywhere *en route*, particularly at the entries and exits to the towns and villages. It was strange to see Catholic churches, and women in costume by the roadside, like illustrations from Edith Durham, white wimples over their heads. The fields were high with ripe maize and in the wheat fields men with white turbans were harvesting with scythes. Cows and donkeys stood, lay or wandered slowly in the middle of the road; we would slow and shudder past them. A lorry had jack-knifed across the road and into the ditch; police waved us by slowly, their machine-guns unslung. They were obviously there to prevent looters pillaging the wreck.

It was very hot. The driver kept the front door open to let the breeze in when he could; he shut it when he saw a police post coming up. It was a $5 fine if they caught a bus with the door open. At the front a group of middle-aged men had formed round the driver, like a Spanish tertulia, discussing politics and the way of the world. I had brought my water-bottle with me but it was soon emptied. We did not stop except to take passengers on or drop them. I was in agony for the last couple of hours, my innards jolted to pieces by the pot-holes.

It was such a relief to be back in Tirana again. I walked through the familiar streets as if I were in London again, almost. I had a key to Alexei and Alicia's flat, and walked up the stairs slowly, pausing on each floor to catch my breath.

I let myself in and flopped down on the bed in the spare room, where all my clothes and things lay untouched, just as I'd left them. Then I went to sleep and didn't awake until after dark.

*

Alexei and Alicia were relieved to see me. I had promised to phone them when I got to Shkodra from the Accursed Mountains to say I was all right, but the lines had been down between the north and Tirana. They had been worried. Rumours of the chaos and violence spreading across Ghegeria had started to reach Tirana.

Newspapers were still appearing, ostensibly uncensored, but nothing of conditions in Djakova was ever mentioned. I told Alexei and Alicia about the brigands of Lekbibaj, the murdered Dutchman, the shot Hungarian doctor, the thefts and murders, the cowardly police. They were shocked but not surprised.

'Sali Berisha!' they said, and cut the air with the flat of their hands. I told them about the strong colours of Dibra, of the hidden life of the women. They were fascinated.

'E qualcosa de Edith Durham, veramente!' Alexei exclaimed. 'Io non ho creduto che questi tradizzione existono sempre in Albania.'

He had been to Dibra when in the army, thirty years ago, *en plein communisme*. But then he had stayed in barracks and not with a family. I realised how lucky I had been in my travels. Perhaps not since Julian Amery in 1942-3 had an English author been able to live so close to ordinary Albanians in their own houses. Even he had been surrounded by spies and orderlies much of the time.

I didn't go out for three days. I slept and drank water and Earl Grey tea with lemon. I didn't want to eat. My room was very hot: it got the sun full on the window side all day, and was on the top floor. I soaked my top sheet in water and put it over me; the evaporation kept me cool for a hour or so. Alexei and Alicia left me alone.

*

Getting into Albania had been one thing; getting out was proving another. The few airlines which serviced Tirana were booked solid for the next six months – so many diplomatists, military and aid workers going in and out, not to mention the Democrat Party fat cats. There was a ferry service to Italy from Durrës, but there were rumours that this had been 'suspended' owing to repeated hijack attempts. The ferry ticket office knew nothing, but were not optimistic. The land borders with Montenegro, Serbia and Slavo-Macedonia were sealed tight.

This left the dreaded bus service from Tirana to Athens, via the notorious frontier crossing at Kakavia, or a return via Korça to Salonika. Neither was an attractive prospect. The journey to Athens took twenty-four hours, most of it sheer bone-shaking in an unair-conditioned and very old bus. The temperature in Athens was currently 40 degrees. People were dying of the heat; taxis and private cars alike had been banned from the centre in an attempt to reduce pollution. The bus arrived in a suburb of Athens miles away from the airport. More to the point, there were reports that two Athens-bound buses from Tirana had been held up recently near the border and everyone robbed.

The only other alternative was Dada Airways. The advertisements were in *Zeri i Populitt* every day: fly to Athens for just $100 one-way on 'Albania's newest independent airline'. Albania's only independent airline, they could have said just as accurately.

I had asked Carruthers about Dada Airways before I'd left for the north.

'I believe they go when the plane is full', he'd replied. 'Something of a hedge-service. If a passenger wants the driver to put him down in Gjirokastra or Jannina, say, he just pulls his pistol on the feller, or so I've heard.'

I had convinced myself that this was Carruthers' attempt at a joke. What planes did Dada Airways have?

'One World War II vintage, prop-driven Tupolev, ex-Turkmenistan Aeroflot, which some mercenaries were using to bomb one of the factions in the Afghan civil war, before the Albanians got hold of them', Carruthers said slowly, examining his fingernails with care. 'Known as "flying-coffins" in Central Asia, I believe, those particular prop-driven Tupolevs. Two fell out of the sky recently over New Delhi. No survivors.'

This surely couldn't be correct. I went to the Dada Airways head office in down-town Tirana to check it out. The plane was indeed a Tupolev, but a jet borrowed from Hemas Bulgarian Airways. No one knew anything about Afghan mercenaries. I thought that Hemas sounded like some terrible liver disease, but kept this to myself. The flights went twice a week, if the plane was in service and not grounded, awaiting spare parts from the depot in Tashkent.

On trying to book a ticket to Athens on Dada, however, I was informed that the price for a non-Albanian was $200, not $100. The bus only cost $50. I waxed wroth, protested, waved my arms – to no avail. The girl at the ticket desk was adamant. No $200, no ticket. I went back to Alexei's flat ticketless and fuming.

'You must see the manager and show them your card telling them you are a big BBC journalist', Alexei advised. 'Last week an Italian girl from RAI did this, and got a Dada ticket for $100.'

I recognised sage advice when I heard it. So I decided to push chutzpah even further, into the realms of sheer, naked gall.

The next day, dressed in neat shirt and tie, I respectfully requested an interview with the manager of Dada Airways, proferring my bullshit-encrusted visiting card to the receptionist. This evidently did the trick. I was ushered into his office immediately.

'I am writing an important article on tourism in Albania, and I want to interview you, sir, to make a big publicity for Dada Airways in the West', I lied cheerfully, taking out my pad and pencil ostentatiously.

Now, if there is one thing no Albanian can resist it is being interviewed. To talk and talk and talk and have a Westerner take it all down is demi-paradise.

The manager, a short man in his late thirties with dark hair and a twelve o'clock shadow, lapped it up. He spoke good, fluent English, for he had been a flight controller at Tirana Airport in the Communist days. Now he was the big cheese at Dada Airways.

I asked him question after question, writing all his answers down with great enthusiasm in my notebook. Dada Airways were going places: New York, Moscow, London, Bonn, San Francisco, Tokyo, Mogadishu (the manager's brother lived there), Rome, Paris and Geneva – when they got more investment money to buy more planes and hire more staff. Until then, well, there was just the Tirana-Athens service, twice a week, spare parts permitting. The Tashkent factory's fax machine was a Soviet fax and didn't work very well; in fact, often if you sent them a fax their machine sent your own fax back to you again, instead of a reply, he told me. This caused delays and confusion.

'Very Soviet', I commented, but surely Russia didn't manufacture fax machines of its own.

That he couldn't say, but the Tashkent depot's fax machine had printed on the top of its fax paper 'Soviet-made Fax Machine'. Perhaps someone, somewhere in the ex-Soviet Union had kept their sense of humour.

This reminded me of the – apparently true – story of the plastic Irish leprechauns for sale at Shannon Airport souvenir shop which had 'Made in Japan' printed on the underside of the base, but in Gaelic.

When the manager finally started to run out of steam, I put my proposal to him.

'Do you think it would be possible for me to travel myself on Dada Airways, to sample the lavish Albanian hospitality and superb modern comfort of your bold new independent, international airline?' I suggested.

He leapt like a prime speckled trout at my fly. But of course! Any time! He would be delighted!

Could he arrange a small discount, perhaps, as I was a journalist on a goodwill mission to promote tourism in Albania? Perhaps allowing me to travel at the Albanian price?

But of course! He would arrange it straight away! He telephoned the girl in the office outside, who had refused me a $100 ticket the day before, and told her to issue me one now.

I bowed and scraped my way out of his office. The girl bathed me with respectful smiles, and wrote out my ticket then and there, a $100 note that had been up to Lake Gashit and back in my emergency money belt changing hands with ease and pleasantness. I went back to Alex's light-hearted. At least I would not have to suffer the Athens bus.

I had to go to another airline office to check an onward reservation to London from Athens. There I saw a true wonder, a telephone computer link between Tirana and Athens, which worked. Ahead of me in the queue was an elderly American man who was having a hard time. The Albanian cashier was waving a $100 note at him.

'I do not think this note is a good one', she said in English, 'I think it is a fake.'

'But I just got it from the State Bank of Albania!' the American said in exasperation.

'Then it almost certainly IS a fake!' the woman replied with triumph. 'I will accept this note only provisionally, and issue you with your ticket, then send the note over to be officially checked. If it is a fake you will have to pay again.'

The man nodded dumbly. What could he do?

It was easy to see how this scam worked. The woman would exchange the genuine $100 he had given her for a false one she could buy for $5. He would be presented with the false one later on when he wanted to leave, and told he had to pay up again or he couldn't travel. The woman would thus make $95 profit. Foreigners were so easy to cheat. Cashiers in airline offices earned about $50 a month, so this was almost two months' wages to her.

I said nothing. What did I know? I might have become too cynical, after all.

*

I spent my last few days in Tirana resting. I had found two Hoxha-era pirated paperbacks in English, Graham Greene's *The Comedians* and *The Quiet American*. They were copied from the Penguin edition: I could tell from the print and the list of other Graham Greene books at the back. When they had been printed they had cost 8½ lek each – 8½ cents. Now they were $2 each.

So I lay on my bed at Alexei's and drank *Shesh-izi* red wine and smoked my *Tarabosh* tobacco and read about Haiti and South Vietnam of the 1950s in the Tirana of the late 1990s. Saturated in self-pity and bourgeois existentialism, what a remote yet familiar world these two novels conjured up!

As the gunfire at night drew ever closer to the centre of Tirana, and I strained to read the fading text in the dwindling daylight, I mused on how the world changed so much, yet stayed so much the same. Here I was in classic Greene-land: a corrupt, violent, Third World country about to be engulfed in chaos and revolution, a cast of seedy misfits from Europe and America all round me. Yet all this was the product of fifty years of 'Socialism', of Enver Hoxha's brave new world. How feeble and amateur the Haitian tonton macoutes sounded compared to the Sigurimi! How gentle and cautious the South Vietnamese and their American advisors compared with the Albanian Communists!

On the day before I left, I steeled myself to go to the Communist Genocide Exhibition which was on at the Palace of Culture. I had seen Auschwitz, Birkenau and Theresienstadt, so I knew what to expect; the industrial relics of mass murder vary only in their presentation. There were blood-stained uniforms, bones, rags, identity cards with bullet holes, photographs of torture chambers and mass hangings, open graves, firing-squad walls, emaciated bodies, staring eyes, the legions of the unjustly slaughtered. There were huge TV screens showing films of the camps, the places of murder, the grim remains. Over the river at Spaç they used to hang naked prisoners inside an iron cage in midwinter as a punishment. The gallows with the hanged bodies on were the portable three-legged triangular Ottoman models on which I'd seen Adnan Menderes executed in the '60s in Turkey, and which the Sultans used to carry around with them on campaign.

The exhibition was Democrat Party propaganda, of course, but that didn't make it less true. I went on a Sunday, a public holiday. I was the only person there. The Albanians knew all about Communist persecution. They didn't need exhibitions; they had lived it.

The next day Alexei walked me to the bus which took the workers out to Rinas Airport at 6 a.m.; the ticket cost 60 cents. If a foreigner got a cab it cost $50. We had an armed police guard all the way. There had been a hold-up of a bus on the airport road just the day before, it was rumoured. The banditry and highway robbery were creeping closer and closer to Tirana.

'Ring me from London to let me know you have arrived safely', Alexei said as I climbed aboard. For him travel outside Albania seemed as dangerous as he knew it to be inside the country. I could not explain to him that Athens to London was like a bus ride down a country lane. He had never been further than Jannina.

'I will if I can', I replied, 'but you know the phones often don't work.' If you ever read this, Alexei, I did try, but the phone connection was impossible. I'm sorry.

Rinas was tiny, a collection of miniature concrete boxes, like Nicosia Airport in the early 1950s, when I first arrived in Cyprus as a child – smaller even. It felt as if it had been built by the Chinese; even the pastel pinks and blues on the walls were redolent of Cathay.

There was no airport café, no staff, no shops, no water tap, no lavatory even. No security machines to X-ray your bag, no advertisements, no airline offices. There were six uniformed policemen, though, lounging around smoking and hitting each other not so gently on the back out of camaraderie and boredom.

Ten minutes before our flight was due to leave the passengers, the air crew and the one check-in official all arrived in the same minibus from Tirana, guarded by a police car, four uniformed cops with machine-guns. All those foreign passports to protect on an open road half an hour away from the capital.

I checked in and then paid my $10 tax to leave and passed through into transit. Five dollars to enter Albania, ten to leave. There was no customs control: what could I possibly be taking out?

There was a duty-free shop in the transit lounge loaded with goods you never saw in the rest of Albania: gold jewellery, silver, rich oriental carpets, embroidered traditional waistcoats. Was this a Communist-era shop for the *nomenklatura* which had somehow survived, or a new capitalist hard-currency venture? The shop was closed and there was no one around. Who would bother opening it for a Dada exit flight?

All the passengers for Dada Airways were Albanians who had obtained foreign passports and therefore foreign currency, and were thus able to pass through that looking-glass of the late twentieth century, the invisible barrier between the Third World and the First.

The grounds of the airport had been laid out neatly and planted with flowers and shrubs; there were palm trees and well-tended pathways. Beyond loomed the mountains. Where were we? Central Asia somewhere, surely.

The Tupolev was very small. It sat alone on the tarmac, away from the main buildings, as if ashamed. It was painted Soviet-olive drab, and had the name 'Tristan Tzara' painted on the nose-cone; it wobbled on its wheels when we climbed up through its bottom on a spindly metal ladder. The seats were as if designed for children. The gangway could barely accommodate one person, even moving sideways. It was the smallest plane I'd ever been on in my life. There were thirty seats, fifteen a side, like two teams for some bizarre aerial contest. When I sat down I noticed there was a printed sign in Bulgarian and English in front of me. The English read: LIVE VESTS UNDER YOUR SEAT.

The door was shut and the engines revved up and away we went, into the air with a whoosh. I looked at my watch. We had left exactly on time, another example of the amazing Albanian punctuality. The whole plane-load of passengers clapped vigorously as we rose across the brown, summer-burnt mountains, though whether to laud the pilot's skill or their own escape from Albania wasn't clear.

A steward in uniform served us sandwiches, and soft drinks in paper cups. I looked down below me at the mountainous land through which I had so laboriously travailed for the last three months. It looked like Afghanistan.

*

There was heartfelt applause once again from all the passengers when we landed at Athens Airport. We were out of the clutches of Ali Pasha and his spiritual descendants.

Our Tupolev appeared tiny, absurd even against the great bulk of the international airliners on the tarmac. We were shunted to a remote part of the airport where we would not embarrass anyone.

Air-conditioned, calm, ordered, peaceable, loaded to the gunwales with luxury products of all sorts from all over the world, Athens Airport transit lounge appeared as a wholly unreal vision. Where were the snot-covered children, the policemen with machine-guns, the goats and saddle-sore mules, the empty, ruined buildings and tiny shops bereft of goods? I wandered around in a daze feeling very small.

Albania had been my world for almost three months. But it was a country no bigger than Wales. I remembered a Russian friend who had been taken to a supermarket in Chiswick on her first day in London in 1990 and had fallen on the floor in hysterics. She had had to have a sedative injected by a doctor: all those products freely available to everyone. I had asked an intellectual in Leningrad what he thought the West was really like back in 1990: 'I don't believe all our propaganda about you starving in the West', he had told me, 'I think you have queues at your shops, like us, but that they are not as long as ours.'

So how could you explain Albania to the West? I tried, on getting back to London, but a bored look of incomprehension and disbelief came over people's faces. Travellers' tales! The Balkans – bandits, wolves, derring-do in the mountains!

I met Peter Hopkirk at an Italian café in central London; he more than anyone had been instrumental in my going to Albania with the idea of writing a book about my travels. He was the first person who had believed in the project. We sat over *cappuccini* for two hours while I let Albania gush out of me without respite.

'Well', he said, when I had finished, 'how are you going to tackle it?'

I mumbled something about current fears that the travel book had become an exhausted form, mannered and self-regarding, waffling Old Etonians on bicycles; about having to re-invent the genre after Bruce Chatwin, that sort of thing.

'Never mind all that', he said, 'just go away and write it down the way you've told it to me, with all the voices – the ordinary people's voices.'

So that's what I did.

Postscript

The Dance of the Kalashnikovs

'A time is coming when men will go mad, and when they see someone who is not mad they will attack him, saying: "You are mad, you are not like us."'

from *The Sayings of the Desert Fathers*
Anthony the Great

IN MARCH 1997 Albania's short-lived post-Communist, Democrat government collapsed in a welter of violence, looting and destruction.

The pyramid schemes in which Albanians had placed 95% of their savings collapsed, leaving virtually the whole country penniless. Riots broke out in the south, in Vlora, Gjirokastra and Saranda, and eventually spread across the whole country. The police and army melted away and the state arsenals were looted. Vast stocks of Kalashnikovs, mortars, heavy machine-guns, landmines, tanks, rockets and ammunition passed into the hands of the people, who used them to settle scores with the SHIK and their clan enemies, or simply to rob and kill.

Anarchy reigned. On TV, children of six were seen loosing off volleys from machine-guns, the wooden handles sawn off to accommodate their pygmy arms. The price of a Kalashnikov fell from $1,000 to $3. Many of these weapons were immediately smuggled and sold to ethnic Albanians in Serbian-occupied Kosovo. In all, an estimated 4 million automatic weapons were looted, more than one each for every Albanian man, woman and child. All the prisoners escaped from the gaols, including Fatos Nano, leader of the Socialist Party, and Enver Hoxha's widow. Some criminals stole police uniforms and robbed banks with armoured cars and tanks, or else held up private citizens with pistols and machine-guns.

Democrat Party government was replaced by gangster rule; bloody turf wars between rival bands of mafiosi engulfed the country. Children were kidnapped and held to ransom or murdered; women and children were raped; stores, factories and food depots were pillaged and burnt. Whole residential blocks barricaded themselves in with burnt-out cars to prevent the bandits getting at them.

Anything that could be looted and destroyed was, including the hospitals and schools. Two and a half billion dollars of damage was done and more than 2,000 people were killed. It had taken the combined efforts of the Ottomans, King Zog and Enver Hoxha 150 years to disarm the ordinary Albanian; in a few weeks the clock was turned back two centuries. Mobs of armed Albanians shouting 'Take us to America!' now fired their Kalashnikovs at US helicopters, which landed in Tirana to take out their citizens.

Western diplomatists and refugees were taken off by warship from Durrës after a night surrounded by armed looters on the beaches. A force of foreign intervention was landed to oversee fresh elections and food aid distribution. Sultan Zani, known as 'the King of Vlora' and the country's most notorious gangster, declared for the Socialist Party. Victory for Berisha would mean 'the dance of the Kalashnikovs', he claimed. In his fortified headquarters lay a great arsenal of thousands of anti-tank rockets, grenades and machine-guns.

Berisha's Democrats lost the election: the former Communists were back in power again. The new prime minister was the convicted foreign-aid fraudster and ex-gaolbird Fatos Nano. The only growth area in the economy was drug growing and processing; the mafia distributed marijuana seeds to the peasants and bought the crop at $200 a kilo for export to Italy. Hundreds of thousands of Albanians tried to flee the country to Italy and Greece, including the whole of the Albanian navy still afloat. Seventeen Italian cities were reported to be controlled by the Albanian mafia; twenty thousand under-age Albanian prostitutes were estimated to be working the Italian streets. The Italian navy was accused of deliberately sinking Albanian refugee ships to stem the flood.

*

Slowly news began to filter through to me.

Karl and Thomas, the missionaries I stayed with in Bajram Curri, had managed to get out on literally the last plane with their families. They had to leave everything behind – cars, computers, clothes, books and personal effects – to be looted by the mob.

From Shkodra a letter got through to England from Mehmet Yezidi: 'Thank God, we are well after all that catastrophe. I've never before heard of people fighting against nothing, but destructing [sic] and terrorising women and children – the innocent people. There is no more hope for this country as there are some individuals who want no help, no education, no progress and no peace. Did you hear about the destruction of the Agricultural Institute and Vet Clinic as well? They even stolen [sic] the contaminated refrigerator!'

From Korça came the news that a woman had recognised a man in a bar who had raped her; he was sitting drinking with six friends. She went in, pulled out her pistol and shot all seven of them dead. Then she went into hiding as the dead men's relatives and friends tried to hunt down her family and murder them all. According to Gabriel, who confirmed this report, three of the men she killed were innocent bystanders, refugees from Vlora. Blood feuds and vendettas now engulfed the whole of Albania; *gjak per gjak, kok per kokë*, blood for blood, a head for a head. Old Albania was back with no restraints. Everyone was armed, everyone's home a fortress. There was no law and no security save in family and guns. *Hakmarre* and *gjakmaria* ruled, from the political leadership down to the man on the street. There had been nothing like this since the worst days of the Ottomans. In the new parliament a Socialist deputy pulled out his automatic in the debating chamber itself, and shot a Democrat deputy – a Gheg blood feud, it transpired. All charges against the old Communists were dropped by the new government, which proposed to reintroduce the death penalty 'as a matter of urgency'. In the villages peasants started putting up statues of Enver Hoxha again.

From Korça Gabriel reported that he had got hold of two tanks and some heavy machine-guns during the looting of the arsenals. He had deployed these to fend off the mob which was bent on ransacking his brother-in-law's Jolly Roger factory. The legion of mercenaries manning these weapons had been paid 'ten times the daily wage of the factory workers'. They had fought a series of pitched battles outside the factory gates over several days, with many dead and wounded. The factory was still intact and in production, Gabriel said. They had looted a generator for electricity, and the cloth from Germany was now trucked in under armed guard from Greece, the finished clothes trucked out the same way. 'I'm not sure I quite believe Gabriel on the factory still operating', his English benefactor told me. 'He might just be putting a positive spin on things.'

Gabriel was also alleged to have been in the forefront of the general looting, machine-gun ever at the ready. His children had not been allowed out of the family apartment for several months, for fear of kidnapping. 'I would never have believed all this could come again in Albania', Gabriel had commented, on the chaos. He had, however, managed to get a volume of his own poetry published, in English and Albanian, and this slim volume was reported to be selling well among his ex-pupils. Armed looting and bilingual poetry, high culture amidst bloody tank battles – a very Albanian blend, this.

Popi, Gabriel's sister, had managed to get her precious English sewing-machine out of her apartment; she was now up in a remote village, with the machine, still making shoes for a living.

Rahman the hairdresser had managed to get his Western equipment out of the salon before the building was looted and burnt out; he was now styling hair from home, his children manning Kalashnikovs at the windows to protect the clientele inside.

From Gjirokastra, Dr Shkrelli was reported to be safe, but barricaded into his house, gloomily chain-smoking cigarettes, his jacket festooned with hand grenades; the Macedonian job had fallen through and he was waiting for something to turn up.

A letter from Dr Cider informed me that Mimoza's efforts to secure a visa for her son Egrem had finally borne fruit; he had escaped from Albania and was now studying in England at the Wormwood Scrubs Business School. Who was paying for this wasn't clear – 'not me, certainly', added the doctor. Ominously, Egrem had already been in 'a spot of bother with the police', Cider revealed, this down in the West Country where he had been staying with one of his now disillusioned English benefactors.

Natasha managed to get out to England on a 'study visa', too. She left a breathless message on my telephone answering machine. She sounded very sexy, and expressed her keenness to see me; the wheel of fortune had turned once again. She said she was staying 'with some Albanian friends in London'. The number she gave me was odd, neither 0181 nor 0171 prefixed. When I rang, the phone was answered by altogether another girl, with a marked South London accent. In the background rose a babble of female gossip. 'Nah, nah, we 'ain't got no Albanian girls 'ere, darlin' – but if you come round I bet I've got what you're lookin' for . . .'

Evidently I was through to a Brixton cat-house. Perhaps Natasha had given me the wrong number. Then I remembered the fate of her last older lover, warned off by the Sigurimi. I didn't try to ring back again.

From Bajram Curri came an unconfirmed report that a promising career in the international heroin trade had been nipped in the bud; Jules had stopped a stray machine-gun bullet during the March disturbances.

In June BBC radio news reported that Carruthers had been stabbed by his Albanian fiancée in Tirana. The *Daily Telegraph* claimed the next day that he had been followed by the Berisha secret police, the SHIK, suspected of having been a British secret agent. His apartment had been burgled, perhaps by SHIK. Carruthers had gained something of a louche reputation for himself among foreign correspondents, allegedly offering to take them to 'the largest disco floor in the Balkans'. His fiancée had knifed him in the chest and the side. He had been evacuated to a hospital in Brindisi, leaving an empty, fortified British Embassy guarded by the SAS. The Ambassador had been recalled to London for 'consultations'. There was no reason suggested as to why Carruthers' fiancée might have attacked him.

In December 1998 I heard from Bajram Curri that Major-Doctor Muharrem Bajraktar had been ambushed, murdered, and robbed in July 1998 while en route into Kosovo through the Accursed Mountains. With a group of Kosovars he had been taking a clandestine cargo of guns and money into Serb-controlled Kosovo for the Kosovo Liberation Army. The two brothers who ambushed and shot him were themselves later murdered in a blood-feud by Fatmir Haklaj, the former Police Chief of B. C. The Major-Doctor's son

Aryan, my demented driver, was later ambushed and murdered, also in a blood-feud, while he was on his way from Bajram Curri to Dushaj.

*

The Albania I saw in the summer of 1996 is now as much of a historical epoch as the world of Hoxha or Zog. It vanished forever during the maelstrom of destruction in March 1997.

ORGANISM, DISCIPLINE, EMULACION was the Communist slogan displayed in large outside an apartment block opposite the Hotel Apollonia in the Hoxha years. To make these qualities stick in Albania was never more than a dream.

DISORGANISM, INDISCIPLINE, DISEMULACION must surely be an apposite epitaph for the short-lived Berisha regime I saw, which failed not from being too repressive but, like that of King Zog, from not being brutal enough.

Albania has retreated once again into silence, isolation and conjecture, hidden behind its impenetrable curtain of mountains and lawlessness. My journeys would be as impossible today as in the years before 1991.

I had the great good luck to see more than most outsiders of this enigmatic, this extraordinary and, when all is said and done, this fascinating country. I enjoyed great traditional hospitality from a bygone age, a genuinely warm welcome, and encountered much kindness and many fascinating characters. I was supremely fortunate.

But I was also lucky to get out alive.

In dealing with the Land of the Eagle and its undeniably proud and warlike Sons, that anarchic mix of smiling murderers and honourable kidnappers, hospitable rapists and elegant torturers, welcoming robbers and wife-beating family men, kindly blood feuders and generous headhunters, sophisticated forgers and multilingual embezzlers, perhaps the best words of guidance come in the form of two traditional Albanian proverbs: 'First buy the horse, then the saddle' and 'Only the owner can pull his donkey from the mire.'

Index

Index

Assos 65, 127
Ataturk, Kemal 42, 94, 95
Athens 6, 60, 81, 324
Athens Airport 330
Auschwitz 328
Azem 63–4

Babaliou, Emira 54–5
Baha'i faith 164, 187
Baikal, Lake 49, 291
Bajraktar, Aryan 282–3, 299, 300, 336
Bajraktar, Baçkim 289, 292, 294
Bajraktar *fis* 281, 288
Bajraktar, Lorelei 279–300
Bajraktar, Major-Doctor Muharrem
    278–300, 336
Bajram Curri (B. C.) 155, 176, 186, 226,
    229, 240, 242, 243, 247–71, 273–7,
    281, 282, 298, 299, 306, 334, 336
Baker, Sir Samuel 222
BALFORCE 163, 172–3, 179
Balli Kombetar Party 22, 74, 93, 126,
    143–4, 219, 302, 304
Ballsh 139
bandits 193, 230, 243–61, 265, 266, 272,
    282, 295, 297, 328, 333
Bangladesh 192
Baptist Church 186, 194
Barbara, Aunt 168
Barber, T. 165
Bardhyl 106
Baudelaire 183
BBC 1, 75, 159, 162, 195, 217, 231, 256,
    325, 336
BBC World Service 22–3, 67, 149, 165,
    182, 187–8, 203, 223–4
beards and moustaches 61, 89, 215
bears 85, 163, 165, 214, 226, 278–9
Beatles, The 73
Beden Camp 304
begging 180
Bektashi tribe 298
Berat 80, 93, 109, 114, 135
Berisha, President Dr Sali 62, 108,
    113–14, 121, 122, 123, 126, 127, 140,
    152, 176, 195, 309, 323

general election 18, 20, 32, 69, 71, 82,
    157, 159, 161, 167, 218, 333
Gheg background 28, 216, 231
regime 20, 36, 46, 71, 111, 112, 134,
    173, 180, 225, 246, 254, 336–7
besa 9, 52, 186, 225, 238
Bey, Etem 163
Bey, Mehti 145
Bible, The 189–90, 193, 194–5
Bible in Spain, The 193
Bicycle Thieves, The 29
biographi, 22, 73, 135, 179, 304
birds, lore concerning 210
Birkenau 328
black market 108–9, 116, 122, 167,
    234–5
Blake, William 182
Blood Feud Reconciliation Committee
    302–7
blood feuding (*gjakmaria*) 124, 160, 186,
    191, 209, 215, 226, 235, 239, 252–3,
    255, 257, 262, 265, 276, 284, 285,
    286, 296, 302–12, 317, 334
Blue Danube Radio 264
BMW 129
Bogart, Humphrey 245
borders 277, 279
    with Greece 5–6, 8, 10, 11–17, 60–1,
    83, 108
    with Montenegro 173, 261, 280, 291,
    318, 324
    with Serbia 173, 213, 216–17, 253,
    261, 270, 275, 280, 283, 285, 286–7,
    291, 324
    with Slavo-Macedonia 51, 173, 213,
    217, 324
Borrow, George 193
Bosnia 223, 277
bread, superstitions about 207
Brecht, Bertolt 171
bribery and corruption 99–100, 107–9,
    115–16, 122–3, 134–5, 138, 141, 169,
    173–4, 191, 192, 247, 275, 277
Brindisi 129
Britain 120, 128, 167–8, 174–5, 184, 210,
    258–9, 286, 318, 322

Index

Index

Index

Index

prisons and prison camps 42, 89, 302–7, 328, 332]
propaganda 75, 95, 127, 160, 328
proverbs 178, 337
prostitution 105, 106–7, 191, 192, 256–7, 333
Psarades 6, 11, 12–14
punctuality 227, 330
pyramid selling schemes 71, 332

Qiriazi, Dhori 79–86
Qiriazi, Gjerasim 193
Quiet American, The 327
Quiller, Paul 186, 189, 190

Radio Moscow 67
Radio Peking 67
Radomirë 203, 213–14, 219, 223
Rafiq 213–28
Rahman 59–63, 115, 335
RAI 40, 75, 325
Rambo 271
rape 135, 192, 222, 256, 334
Refah 72
refugees 83–5, 94, 333, 334
religion 10, 35, 60–1, 68, 69–70, 95, 186–95, 297, 305
revenge killings *see* blood feuding
Riefenstahl, Leni 258
Rimbaud 183
Rinas Airport 325, 328–9
riots 332
Ritz Hotel, London 146
roads 76, 79–80, 85–6, 137, 186, 192, 230, 232, 322
Roberts, David 232
Rogem 270
Rogner Hotel, Tirana 165–6
Roman Catholic Church 61, 95, 193, 195, 215, 256, 305
Roman civilization 209, 289
Rome, Open City 29
Royal Air Force 168
Russia 2, 10, 67, 75, 100, 123–4, 143, 298, 316, 325–6, 330
Rustem 213–14, 221, 222–8

St Nicholas Church, Voskopoja 35
St Paul's Cathedral, London 194
Sally 251, 258, 261, 264, 265, 274–5, 299, 300
Salonika 8, 10, 12, 51, 60, 64, 94, 319, 324
Saranda 86, 98–100, 104, 117, 121, 135, 332
SAS (UK) 154, 175, 288, 336
Saudi Arabia 140
Save the Children 184
Saxon 271
Saying of the Desert Fathers, The 332
Schindler's List 44
Scott, Walter 119
Serbia 8, 12, 67, 144, 232, 254, 268, 296, 297
   border with Albania 173, 213, 216–17, 253, 261, 270, 275, 280, 283, 285, 286–7, 291, 324
Seymour, Captain 219
Shakespeare, William 190
shame 124, 160–1, 207–8, 210, 220, 271, 272, 308–12
Shannon Airport 326
Shehu, Mehmet 111, 147, 178, 304
Shelley 182
shepherds 85, 261, 211–12, 296
Sheraton Hotel 150
Shia Muslims 277
SHIK 134–5, 137, 148, 158, 159, 179, 243–4, 252, 332, 336
Shkumbin, River 7
Shkodra (Scutari) 61, 150, 158, 204, 230, 253, 256, 264, 265, 301, 302, 306, 313–23, 334
Shkrelli, Dr 92–5, 98–104, 123, 126, 127, 132–3, 136, 231, 241, 318, 335
shooting accidents 284
shortages (1991–3) 21, 39, 67, 78, 143
Shoshan 270
Sicily 176
Sigurimi (Secret Police) 22, 42, 65, 68, 96–7, 122, 158, 176, 179–80,252, 304, 312, 327, 336
SIS (UK) 174

Index

Index

Wilfred Thesiger

My Kenya Days

Wilfred Thesiger is one of this country's greatest travellers and explorers. His books *Arabian Sands* and *The Marsh Arabs* have been hailed as classics of modern travel writing. This book, which follows on from his bestselling autobiography, *The Life of My Choice*, provides a compelling record of Thesiger's thirty years in Kenya.

My Kenya Days offers fresh insights into Thesiger's motivations and enigmatic personality. Lavishly illustrated with his extraordinary photographs, it contains superb evocations of Kenya's vanishing tribal heritage, of the dramatic landscapes of Thesiger's Kenya journeys, and intimately portrays his Samburu companions and surroundings at Maralal, where he made his home.

'A remarkable man whose love for Africa shines through this book'   *The Times*

'Magnificent photographs . . . almost religious in nature, displaying a reverence for their subject matter, both human and inanimate'   *Sunday Telegraph*

'A book worth pondering deeply' FRANK McLYNN, *Guardian*

'More than a sum of its parts: it reads as a threnody for a world we have lost and which will never be recreated'
ANTHONY DANIELS, *Sunday Telegraph*

0 00 638392 0

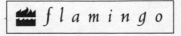

William Dalrymple

In Xanadu

A Quest

'A classic.'   *Sunday Express*

'William Dalrymple's *In Xanadu* carries us breakneck from a
pre-dawn glimmer in the Holy Sepulchre right across Asia to a
bleak wind in Kubla Khan's palace . . . it is learned and comic,
and a most gifted first book touched by the spirits of Kinglake,
Robert Byron and E. Waugh.'

PATRICK LEIGH FERMOR, *Spectator* Books of the Year

'*In Xanadu* is, without doubt, one of the best travel books produced in the last 20 years. It is witty and intelligent, brilliantly
observed, deftly constructed and extremely entertaining . . .
Dalrymple's gift for transforming ordinary, humdrum experience into something extraordinary and timeless suggests that
he will go from strength to strength.'

ALEXANDER MAITLAND, *Scotland on Sunday*

'Exuberant.'   COLIN THUBRON

'Dalrymple writes beautifully, is amazingly erudite, brave and
honest, and can be extremely funny.'

QUENTIN CREWE, *Sunday Telegraph*

'The delightful, and funny, surprise mystery tour of the year.'

SIR ALEC GUINNESS, *Sunday Times*

'Erudite, adventurous and amusing . . . reminded me of Evelyn
Waugh.'   PIERS PAUL READ

0 00 654415 0

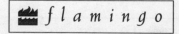

Dervla Murphy

The Ukimwi Road
From Kenya to Zimbabwe

For travellers who wish to remain carefree, Africa is the wrong continent.

Embarking on a three-thousand mile solo cycle ride across sub-Saharan Africa, Dervla Murphy, at sixty 'the toughest female travel writer of our age', had hoped to escape from the mental and emotional shackles of home. But as she pedalled and pushed her bicycle over some of the roughest roads from Kenya through Uganda, Tanzania, Malawi and Zambia to Zimbabwe, inevitably the harrowing problems of the peoples among whom she travelled rose up to take their place. In particular, the mysterious threat of AIDS ('Ukimwi' in Swahili) was talked about wherever she went, by both men and women.

Finding comfort in the beauty of the contrasting landscapes of the countries she passed through, in the space and the solitude, and entertained by the talkative, welcoming local people, Murphy survived starvation, a beating by paramilitaries and a bout of malaria. As ever, she was sustained by her extraordinary compassion, humour and sense of adventure. What emerges from her journey along the Ukimwi Road is a personal, often controversial, always compelling view of Africa, its peoples and its future.

'The essence of good travel writing'

IMOGEN LYCETT-GREEN, *Daily Mail*

'[Dervla Murphy] belongs firmly to that fine tradition of eccentric women travellers . . . endearingly self-deprecating'

ANTHONY DANIELS, *Spectator*

0 00 654802 4
£6.99

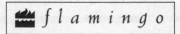